T0336730

Cyber Security, Cyber Crime and Cyber Forensics:

Applications and Perspectives

Raghu Santanam
Arizona State University, USA

M. Sethumadhavan
Amrita University, India

Mohit Virendra
Brocade Communications Systems, USA

A volume in the Advances in Digital
Crime, Forensics, and Cyber Terrorism
(ADCFCT) Book Series

Information Science
REFERENCE

Senior Editorial Director:	Kristin Klinger
Director of Book Publications:	Julia Mosemann
Editorial Director:	Lindsay Johnston
Acquisitions Editor:	Erika Carter
Development Editor:	Myla Harty
Production Coordinator:	Jamie Snavely
Typesetters:	Casey Conapitski, Julia Mosemann & Deanna Zombro
Cover Design:	Nick Newcomer

Published in the United States of America by
Information Science Reference (an imprint of IGI Global)
701 E. Chocolate Avenue
Hershey PA 17033
Tel: 717-533-8845
Fax: 717-533-8661
E-mail: cust@igi-global.com
Web site: http://www.igi-global.com

Library of Congress Cataloging-in-Publication Data

Cyber security, cyber crime and cyber forensics : applications and perspectives / Raghu Santanam, M. Sethumadhavan and Mohit Virendra, editors.
    p. cm.
 Includes bibliographical references and index.
 Summary: "This book provides broad coverage of technical and socio-economic perspectives for utilizing information and communication technologies and developing practical solutions in cyber security, cyber crime and cyber forensics"--Provided by publisher.
  ISBN 978-1-60960-123-2 (hbk.) -- ISBN 978-1-60960-125-6 (ebook) 1. Computer security. 2. Cyberspace--Security measures. 3. Computer crimes. 4. Computer crimes--Investigation. I. Santanam, Raghu, 1969- II. Sethumadhavan, M., 1966- III. Virendra, Mohit.
  QA76.9.A25C919 2011
  005.8--dc22
                          2010040615

This book is published in the IGI Global book series Advances in Digital Crime, Forensics, and Cyber Terrorism (ADCF-CT) Book Series (ISSN: 2327-0381; eISSN: 2327-0373)

British Cataloguing in Publication Data
A Cataloguing in Publication record for this book is available from the British Library.

Advances in Digital Crime, Forensics, and Cyber Terrorism (ADCFCT) Book Series

ISSN: 2327-0381
EISSN: 2327-0373

MISSION

The digital revolution has allowed for greater global connectivity and has improved the way we share and present information. With this new ease of communication and access also come many new challenges and threats as cyber crime and digital perpetrators are constantly developing new ways to attack systems and gain access to private information.

The **Advances in Digital Crime, Forensics, and Cyber Terrorism (ADCFCT) Book Series** seeks to publish the latest research in diverse fields pertaining to crime, warfare, terrorism and forensics in the digital sphere. By advancing research available in these fields, the **ADCFCT** aims to present researchers, academicians, and students with the most current available knowledge and assist security and law enforcement professionals with a better understanding of the current tools, applications, and methodologies being implemented and discussed in the field.

COVERAGE

- Computer Virology
- Cryptography
- Cyber Warfare
- Database Forensics
- Digital Crime
- Encryption
- Identity Theft
- Malware
- Telecommunications Fraud
- Watermarking

IGI Global is currently accepting manuscripts for publication within this series. To submit a proposal for a volume in this series, please contact our Acquisition Editors at Acquisitions@igi-global.com or visit: http://www.igi-global.com/publish/.

Titles in this Series

For a list of additional titles in this series, please visit: www.igi-global.com

The Psychology of Cyber Crime Concepts and Principles
Gráinne Kirwan (Dun Laoghaire Institute of Art, Design and Technology, Ireland) and Andrew Power (Dun Laoghaire Institute of Art, Design and Technology, Ireland)
Information Science Reference • copyright 2012 • 372pp • H/C (ISBN: 9781613503508) • US $195.00 (our price)

Cyber Crime and the Victimization of Women Laws, Rights and Regulations
Debarati Halder (Centre for Cyber Victim Counselling (CCVC), India) and K. Jaishankar (Manonmaniam Sundaranar University, India)
Information Science Reference • copyright 2012 • 264pp • H/C (ISBN: 9781609608309) • US $195.00 (our price)

Digital Forensics for the Health Sciences Applications in Practice and Research
Andriani Daskalaki (Max Planck Institute for Molecular Genetics, Germany)
Medical Information Science Reference • copyright 2011 • 418pp • H/C (ISBN: 9781609604837) • US $245.00 (our price)

Cyber Security, Cyber Crime and Cyber Forensics Applications and Perspectives
Raghu Santanam (Arizona State University, USA) M. Sethumadhavan (Amrita University, India) and Mohit Virendra (Brocade Communications Systems, USA)
Information Science Reference • copyright 2011 • 296pp • H/C (ISBN: 9781609601232) • US $180.00 (our price)

Handbook of Research on Computational Forensics, Digital Crime, and Investigation Methods and Solutions
Chang-Tsun Li (University of Warwick, UK)
Information Science Reference • copyright 2010 • 620pp • H/C (ISBN: 9781605668369) • US $295.00 (our price)

Homeland Security Preparedness and Information Systems Strategies for Managing Public Policy
Christopher G. Reddick (University of Texas at San Antonio, USA)
Information Science Reference • copyright 2010 • 274pp • H/C (ISBN: 9781605668345) • US $180.00 (our price)

www.igi-global.com

701 E. Chocolate Ave., Hershey, PA 17033
Order online at www.igi-global.com or call 717-533-8845 x100
To place a standing order for titles released in this series, contact: cust@igi-global.com
Mon-Fri 8:00 am - 5:00 pm (est) or fax 24 hours a day 717-533-8661

Table of Contents

Section 1
Cyber-Crime: Policies and Implications

Chapter 1

Rajarshi Chakraborthy, University of Buffalo at SUNY New York, USA
Haricharan Rengamani, University of Buffalo at SUNY New York, USA
Ponnurangam Kumaraguru, Indraprastha Institute of Information Technology, India
Raghav Rao, University of Buffalo at SUNY New York, USA

Chapter 2

C. Warren Axelrod, Delta Risk, USA
Sukumar Haldar, Anshinsoft Inc., USA

Chapter 3

Himanshu Maheshwari, University of South Florida, USA
H. S. Hyman, University of South Florida, USA
Manish Agrawal, University of South Florida, USA

Chapter 4

Divya Shankar, University of Buffalo at SUNY New York, USA
Manish Agrawal, University of South Florida, USA
H. Raghav Rao, University of Buffalo at SUNY New York, USA

Section 3
Cyber-Security: Methods and Algorithms

Detailed Table of Contents

Section 1
Cyber-Crime: Policies and Implications

Chapter 1

Rajarshi Chakraborthy, University of Buffalo at SUNY New York, USA
Haricharan Rengamani, University of Buffalo at SUNY New York, USA
Ponnurangam Kumaraguru, Indraprastha Institute of Information Technology, India
Raghav Rao, University of Buffalo at SUNY New York, USA

The Indian government has undertaken a major effort to issue Unique Identification Numbers (UID) to its citizens. This chapter examines the Social Security Number system in the US, and investigates other UID projects in Europe. Based on these understanding and other information around UID systems, the authors discuss possible issues that are expected to arise in the implementation of UID system in India. They articulate how biometrics is being advocated by the proponents of the system in India for unique identification. The authors elucidate the social, ethical, cultural, technical, and legal implications / challenges around the implementation of a unique identification project in India.

Chapter 2

C. Warren Axelrod, Delta Risk, USA
Sukumar Haldar, Anshinsoft Inc., USA

The security of business processes, particularly those based on IT (information technology) systems, is at increased risk when the processes are outsourced, especially during difficult economic times. This chapter examines factors affecting the cyber security of BPO (business process outsourcing) and argues that the combination of effects of outsourcing and the economic environment leads to even greater levels of risk than do the individual components. Suggestions are made as to how the risks might be mitigated.

Chapter 3

Himanshu Maheshwari, University of South Florida, USA
H. S. Hyman, University of South Florida, USA
Manish Agrawal, University of South Florida, USA

Unlike traditional crimes, it is difficult to define legal jurisdiction and authority for prosecuting cyber crimes. This issue is further complicated by differences in definitions of cyber crime in different countries. This chapter motivates the issue with an example of the ILOVEYOU virus and compares the legal provisions to combat cyber-crime in the US and India. The authors find that there are significant differences between India and the US in definitions of cybercrimes. It appears that in the United States, it is a crime to access information that has been declared to be confidential. In India, criminality requires dissemination of the information obtained without authorization. Another notable difference between the prosecutions of cybercrimes in the two countries relates to obscenity and decency laws.

Chapter 4

Divya Shankar, University of Buffalo at SUNY New York, USA
Manish Agrawal, University of South Florida, USA
H. Raghav Rao, University of Buffalo at SUNY New York, USA

The Mumbai terror attacks of November 2008 lasted for over 60 hours and resulted in the death of over 172 people. The attack revealed several shortcomings of the emergency response preparedness in Mumbai. This chapter concentrates on the emergency response provided and uses activity theory to analyze it. We explore the diverse dimensions of emergency, determine the lessons learned from the incident and evaluate the emergency response. We suggest how operations could be improved thus setting a standard for any future emergency response

Chapter 5

Charulata Chaudhary, Rajiv Gandhi National University of Law, India
Ishupal Singh Kang, Rajiv Gandhi National University of Law, India

The chapter discusses the issues involved in the protection of copyrights of intellectual creation over the Internet. The chapter focuses upon concept of liability and jurisdiction in cyberspace in context of the threat of violation of the rights of copyright holders. The chapter examines the role of technological advancement vis-à-vis the legal scenario make several observations and suggestions in regard.

In this chapter, we propose an ontology based approach to classify the anomalous events occurring in a number of hosts, thus filtering the interesting or non-trivial events requiring immediate attention from a set of events. An ontology is developed to structure the domain of anomaly detection. It expresses the semantic relationships among the attributes of an anomaly detection system and events collected by it. The system harnesses the reasoning capability of ontology and that of inference engine to make meaningful assumptions about anomaly events. This enables automatic classification of the reported anomalies based on the functionality and significance of the originating host as well as the associated system resource or parameter.

In Next Generation Internet (NGI), internet will graduate from being just a network of networks to network of interoperable services. Security in NGI must cover all 7 layers of the OSI model instead of just 3 bottom layers as in the past. This chapter discusses the security issues in NGI and proposes a methodology for security countermeasures in NGI.

The purpose of this chapter is to examine the strengths and weaknesses of the most commonly used model for digital identities. It is compared to other models which have preceded it, thus giving a background on its development. The models are measured against a set of criteria which it is desirable for an identity management system to have. The underlying hope is that understanding this model will help improve it or even lead to a different model.

Chapter 9

N. Harini, Amrita Vishwa Vidyapeetham, India
C. K. Shyamala, Amrita Vishwa Vidyapeetham, India
T. R. Padmanabhan, Amrita Vishwa Vidyapeetham, India

Cloud Computing has rapidly emerged as a new computing paradigm that arrays massive numbers of computers in centralized and distributed data centers to deliver web-based applications, application platforms, and services via a utility model. Cloud computing technologies include grid computing, utility computing and virtualization. It is very much essential to make computations of the virtual machines confidential and secured. Challenges that cloud computing currently face, when deployed on a large enterprise scale, include self-healing, multi-tenancy, service-orientation, virtualization, scalability and data management. Undoubtedly, any model which involves data assets residing on equipment not within users' immediate control needs to address security and privacy. Securing the cloud environment encompasses many different things, including standard enterprise security policies on access control, activity monitoring, patch management, etc. This chapter focuses on the approaches to secure the cloud environment.

Chapter 10

Rajbir Kaur, Malaviya National Institute of Technology, India
M. S. Gaur, Malaviya National Institute of Technology, India
Lalith Suresh, Malaviya National Institute of Technology, India
V. Laxmi, Malaviya National Institute of Technology, India

A mobile ad hoc network (MANET) is a collection of mobile devices that communicate with each other without any fixed infrastructure or centralized administration. The characteristics specific to MANET (1) dynamic network topology, (2) limited bandwidth, (3) limited computational resources, and (4) limited battery power pose challenges in achieving goals of security and availability. MANETs are vulnerable to Denial of Service (DoS) attacks that can adversely affect performance of MANET. In this chapter we present a survey of DoS attacks at various layers, their detection and respective countermeasure.

Chapter 11

Mohit Virendra, State University of New York at Buffalo, USA
Qi Duan, State University of New York at Buffalo, USA
Shambhu Upadhyaya, State University of New York at Buffalo, USA

This chapter focuses on an important, challenging and yet largely unaddressed problem in Wireless Sensor Networks (WSN) data communication: detecting cheating aggregators and malicious/selfish discarding of data reports en route to the Base Stations (BSs). If undetected, such attacks can significantly affect the performance of applications. The goal is to make the aggregation process tamper-resistant so that the aggregator cannot report arbitrary values, and to ensure that silent discarding of data reports by intermediate en-route nodes is detected in a bounded fashion. In our model, individual node readings are aggregated into data reports by Aggregator Nodes or Cluster Heads and forwarded to the BS. BS performs a two-stage analysis on these reports: (a) Verification through attached proofs, (b) Comparison with Proxy Reports for ensuring arrival accuracy. Proofs are non-interactive verifiers sent with reports to attest correctness of reported values. Proxy Reports are periodically sent along alternate paths by non-aggregator nodes, piggybacked on data reports from other nodes. The model is intended as a guide for implementing security in real sensor network applications. It is simple and comprehensive, covering a variety of data formats and aggregation models: numeric and non-numeric data and aggregators located across one or multiple hops. Security analysis shows that the reports, both primary and proxy, cannot be forged by any outsiders and the contents of the reports are held confidential and the scheme is robust against collusion attacks. Lightweight design aims at minimal additional control and energy overhead. Simulation results show its fault tolerance against random and patterned node failures.

Chapter 12

S. Sajan Kumar, Amrita Vishwa Vidyapeetham, India
M. Hari Krishna Prasad, Amrita Vishwa Vidyapeetham, India
Suresh Raju Pilli, Amrita Vishwa Vidyapeetham, India

Till date there are no systems which promise to efficiently store and retrieve high volume network traffic. Like Time Machine, this efficiently records and retrieves high volume network traffic. But the bottleneck of such systems has been to capture packets at such high speed without dropping and to write that big amount of data to disk sufficiently quickly, without impact on integrity of the captured data (Ref. Cooke.E., Myrick.A., Rusek.D., & Jahanian.F (2006)). Certain hardware and software parts of the operating system (like drivers, input/output interfaces) cannot cope with such a high volume of data from network, which may cause loss of data. Based on such experiences we have come up with a redesigned implementation of the system which has specialized capture hardware with its own Application Programming Interface for overcoming loss of data and improving efficiency in recording mechanisms.

Chapter 13

Vinod P., Malaviya National Institute of Technology, India
V. Laxmi, Malaviya National Institute of Technology, India
M. S. Gaur, Malaviya National Institute of Technology, India

The term 'malware' is collectively used for any program which accesses the system through surreptitious (often unauthorized) means, with malicious intent, resulting in data loss and/or corruption. Some examples are viruses, worms, trojans, botnets etc. Malware is becoming a world-wide epidemic as one infected computer system may compromise all networked systems. Millions of computers connected to the Internet exchange useful data and information and are exposed to malware threats. Malware programs may apply different techniques for unauthorized access, but all of them compromise the system in one way or another. In order to protect from the threats imposed by the malware, we need to understand the techniques used by them in exploiting system vulnerabilities and build an effective detection system. This contribution chapter surveys various malware types, infection mechanisms, detection techniques and metamorphic viruses. This chapter also presents a Longest Common Subsequence (LCS) based methodology for metamorphic malware detection.

Section 3
Cyber-Security: Methods and Algorithms

Chapter 14

N. V. Narendra Kumar, Tata Institute of Fundamental Research, India
Harshit Shah, Amrita Vishwa Vidyapeetham, India
R. K. Shyamasundar, Tata Institute of Fundamental Research, India

Assuring integrity of software is a very challenging issue. Different manifestations of tampering exist such as intentional attack with the aim of harming the user (through some kind of a malware; Baker, 1995) or the user himself tampers with the software to gain features he is not authorized with (Baxter, Yahin, Moura, Sant'Anna, & Bier, 1998). In this chapter, we make a survey of various strategies used to assure the integrity of software such as trusted computing platform, software attestation, software similarity, software watermark, software birthmark etc. Subsequently, we present a novel method for malware detection from a semantic approach that can be adapted for checking the integrity of software. We shall discuss some of the initial experimental results in this direction.

Chapter 15

Chungath Srinivasan, Amrita Vishwa Vidyapeetham, India
Lakshmy K. V., Amrita Vishwa Vidyapeetham, India
M. Sethumadhavan, Amrita Vishwa Vidyapeetham, India

Boolean functions are used in modern cryptosystems for providing confusion and diffusion. To achieve required security by resistance to various attacks such as algebraic attacks, correlation attacks, linear, differential attacks, several criteria for Boolean functions have been established over years by cryptographic community. These criteria include nonlinearity, avalanche criterion and correlation immunity and the like. The chapter is an attempt to present state of the art on properties of such Boolean functions and to suggest several directions for further research.

Chapter 16

Narayanankutty Karuppath, Amrita Vishwa Vidyapeetham, India
P. Achuthan, Amrita Vishwa Vidyapeetham, India

The developments in quantum computing or any breakthrough in factorization algorithm would have far-reaching consequences in cryptology. For instance, Shor algorithm of factorizing in quantum computing might render the RSA type classical cryptography almost obsolete since it mainly depends on the computational complexity of factorization. Therefore, quantum cryptography is of immense importance and value in the modern context of recent scientific revolution. In this chapter, we discuss in brief certain fascinating aspects of Einstein-Podolsky-Rosen (EPR) paradox in the context of quantum cryptology. The EPR protocol and its connections to the famous Bell's inequality are also considered in here.

Chapter 17

The joint linear complexity and k - error joint linear complexity of an m - fold 2^n periodic multisequence can be efficiently computed using Modified Games Chan algorithm and Extended Stamp Martin Algorithm respectively. In this chapter we derive an algorithm which, given a constant c and an m – fold 2^n periodic binary multisequence S, computes the minimum number k of errors and the associated error multisequence needed over a period of S for bringing the joint linear complexity of S below c. We derived another algorithm for finding the joint linear complexity of 3.2^v periodic binary multisequence

Steganography is the art of hiding information in ways that prevent the detection of hidden message, where as cryptographic techniques try to conceal the contents of a message. In steganography, the object of communication is the hidden message while the cover data is only the means of sending it. The secret information as well as the cover data can be any medium like text, image, audio, video etc. The objective of this chapter is to report various steganographic embedding schemes that can provide provable security with high computing speed and embed secret messages into images without producing noticeable changes. The embedding schemes utilizes the characteristic of the human vision's sensitivity to color value variations and resistant to all known steganalysis methods. The main requirement of steganography is undetectability, which loosely defines that no algorithm exists that can determine whether a work contains a hidden message.

Preface

INTRODUCTION

The main objective of this edited volume is to provide a broad coverage of technical as well as socio-economic perspectives of utilizing Information and Communication Technologies to provide practical solutions in Cyber Security, Cyber Crime and Cyber Forensics for a multitude of industrial applications. Recent developments in this domain have attracted researcher and practitioner interests from technological, organizational and policy-making perspectives. Technological advances address challenges in information sharing, surveillance and analysis. However, organizational advances are much needed in fostering collaborative arrangements between federal, state and local agencies as well as the private sector. Initiatives to strengthen security clearly benefit from well-designed policies that address developments in science & technology and collaborations between entities. Much of the literature in this area is fragmented and often narrowly focused within specific domains. This edited volume strives to address a wide range of perspectives in cyber security, cyber crime and cyber forensics. We have assembled insights from a representative sample of academicians and practitioners and addressed this topic from a variety of perspectives ranging from technologies, economics and social studies, organizational and group behavior, and policy-making.

Many of the chapters in this book are based on research and position papers presented at the Indo-US conference & workshop on cyber-security, cyber-crime and cyber-forensics held at Amrita Vishwa Vidyapeetham, Kochi, India in August 2009. This conference and workshop received over 100 papers on a wide-range of topics related to cyber security, cyber crime and cyber forensics. A select set of authors from the conference was asked to submit extended versions of their work for publication consideration in this Book. In addition to the peer-reviews conducted as part of the Indo-US conference, each chapter went through a peer-review process from the editors when it was submitted for the book chapter.

The chapters in the book are divided into three main sections – *Cyber Crime: Policies and Implications, Cyber Security: Technology Review, and Cyber Security: Methods and Algorithms*. The chapters addressing policies and implications are intended to address broad range of issues in the area. The chapters in this section discuss the significant challenges that governments and societies face when information access and usage becomes ubiquitous. The ubiquity raises legal challenges for business entities that engage with each other, and raises unique challenges for law enforcement and policy makers in designing new rules and policies and enforcing them. The chapters in the section, *Cyber security: Technology Review*, analyze the potential of emerging technologies for providing information assurance in the cyber world. The discussion here provides a good sample of various types of application contexts and solutions. The section on *Cyber Security: Methods and Algorithms* dives deep into review and analysis of techniques and approaches that secure information at its fundamental level. Overall, the selection of chapters demonstrates the kind of multi-disciplinary research effort needed to address the wide range of challenges facing us today in the Information Age.

INTENDED AUDIENCE & USE

The intended audience for this book includes:

- Graduate and advanced undergraduate level students in Information Sciences, Information Systems, Computer Science, Systems Engineering, Social Studies, and Public Policy.
- Researchers engaged in cyber security related research from a wide range of perspectives including but not limited to informatics, decision sciences, organizational behavior and social studies, and public administration.

This book is intended for use as both a textbook and a comprehensive research handbook. The contributors to this edited volume are renowned experts in their respective fields. Most of the chapters contained in this book provide an updated comprehensive survey of the related field and also specific findings from cutting-edging innovative research.

CHAPTER SUMMARIES

Cyber-Crime: Policies and Implications

The first chapter in this Section by Chakraborthy, Rengamani, Kamaraguru and Rao *The Unique Identification Number Project: Issues and Analysis* discusses the unique ID project initiated in India recently. While similar types of citizen identification approaches have operated in other countries for a number of years (e.g., USA, UK, etc.), the population of India and geography present interesting and unique challenges in making this project a success. The authors present a comprehensive review of the technological, administrative and legal challenges. The enormous scale of this project prompts the authors to call for a unit specifically tasked with fighting cyber crime incidents.

The second Chapter in this section by Axelrod and Haldar *Combined Impact of Outsourcing and Hard Times on BPO Risk and Security* examines security risks of business process outsourcing. The authors argue that cyber risks in outsourced processes escalate when the general economic conditions worsen. Risk mitigation strategies related to provider viability, quality of service, loss of control, and other significant issues are discussed in detail in this Chapter.

The third chapter by Maheshwari, Hyman and Agrawal *A Comparison of Cyber-crime Definitions in India and the United States* tackle the inconsistent and often incompatible definitions of cyber crime in India and the United States. The impact of inconsistencies can be significant due to the increasing business relationships and information exchange between India and the United States. The authors draw a distinction in the approach of United States, which treats cybercrimes by extending traditional criminal codes, and India, which has passed a separate set of laws dedicated to addressing electronic commerce, communication and information technology.

The fourth chapter in this section by Shankar, Agrawal and Rao *Emergency Response to Mumbai Terror Attacks: An Activity Theory Analysis* presents a unique approach analyzing the use of Information and Communication Technologies in a large-scale terrorist attack incident. Using activity theory based analysis of the response by various law enforcement agencies, the authors examine the coordination dimension requirements of emergency response that includes the concurrency and interdependence dimensions.

The final chapter in this section by Chaudhury and Kang *Pirates of the Copyright and Cyberspace: Issues Involved* explore the legal aspects of copyright violations in an inter-connected world. Protecting intellectual property, especially digital works, is a vexing issue for governments across the world. A big challenge is the myriad of legal frameworks and enforcement approaches. The authors suggest an international dispute resolution system to handle copyright issues across national boundaries.

Cyber Security: Technology Review

The first chapter in this section by Ramachandran, Mundada, Bhattacharjee, Murthy and Sharma *Classifying Host Anomalies: Using Ontology in Information Security Monitoring* argue for automating information filtering in security environments to reduce the burden on security analysts. The authors examine the feasibility of using an Ontology based approach to information filtering. An ontology based approach allows explicit representation of domain knowledge and cause-effect relationship modeling.

The chapter by Talukder *Securing Next Generation Internet Services* defines next generation internet services as "computer communication, telecommunication, or consumer entertainment services that are user-agent agnostic, device agnostic, network agnostic, and location agnostic over Internet." The chapter argues that security must be defined at each of the seven levels of the Open Systems Interface (OSI) model. The author presents a framework for defining security for next generation internet services.

Giuliani and Murty *An Examination of Identity Management Models in an Internet Setting* examine the criteria for identity management systems and present arguments for better identity management models for use on the Internet. A key aspect of the model is to move from a centralized system of identity management to a federated model in which identity providers also play a role in transactions.

Continuing the theme of security in services oriented environments, Harini, Shyamala and Padmanabhan *Securing Cloud Environment* present a review of challenges faced by adopters of cloud computing technologies. A secure architecture framework is utilized to present the overarching security related issues in this environment.

While the first four chapters discuss security issues in enterprise environments, Kaur, Gaur, Suresh and Laxmi *DoS Attacks in MANETs: Detection and Countermeasures* focus specifically on mobile ad hoc networks (MANETs). Ad hoc networks, by their very nature are vulnerable to denial of service (DoS) attacks. The authors present an overview of DoS attacks and countermeasures using the protocol stack as the underlying framework.

The Chapter by Virendra, Duan and Upadhyaya *Detecting Cheating Aggregators and Report Dropping Attacks in Wireless Sensor Networks* tackle the issues of misaggregating and dropping attacks in wireless sensor networks. The authors develop cryptographic techniques to address the security issues. A unique contribution of this chapter is that unlike conventional reliability and security schemes, the security model is tunable to obtain a desired tradeoff between control overhead and the accuracy of detection.

Investigating cyber security related events require that systems store and process massive amounts of data. However, storing high volume data in heavy traffic environments is difficult, if not infeasible. To address this problem, Kumar, Prasad and Pilli *Extended Time Machine Design using Reconfigurable Computing for Efficient Recording and Retrieval of Gigabit Network Traffic* present the design and implementation of a system that efficiently records gigabit network traffic. The system features both dedicated hardware and application programming interface.

The final chapter in this section by Vinod, Laxmi and Gaur *Metamorphic Malware Analysis and Detection Methods* presents a survey of different malware identification techniques. A key distinguishing feature of metamorphic malware is that they mutate and generates new variants of the code that are structurally different from the original. The authors present a survey of metamorphic malware detection techniques and present directions for future research.

Cyber Security: Methods and Algorithms

The first Chapter by Narendra Kumar, Harshit Shah and Shyamasundar *Towards Checking Tampering of Software* surveyed issues, strategies and techniques that have been used to check tampering of software. It also discusses how semantic malware detection approach can be effectively applied to arrive at notions of birthmark.

The second Chapter in this section by Srinivasan, Lakshmy and Sethumadhavan *Complexity Measures of Cryptographically Secure Boolean Functions* discusses various complexity measures of cryptographically secure Boolean functions and the major tradeoffs between them, which will help to get an insight into study of such functions and to design stream ciphers.

The third Chapter by Narayanankutty and Achuthan *Einstein-Podolsky-Rosen Paradox and Certain Aspects of Quantum Cryptology with Some Applications* presents some factors preventing wider adoption of Quantum Cryptology outside high security areas. They include equipment costs, lack of demonstrated threat to existing key exchange protocols etc.

The fourth Chapter by Sindhu, Sajan Kumar and Sethumadhavan *Error Linear Complexity Measures of Binary Multisequences* presents two algorithms for finding the joint linear complexity of periodic binary m-fold multisequences and an algorithm for finding error multisequence which are extensions to the case of single sequence

The final Chapter by Amritha and Giresh Kumar *A Survey on Digital Image Steganographic Methods* provides a state of the art review of different existing embedding methods of steganography drawn from the literature and gives a survey on the usual struggle of steganographic methods with achieving a high embedding rate and good imperceptibility.

CONCLUDING REMARKS

Cyber security and cyber crime are at the center of research and practitioner interests in an increasingly inter-connected world. Information and communication technologies are embedded into the daily life of citizens and therefore the risks inherent in their use understood and acted upon by all stakeholders.

The main objective of this book is bringing attention to the multi-disciplinary approach needed engage all stakeholders in a collaborative fashion. The contributing authors in this book have taken the initial steps to define and explore the underlying issues related to cyber security and cyber crime. We hope that this book continues to engage practitioners and researchers on this important topic.

Raghu Santanam
Arizona State University, USA

M. Sethumadhavan
Amrita Vishwa Vidyapeetham, India

Mohit Virendra
State University of New York at Buffalo, USA

Acknowledgment

We would like to thank the Indo-US Science and Technology Forum (IUSSTF) and the National Science Foundation (NSF), USA for sponsoring the Indo-US conference & Workshop on cyber security, cyber crime and cyber forensics. A number of chapters in this book owe their origins to the thought provoking discussions at the Workshop.

We thank all of the authors of the chapters for their commitment to this endeavor and their timely response to our incessant requests for revisions. The editors would like to recognize the contributions of editorial board in shaping the nature of the chapters in this book. In addition, we wish to thank the editorial staff at IGI Global for their professional assistance and patience.

Raghu Santanam
Arizona State University, USA

M. Sethumadhavan
Amrita Vishwa Vidyapeetham, India

Mohit Virendra
State University of New York at Buffalo, USA

Section 1
Cyber–Crime:
Policies and Implications

Chapter 1
The UID Project:
Lessons Learned from the West and Challenges Identified for India

Rajarshi Chakraborthy
University of Buffalo at SUNY New York, USA

Haricharan Rengamani
University of Buffalo at SUNY New York, USA

Ponnurangam Kumaraguru
Indraprastha Institute of Information Technology, India

Raghav Rao
University of Buffalo at SUNY New York, USA

ABSTRACT

The Indian government has undertaken a major effort to issue Unique Identification Numbers (UID) to its citizens. This chapter examines the Social Security Number system in the US, and investigates other UID projects in Europe. Based on these understanding and other information around UID systems, the authors discuss possible issues that are expected to arise in the implementation of UID system in India. They articulate how biometrics is being advocated by the proponents of the system in India for unique identification. The authors elucidate the social, ethical, cultural, technical, and legal implications / challenges around the implementation of a unique identification project in India.

1 INTRODUCTION

The Unique Identification (UID) initiative is a forthcoming and highly ambitious project in India where each resident of India will be issued a unique number that can be used lifelong and anywhere (Rai, 2009). The central government under the leadership of Mr. Nandan Nilekani,

Minister of State, created the Unique Identification Authority of India (UIDAI), an agency responsible for implementing the envisioned Multipurpose National Identity or Unique Identification (UID Card) project in India. UIDAI will be responsible for issuing the numbers; but individual government ministries and agencies will be responsible for integrating the numbers with their respective databases (e.g. The Union Labor Ministry will

DOI: 10.4018/978-1-60960-123-2.ch001

be responsible for Employment Provident Fund). The Indian government believes this unique identification will save identity verification costs for businesses (Hindu, 2009), especially by virtue of a system that facilitates online verification of authentication of an identity. To enable this fast verification, UIDAI will be building a central database on details of every Indian citizen including demographic and biometric information (Thapar, 2009). Such a centralized system invites the questions about single point of failure and potential abuse from inside the central government. Given that UIDAI aims to make verification easier for both organizations in both private and public sectors through a central database, it is important to understand potential loopholes that include breach of privacy, and targeted advertising in the context of cultural, administrative and bureaucratic practices as well as the contemporary technological and legal issues in India.

For the purpose of this paper, we assume that the Unique Identifier is similar to the Social Security Number in the US and to the proposed but now scrapped National Identity scheme in the UK as well as similar but active systems in some other EU countries. Even though the motivation for the UID in India is to provide services to citizens living in rural parts of India, at a broad level the idea is to create unique identifier which is same as in other countries. Based on this assumption we draw inferences that can be helpful in designing and deploying the UID scheme in India.

We discuss the evolution of SSN (Puckett, 2009). Although the Social Security Administration (SSA) has made the card counterfeit-resistant, the card does not contain information that would allow it to be used as proof of identity. However, the simplicity and efficiency of using a unique number that most people already possess has encouraged widespread use of the SSN by both government agencies and private enterprises, especially as they have adapted their recordkeeping and business systems to automated data processing. Apart from US (Rengamani, et al., 2010), we also study

similar initiatives in several European countries and have discussed the ethical, social and other challenges faced in their respective countries. In particular we will look at the challenges faced in the UK that proved too high to overcome for their proposed National Identity Card and Registry system. These will be synthesized into a broad set of challenges that Indian authorities must look out for when designing and implementing UID.

In Sections 2, 3 and 4 we discuss briefly the issues faced in SSN in the US, describe the National identity schemes in the UK (proposed but not cancelled) and other EU countries. In Section 5, we discuss in detail the challenges that we anticipate in implementing UID in India and then in Section 6, we provide specific recommendations based on our analysis. We also discuss issues that impact a biometric unique identifier initiative. Finally, in Section 7, we conclude the paper with our observations.

2 SOCIAL SECURITY NUMBER (SSN) IN THE US

Before citing the similarities and differences of the SSN, it is important to study the evolution of SSN. The SSN was primarily designed to enable the Social Security Board to maintain accurate records of the earnings of individuals who worked in jobs covered under the Social Security program (Acquisti & Gross, 2009). The card was never intended to serve as a personal identification document - that is, it does not establish that the person presenting the card is actually the person whose name and SSN appear on the card. Although Social Security Administration (SSA) has made the card counterfeit-resistant, the card does not contain information that would allow it to be used as proof of identity. However, the simplicity and efficiency of using a unique number that most people already possess has encouraged widespread use of the SSN by both government agencies and private enterprises, especially as they have adapted their recordkeeping and business systems to automated data processing. Use of the SSN as a convenient means of identifying people in large systems of records has increased over the years and its expanded use appears to be an enduring trend. The evolution is best explained through Table 1 as articulated by Carolyn Puckett in 2009.

It is thus quite evident from the above table that SSN has gradually evolved from a simple form of identity of older citizens to an all purpose tax identification that is now governed by rules and regulations designed to help in the current world of crime and terrorism which is strongly interconnected at the same time. In fact, SSN became the single most important identifier for check the credit history of any person living in the US which in turn serves as the key metric for application processes for loans, rentals, credit cards, cell phones and many other services. The increase in implementation of SSN across all domains has repercussions in other areas such as: privacy (Todorova), identity theft (RHIOs, 2006) and terror related crimes (van der Ploeg, 2007).

There have been many incidents reported owing to loss of SSN Numbers. Attackers can exploit various public and private-sector online services, such as online "instant" credit approval sites, to test subsets of variations to verify which

Table 1. Changes in Social Security card evidence requirements, 1936–2008 (Puckett, 2009)

Date	Evidence requirements
1936	The first SSNs were assigned.
1972	Evidence required establishing age, true identity, and citizenship or alien status of SSN applicants.
1974	Evidence required establishing age, identity, and citizenship or alien status of U.S born applicants aged 18 or older for original SSNs and all foreign-born applicants for original SSNs.
1978	All applicants are required to provide evidence of: Age, identity, and U.S. citizenship or lawful alien status for original SSNs; and Identity for replacement cards. In-person interviews are required for individuals aged 18 or older applying for original or new SSNs.
1987- 1988	Aliens living in the United States since before 1982 are offered lawful temporary resident status. Because many aliens were unable to submit the proper identity documents, SSA accepted Immigration and Naturalization Service (INS) documents as proof of identity.
2002	SSA begins verifying birth records for all U.S born individuals aged 1 or older when requesting an original SSN or when changing the date of birth on the Numident record. The Numident record is a computer extract of information from the original application for a Social Security card.
2002	SSA begins verifying all immigration documents for all aliens requesting original or new SSNs, or replacement cards.
2003 2004	In-person interviews are required of all applicants aged 12 or older applying for original SSNs. Evidence of identity is required of all applicants regardless of age. SSNs are no longer assigned for the sole purpose of obtaining a driver's license. Foreign students, who do not have an employment authorization document from the Department of Human Services (DHS) and are not authorized for curricular practical training (CPT) as shown on the student's Student and Exchange Visitor Information System (SEVIS) Form I-20, Certificate of Eligibility for Nonimmigrant (F-1) Student Status, will no longer be presumed to have authority to work without additional evidence. Before SSA will assign an SSN that is valid for work in such cases, the F-1 student must provide evidence that he or she has been authorized by the school to work and has secured employment
2005	Intelligence Reform and Terrorism Prevention Act [IRTPA] of 2004 changes evidence requirements for SSN applications and sets limits on the number of replacement cards an individual may receive: SSA verifies birth records for all U.S born individuals requesting an original SSN (except for those who obtain an original SSN through the Enumeration At Birth (EAB) process).
2008	Domestic birth records are no longer verified with the custodian of the record unless the document appears to have been modified or is questionable. (Change is based on study results). For foreign-born individuals requesting a change to the Numident date of birth, SSA continues to verify with DHS any immigration document presented as evidence.

number corresponds to an individual with a given birth date. ID theft is one of the fastest growing financial crimes and has affected nearly 10 million Americans and it amounts to 42% of complaints received in 2003 by Federal trade commission (Thomas, 2004). The danger of identity theft is illustrated in Triwest HealthCare Alliance where several Triwest beneficiaries became victims of the identity theft in 2003 (RHIOs, 2006).

Terrorists have used Social Security number fraud and ID theft to assimilate themselves into society. According to FBI testimony before the Senate Committee on the Judiciary, "Terrorists have long utilized ID theft as well as Social Security number fraud to enable them to obtain such things as cover employment and access to secure locations" (Thomas, 2004).

Researchers have shown that Social Security Number can be predicted using publicly available data (Acquisti & Gross, 2009). One of the big privacy concerns regarding sharing of the SSN with untrustworthy parties was that this number in conjunction with other personally identifiable information could have been sold as a "credit header" by a credit bureau to "information brokers". This flaw in the Fair Credit Reporting Act (FCRA) was removed through an amendment in 1997.

3 NATIONAL IDENTITY CARD AND NATIONAL IDENTITY REGISTRY IN UK

The National Identity Card in UK was proposed through the Identity Card Act of 2006. However due to widespread criticism of the cost of this program along with concerns about privacy and other human rights, especially for ethnic minorities, the newly elected British Government of 2010 scrapped the program by passing the Identity Documents Bill 2010. All data collected prior to this development to populate the National Identity Register would be scrapped according to the Identity Documents Bill. The proposed program would have required the National Identity Register to contain 50 different categories of information pertaining to every British citizen. These would include biometric information like fingerprints and facial and iris scans. The proponents of this program proposed that the National Identity Card would be used as a proof of citizenship and a travel document. Similar to the SSN in the United States, prior to being ultimately scrapped, the implementation of the national identification card in 2009 came about through an evolutionary path.

Historically, UK has passed laws and later, repealed the need for a national identifier. The UK had national identifiers as early as 1915 (Beynon-Davies, 2006). During the World War II, the political leadership realized a need for a national identifier. Once the war was over, the use of national identification cards were shunned and associated legislations were repealed. In its modern form, the UK Home Secretary David Blunkett resurrected the idea of introducing a national identity card called the "*Entitlements Card*." This universal identifier is described to address a four-fold purpose, as below (Beynon-Davies, 2006):

1. To provide lawful UK residents with a means of confirming their identity.
2. To establish a single record of identity for official purposes.
3. To give people easy entitlement to products and services provided by the public and private sectors.
4. To help private and public sector organizations to validate a person's identity / eligibility to work in UK.

According to the National Identity Card scheme it would not be mandatory for UK nationals to hold a card; however the Government has made it compulsory for foreign nationals in UK to hold one. The card itself is not as significant as the national registry it is linked to, this registry is known as the National Identity Registry (NIR). UK nationals can either apply for the card or surrender their old passports and apply for a new one. Once they do it, their details would have been automatically saved on to the NIR and their card / new passport details would be linked to the NIR. The Labor ruled British Government that promoted this scheme targeted that by 2015, 90% of the foreign workers would have been registered with the NIR. Though the possession of a card is meant to be an option, there would be no option of being left out from registering with the NIR.

Anticipated Benefits and Costs with the UK National Identifier

The proponents of the National Identity Card anticipated the primary benefit of this scheme as helping in effectively *combating identity thefts* in UK. Currently it is estimated that identity thefts cost UK nearly 1.3 Billion pounds per annum. It was thought that a national identifier when associated with a sound authentication, identification and enrolment process would significantly improve combating identity thefts. It was also believed that the lack of a national identifier makes the UK an attractive target for illegal immigrants who tend to work and access welfare benefits fraudulently. National identity cards were expected to alleviate the UK issues of *illegal immigration* to considerable degree. These cards were also expected to help UK Criminal Records Bureau maintain accurate records of criminal activity, as the NIR would have also been a database of fingerprints. This database would help in establishing extra authentication of an individual whose DNA sample is taken for mass screening (*UK 'national identity register' is a national database of fingerprints*, 2005).

Potential misuse of data privacy and increased fraudulent activity were of course perceived as potential costs to the National ID scheme. Data protection and other significant organizational costs such as large investments for information systems upgrade and maintenance were an-

ticipated to outweigh the benefits of the national identification card project.

Concerns about the National Identity Register

The London School of Economics submitted a report (LSE, 2005) with alternative models for an identity card scheme keeping in mind the need to establish an identity system, which is trusted, secure and cost-effective. The report stated that the Government could achieve the goals of terror-management and national security by allowing individuals to have greater control over disclosure of private information; and by strengthening its borders. The report estimated the cost of a ten-year roll out to be between 10.6 and 19.2 Billion pounds without taking into consideration any cost overruns.

Traditionally, criminals have been the ones whose biometric data such as fingerprints were collected. Biometric data collection must precede the issuance of cards. The big concern in this context was whether collecting data from every citizen for populating the NIR would turn him/her into potential suspects. Security and identity ethics thus played a major role in this criticism. The existence of a large database containing up-to-date information on personal data, fingerprints might make it attractive to other companies to feed off data from the repository. This data might hold keys to exploiting and expanding their customer base. They might even be willing to pay a huge sum for the same. It was also feared that such data might be used by the British Government, based on political or tactical reasons, in monitoring citizens and their movements.

Regarding the technological environment, the report stated that the technology being used is largely untested and unreliable. The report says that the new tier of technological and organizational infrastructure could itself become a target for terrorists or others.

Legally, the Identity cards bill appears to be unsafe. A number of elements potentially compromise Article 8 (privacy) and Article 14 (discrimination) of the European Convention on Human Rights. The interim report of the LSE Identity Project in March 2005 revealed that potential conflict with laws such as Disability Discrimination Act and Race Relations Act is expected to arise when individuals face difficulty with biometrics registration or verification.

With the introduction of fingerprints capture in passports, exceptions to the Immigration Act need to be provided. The Bill also could conflict with the movement of freedom for the non-UK EU workers. The current population of oversight bodies in the UK is complex, inefficient and frequently in conflict. Commissioners responsible for various aspects of privacy and surveillance, for example, rarely cooperate with each other.

4 NATIONAL ID IN EUROPEAN UNION (EU) COUNTRIES

Identity management in EU Countries is handled along with other entities in the "e-Government policies". eID (electronic Identity) is aimed for easier access to public services across the EU. In general E-Government in European Union countries is about using the tools and systems made possible by Information and Communication Technologies (ICTs) which will provide better public services to businesses and citizens. Effective e-Government involves rearranging organizations and policies so that public services can be rendered more effectively (*ICT for Government and Public Services*, 2010).

Project STORK (Secure identity across borders linked) was initiated to aid business, citizens and government employees to utilize their national electronic identities in any member state. Member state partners of this initiative includes fourteen countries and they are Austria, Belgium, Estonia, France, Germany, Italy, Luxembourg,

Netherlands, Portugal, Slovenia, Spain, Sweden, United Kingdom and Iceland (EEA) (*eID - Easier Access to Public Services Across the EU*, 2010). The objective of this project is to achieve the pan-European recognition of IDs existing across EU. Instead of finding one single solution it will allow all national systems to work together.

Various countries which are participating in STORK will use their respective national identity cards and test a host of services using open standards and they are (*eID - Easier Access to Public Services Across the EU*, 2010):

- By forming a common architecture that allows citizens to use their own national eIDs and to access e- Government portals across borders.
- This provides a platform that in turn offers safer browsing and online communications especially for children using eIDs
- Mobility of students for various purposes across Europe is more flexible and easy with the use of common identity system.
- eID can be used for cross-border electronic delivery for citizens and for businesses activities.
- Finally eID can be used for testing the electronic process of address change for EU citizens who move to other member states.

To further examine the individual implementation of national identification process in the European Union, few of the nations are taken into account and they are: Belgium, Estonia and the Netherlands [Members of STORK Project]. Challenges and evolution of the identity management system are discussed for each of these countries (Figure 1).

National e-Id Card (BELPIC) in Belgium

Belgian Personal Identity Card (BELPIC) is the largest e-ID scheme in Europe and one of the most

Figure 1. The EU's main policy initiative in this field is the e-Government Action Plan, which focuses efforts on five priorities: Adapted from (ICT for Government and Public Services, 2010)

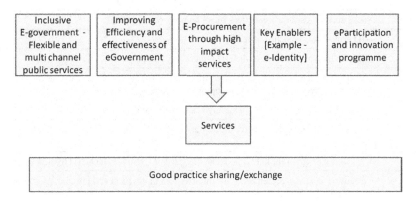

successful initiatives too. By the end of 2008, they had issued around 8 million cards and e-ID had become the electronic key for more than 600 applications (Gemalto, 2009). It started in the year of 2001, when the Belgian Council of Ministers made the decision to introduce an eID card to all the citizens of Belgium in an effort to simplify administrative processes and modernize public services. After approval from the parliament, the project was officially launched in March 2003. eID is used for multiple purposes. It is used to authenticate the citizen and involves digital signing with advanced electronic signatures and has card authentication, which includes third key pair generation, thereby ensuring the authenticity of the card.

The key events and developments of this project are mentioned in the Table 2 adapted from (Gemalto, 2009).

e-ID card is an electronic identity card which officially recognizes a person as citizen of Belgium. Being one of the first countries to implement e-government programs and services at a national level, Belgium doesn't have the luxury to look at working models in other countries to benchmark it. So it is pushed to a state where it has to experiment with many of its challenges such as security, infrastructure, technical framework and organizational challenges.

In addition to providing an e-identity for every citizen, the e-ID card can also be used for storing electronic signature, which can be used for authentication for accessing e-government applications (Gemalto, 2009). Apart from e-government services, the e-ID card can also be used as library card, key for computer network security in a company, e-signature for the Internet purchases and as key for security cupboards etc (Belgium, 2010).

Belgium's present focus is on the interoperability of e-IDs across different units of administration with in Belgium (Municipality, Regional, Community, Federal) (Arora, 2008).

National e-ID in Estonia

Ninety percent of Estonians have a national ID card issued by the Government (Dutta, 2006) with a legally binding digital signature embedded in the card. The card is used for various purposes such as declaring taxes online, obtaining e-services (such as validity of insurance, address, and family physician) obtaining sickness benefits, and authenticating voters for online voting. Permanent residents above the age of 15 living inside Estonia are also required to carry the National ID card (Aadel, 2007).

Table 2. Changes in BELPIC requirements, 2001–2008 (Gemalto, 2009)

Date	Evidence requirements
2001	Social security card for a paperless social security was launched
2003	e-ID project was launched officially
2004	Decree to expand the use of the eID project was passed.
	Be-Health (Belgium Health) platform offering on-line healthcare services, using e-ID and the Social Information System (SIS) card was approved from the government.
2005	Launch of the Federal Interoperability Framework for e- Government (BELGIF) was launched.
2006	Salaries enabled through social security are recorded online. This is the first e-Democracy project of its kind.
2006	A specific program for kids called Kids-ID Card program was launched to protect children.
2007	e-Government was presented by the minister for employment and information and strategic plan 2007 for knowledge society was initiated.
2008	www.belgium.be was released [federal portal]
2008	Citizens were given access to request police to monitor their homes in their absence and while they were away using their eID through the Police- on- Web application for on-line crime reports.
2008	Foreign nationals who are residing in Belgium and became citizens have become entitled to replace their old paper identity with electronic residence permit cards.
2008	Circulation of eID cards approaches 8 million.

These cards are issued by an organization called as *Sertifitseerimiskeskus* (or "Certification Center"), which was not founded by the Government but banks and telecom companies. They produce the software and electronic services associated with the ID card while a subsidiary of a Swiss company personalizes the card. Such services include LDAP directory services and various validity and signature matching and confirmation services. This Certification Center (called SK in short by Estonians) acts the Certification Authority (CA). Although the principles of privacy in identity management are: anonymity; unlinkability; unobservability; and pseudonymity (Arora, 2008), the Estonian national ID card system does not emphasize privacy beyond data protection and retention. In fact, the name and national ID code of a person is considered *public*. Data protection is not a major issue in Estonia in the context of the ID cards themselves since the general philosophy is to store as little private data as possible on the cards. Instead data are stored on the databases that are controlled by the relevant authorities.

The "public" data, which is the name and the ID code, is not available online; it is only available when the card is physically presented.

Estonian Certification Service Providers (CSP) certifies real persons identified by name and ID code. Time Stamp Providers (TSP) assigns time-stamps to data in a way that they are unalterable. National Registry of Certificate Service Providers confirms the public keys of the CSPs and TSPs. They are a supervisory organization, which works under Ministry of Economy and Communications. Both the providers above, as well as their supervisory registry, are regulated by the *Digital Signature Act* (DSA).

According to the DSA, it is mandatory for all Estonians and foreigners residing in Estonia to carry an ID card. Furthermore, this ID card does not guarantee citizenship.

Nor is there any legal/monetary sanction for not carrying this card. The rationale behind this is that when people who simply own a passport will have to renew that passport, they will either have to get just an ID card or an ID card along with a renewed passport. When DSA was passed, it was estimated that by the end of 2006, one million ID cards would be given out. However, in spite of widespread penetration of the national ID card, as of 2006 only 65% of the citizens file their taxes online using e-banking applications. People are allowed to opt out of the electronic use of the ID card, which is achieved by disabling the validity of the certificates. The result is that the user's data are completely removed from the *public certificate directory*.

According to ("ID-ticket," 2007), tickets for transportation can be substituted with the National ID card in Estonia, where the fare would be paid over the Internet, cell phones or landline phones as well as using cash over select service points.

Problems solved through the implementation of the Estonian ID card and digital signature infrastructure are presented below:

Verification of the validity of digital certificates is the key issue to be addressed by any digital signature infrastructure. Certification Revocation Lists (CRL) was first being used for suspended and revoked certificates to help in checking validity of certificates. But since these lists grew in size, LDAP directory began to be used for validity verification purposes. This directory contains only the valid certificates and they also help in retrieving the email addresses of cardholders. Another method of validity verification now adopted by Estonia is a service based on the Online Certificate Status Protocol (OCSP). This RFC 2560 compliant Internet protocol is used for obtaining the revocation status of an X.509 digital certificate (Myers, et al.). Compared to CRL, the OCSP responses reflect real-time certificate status. Furthermore it does not require an unnecessary public exposure of those whose certificates have been revoked. OCSP is also used for time stamping of digital signatures while the signed responses are logged to serve as evidence (perhaps against investigations by authorities and challenges from card holders). All of these enable the digital signature to be valid for a long time.

Signature must be valid even if a card is revoked or has expired allowing easy reactivation at a "bank office". Due to the lack of availability of a wholesome implementation for digital signatures, especially inside Estonia, there was a push for an entirely new software architecture called DigiDoc, which was developed by SK and its partners. DigiDoc performs different activities on the server-side and the client-side. Both windows-based and online interfaces exist for signature verification. This was achieved by implementing common DigiDoc libraries.

Potential interoperability and scalability issues, stemming from allocation of different certificates for different roles for the same person, especially when roles are added, were resolved by the Estonian DSA by mandating that roles cannot be embedded in the certificate. Instead roles and authorization information would be stored in online databases for example.

The issue of replacement of cards was being discussed from 2003 onwards. A 30-day time frame to issue a new card could jeopardize a person's regular every day activity that required digital signature verification. It was proposed that this problem be addressed through a "backup card" but the latter never got implemented.

Since many companies are multinational today and many non-Estonians reside in Estonia, there was a problem with restricting digital signatures only to a National ID card. Hence an "alternative card" can be issued by SK where of course the Registration Authority would be the private sector (e.g. a company requiring use of smartcards for internal purposes).

Not every country implements the same system of using of digital signatures; the scope of such a system thus becomes narrow in a continuously globalizing environment. Also in the international context, there is a multitude of standards of PKI. However, the understanding of legally binding should be fairly universal everywhere regardless of the nature of signing, digital or otherwise. International interoperability is being addressed through the OpenXAdes project whose mission is to comply with "different legislations and technology standards".

National ID (BSN) in Netherlands

Netherlands assigns a unique Citizen Service Number (in Dutch Burgerservicenummer or BSN) to every citizen or resident (living or working) who is registered with the Municipal Authorities (Municipal Personal Records Database). This system was adopted in July 2007. This identifier is used by all government organizations and it succeeds another form of ID called the *SoFi* number. The latter system apparently became unfit for many tasks it was intended for and thus was replaced with the BSN system along with a complete overhaul of the "legal, technical and organizational conditions" that are necessary for all ID-related activities starting from number issue to number usage (Koninkrijksrelaties). The Municipality is in charge of handling requests for corrections related to the BSN number (and not for the data which the number links to). BSN is not assigned to non-EU resident aliens.

This number, assigned by the Office of Tax Administration, is needed for being eligible for any kind of insurance, opening bank accounts and receiving a salary and any kind of benefits. In many places it is referred to as the personal tax identification number as well which is similar to the SSN number's connotation in the US. However BSN is not a substitute for a valid work permit in the Netherlands ("Disclaimer,").

Unlike Estonia, the use of BSN is extremely limited for private organizations and individuals who can use it for activities related to income data that are relevant to the Government. The philosophy behind this approach seems to be driven by the fact that the number is easily linked to personal data which is not the case in Estonia where the ID was simply a key for authentication. The BSN system appears similar to the SSN system of the US in this regard. In other words,

this number alone cannot identify a person and hence is "privacy insensitive." The government does not store the name of the BSN user in their databases providing further privacy assurance (Starre, 2006).

A slight difference between the two systems is that the Health Insurance Act of the Netherlands requires all family members to have a BSN for all insurance benefits. The BSN is supposed to appear on resident's passport, identity card and driver's license in order to be always handy ("Citizen's service number," 2009). This is quite in contrast with the SSN system where users are discouraged from carrying the number in printed form. Also, in order to give patients better control over their individual health records, the Netherlands has implemented the Electronic Health Record system wherefrom records will be accessible using the BSN along with a personal code (Groot, et al., 2007; Manders-Huits & van den Hoven, 2008).

Different government agencies collect different kinds of information and these are all indexed primarily by the BSN, where the latter is intended to facilitate easy exchange of data within these agencies. This intention does make BSN a single point of failure, although the efficiency and effectiveness benefits are extremely important as well. However this problem is handled by the fact that BSN cannot be used simply as a key to the databases, which are supposed to be protected by the Personal Data Protection Act. In other words, the handling of a potential theft of BSN ID is dependent on the context-specific security mechanism for the access to databases (Koninkrijksrelaties).

The Citizen Service Number Management Facility is responsible for properly matching the number holder and the actual number before processing any data request and hence this is expected to help better in curbing identity theft as compared to the SoFi number system. Furthermore, there is an improvement in the number issuing system which can establish a one-to-one mapping better than the SoFi system could (Koninkrijksrelaties) (see Table 3).

Table 3.

Country	Population Size	Population Growth Rate	Challenges
USA	310,232,863	0.97%	Identity Theft, Terrorism, Prediction of SSN using many other factors
UK	61,284,806	0.282%	Potential to treat everybody like a criminal, Untested infrastructure, Potential racial and other forms of discrimination based on biometrics, Cost
Belgium	10,423,493	0.082%	Lack of benchmarking as an early-adopter, security, infrastructure, technical framework and organizational challenges, interoperability across units of administration.
Netherlands	16,783,092	0.39%	All information indexed by ID, single point of failure, Identity theft dependent on security mechanism to the database.
Estonia	1,291,170	-0.635%	Verification of validity of ID, digital signature infrastructure not well developed, card replacement, interoperability with other countries

5 CHALLENGES ANTICIPATED IN UID IN INDIA

Given that we have seen UID systems around the world, in this section we look at various challenges with respect to UID system in India. For the implementation of the UID project in a country with a population of a billion people and upwards, challenges are manifold. Several challenges are anticipated and they can be broadly classified as Legal, Administrative, and Technological challenges.

Legal Challenges: In the US, the SSN was primarily used for tracking benefits and income of citizens / migrant workers. As time went by, SSN became the primary identifier and a supporting document that facilitated applying for loans or insurance or even to apply for a driver's license. As for the UID project, the legal system in the country should decide / mandate / regulate the benefits that citizens can acquire through the use of the UID. While the SSN is an identifier for both migrant workers and citizens, the UID is planned to be for the citizens/residents of the country. The judicial and executive machinery of the country needs to stipulate eligibility criteria for allotting the UID to a given person. Apart from this, the system could also be extended to include migrants to the nation.

Although the UID system is intended to provide an identity for every citizen, it can also be used by the government to ensure the availability of various services for a citizen such as health care, pension, voting, income tax and school /work ID. Before listing out the services, the various services offered by the respective state and central governments should be analyzed and then amendments to the corresponding act should be passed based on the requirements.

With the existing legal system, registration of vehicle to the owner's name does not demand any unique ID, but only requires the vehicle registration documents, sale receipt and any proof of date of birth. Therefore amendments can be made for "Motor Vehicles Act, 1988" to facilitate the inclusion of UID of a citizen, which can be then de made as a mandatory requirement.

In a similar way, respective departments in various fields such as Healthcare, Banking, Postal, Railways, Industry, Retail, Agriculture and other sectors should be identified and the corresponding acts should be amended to support the UID system. This will bring more transparency to the existing legal system and provides more scope for efficiency and reliability in a system.

Besides this, a separate act for UID [say national identity act] can be enacted which will ensure the ownership of data, protection of data, services associated with it, issuing bodies, and effects of misuse ("Belgium eID card Website," 2010). Identity theft has been identified as one of the primary issues to be addressed through the UID program. That can however be accomplished successfully only when India both at the Central and State level introduces serious legal repercussions for stealing the UID card, using someone else's ID without proper authorization, tampering with someone else's UID card (or any other form of identification container) or attempts of tampering with the UID database for malicious purposes like avoiding charges through investigation. One of the biggest challenges to the introduction and implementation of such a legal framework is to specify concretely the acceptable forms of evidence related to the UID as well as the penalties of such tampered evidence. This would require the lawmakers to fully appreciate the intricacies of the implementation of the UID system. For example, if a UID number is obtained by a hacker through some malicious means and misused in seeking approval for a bank loan, the law should require establishing the ownership of the UID as well as evidence of access to the UID database for authentication activities performed by the hacker or on behalf of the hacker during the loan approval process.

Administrative Challenges: Considering the current population and its growth rate in India, data collection for the purpose of populating the UID database is a massive task. Data collection can also be influenced by other factors like ethnic diversity, geographical variation, accessibility, gender, and climatic conditions. Data Collection is defined as the process of manually gathering data such as age, gender, and marriage status etc. It can also be facilitated by the existing Identifica-

tion cards used currently. It is debatable whether a separate body overseeing the data collection should be constituted and branches acting as direct data collecting agents have to be established. Whatever be the model, the prime body (UIDAI) governing the UID program should mandate the necessary manual proofs/documents needed to corroborate the identity of an individual. The first administrative challenge in the data collection process would be to coordinate the consistency of data collected within the same branch/agent as well as across them. The second administrative challenge that is bound to arise in the context of data collection, especially from a privacy and assurance standpoint, is the process of recruiting agents and laying down policies with sufficient protection mechanism for the citizens from data collection fraud possibly committed by any agent.

Identification of stakeholders is another conceivable challenge. For example, the Ministry of Home Affairs (MHA) and the Bureau of Immigration must work in tandem to decide what information must be used in asserting alien rights and how they will change their immigration process workflows. Similarly the Ministry of rural development and the Ministry of Panchayat Raj ("Belgium eID card Website," 2010) must be able to work closely to align their functions and reach out to the rural population using the UID linked schemes.

While each department or ministry works on delivering particular services, they must be able to use the UID to carry out their work targeted at citizen welfare better. Conflict resolution is one other challenge with respect to government bodies (trying to implement their directives).

Facilitating regular update of records is an administrative challenge that is intertwined with the way local governments keep track of deaths and births in a state. Local government officials might need to work closely with the general hospitals, public health centers and other private hospitals to keep track of birth and deaths to ensure there is no anomaly in the UID records. A death and birth registry information system needs to be in place.

Provisions need to be made for people to apply for a replacement card or update or modify the card's details. Processes need to be in place for foolproof update and other activities stated above. Ensuring privacy within the administrative system is in itself a vast area requiring careful study. If privacy is threatened, the purpose of having a secure IT system is defeated.

An administrative framework can be put together with the establishment of a department that might have divisions like Administrative Reforms, Innovation, e-Governance, Policy Reforms, Legal Reforms and more. This implementing agency should be reporting to a national governance advisor who periodically oversees the direction and working of the department. In light of the Government-level corruption often reported in the media in India, it would behoove the administrative framework to establish a separation of power as well as separation of information. The latter would possibly help in curbing corruption where a corrupt Government official could have sold information to the black market.

Technological Challenges: Based on the legal and administrative scope of the UID project, the requirements for the design and implementation of the project will vary. Given the scale of complexity of the project, it can be broken down to many sub projects which in turn spans many modules. Depending on the functional requirements of the modules, each can follow its own software lifecycle models; integrating all subprojects will be an ambitious task. The core of the UID project's technological aspect should be devoted to data gathering from several types of clients for example laptops, PDA and other electronic devices. The design or choice every piece of UID-related technology should be governed by factors like robustness, scalability, performance, complexity, extensibility, maintenance and cost.

Given that the UID-related technology would have functionalities that range from interfacing to data-related processes and functions including some kind of governance mechanism, we postulate that the N-tier architecture is a plausible choice for project modularization. Furthermore, N-tier architecture improves robustness by allowing each tier to grow and adapt to additional challenges arising from global technological innovations as well as philosophical debates about data collection, retention and utilization. In other words, every layer of the UID system can be impacted separately from new challenges that enforce separate requirements. N-tier architecture is also known for promoting Reliability, Availability, Serviceability and Innovation and these are characteristics that we deem essential for the UID-related technological implementation to posses. Finally interoperability is one very challenging aspect of this project as integration of various tiers needs to be done without breaking the chain and flow of data. Based on the proposed model in (Garhwal, 2009), the N-tier architecture for a proposed UID system could consist of the following layers (or tiers):

Presentation Layer: This will be primarily the User Interface screen wherein the data entry is involved. Placeholders for a citizen's name, date of birth, sex and other personal details will be used in this layer for data input. This will be validated for all business rules designed by the UID Technical committee. Mandatory fields and other regular expression validations (Date/month/year pattern) will be dealt in this layer as well.

Business Layer: This involves the actual business implementation of the project. Business logic and other fields that are associated with data entry are validated and a request call is made to the database for any of the following operations such as viewing a record, inserting a record, updating a record, and deleting a record. Furthermore and perhaps most importantly, this layer will itself be majorly impacted by philosophical and legislative requirements about handling of personally identifiable information about private citizens. The business logic of the system will be significantly affected by challenges of interoperability with systems outside UID as will be the other layers in order to help the UID scheme meet its fundamental universal-usability goal.

Data Access Layer and Database Layer: Based on the UID system requirements, these layers can be together viewed as a data warehouse database or as a Online Transaction Processing database (OLTP). Each database has its own list of pros and cons.

While designing a data warehouse, it is imperative that the architecture goals of the project should be clear and understood. This project should also leave some scope for future upgrading. On the whole, some of the best practices that should be taken care in designing a data warehouse are (Browning & Mundy, 2001):

- To deliver a great user experience i.e. user acceptance is the measure of success (Depends on the user roles defined for the UID project)
- Functions without interfering on other OLTP systems
- Focusing on providing consistent data
- To handle ad-hoc queries and requirements
- To generate reports for business intelligence which can be used to make some key decision for example, to generate report of the percentage of population who fall under Below Poverty Line (BPL). This report can then be used to take appropriate measures.

Also while designing database, much focus and attention should be given for replication for high availability and Disaster recovery. Few of the guidelines are mentioned below: (Garhwal, 2009)

- Manual fail over and fail back operation support
- Support for high availability and remote disaster recovery configurations.
- Integrated monitoring with email alerts
- Protection against database corruption

- Configuring for ensuring minimal data loss
- Automated logging and generating alert with the respective centers

In addition, datacenters should be distributed geographically and natural disaster threats should be eliminated by positioning the datacenters in a flood, hurricane, tsunami and earth quake free zones with in the country.

Security Aspect for UID Project

Some of the security enhancements (Noordergraaf, 2000) we propose for the N-Tier UID project architecture are:

- Physical segmentation
- Automated OS installation
- Dedicated network segments
- Host- Based firewalls
- IP forwarding and Encryption
- Backups
- Intrusion Detection
- Layered Environment
- Centralized logging

The primary focus should be on designing a highly secure N-Tier architecture with no particular component being a single point of failure for the entire environment. The above-mentioned items can be implemented in the following areas:

Physical segmentation: Segregation of Systems into multiple tiers of similar functionality, services, risk and exposure is critical to the overall security of the architecture. This grouping of systems forms the fundamental building block of the N-Tier architecture of UID project, thereby ensuring more security.

Requirements for building a system: Every system in the architecture must be secured. As such every system is exposed to different kinds of risk and so the requirements of every layer in N-Tier architecture differ. Securing systems requires the following action items such as: Dedicated functionality - Providing only one service to the environment and enhancing security through server customization

- **Hardening:** Configuring the Security settings and improving the resilience of system to unauthorized manipulation,
- **Host Based Firewall:** The implementation of firewalls has to be done in a careful manner as it can lead to a host of problems such as network congestion, maintenance and other scalability issues. Firewalls can be installed in individual servers and in this way, they can provide the fine level of granularity needed to allow services to particular network and minimized the network impact too.
- **Minimization:** Components that are required for a particular module of UID Project should alone be installed. As such, configuring every option in a server can complicate the architecture and increase the risk level of the module. But the process of determining the necessary components for a module is time consuming and so this is recommended for systems which are susceptible for possible security breaches.

Encryption: Protocols that are used in the UID project such as Telnet, FTP should be replaced by encrypted versions such as SSH or SEAM. In case of Remote procedure calls (RPC), Secure RPC protocol should be implemented. With respect to Privacy of data, data needs to be protected by secure encryption methods, security certificates and implementation of self-check digits is recommended.

Backup: This is one significant phase of the project as it is very necessary to consider the importance of data and ways of storing the same. Sensitive information such as User account and password must be encrypted.

Intrusion Detection: Since the nature of networks in the architecture is well defined, intrusion detection can function more effectively as every network segment is segregated and has some known number of protocols working across it. Based on this flow, the intrusion detection system has to possibly identify the unknown protocols and malicious traffic in these areas. All the systems, servers, devices and applications should be monitored and logs have to be created by the respfective items. Only through logging, intrusion detection can be effectively implemented. This information will serve vital for tracking any changes or activities across the systems.

Defense-In–Depth for UID project: Premise of designing such architecture is that no device or module should be a single point of security failure in the organization. Thus by isolating the layers and servers, chances of gaining access to the sensitive confidential data becomes remote and data is more secured especially with the combination of logging and other features.

Other Factors for Consideration: The UID system should be capable of thwarting any Denial Of Service attacks and other unethical attacks. Risk factors needs to be identified and risk mitigation plans should be built around the same. Risk factors may include natural calamities such as earthquakes, floods, tsunami and unwanted acts of crime etc. Information recovery needs to be included in the risk mitigation plan in the event of critical data loss. Other technology considerations include standard secure ways to store and to retrieve the data in a microchip format, where in a single swipe of the card facilitates authorized persons to view the person's details. The architecture for the database should be designed in a way by which it handles more than a billion unique entries in a reliable way. Provisions can be made for avoiding misuse/reuse of the UID card in case of death by maintaining death master file of the individual.

There have been many advocates regarding the implementation of biometrics in the UID project.

In the next section we shall review the biometric mechanisms and discuss the challenges involved.

5.1 Biometric Approach to UID

One of information technology's many offerings, the biometric identification system, provides a way to uniquely identify individuals. The Government of India's UID venture also plans to use biometric identification to identify its citizens uniquely. The UID system is perceived to allot unique identification numbers and verify its citizens' identity through the use of biometric identification techniques. In this section we discuss the idea of biometrics, its varied use, best practices and some concerns with the use of this technology.

Since the first forms of biometric identification, biometric technology has undergone numerous advancements. Today there are different types of biometrics that can be used to accurately identify a person. Facial recognition, vocal recognition and iris scanning are a few biometric identification methods widely used today, apart from finger printing. Today, biometrics mainly finds its use in identity access management and access control (Jain, et al., 2008; Rhodes, 2003). Biometric characteristics based on shape of the body and other physical traits. Examples include face recognition, DNA, hand and finger geometry. Biometrics based on the behavior of an individual. Examples include gait, voice. Voice is generally a physiological trait but voice recognition is mainly based on the study of the way a person speaks, commonly classified as behavioral. Human characteristics can be used as a biometric based on parameters such as uniqueness (how well the biometric identifies an individual from another), permanence (measures how far a biometric resists variance over time), collectability (ease of data capture for measurement), performance (robustness of technology, accuracy), etc.,

Because biometric systems based solely on single biometric information may not always meet performance requirements, the development of systems that integrate two or more biometrics is emerging as a trend. Multiple biometrics could be two types of biometrics, such as combining facial and Iris recognition. Multiple biometrics could also involve multiple instances of a single biometric, such as 1, 2, or 10 fingerprints, 2 hands, and 2 eyes. Prototype systems are trying to integrate fingerprint and facial recognition technologies to improve identification.

Biometrics comes with several challenges. Accuracy challenges are one of the key challenges of relying on biometrics for authentication. Just like accuracy can be a problem in authenticating a legitimate identity holder through false negatives, it can also authenticate a fraudulent person through false positives. The next set of challenges pertains to security and privacy, especially during the collection, transmission and storage of biometric data to the database. These challenges will require expensive safeguards, protocol implementation as well as personnel training. This could be a tall order for a developing country. Finally, there are several challenges in the Indian Socio-Political system that could impede the biometric approach (*Security and Privacy Challenges in the Unique Identification Number Project,*, 2010). One of the key aspects of this group of challenges is that the UID will be available to some departments of the Indian Government. Given the Corruption Perception Index of 2009 where the Indian Government scored quite high (3.4) in corruption, some group of citizens might be vulnerable to malicious misuse by members who might have a legitimate access to the UID database or might be able to establish access through monetary means. The latter has been known to be quite common in India. Even if the access is not for malicious purposes, the fact that UID uniquely identifies a person might create a fertile ground for profiling of citizens. This was in fact one of the prime arguments against the National Identity Card scheme in UK, which ultimately got scrapped. One of the means of dealing with this challenge is to implement very strong but at the same time very little bureaucratic mechanisms to deal with potential misuse from inside the Government, where an extra layer of authentication may be needed to access the database.

Being extremely diverse in its population, language, geography while at the same time struggling with checks and balances in the Government along with monetary resources, India does indeed sound like the last place that should be worrying about biometrics for unique citizen identification. All the challenges identified here should still be worth adopting biometrics because its utility can be extremely beneficial in the type of environment that exists in India along with the progression towards individualistic culture. Strong authentication mechanism achieved through biometrics can reduce fraud much better than existing mechanisms. Biometrics can help in better forensic outcomes for criminal investigations.

Advanced Biometric Technologies

Besides the existing list of Biometric technologies, there exist some next generation technologies that can be considered during the implementation of UID, which will enhance the security and improve the accuracy rate of detection in biometric systems. These technologies are especially very much useful to nab the criminals and other offenders of Law who involve in illegal activities. A few of the technologies that have been used to combat terrorism are discussed below (FBI, 2009):

Quality Check Automation (QCA)
This has eliminated the Manual quality check review and successfully enables faster response times for the majority of the finger print transactions. This involves lots of business rules which provide an automated quality check review, thereby automating the decision process and is more consistent than the traditional system.

The average processing of QCA is approximately .7 seconds as compared to manual QC processing time which takes about 16.1 seconds.

Interstate Photo System Enhancements (IPS)
This will allow users to add photographs for various scenarios such as previously submitted arrested data, loading data in bulk manner and also submitting photo with civil submissions. This has some special search mechanisms such as searching for scars, marks and tattoos and has explored the use of facial recognition technology to a varied extent.

Advanced Finger Print Identification Technology (AFIT)
This enhanced facility will provide a rapid identification search of a limited population using a minimum of two rolled or flat finger prints. Limited population mainly comprises of wanted persons, suspected terrorists, sex offenders and other criminals. This system ultimately increases the accuracy, daily finger print processing capacity and improves system availability.

National Palm Print System (NPPS)
Main objective of this system is to create a centralized repository for palm print data by facilitating the storage of both known and unknown palm prints. This data will be made available for all authorized centers' who involves in scanning. Palm prints obtained from crime scenes will also be loaded and thus increases the chances of nabbing the criminals.

Disposition Reporting Improvements (DRI)
This provides an exclusive list and a complete criminal history repository. This involves using latest technologies and has methods of modernizing the Machine readable data (MRD) process which allows submissions of disposition via Compact Disc read only memory (CD-ROM). Future enhancement includes using Digital Versatile Disc (DVD) and other Internet materials. Thus the repository is built around latest technologies and is updated every now and then with all futuristic requirements.

Although implementation of these technologies given a nationwide scenario is cumbersome, this can definitely be tested for a limited population (mainly criminal, Terrorists and other Law offenders) and this can definitely further enhance the security aspect of the existing system.

6. RECOMMENDATIONS

While designing and implementing the UID, we suggest the following factors to be taken for consideration.

- Access should be restricted or if possible prohibited to public and private sectors for accessing UID and any means of exploiting UID should be prevented.
- UID Lookup, if provided through online should be dealt with more security measures and validations and individuals bearing UID should be protected by prohibiting persons from obtaining their Id's to find a person with the intent to physically injure or harm them.
- Process of issuing UID should be tightened by some simplistic measures say, requiring photo ID to get an UID or replacement card. Restricting issuance of multiple replacement cards, and to push for verification of birth records at the time of issuance.
- Self check-digit should be implemented to prevent transcription errors and to ensure accuracy in the system.
- Encryption and Decryption Scheme should be implemented to protect the privacy of the identifier. The proposed Enhanced SSN encryption and decryption scheme is intended to aid the access security without compromising an individual's privacy.
- While designing the numbers, certain algorithm (Random number generation) should be implemented rather than developing numbers based on the date of birth, state

and other known fields. This will resolve issues through "Content-free Identifier" thereby improving security ("Enhanced Social Security Number,").

- Certain Process/Mechanism should be introduced to handle persons who don't have an UID (Immigrants, Dual Citizenship holders).
- Creating a public awareness about the importance of this system through a nationwide campaign and public should be alerted about its misuse about other fraudulent activities.
- The UID card can be made with lots of inbuilt security features and functionality say, a plastic card with picture having a magnetic strip and a secure bar code stripe with optical memory stripe.
- IT Infrastructure should be designed in a manner that any disruptions in the operations of information systems that are critical to the Infrastructure of the nation should be infrequent, manageable of minimum duration and result in least damage possible with effective backup measures and contingency plans.

The greatest social concern with respect to the implementation of UID with biometric information is the misuse and possible profiling with respect to gender or a specific race or sector of people. Judicial regulation and executive supervision needs to be in place to avoid misuse of biometric information, subsequently avoiding privacy invasion. A second factor of concern is the cost involved. Billions of dollars could be spent just on the first phase of the project. This doesn't cover recurring costs. Privacy advocates might protest the "informatization of the human body" (O'Carroll, 2004); where the human body is seen as an entity of information. Centralization of private information is also a security concern (see Table 4).

Table 4. Privacy aspects with respect to various biometric technologies

Technology	Positive privacy aspects	Negative privacy aspects
Finger print	Can provide different fingers for different systems; large variety of vendors with different templates and algorithms	Strong de-identification capabilities
Face recognition	Changes in hairstyle, facial hair, texture, position, lighting reduce ability of technology to match without user intervention	Easily captured without user consent or knowledge
Iris recognition	Current technology requires high degree of user co-operation - difficult to acquire image without consent	Very strong de-identification capabilities; development of technology may lead to covert acquisition capability; most iris templates can be compared against each other - no vendor heterogeneity
Retina scan	Requires high degree of user cooperation; image cannot be captured without user consent	Very strong de-identification capabilities
Voice scan	Voice is text dependent, the user has to speak the enrollment password to be verified	Can be captured without consent or knowledge of the user
Hand geometry	Physiological biometric, but not capable of identification yet; requires proprietary device	None

This technology when combined with other technologies can allow covert monitoring citizens at any given place or time. This could well be the most dramatic surveillance technology that can emerge as a standard for terrorism prevention. Some specific implications for UID are:

- **Privacy invasion**: Billions of records can be linked to people with respect to their identity, health information and/or other private information. Sophisticated data-mining techniques can enable discovery of unknown and non-obvious relationships amongst these data sets; arising concerns of social insecurity amongst people. Efficiency and convenience of this high technology also enables traceability of privacy data and subsequent loss of the same (Prabhakar, et al., 2003).

- **Social implications**: Europe has instituted directives with respect to data processing that reveals any racial or ethnic origin ("Biometric Identification Technology Ethics (BITE) project,"). Other sensitive data might include political opinions, religious beliefs and/or anything concerning health information. European union "charter of fundamental rights" addresses some of the issues that affect Biometric technologies. It mandates that everyone must have the right to protect and access his/her personal data. It also ordains the right to edit personal data. If not safeguarded, data collected during screening procedures and identification might be a tool for racial or ethnic classifications that might render appalling political consequences ("Biometric Identification and Personal Detection Ethics (HIDE) project,"). In India, where caste and religion is not necessarily a taboo subject in the mainstream with many official documents asking for sharing of such information, directives similar to the above in Europe need not be effective. What this implies is that the Indian Government can possibly save money and other forms of resources by allowing some of the biometric methods of identification to give away race or skin tone. In a country like India which is not necessarily a melting pot like the US, racial differences are very negligible in the visual sense. There are some visual identifiers of religion like the turban for Sikhs and the caps and veils donned by some Muslim practitioners (males and females, respectively). However, the main discriminating factor between the majority of Indians is the caste system as well as their political beliefs. These factors cannot be identified from fingerprints or DNA blueprints or pictures of the face. Thus the Indian Government has to worry relatively less about biometrics putting minority Indian citizens in a position of discrimination, except for Sikhs and Muslims. Of course in the Indian society, skin tone can still be a basis of discrimination (Jordan, 1998) and thus facial recognition can at times make some people even from a dominant majority group in a vulnerable position. In light of these possible vulnerabilities of biometrics enabled unique identification in the Indian society, there has to be adequate directives from the Indian Government to ask the private sector adopters of the UID to compensate for the lack of controls that prevent discrimination of the above kind through strictly implemented policies. For example, if an facial identification is used for the purpose of authentication, the institution should have policies that instruct the persons in charge of that authentication process to report the skin tone and any other significant indicators of faith.

- **Ethics**: It also stems from medical research that certain medical disorders are directly associated with certain behavioral characteristics. In such cases biometrics might not only become an identifier for an individual; it could also prove to be a source of individual's information. Furthermore, DNA profiles might bear risk of discrimination and multiplication of compulsory testing procedures. These ethical reasons might justify the need for a strong legal framework. Instances where biometric information is being used for reasons beyond its original purpose and without the consent of the participants whose data is involved are some areas of major ethical concern.

7. CONCLUSION

Introduction of UID in India has a potential to enable citizens to have better access to a host of government services. While this forces the governments to better their citizen services, it also tries to eliminate fake and duplicate identities under various government schemes. This will help governments stem exchequer losses arising out of ghost identities or duplication. Generally lack of ID proof results in harassment and denial of services and the introduction of UID would specifically improve delivery of flagship schemes. Indian banking rules mandate the use of a document to verify the identity of an individual before opening a bank account. This can also be extended to securing loans and other financial products. Use of the UID card as a means of identifying an individual will quicken the process of securing a credit card or a loan. This will pave way for Governments effectively build new schemes (employment generation, food and nutrition, disability benefits) and ensure that they reach the targeted strata of the country; thereby cleaning up delivery of social sector services and subsidies. Issuance of passports and driving licenses can be facilitated through the use of UIDs which will be a photo id card. The ensuing text elucidates the impact UID cards are expected to bring in India.

Issuance of the cards will also help the government gain a clearer view of population and other demographic indicators. UID cards can be a major impetus to e-governance programs and services. When the UID system matures, technology systems can be built around the UID framework to formalize a 'grievances cell' where basic amenities such as public sanitation, roads, and power may be fulfilled or grievances redressed. The internal security scenario in the state can also be monitored with UIDs being used to track criminals. UID can help deter illegal-immigration and help curb terrorism. Citizens need not carry multiple documentary proofs of his/her identity for availing government services. Even though in an Indian scenario, patient health information is not linked to any specific financial records, similar scenarios might arise if the UID is used to track a variety of purposes. The judiciary and executive must bring out laws and legislations to stipulate the use and scope of UIDs in each sector.

Another recommendation is to form a dedicated Cyber wing post implementation of the project. This wing can deal with all sorts of Cyber security related issues and can design a Forensic Response Plan. This plan should mandate how groups can form a resource pool that is well aware of the UID System and they can closely work with the Cyber wing to combat any issues involving breach of security and others, without disrupting the normal functioning. These kinds of mitigation plans can then be amended frequently to facilitate requirements that arise out of many scenarios. Also these professionals should be included in the review committee and their inputs should be considered for any up gradation or optimization activities.

Even though we have cited many issues related to UID, we believe that this project can be successful if these issues are considered while designing the system. If the UIDAI takes an inclusive approach of brining different stakeholders together to provide a solution, it would be very helpful for the project.

7.1 A Final Note

India had a major identification launch about 15 years ago when Mr. Seshan, the then Election Commissioner distinguished himself by operating a scheme under which he tried to provide what are popularly called "Vote Cards." These are photo i.d. cards with the name and address and a photo with records kept in the local county offices. The scheme was by and large, surprisingly successful because there was widespread acceptance of the democratic function of voting. Mr. Seshan was able to implement the scheme with comparatively limited expenditure availing of the existing administrative machinery, and within a meaningful time frame such that the Voters had these identification cards for the coming elections. Mr. Seshan's scheme, despite being the first of its kind, has thus been an outstanding achievement, considering the dimensions of the country, the diversity of the population, the large population that had to be covered and the inadequate literacy. It stands out in modern Indian history as an outstanding example of identity coverage and it appears to have succeeded because of people's participation.

In contrast, the Chairperson of UIDAI, Mr. Nandan Nelkani's proposals have already sought a very large budget. People's acceptance has not been adequately factored into the scheme, nor has it been mobilized. Questions are likely to arise as to whether the biometric tools like iris identification and fingerprinting will invite the cooperation of large sections of people who have traditionally looked upon the Government agencies with suspicion and hostility. Pardanasin ladies in the Muslim community (those who according to the customs and manners of their community do not appear in public), tribal populations and literacy deprived elderly, generally are apprehensive about lodging their fingerprints, and large sections of the population may thus see the whole activity as an instrument of domination and exploitation. Government has first to be seen by all as a friend of the people and not as an exploitative authority before commanding widespread and voluntary acceptance. There is therefore a legitimacy in raising a question as to whether biometric means although technologically most suitable, will gain universal people's acceptance without which the Project may not meaningfully succeed.

ACKNOWLEDGMENT

This research is supported in part by NSF Grant Numbers 0916612 and 0929775. Any opinions, findings, and conclusions or recommendations expressed in this material are those of the author(s) and do not necessarily reflect the views of the National Science Foundation.

REFERENCES

Aadel, L. (2007). *Are National and Local Information and Communication Technology Policies Based on Adequate Assessment of Real Situation?* Tallinn University of Technology.

Acquisti, A., & Gross, R. (2009). Predicting Social Security numbers from public data. *Proceedings of the National Academy of Sciences of the United States of America, 106*(27), 10975. doi:10.1073/pnas.0904891106

Arora, S. (2008). *Review and Analysis of Current and Future European e-ID Card Schemes.* London: University of London. Belgium. (2010). Taalkeuze eid.belgium.be.

Belgium eID card Website. (2010). Retrieved from http://eid.belgium.be/

Beynon-Davies, P. (2006). Personal identity management in the information polity: The case of the UK national identity card. *Information polity, 11*(1), 3-19.

Biometric Identification and Personal Detection Ethics (HIDE) project. (2010) Retrieved from http://www.hideproject.org/

Biometric Identification Technology Ethics (BITE) project. (2010). Retrieved from http://www.biteproject.org

Browning, D., & Mundy, J. (2001). *Data Warehouse Design Considerations.* Microsoft Corporation MSDN Library.

Citizen's service number. (2009). *Gemeente Amstelveen*, from http://www.amstelveen.nl/web/show?id=174916&langid=43&dbid=850&typeofpage=44744

Disclaimer. *Expat Guide Holland*(n.d.). Retrieved from http://www.expatguideholland.com/disclaimer/?region=tilburg

Dutta, S. (2006). Estonia: A Sustainable Success in Networked Readiness? *The global information technology report, 2007*, 81-90.

eID - Easier Access to Public Services Across the EU. (2010). European Commission – Information Society and Media.

Enhanced Social Security Number. (n.d.). *National Committee on Vital and Health Statistics*, from http://www.ncvhs.hhs.gov/app7-1.htm

FBI. (2009). *Next Generation Identification.* Retrieved from http://www.fbi.gov/hq/cjisd/ngi.htm

Garhwal, T. (2009). Logical building blocks in n-tier application architecture. *Tejpal Garhwal.* fRetrieved from http://tgarhwal.wordpress.com/

Gemalto. (2009). *Belgium – the national eID Card: A true e-Government building block.* Retrieved from http://www.gemalto.com/brochures/download/belgium.pdf

Groot, P., Bruijsten, F., Oostdijk, M., Dastani, M., & Jong, E. (2007, November 5-6). *Patient Data Confidentiality Issues of the Dutch Electronic Health Care Record.* Paper presented at the Proceedings of the 19th Belgium-Netherlands Artificial Intelligence Conference, Utrecht, The Netherlands.

Hindu. (2009). Businesses will gain from Unique ID project. *The Hindu.*

ICT for Government and Public Services. (2010). European Commission Information Society.

ID-ticket. (2007). *Sertifitseerimiskeskus*

Jain, A., Flynn, P., & Ross, A. (2008). *Handbook of biometrics*. New York: Springer. doi:10.1007/978-0-387-71041-9

Jordan, M. (1998, 1998, April 24). Especially in India/Fair Color as a Cultural Virtue: Creams for a Lighter Skin Capture the Asian Market. *The New York Times*. Retrieved from http://www.nytimes.com/1998/04/24/news/24iht-light.t.html

Koninkrijksrelaties, M. v. B. Z. e. Frequently Asked Questions. *Burgerservicenummer*

LSE. (2005). *The LSE Identity Project Report*. LSE Information Systems and Innovation Group.

Manders-Huits, N., & van den Hoven, J. (2008). Moral identification in Identity Management Systems. *The Future of Identity in the Information Society*, 77-91.

Myers, M., Ankney, R., Malpani, A., Galperin, S., & Adams, C. RFC 2560: X. 509 Internet Public Key Infrastructure Online Certificate Status Protocol ñOCSP, 1999. *Found at* http://www. faqs. org/rfcs/rfc2560. html.

Noordergraaf, A. (2000). *Enterprise Engineering Sunblueprints™ Online*. Retrieved from http://www.sun,com/blueprint

O'Carroll, P. (2004). *Testimony Before the Subcommittee on Social Security of the House*. Committee on Ways and Means. Social Security Administration.

Prabhakar, S., Pankanti, S., & Jain, A. (2003). Biometric recognition: Security and privacy concerns. *IEEE Security & Privacy*, *1*(2), 33–42. doi:10.1109/MSECP.2003.1193209

Puckett, C. (2009). Story of the Social Security Number, The. *Social Security Bulletin, 69*, 35.

Rai, A. (2009). Here to make a difference, not to give Infy contracts: Nilekani. *The Times of India*.

Rengamani, H., Kumaraguru, P., Chakraborty, R., & Rao, H. (2010). The Unique Identification Number Project: Challenges and Recommendations. *Ethics and Policy of Biometrics*, 146-153.

RHIOs. (2006). Using the SSN as a Patient Identifier. *Journal of AHIMA, 77*(3), 56A-D.

Rhodes, K. (2003). *Information Security: Challenges in Using Biometrics*. United States General Accounting Office.

Security and Privacy Challenges in the Unique Identification Number Project,. (2010). Data Security Council of India.

Starre, L. (2006). *The electronic government and its client systems*. University of Groningen.

Thapar, K. (2009). *Unique ID will enable more effective public delivery*. The Hindu.

Thomas, B. (2004). *Fact Sheet: Social Security Identity Theft*. Committee on Ways and Means.

Todorova, A. (2009, July 24). Is Hiding Your Social Security Number Worth It? *The Wall Street Journal*.

UK 'national identity register' is a national database of fingerprints. (2005). Privacy International.

van der Ploeg, I. (2007). Genetics, biometrics and the informatization of the body. *ANN IST SUPER SANIT, 43*(1), 44–50.

Chapter 2
Combined Impact of Outsourcing and Hard Times on BPO Risk and Security

C. Warren Axelrod
Delta Risk, USA

Sukumar Haldar
Anshinsoft Inc., USA

ABSTRACT

The security of business processes, particularly those based on IT (information technology) systems, is at increased risk when the processes are outsourced, especially during difficult economic times. This chapter examines factors affecting the cyber security of BPO (business process outsourcing) and argues that the combination of effects of outsourcing and the economic environment leads to even greater levels of risk than do the individual components. Suggestions are made as to how the risks might be mitigated.

INTRODUCTION

IT-based BPO arrangements continue to proliferate in the current difficult economic conditions, as private companies, government agencies, and other organizations seek to reduce their costs. The potential for compromise from cyber security exploits also increases, however. Over the past decade, the expansion of BPO, particularly offshore, was during times of continued economic growth, save for the recession around 2001 when a number of major outsourcers failed, giving little or no notice, as described in (Berinato, 2001). Prosperous times tend hide nefarious activity. However, when the tide recedes, questionable activities are exposed, as for example with Satyam. Motivation for exploiting outsourced services generally rises.

Threats posed by insiders, in particular, are thought to increase considerably as employees are fired and remaining employees are both disgruntled and feel threatened economically. Insider threat is difficult to measure since insiders operate using authorized access and practices. Consequently, while one might expect computer crime generally to increase when individuals are

DOI: 10.4018/978-1-60960-123-2.ch002

suffering economic hardship, any measures of such increases will be called into question since many exploits by insiders are not detected, and many of those that are detected most often go unreported.

RISKS OF OUTSOURCING

As business processes are moved outside the organization domestically or offshore, they usually become more dependent than previously on communications networks in order to connect outsourcers and client organizations. The economics for long-distance and international communications greatly favor the use of the Internet public network over private networks. Even when the communications are between known and trusted entities and individuals, the use of public networks exposes systems to cyber attack by others.

Often, outsourced business processes rely on computer systems that were developed for internal use by trusted employees. When access to these systems is granted to a service provider's employees, different access rights may be appropriate. However, restrictions on access to sensitive data, and on the handling of such data, may not be feasible with the current systems nor may the client organization realize the need to restrict data access and the functional capabilities of computer applications.

Another important, if not the most important, risk of outsourcing is that which relates to humans. Third-party service providers' employees may not have the same commitment to the client company that internal employees do. They may not have the understanding of the business environment and processes of the client company, nor sufficient training in regard to security and privacy. When the service provider is located offshore, other factors must be considered relating to differences in culture, language, physical and cyber infrastructures, legal and regulatory requirements, time zones, travel distances, and so on.

While there are certainly variations among researchers with respect to specific risk categories and their scope, for the most part there is commonality, as the mapping in Table 1 illustrates.

RISKS OF ECONOMIC DISTRESS

There are a number of threats that, while always present, are exacerbated by significant changes and economic stress, as described in a series of blogs (Axelrod, 2008). That these concerns are now mainstream is illustrated by the summary of many of these threats and their potential impact in recent articles (Campbell, 2009) and (Zarrella, 2009).

They include the following:

- Propensity to engage in fraudulent activities (for financial gain)
- Propensity to engage in destructive activities as a result of feeling disgruntled, wronged, etc. (for revenge)
- Increased opportunity for crime due to less stringent controls and employee apathy
- Increased vulnerabilities due to change and confusion relating to bankruptcies, mergers, and acquisitions

As can be seen from the above, risks in hard times derive from increasing numbers of vulnerabilities, opportunities, and propensities. The propensity to engage in fraudulent and other criminal activities is significantly increased in hard times as the pressure to continue to maintain a particular lifestyle or to pay off debts lowers the resistance of law-abiding citizens to overtures by predatory criminals. At the same time, people are more distracted and therefore less likely to recognize social engineering exploits. These factors are addressed elsewhere (Axelrod, 2009)

Table 1. Lists of risk categories from different reference sources

(Axelrod, 2004)	(Tho, 2005)	(Rost, 2006)
Loss of control	Loss of organizational competencies	Inadequate governance Loss of control over key information, crucial knowledge, and technical staff
Viability of service provider	Business uncertainty*	Buyer's business continuity
Relative size of client and service provider	Dangers of eternal triangle*	Loss of leadership in business relations Distribution of risks between buyer and seller
Quality of service	Service debasement	
Empathy		Underestimating backlash and resistance of the existing in-house team
Trust		Sly and unfair providers Vendors working for competitors
Performance	Possibility of weak management* Fuzzy focus*	Risk of failed projects Management of distributed projects might turn out more challenging than expected
Lack of expertise	Inexperienced staff*	Outsourcing unsuitable projects
Hidden and uncertain costs	Transition/management cost Increased cost of services Hidden costs Endemic uncertainty*	Underestimating communications costs Dynamic of costs
Limited customization and enhancements	Loss of innovative capacity* Technological indivisibility*	
Knowledge transfer	Loss of organizational competencies Lack of organizational learning*	Loss of control over key information, crucial knowledge, and technical staff
Shared environments		
Legal and regulatory matters	Disputes and litigation	International litigation may turn challenging
Extrication	Lock-in	

* Source: (Earl 1996)

RISKS DUE TO OUTSOURCING AND ECONOMIC DISTRESS

When we experience the confluence of expanding outsourcing and deteriorating economic conditions, as currently, we see enhanced risk due to the combined effects of each and the impact of the convergence of the two factors. This mutuality is illustrated in Figure 1, where we show risks that are attributable to outsourcing, risks that derive from economic distress, and risks that result from outsourcing during times of economic difficulties.

There are a number of scenarios that can be envisaged here. For example, displaced internal employees may believe that the chances of landing a new job are greatly diminished in a bad economy. This might result in their prolonging the transition to an outsourcer, and/or subverting the outsourcers' services after conversion.

In another situation, the outsourcer might be in distress due to the loss of business from clients' bankruptcies, mergers or acquisitions or downsizing, and clients may be concerned about similar events experienced by their outsourcers. The outsourcers' employees might think that their jobs are in jeopardy and may not provide the usual level of support. Conversely, the clients' employees may be disinterested in demanding the agreed-upon level of service if they themselves are threatened.

Figure 1. The Intersection of Risks due to Outsourcing and Economic Distress

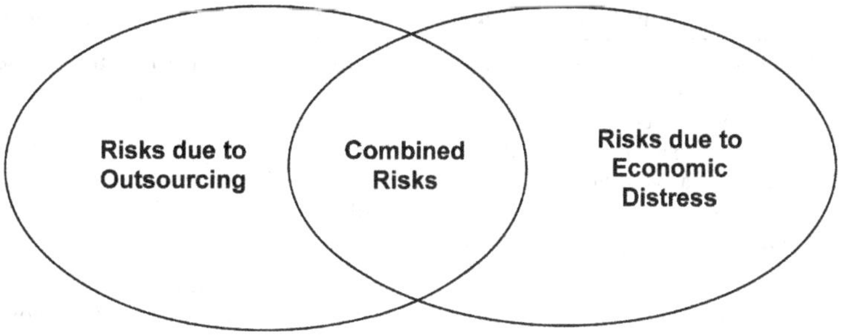

OUTSOURCING RISKS AND THEIR MITIGATION

A good summary of the legal and regulatory requirements, particularly in the U.S., for vendor due diligence, how issues should be addressed and what the related costs might be, are provided in (Bayuk, 2009).

In this chapter we suggest risk mitigation activities specifically related to economic distress, outsourcing and their combination, as shown in Table 2. Here we take the list of outsourcing risk categories shown in Table 1 and indicate how they are affected by economic hardship. We also indicate what remediating actions should be taken.

Loss of Control

When loss of control is due to low morale and motivation, both customer and provider organizations can make an effort to lift morale by such approaches as providing some additional benefits and arranging for community events, such as picnics, that go beyond the everyday norm. Control may be further wrested from client organizations due to fears by the providers that they might lose clients. This fear may translate into "game playing" wherein the provider extends its control over clients' activities so as to lock in the client.

Provider Viability

A key factor when considering which outsourcer to use is the anticipated viability of the service provider. While, even in good economic times, there are always some businesses that run into trouble, or are acquired by another company that has a different view of the outsourcing business, economic downturns generally lead to a greater number of bankruptcies, distress acquisitions, and the like. This suggests that more in-depth due diligence, including specific consideration of the failure of the service provider, is needed. Also, it is recommended that the risk should be spread across two or more vendors, subject to the criticality of the service, the efficiency of such an arrangement and the number of workable choices in a particular marketplace.

Relative Sizes of Customers and Outsourcers

There are concerns by customers that small providers may not survive. Another customer concern is that larger providers may decide to terminate arrangements with less profitable clients, or raise the latter's charges. Client organizations should select their portfolio of outsourcers ased upon consideration of such eventualities.

Table 2. Outsourcing Risk Categories, Impact of Economic Stress and Mitigation

Risk Category	Impact of Economic Stress	Mitigation Strategy
Loss of control	Motivation lower due to lack of job security, resulting in less interest in controlling environment by client or provider. Provider might intentionally increase control because of concern about losing client. Client might try to get more control because of potential decision to insource the process.	Introduce incentive bonuses and try to lift employee morale by being open with employees and fair with them if severance occurs. Take action to prevent "game playing" in an attempt to lock in business and discourage job protection activities.
Viability of service provider	Greater chance that service will file for bankruptcy or be acquired.	Perform detailed due diligence on critical existing and potential service providers. Spread services across a number of providers. Insurance should be written against compromise of systems and data and/or discontinuation of services.
Relative size of client and service provider	Generally larger providers with diverse client populations have relatively good chances of surviving Larger providers may use hard times to push out small providers.	Rank service providers by size, viability and diversity of clients and select those who score highly. This is no guarantee against fraud or other hidden problems, as in the case of Satyam, for example.
Quality of service	Likely that service providers will cut staff and try to meet service levels with fewer individuals. Also, other aspects of service may be cut.	Negotiate and enforce service level agreements that contemplate fluctuations in the market and business volumes.
Empathy	Service provider may cut hours of service, limit personal attention, not provide for specific user needs, etc.	Negotiate and enforce agreements that specify these service characteristics clearly.
Trust (Security, Privacy)	Insiders and others within the client and outsourcing organizations may be under financial pressure and look for or take opportunities for fraud, blackmail, etc.	Increase oversight of identity (authentication) and access (authorization) management. Increase enforcement and deterrence.
Performance (business continuity, data integrity)	Outsourcer might lower performance so as to reduce costs. Outsourcer might cut corners on backup, incident management and recovery in order to cut costs and remain competitive. Client and outsourcer may reduce checking of results under resource pressures making for higher error rates.	Client needs to enforce agreed-upon service level agreements. Client should increase oversight in order to reduce the possibility of being short-changed regarding backup and recovery and to ensure that the data checking and verification functions are not reduced. If anything they should be increased.
Lack of expertise	Highly qualified individuals in both the client and outsourcer organizations are more likely to leave organizations for more secure positions.	Communicate to key employees their importance to the arrangement and provide whatever incentives to stay that are available.
Hidden and uncertain costs	New costs related to unpredictable business levels might appear.	Continue to manage costs and investigate any unusual or unexpected changes.
Limited customization and enhancements	Both parties may be reluctant to spend on changes unless there are very clear economic benefits.	Sometimes it pays to invest in bad times in order to be able to take advantage in the turnaround.
Knowledge transfer	Outsourcers might be less inclined to share knowledge due to the belief that it will capture the client more effectively.	Policy and procedures to ensure that relevant knowledge is shared appropriately need to be defined and enforced.
Shared environments	Outsourcers have increased incentive to share resources so as to reduce their costs.	Clients must be specific in their demands to not have resources shared where sharing might impact security, privacy, performance, service, etc

continued on following page

Table 2. continued

Risk Category	Impact of Economic Stress	Mitigation Strategy
Legal and regulatory matters	Lawyers and regulators may become more active and pedantic in hard times.	The best protection is to have a clear, comprehensive agreed-upon set of terms and conditions in the agreement.
Extrication	Service providers are likely to be more resistant to requests to terminate the arrangement in difficult times and will present more obstacles to doing so.	The best protection is to have negotiated a contract that clearly describes the terms and conditions of termination of the contracted services.

Quality of Service

Quality of service may well be hit hard during difficult economic times because of the need for providers to cut staff and other resources to remain competitive and profitable in the face of falling revenues due to lower transaction volumes, fewer business projects, loss of clients and difficulty in attracting new clients. From the client perspective, it might become increasingly necessary to enforce existing service level agreements and, if possible, enhance agreements to account for the cost pressures on providers and clients themselves.

Empathy

Another aspect of service quality is empathy between client and provider staff members. Often, in difficult times, both parties are likely to cut staff and reassign some staff. Consequently, the interpersonal relationships among those who might have been interfacing for some time, often years, will be broken. Replacement staff may not have the same feeling of responsibiility as their predecessors or be willing to "go the extra mile," so that certain niceties, considered indicative of empathetic service, may well suffer. In such cases, it is often necessary to revert to the specific temrs of the service agreementm which may or may not adequately account for change. Service relationships need to be explicit and clear in the wording of contracts.

Trust

Trust, which emanates from the perception of security and privacy posture, is at increased risk when there is rapiid change and when ther is a propensity to circumvent security measures and controls. The tasks of authenticating and authorizing staff becomes much more difficult when organziations are cutting back. Also, with mergers and acquisitions of both clients and providers, roles and responsibilities change rapidly.

Since the risk of fraud, theft, and other misdeeds increase when economic times are hard and there is increased turbulence, it behooves clients to ratchet up the security oversight and enforcement as they relate to service providers.

Performance

In looking to cut back on expenses, providers may reduce certain aspects of service that do not necessarily show up in day-to-day performance figures for some time, but might have serious consequences and repercussions were a security incident to occur. In order to ensure that the expected levels of quality assurance, incident response, backup and recovery are maintained, clients should step up their oversight and, for example, verify that resiliency has not been compromised by cost reduction efforts. Clients must also decide how much providers should invest in resiliency (Axelrod, 2009b).

Lack of Expertise

Some organizations suffer more than others in a recession. As a consequence, better qualified, more experienced, and more productive individuals are more likely to transfer to other organizations and other sectors, which may be faring better in the generally poor economy. For example, it is possible that cloud computing service providers might draw experts from more traditional outsourcers. This can result in serious deterioration in clients' and providers' ability to maintain and improve systems and services. Both client organizations and providers should communicate with valued employees in particular and provide incentives where possible to encourage them to remain on staff.

Hidden and Unexpected Costs

The reduction of services and other forms of retrenchment can result in unexpected costs that can further exacerbate a bad situation. This might apply when there are discounts for higher volumes. Volume reductions might result in higher per unit costs. The benefits of volum discounts are a major driver in cloud computing where the largest providers can benefit hugely from their purchasing power and economies of scale. Clients, in particular, should stay on top of costs and investigate any changes in charges to verify that they are valid. If the current service agreements do not adequately account for volume reductions, then there may be a possibility to renegotiate some of the terms of the agreements.

Another consideration in reducing costs is to move fixed assets from client organizations to providers and rent back the resources on a variable basis. Another flavor of this same approach is to eliminate fixed assets and staff and replace the services with those from a third party.

Limited Enhancements

With money tight, organizations are less likely to invest in changes and enhancements, even when the changes can be shown to deliver considerable potential returns. In such cases, the return on investment might be high but there may not be any budget to pursue these investments. Both parties should evaluate changes and enhancements and try to obtain funds for such activities that may offer significant added value. Also, by not enhancing products and services, providers may lose significant amounts of new business and renewals to competitors. Similarly clients may lose to competitors if their outsourcers do not provide up-to-date systems, services and products.

Knowledge Transfer

When the economic environment threatens job security, employees of both clients and providers are generally less willing to share information in the belief that, by keeping certain knowledge to themselves, it is less likely that they will be fired. This ploy often backfires in that the employees might be viewed as obstructionist and be fired because of that.

When the retention of clients is at risk, providers are often reluctant to share knowledge if they are not contractually obligated to do so. This is due to the belief that knowledge sharing might reduce the grip a provider has on clients. Providers want to lock clients in even in prosperous times, so that in hard times, the desire for client lock-in increases.

Management needs to enforce knowledge sharing where the lack of sharing can be detrimental to one or both parties.

Shared Environments

There is increased incentive for providers to share resources across more clients so as to reduce costs. In fact resource sharing and virtualization are major drivers in cloud computing economics. However, such sharing will increase the risks if inadvertent disclosure of one client's data to another client. Also, if the underlying system were to fail, the impact would be =on a number of clients rather than just one, except if the provider has implemented adequate resiliency and redundancy in its applications, systems and network architecture.

The inadvertent sharing of personal information leads to obvious privacy concerns and the unintended sharing of intellectual property can adversely impact the competitiveness of clients. It is incumbent on clients to ensure that resources are not being shared in such ways that sensitive data might be compromised and performance might suffer.

Legal Activity

During difficult times there is a potential for increased crime, although there is a reduction in the likelihood that crimes will be detected due to distractions and reduced staff. Thus the increased criminal activity that is being made public is probably a smaller percentage of actual crimes than during better times, so that the real increase in detected and undetected crime combined is likely to be much higher than generally believed.

The increased crime results in not only more legal proceedings but also greater activity by legislative bodies in response to the growth of perceived crime, especially in regard to identity theft and fraud. Thus legislators tend to intensify their efforts in enacting laws to deter perpetrators from committing certain crimes. From the perspective of clients, it is important that they try to ensure that providers will comply with all relevant laws. This has become a major issue in the cloud computing arena.

Regulatory Responses

As has been seen over the past year or so, with a number of high profile frauds in the news, economic downturns expose fraudulent activities that might otherwise have been hidden in boom times. Sometimes the fact that certain frauds were not caught early by auditors, regulators and other overseers serves to induce a knee-jerk reaction from the those whose mission it is to ferret out such behavior. The reaction often swings the overseers to the other extreme in that they become much more active and much less permissive in their reviews, assessments and examinations.

As a result both clients and providers must be particularly careful to include compliance with regulations, guidance and rules in their agreements. Further they must put in place procedures to enforce adherence to these requirements.

Exit Strategy

The exit strategy is considered by many (particularly lawyers) to be one of the most important areas of a service agreement. In difficult economic times, there is an increase in the likelihood that both clients and providers will want to invoke the termination clauses in their contracts. Sometimes the conditions under which the termination is requested were not contemplated at the time the agreement was made. For example, there may be charges incurred for early termination. It is clearly much better to have tried to anticipate events and account for such exigencies when the contract was being negotiated. If this is not done, then the consequences might be harsh.

CONCLUSION

Even in good economic times, there are many risks relating to outsourcing that need to be addressed. However, in difficult economic environments, as the World economies have been experiencing in recent years, these risks are greatly amplified, leading not only to additional losses from economic distress, but also amplifying particular risks that result from the combination of outsourcing and the economies of the client and outsourcing countries. This necessitates greater due diligence and oversight by clients and outsourcers, even though resources may be severely restricted.

There are some risks that may be relatively rare in good economic times but are particularly damaging when economies take a turn for the worse. Whereas in good times, poor worker morale may be seen in relatively few organizations or may be confined to small ppickets within entities, in down economies the occurrence of bad morale is much more prevalent. We see negative views and actions proliferate when times are bad. As a result, some areas of risk, which previously could be ignored with some measure of assurance that any impact will remain small, will proliferate when hard times appear and much receive much more attention.

By trying to avoid the risk issues particular to difficult economic times, both client companies and service providers only exacerbate the situation. It is much better to be aware of how certain outsourcing risks might greatly increase in times of economic stress and to address them as best one can under the circumstances. In order to reduce the number and higher levels of risk, organizations must increase their risk mitigation activities, such as oversight and enforcement, over what would prevail in normal times.

REFERENCES

Axelrod, C. W. (2004). *Outsourcing Information Security*. Boston: Artech House.

Axelrod, C. W. (2008). Security and Change (pt. 1): Blackouts. Retrieved from www.bloginfosec.com

Axelrod, C. W. (2008b). Security and Change (pt. 2): Black Swans. Retrieved from www. bloginfosec.com

Axelrod, C. W. (2008c). Security and Change (pt. 3): White Knights. Retrieved from www. bloginfosec.com

Axelrod, C. W. (2008d). Security in Times of Crisis. Retrieved from www.bloginfosec.com

Axelrod, C. W. (2009a). An Adaptive Threat-Vulnerability Model and the Economics of Protection. In Gupta, M., & Sharman, R. (Eds.), *Social and Human Elements of Information Security: Emerging Trends and Countermeasures*. Hershey, PA: IGI Global.

Axelrod, C. W. (2009b). Investing in Software Resiliency. *CrossTalk Magazine*, *22*(6), 20–25.

Bayuk, J. (2009). Vendor Due Diligence. *ISACA Journal, 3*, 34-38. Available at www.isaca.org (membership required).

Berinato, S. (August, 2001). Security Outsourcing: Exposed! *CIO Magazine*. Available at www. cio.com.

Campbell, G. K., & Lefler, R. A. (2009). Security Alert: When the economy's down – and budgets are stressed – the threat level rises. *Harvard Business Review*, ▪▪▪, 104–105.

Earl, M. J. (1996). The risks of outsourcing IT. *Sloan Management Review*, *47*(3), 57–74.

Rost, J. (2005). *The Insider's Guide to Outsourcing Risks and Rewards*. Boca Raton, FL: Auerbach Publications.

Tho, I. (2005). *Managing the Risks of Outsourcing*. Burlington, MA: Elsevier.

Zarrella, E. (2009). Managing IT Governance Through Market Turbulence. *ISACA Journal, 4*. Available at www.isaca.org (membership required).

Chapter 3

A Comparison of Cyber–Crime Definitions in India and the United States

Himanshu Maheshwari
University of South Florida, USA

H.S. Hyman
University of South Florida, USA

Manish Agrawal
University of South Florida, USA

ABSTRACT

Unlike traditional crimes, it is difficult to define legal jurisdiction and authority for prosecuting cyber crimes. This issue is further complicated by differences in definitions of cyber crime in different countries. This chapter motivates the issue with an example of the ILOVEYOU virus and compares the legal provisions to combat cyber-crime in the US and India. The authors find that there are significant differences between India and the US in definitions of cybercrimes. It appears that in the United States, it is a crime to access information that has been declared to be confidential. In India, criminality requires dissemination of the information obtained without authorization. Another notable difference between the prosecutions of cybercrimes in the two countries relates to obscenity and decency laws.

INTRODUCTION

While most individuals and businesses use the Internet as a communication medium to learn and to socialize, other individuals and groups use the Internet as a medium for criminal purposes. The Internet has positively transformed many legitimate business activities, lowering costs and accelerating transaction speed. It has also served as a platform for criminals who strategize online and attack valuable targets at a remote distance from the crime scene. (Phil Williams)

Successful investigation, apprehension and prosecution of cyber-crime require an extension of existing attitudes and assumptions of legal

DOI: 10.4018/978-1-60960-123-2.ch003

boundaries, and methods used by law enforcement to solve crimes. One traditional assumption associated with investigating crime is the physical proximity of victim and perpetrator. Many personal crimes occur face to face, such as robbery or assault. Property crimes such as burglaries and thefts occur locally and the perpetrators are usually, but not always, present at the scene of the crime.

Some exceptions to this usual occurrence are instances of conspiracy, and principal theory; both provide for prosecution of participants to a crime, who may not be present at the time of its occurrence. Perpetrators of cybercrime, by the very nature of the offences committed, are located remotely, and quite often in other countries, where it is difficult to determine legal jurisdiction. Which country has the authority to prosecute? Is it the country of the victim or the defendant? Where did the crime actually take place?

By now many readers are familiar with scams originating in Nigeria, in which the criminal claims to have access to millions of dollars, and all that is needed from the victim is a few thousand dollars to pay the transfer taxes. If a person from Nigeria sends an email to an individual in the United States, requesting money and the individual sends the money to Canada, where did the crime take place, in one, two, or all three countries?

Remotely perpetrated financial scams are not new phenomena. There are many laws and agencies in the United States specifically mandated to target crimes such as wire fraud (18 USC 1343, mail fraud (18 USC, Chapter 63), and money laundering (Bank Secrecy Act of 1970, Patriot Act of 2001). However, resources now must consider the impact of crimes that are launched from remote locations far beyond the borders of the victim country. For example, the Love Bug virus, which was launched from the Philippines in 2000, caused damage to computers in more than twenty countries, causing damage estimated to be in the billions of dollars. As described later in the paper, the perpetrators were caught in no

time, but authorities could do little to prosecute them because of weaknesses in cybercrime laws.

Definitions of cybercrime are not uniform across countries, so behavior legally defined as a crime in the victim's country may not be defined as such in the perpetrator's country. For example, while it was relatively easy for US agencies to trace the origins of the ILOVEYOU virus to an apartment in Manila in the Philippines. Prosecution was another matter because at the time of the offense, no law existed in The Philippines that made this behaviour illegal. The behaviour in this case was the creation of a software virus.

In discussing cybercrime, it becomes necessary to begin with a clear listing of cybercrimes defined within each jurisdiction. This paper examines the definitions of cybercrimes in India and the United States. We draw upon the US Code and the Indian IT Act. The paper is organized as follows we begin with an introduction to cybercrime, cyber law and cyber forensics we then report current statistics on reported cybercrime. This is followed by a comparison of legal provisions to help prosecute cybercrime in India and the United States.

CYBER CRIME

Cybercrime is defined as crimes committed on the Internet using the computer either as a tool or a targeted victim. However, some overlap occurs in many cases and it is difficult to have a clear cut classification system. We breakdown cybercrime along two dimensions. The first dimension the computer as a tool and as a target. The second dimension is the classification of crime itself: Person, Property, and Victimless/Vice.

In our first dimension, we divide cybercrime between the following two categories:

a. Using the computer as a tool: In this case, the target of the cybercrime is an individual. Such crimes usually do not require a high level of technical expertise; the target is somebody in the real world. The objective is to attack a person in a very subtle manner and on the psychological level. This situation is similar to criminal stalking cases. Quite often law enforcement is befuddled by the lack of a clear, unambiguous act on the part of the criminal in order to prosecute. How many times do we read about the ex-girlfriend killed by the jealous boyfriend? When witnesses are interviewed after the fact, everyone recalls some incident that "was not quite right." So why are the police not able to prevent such a tragedy? The answer is that incidents that are subtle and ambiguous are simply difficult to sustain a prosecution. Cybercriminals take advantage of these types of seams in the fabric of the law. Perpetrators are usually harder to trace and apprehend, given the remote, often international origin of attack, and have typically been operating for a significant period of time, honing their skills. Take the Nigerian scam example. How many people still fall victim to that offense, despite the attention it has been given. A successful financial crime takes practice. Numerous failed attempts serve as valuable lessons for future innovations. Cybercrime is well suited to an iterative approach to crime. The world has billions of people with millions of IP addresses just waiting to be harassed, conned, or otherwise victimized.

b. Using the computer as a target: These crimes are usually committed by groups of collaborating individuals. Unlike the previous category, these crimes require the perpetrators to have a high level of technical knowledge and skill. Also, due to the fact these crimes require coordination of numbers of individuals, and orthogonal skill sets, greater sophistication is obtained in the criminal episode. Many catastrophic events are blamed on these uncorroborated conspiracies, but little proof is ever ferreted out. An example of this would be the massive

power grid failure, in the Northeast United States. The second dimension we use to evaluate Cybercrime is the classification of the crime itself. The general legal framework in criminal law divides crimes in three categories by victim type. There are crimes against persons such as, assaults, robberies, stalking. There are crimes against property such as home burglary, theft of unattended property, vandalism. There are crimes considered victimless. Many people consider drug possession and other vice crimes to be in this category. This category is often misunderstood. For instance, many people consider prostitution as victimless given that both parties are consenting. Others believe the crime is a means of abusing women, and imposes hidden costs on society, such as health risks and untaxed wages. We can classify cybercrime using these categories:

1. Cybercrimes against People: These crimes such as harassment via e-mails that can be sexual, racial or religious in nature or financial scams are easy to relate to their everyday physical crime counterparts. Some cybercrimes are difficult to categorize. For instance, transmission of child pornography; is it a crime against the person of the child, or is it a victimless crime because it is only the transmission being prosecuted.

The "Melissa" virus that affected nearly more than 1.2 million users in Dec 1999, in the US itself is a classic example of such a scenario. Cyber harassment as a crime is closely related to another crime area which is violation of privacy of citizens.

2. Cybercrimes against Private Entities: These types of crimes usually include computer vandalism and/or transmission of harmful programs to businesses/people with the intent to cause harm. Businesses have long

been known to spy on their rivals to gain an edge over their competition. The internet is merely providing a new means to accomplish this same illicit goal. What cyber property crimes and physical property crimes have in common is that both seek to attack property that is unattended.

3. Cybercrimes against Government, (also called victimless crimes): The popularity of the internet has given rise to the use of Cyberspace as a tool that can be used against the government and also to terrorize the citizens of a country. Cyber-terrorism is a crime that stands out in this category and is an increasing menace that governments all over are trying to deal with. People cracking into military or government websites or installations are classic examples of cyber terrorism. According to Mr. A.K. Gupta, Deputy Director (Co-ordination), CBI-India, terrorist outfits across the world are increasingly using the internet as a means to communicate and transfer funds without being detected.

Examples of Some Commonly Observed Cyber Crimes:

1. Spamming: Spamming is the act of sending unsolicited e-mails/messages to several users in an instance. It is usually done to advertise products to customers. However, Spamming can also be used to block a users' access to resources. It can used to target an individual/business by sending bulk e-mails to them or their specific IP address. Spammers usually send hundreds of e-mails per second. Most of the spamming scams originate and exist in Nigeria. Spammers are usually characterized into Hucksters and Fraudsters. Hucksters usually have a slow turnaround from the time they send their first message; send a lot of e-mails to harvest stamped addresses and usually send product based spam. The

Fraudsters on the other hand have a quicker turnaround time and usually harvest an e-mail address and send small number of messages to each address at a time.

2. Piracy: This is one of the most common evils faced globally, by most of the manufacturing companies at some point in their life cycle. It involves the unauthorized and illegal distribution (and production) of software applications, games, movies, music etc. These pirates usually buy a genuine version of the software and then make it available to other users either online or through some other means without the permission of the original owner or even notifying them of their activities.

Cybercrime and its Links to Social Media

Web 2.0 has been growing at a steady pace since its inception. The last decade has seen an upsurge of networking sites and social media both locally and globally. Associated with these upsurges in social networking is the upsurge in crimes that have been caused or those that have at least been helped by these social networking sites. A classic example in this case is the problems encountered by Google's social networking site Orkut in Brazil. After the popularity Orkut enjoyed in Brazil, when Google launched advertising on Orkut, it ran into a plethora of troubles. Its troubles ranged from child pornography abuse, aiding in narcotics dealings through the use of Orkut to planned and executed kidnappings and murders over the web.

Brazilian courts ordered Google to share its customer data and other sensitive information to probe these crimes. However, Google refused to co-operate with them, resulting in the Brazilian government imposing a $100,000 per day fine on Google till their compliance requests were not agreed and acted upon by Google. Google in its defense cited absence of international jurisdiction on the part of the Brazilian government, since its servers were in the US and not in Brazil, and hence did not hand over the required information to the Brazilian authorities. This case highlights the need to have a uniform and globally accepted standard for Jurisdiction, Sovereignty, Governance and Net Neutrality, as discussed earlier.

Brazil is not the only country where Orkut has faced legal issues. It has also run into problems with Indian Law Enforcement agencies. Many people also believe there is a moral backlash, due to political motivations in India (Gaurav 2009). These agencies have protested the formation of communities propagating hatred against India, Indian cultures and their religious beliefs on Orkut. Orkut has also had its share of narcotics, kidnapping and murder troubles in India, since the website has been misused to commit these crimes.

However, social media overall has not faced much problems in the US, since there are different laws and legislation that help and prevent such anti-social activities. A classic example in this is the case of a student Ajith D from Kerala, India who started a hate community on Orkut against one of the political parties (Shiv Sena) in India. Though the Indian constitution grants Freedom of Speech to all its citizens in the country, the Supreme Court did not protect this student's rights when he requested that the charges against him by the political party be thrown out of the court. The court cited legal issues and examples, and denied his request (Gaurav 2009). This is in sharp contrast to the US, where such charges would generally not be entertained in courts, since the charter of rights (First Amendment) grants freedom of speech and expression to everyone.

VICTIMS

To have a complete understanding of what makes a cybercrime succeed where a physical crime would fail; one needs to consider the perspective of the victim. For instance, if someone came up to an individual on the street and explained how

they had access to several million dollars, and all they needed from the victim was a few hundred dollars to handle the transfer fees, that crime has very little chance of success. But change the facts from a street conman to an email from Nigeria, and the chances of success have just increased many folds, spelling errors and all. The internet offers the inventor of the above crime two unique advantages. The first is the law of sheer numbers. The criminal can attempt this crime millions of times in a single day. The second is the fact that we live in a heavily transaction based society. It is not unusual to complete entire business dealings over the internet, without ever having established a social foundation with the person we are doing business with. When the email from Nigeria arrives, many victims think nothing of the fact that some stranger is soliciting them to send money to a faraway place, or that the message is riddled with spelling and syntax errors.

So what are the vulnerabilities that make victims fall prey to cybercrime. The most commonly observed categories of cybercrime victims include (Joseph 2006):

1. **Novice:** These people usually have little or no knowledge of the internet. Whereas these people would never give their money to a stranger that knocked on their door, they are ignorant of "Phishing" crimes and the existence of such criminals and hence are most susceptible to fall prey to such crimes.
2. **Credulous:** These are people who usually fall prey to the crimes committed on the Internet, not because of their limited knowledge of the Internet and its darker sides, but rather because the scam seems plausible in their own understanding of how the "new technology driven" world works. Cyber criminals love this group of people since they are the "soft targets" and are usually prone to bring in more prey.
3. **Greedy:** These people usually fall due to their own greed. They believe in the fly-by-night

and get-rich-quick schemes. Luring them is the easiest thing to do for an online criminal into performing any kind of activity.

4. **Unlucky:** There are some people who are just plain unlucky and are usually in the wrong place and at the wrong time (in cyberspace). They usually believe that they are conducting business with genuine people and end up getting scammed into various deals.

As seen in Figure 1, the most common categories of cybercrime complaints relate to breach of trust through frauds at auctions and non-delivery of products purchased online.

Further, as seen in Figure 2, most complainants of cybercrime involve mature adults, not naïve young people. Over 40% of the complaints come from people over 40 years of age. This relates to the information in Figure 1 because this complainant population is relatively prosperous and is more likely to bring issues of non-delivery to the notice of the authorities.

According to the IC3 report, the top 10 countries from where complaints originated were:

1. United States 91.9%
2. Canada 2.10%
3. United Kingdom 1.1%
4. Australia 0.60%
5. India 0.36%
6. Mexico 0.18%
7. South Africa 0.16%
8. Germany 0.14%
9. France 0.14%
10. Philippines 0.11

The reader will notice that the vast majority of registered complaints originate in North America. It would be useful to explore the possible reasons that underlie those numbers so that future research may uncover predictive factors and users could educate themselves to lower their exposure to victimization. Some possible factors include the relative ease with which cyber crime complaints can be filed in North America and the relative popularity of computers among the population, particularly seniors who may be more gullible to phishing and other attacks. Another possibility relates to the extensive use of credit cards in North America and the large-scale attacks on Heartland systems and T J Maxx, which may have compromised credit cards of a large segment of the US population. A cluster analysis of the demographics of the complainants and economic variables as-

Figure 1. Cybercrime complaint categories (2007) (source IC3 report, 2007)

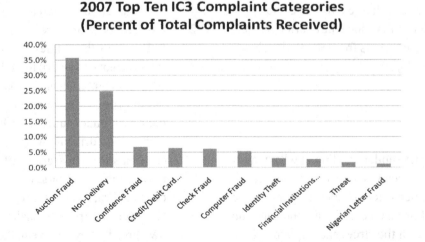

Figure 2. Cybercrime complainant demographics (source IC3 report, 2007)

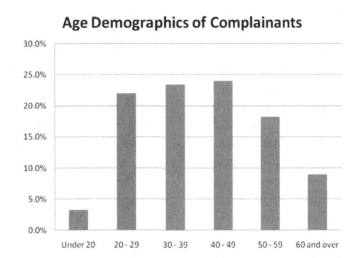

sociated with the crimes may help resolve some of these possibilities.

CYBER LAW

Cyber law is a term that helps describe the legal issues related to use of information and communications technology (ICT), particularly "cyberspace", i.e. the Internet. It is less a distinct field of law in the way that property or contracts are as it is an intersection of many legal fields, including intellectual property, privacy, freedom of expression, and jurisdiction. In essence, cyber law is an attempt to integrate the challenges presented by human activity on the Internet with the legacy system of laws applicable to the physical world.

Need for Cyber Law

When the concept of the Internet was founded and later developed, little did the developers know that the Internet would have the power of being transformed into a monster that could be used for several illegal and immoral activities and it would eventually need to be regulated. There are several disturbing things that happen in

cyberspace ranging from Identity Theft and terrorism to money laundering. Due to the anonymous nature of the Internet, anybody can indulge in a variety of criminal activities with impunity. These "grey areas" are being exploited by individuals, companies and their like to perpetuate criminal activities in cyberspace, thus creating the need for Cyber laws.

Importance of Cyber Law

Cyber laws are important since they cover some if not almost every aspect of the transactions and activities we do over the Internet. Cyber laws may appear to be a very technical field and one may presume that it does not have any bearing on activities conducted in cyberspace. On the contrary, the truth is that whether we realise it or not, every action and reaction in cyberspace has some legal and/or cyber legal perspective associated with it.

Sovereignty

We must research in depth to learn more about the methods, origins and motivations of the growing criminal groups. Policy and decision makers in the government, business and law enforcement must take urgent and necessary steps to prevent such activities from occurring and spreading. They need to have policies, methods, and regulations in place to detect incursions, investigate and prosecute the architects of such crimes and prevent future crimes. They also need to ensure that they protect the sovereignty of the country against such criminal/terrorist groups. In the early 1990s, a survey of 73 global companies found that almost 70% of the respondents had encountered politically-imposed constraints on trans-border data flows. These were primarily related to data privacy law differences between countries. The remedy to this problem is to design a system like Safe Harbor, which was designed to streamline U.S. - EU trans-border data flows.

Jurisdiction: The Case of the ILOVEYOU Virus

The Love Bug virus was disseminated around the world in May 2000. The virus was sent as an email attachment and emails carrying the virus had the text "ILOVEYOU" in their subject line. The virus attachment was a VB script file named "LOVE-LETTER-FOR-YOU.TXT.vbs". Since the 'vbs' extension is hidden by default, users opened it thinking it was a text file. When opened, the worm made a number of malicious changes to the user's system from which the system was generally unrecoverable, and sent a copy of itself to everyone in the victim's Windows Address Book using the victim's address as the sender address. Within hours of its appearance, the Federal Bureau of Investigation had identified Manila as the source of the virus. FBI and the Philippines' National Bureau of Investigation identified Reomel Ramones and his room-mate Onel de Guzman as the persons responsible for disseminating the virus. De Guzman was a student at the AMA computer college in Manila.

What is interesting about the case is that though it was relatively trivial to identify the authors of the virus, it was much more difficult to link them to a crime. Since Philippines had not criminalized virus dissemination at the time, de Guzman could neither be prosecuted in the Philippines nor extradited for prosecution in the United States (Goodman and Brenner 2002).

Eventually the two were charged with violating the Access Device Regulation Act, a law designed mainly to penalize credit card fraud. The act was used because both Ramones and de Guzman had used pre-paid Internet cards to obtain Internet connections. However, upon later investigation, it was decided that the terms of the law could not be extended to Ramones or de Guzman. Eventually the two were charged with malicious mischief. However, this charge too was dismissed because there was only one ISP in the Philippines that filed a complaint in the case. Intent is a necessary ingredient of successful prosecution for the offense and upon investigation, the Department of Justice of the Philippines found no tangible evidence that Ramones or de Guzman specifically intended to damage the ISP's facilities. Both Ramones and de Guzman were released from custody and it is believed that one or both of them now work in the software industry (Severino H. Gana).

Since then, Philippines have criminalized virus dissemination. However, the crime is a minor offense punishable by 2 weeks' imprisonment and a fine equivalent to $100. By comparison, in the United States, disseminating a computer virus is punishable with up to 10 years in prison and a fine of up to $250,000.

COMPARISON OF LEGAL PROVISIONS FOR CYBERCRIME IN INDIA AND THE US

The case of the ILOVEYOU virus shows the importance of being aware of definitions of cyber-crime in different countries. With this background, we can compare the provisions of cybercrime in India and the United States.

In the United States, cybercrime is not defined by one specific law or regulation. In fact, if one searches for the law defining cybercrime, one will be searching for quite some time. The reason is that the United States Code (USC) does not define cybercrime the same way as other crimes such as bank robbery, or kidnapping. In the USC, cybercrime is a method, not a category. So a bank theft could be accomplished, by sneaking in at night and stealing the physical currency, or by using a computer. In fact, the word cybercrime is not a legal term, as much as a legal colloquialism. It is more often listed as a computer related offense, and even then, it is found as a sub-topic in several sources.

An example of this scattered categorization of cybercrime is found in 18 USC, Chapter 47, Fraud and False Statements, not "Cybercrime," or even "Computer Related Crimes." Chapter 47 of 18 USC covers cybercrime by proscribing the actions associated with it, consistent with our descriptions in this chapter. .

For instance, if one wants to find out if stealing someone's back information using a computer is punishable in the United States, one would look to 18 USC 1030, which is not entitled cybercrime, but instead is entitled Fraud and Related Activity in Connection With Computers. The title may be different, but the content covers the same type of actions described. The statute provides that anyone who: "…intentionally accesses a computer without authorization or exceeds authorized access, and thereby obtains[…]information contained in a financial record of a financial institution, or of a card issuer." Accessing another computer without authorization through the medium of email is covered in 18 USC 1037, Fraud and Related Activity in Connection with Electronic Mail.

Hacking is defined by the illegal actions associated with the term as colloquially used. The United States Department of Justice has a web site dedicated to "Cybercrime." It can be found at www.justice.gov/criminal/cybercrime. It is ironic that the web site is dedicated to a term that appears no-where in the USC. The web site is an excellent means of learning what laws may be applied to punish cybercrimes and their associated activities. The site also offers several posted articles by legal professionals offering information and advice in handling cybercrime activity.

"Trafficking" is another loaded term that conjures up illegal drug activity. In fact, the term trafficking is applied to a number of illegal activities including drugs, prostitution, obscene materials, and of particular interest to us, passwords. As it turns out, the applicable laws for password trafficking activities are situational dependent on the accused actions associated with the acquisition and dissemination of the passwords.

An example of this is the 2003 case of Mehdi Rowghani and his co-defendants. They were indicted by the US Attorney for the Northern District of Texas. Their accused crime was password trafficking. The law used to prosecute them, 18 USC 1030 -- Fraud and Related Activity in Connection With Computers. Section 1030 is punishable by 1 year in prison. That does not seem like a significant deterrent. However, Mr. Rowghani and his co-defendants were charged with 15 counts of violation of section 1030 – that is 15 years in prison.

Another example of a traditional crime that has cyber methods of being committed is obscenity. This crime is punishable under the traditional laws associated with possession, or laws making it illegal to transmit. Transmission can be through various media such as fax, mail, or in our case, the computer. Obscenity crime overlaps with indecency and pornography, all of which The United States Congress has attempted to regulate, starting in 1996 with The Communication Decency Act (CDA). It can be found in Title V of The Telecommunications Act of 1996 and is the first legislative attempt to specifically regulate pornography, indecency as related to children, and obscenity on the internet by US federal law. Other legislation soon followed such as the Child On-Line Protection Act (COPA), and the Child

Internet Protection Act (CIPA). These laws deal with the regulation of communications which sometimes run afoul of the First Amendment to the US Constitution dealing with Freedom of Speech. COPA, CIPA and CDA have been challenged in the courts in cases such as *Reno v. Shea, Reno v. American Civil Liberties Union*, and *Nitke v. Gonzalez.*

India's equivalent law to 18 USC 1030 is The Information Technology Act of 2000. The main difference between the USC and the Indian Technology Act is form rather than substance. Both laws seek to prosecute offenses that make use of computers as the tools of the crime. The USC provides for the prosecution of cybercrimes in the same manner as physical crimes, but adds section 1030 to identify the use of a computer or the internet as the means for committing the offense. The Technology Act takes a different approach. The Act specifically states that it is intended to regulate conduct within electronic commerce.

"An Act to provide legal recognition for transactions carried out by means of electronic data interchange and other means of electronic communication, commonly referred to as electronic commerce", which involve the use of alternatives to paper-based methods of communication and storage of information." (Indian Gazette, June 2002).

Whereas, federal authorities in the United States rely on 18 USC as an inclusive component within Chapter 47 of the Code that deals with General Fraud crimes, India has dedicated an entire provision of penal code to electronic commerce. For example, The Technology Act provides definitions for private key, public key, and digital signatures. Title 18 of the USC makes no such distinctions. This is not to say that US federal legislation ignores these definitions -- they are found scattered in numerous laws and publications. For instance, information on digital signatures is found in The Federal Information Processing Standards, Publication 186, not in the USC. A comparison between the Indian Information and

Technology Act of 2002, and its counterpart 18 USC 1030 demonstrates a marked difference in the method each law uses to prosecute offenses by use of computers as the tool of the crime. The United States prosecutes cybercrimes by combining numerous laws to achieve a successful criminal filing. India on the other hand makes use of a uniform law designed specifically for cybercriminal offenses.

One big difference is that the Technology Act has a provision for Cyber-Terrorism, with a penalty of life imprisonment. According to a May, 2009 report in *The Times of India*, a case invoking this section of the Act, has been filed by the Mumbai Police. According to the Police, the case involves the sending of threatening emails. What is significant about the case is that it is the first known attempt to use the cyber-terrorism provision of the Technology Act. (*The Times of India* May 2009).

The US counterpart to the cyber terrorism provision of the Technology Act can be found in the Patriot Act. This was the federal law passed in response to the 911 attacks. Section 814 of the Patriot Act, Entitled Deterrence and Prevention of Cyber terrorism, once again refers itself back to 18 USC 1030.

Table 1 is an attempt to compare the legal provisions against cybercrime in the two countries.

We find that there are significant differences between India and the US in prosecutions of cybercrimes. Though case law in the domain is still emerging, it appears that in the United States, it is a crime to access information that has been declared to be confidential. In India, criminality requires dissemination of the information obtained without authorization.

Another notable difference between the prosecutions of cybercrimes in the two countries relates to obscenity and decency laws. The United States has a long-standing cultural history involving the passionate defense of the right to free speech remaining inviolate. We see many challenges to new laws, by organizations, such as the American

Table 1. Comparison of legal provisions of cybercrime in India and the US

Offence	Legal provisions in India		Legal provisions in the United States	
Unauthorized access	disclose information held in confidence to another person	Up to 2 years or up to Rs. 100,000 or both	Unauthorized access of computer or information deemed by law or executive order to require protection.	Fine and up to 10 years for first offense Fine and up to 20 years for later offenses
Unauthorized access			Financial records Computer or information to cause damage exceeding $5,000 Computer used by govt agency	Fine and up to 1 year for first offense Fine and up to 10 years for later offenses
Unauthorized access			Financial records if laws are violated or goal was private gain	Fine and up to 5 years
Fraud	Forgery for the purpose of cheating	Imprisonment up to 7 years or fine or both.	Unauthorized access that aids fraud	Fine and up to 5 years
Fraud	Forgery for the purpose of harming reputation	Imprisonment up to 3 years or fine or both.		
Unauthorized transmission			program, information, code, or command and damages a protected computer	Fine and up to 10 years for first offense Fine and up to 20 years for later offenses
Damage			Unauthorized access or transmission that causes injury, impaired medical treatment, public safety or national security	Fine and up to 10 years for first offense Fine and up to 20 years for later offenses
Trafficking	Section 366 B IPC	Imprisonment up to 10 years or fine or both	Passwords if it affects commerce or government	
Extortion	Section 383 IPC	Imprisonment up to 3 years or fine or both.	Transmission of threat to cause damage to a protected computer	Fine and up to 5 years
Tampering with source code	conceals, destroys or alters computer source code which is required to be kept or maintained by law	Up to Rs. 200,000 or up to 3 years or both		
Hacking	destroys or deletes or alters or diminishes in value any information residing in a computer resource	Up to Rs. 500,000 or up to 3 years or both		
Obscenity	Publish lascivious material	First Conviction - Up to 3 years and up to Rs. 500,000 Second or subsequent Conviction - Up to 5 years and up to Rs. 1000,000		
Misrepresentation	misrepresentation to obtain any license or Digital Signature Certificate	Up to two years, or up to Rs. 100,000 or both		

continued on following page

Table 1. continued

Offence	Legal provisions in India		Legal provisions in the United States	
False digital certificate	Publishing a revoked or fake digital certificate	Up to two years, or up to Rs. 100,000 or both		
Identity Theft	fraudulently or dishonestly make use of the electronic signature, password or any other unique identification feature	Up to Rs. 100,000 or up to 3 years or both		
Dishonestly receiving stolen computer resource or communication devices	receives or retains any stolen computer resource or communication device	Up to Rs. 100,000 or up to 3 years or both		
Defraud by impersonating using computer resources	Cheats by impersonation using any communication device or computer resource	Up to Rs. 100,000 or up to 3 years or both		
Violation of Privacy	Intentionally captures, publishes or transmits the image of a private area of any person without his or her consent	Up to Rs. 200,000 or up to 3 years or both		
Cyber Terrorism		Imprisonment up to life.		

Civil Liberties Union (ACLU) that have assumed a watch-dog roll to protect free speech. Although the Indian Constitution has a charter of rights, which guarantees freedom of speech, the Country does not have as robust a history challenging newly established federal laws in the name of such freedom.

CONCLUSION

News events and common knowledge suggest that the United States and India both seek to vigorously prosecute cybercrimes. Both countries have broad based laws on the books that empower law enforcement to apprehend and file charges against cybercrime. Laws in both countries appear to encourage law enforcement agencies to deter and prevent cyber attacks and cybercriminal acts. The

main difference is in the forms of the legislation promulgated. The United States treats cybercrimes as an add-on charge to existing traditional criminal codes, creating a scattered incorporation by reference approach. India has chosen to pass an entire body of law dedicated to defining and proscribing the entire electronic method of commerce, communication and technology. It will be interesting to see how the law enforcement agencies of these two countries fare over the next ten to twenty years in their effectiveness in prosecuting cyber based crimes.

ACKNOWLEDGMENT

This research was supported by NSF grant # 0926376. The usual disclaimer applies.

REFERENCES

Gaurav. (2009). *Shiv Sena's Orkut Campaign: The Limits to Freedom of Expression in an Intolerant India.* Retrieved February 20, 2010, from http://www.gauravonomics.com/blog/shiv-senas-orkut-campaign-the-limits-to-freedom-of-expression-in-an-intolerant-india/.

Goodman, M. D., & Brenner, S. W. (2002). The Emerging Consensus on Criminal Conduct in Cyberspace. *UCLA Journal of Law and Technology*, *6*(1), 153.

2007IC3 Report. (2007). Retrieved January 18, 2010, 2010, from http://www.ic3.gov/media/annualreport/2007_IC3Report.pdf.

Joseph, A. E. (2006). *Cybercrime definition.* June 28, 2006. Retrieved January 28, 2010, from http://www.crime-research.org/articles/joseph06/.

Phil Williams, C. C. C. (n.d.). *Organized Crime and Cyber-Crime: Implications for Business.* Retrieved February 21, 2010, 2010, from www.cert.org/archive/pdf/cybercrime-business.pdf.

Severino, H. Gana, J.(n.d.). *Prosecution Of Cyber Crimes Through Appropriate Cyber Legislation In The Republic Of The Philippines.* Retrieved February 20, 2010, 2010, from http://www.acpf.org/WC8th/AgendaItem2/I2%20Pp%20Gana,Phillipine.html

United States Department of Justice. Computer Crime & Intellectual Property Section. (n.d.). Retrieved from http://www.justice.gov/criminal/cybercrime/ccips.html

Chapter 4
Emergency Response to Mumbai Terror Attacks:
An Activity Theory Analysis

Divya Shankar
University of Buffalo at SUNY New York, USA

Manish Agrawal
University of South Florida, USA

H. Raghav Rao
University of Buffalo at SUNY New York, USA

ABSTRACT

The Mumbai terror attacks of November 2008 lasted for over 60 hours and resulted in the death of over 172 people. The attack revealed several shortcomings of the emergency response preparedness in Mumbai. This chapter concentrates on the emergency response provided and uses activity theory to analyze it. The authors explore the diverse dimensions of emergency, determine the lessons learned from the incident and evaluate the emergency response. They suggest how operations could be improved thus setting a standard for any future emergency response.

INTRODUCTION

The balance of safety and wellbeing of the public is disturbed by an emergency situation. Emergency responders try to mitigate this danger and restore the balance of public welfare and security during an emergency. This act is termed as emergency response. These emergencies could occur at a national level and hence they can be large and complex which could necessitate in the cooperation of several agencies. Immediate measures should be taken by emergency responders to ensure safety of people and to mitigate the impact of the emergency. The key to a successful emergency response is how effectively the pre-specified emergency response plan is executed and how well it can dynamically adapt to the change in scope of the crisis. Deviations from the norm can be ex-

DOI: 10.4018/978-1-60960-123-2.ch004

pected in an emergency even when there is a plan in place. Emergencies at a national level require utmost attention and consideration because they involve capably aligning the emergency response processes and ensuring interoperability between systems from different agencies. This could be realized with the help of Activity Theory which assists in framing standards and ideal practices for large scale security operations. Activity Theory is a broad approach that takes a new perspective and develops novel conceptual tools for tackling many of the theoretical and methodological questions (Engestrom 1999).

BACKGROUND

Mumbai is the largest and busiest city in India. Mumbai (formerly known as Bombay) is located on the west coast of India and is the capital of the State of Maharashtra. It is the financial capital of India and serves as its main commercial hub. On 26th November 2008 the city of Mumbai faced a terrorist attack that mercilessly caused the destruction of human life and property.

A group of terrorists attacked several locations in Mumbai including hotels like Taj Mahal Palace hotel & Trident (formerly known as Oberoi) hotel. They also targeted several other popular public locations including the city's main commuter railway station, the Chatrapati Shivaji railway station, formerly known as Victoria Terminus, Leopold Café, Cama hospital & Nariman house. The attack was brought under control two days later on the 28th of November 2008 by the Indian security forces. This attack was well planned and coordinated and it involved the usage of digital technology for communication (Oh, Agrawal and Rao). The terrorists attacked Mumbai in several public locations simultaneously. In addition there was also an incident of misinformation. While the Indian security forces were trying to identify the terrorists, an email from Deccan Mujahideen claimed responsibility for the attacks. It was later

ascertained that the group never existed. Before this attack, terrorism in India did not incorporate many components seen in the Mumbai attacks – multiple locations, extended siege, and use of hand-held weapons. The Mumbai terror attacks of November 2008 underscore the necessity for better emergency preparedness (Rabasa, Blackwill, Chalk, Cragin, Fair, Jackson, Jenkins, Jones, Shestak and Tellis 2008).

Emergency response is the set of actions taken to lessen the impact and minimize danger of an unforeseen incident which threatens public safety. It is a complex activity, typically involving multiple agencies. Activity Theory is a powerful and clarifying descriptive tool with the objective to understand the unity of consciousness and activity (Nardi 1995). This theory gives the flexibility of converting complex tasks into activities which makes it easy to interpret and manage. In this chapter we try to integrate the various activities in emergency response using Activity Theory with specific reference to the Mumbai terror attacks of 2008.

LITERATURE REVIEW

The following literature reviews highlight the usefulness of Activity Theory. We also draw attention to emergency-as-activity and describe the emergency response activities of the Mumbai terror attacks.

Activity Theory may be outlined by five fundamental principles as suggested by Engestrom –

- The first principle is that a collective, artifact-mediated and object-oriented activity system, seen in its network relations to other activity systems, is taken as the prime unit of analysis (Engestrom, Miettinen and Punamaki-Gitai 1999).
- The second principle is the multi-voicedness of activity systems. Every activity system has several perspectives and be-

liefs. The division of labor component in an activity forms diverse positions for all the actors participating in the activity. This component is impressed with the rules and conventions.

• The third principle is termed as historicity. The issues and capabilities of an activity system can only be analyzed by their own history.

• The fourth principle is the central role of contradictions as sources of change and development (Engestrom, Miettinen and Punamaki-Gitai 1999). These contradictions should not be confused with problems or conflicts. Contradictions amass structural tensions within and between activity systems.

• The fifth principle proclaims the possibility of expansive transformations in activity systems. Activity systems generally have lengthy phases of qualitative transformations. Engestrom compares a complete cycle of expansive transformation to a journey through the zone of proximal development of the activity (Engestrom, Miettinen and Punamaki-Gitai 1999).

Activity Theory has been utilized as a framework for human-computer interaction. The basic structure of an activity involves the concepts of subject, object & outcome supported by tools, rules & division of labor. Activity Theory places these concepts into a systematic model. The flexibility of these components and their usefulness in describing any activity are made clear (Kuutti 1995).

Engestrom extends the concept of Activity Theory and gives a specific example of its usage. The example considered is the process of a doctor diagnosing a patient in a hospital. The actions are identified, followed by classifying the components such as subject, object, and outcome. We follow Kuuti and Engestrom to divide the emergency response into activities to plan, analyze and implement them (Engestrom 1999).

The examples above show how Activity Theory has been used in the past to understand routine activities. In this chapter we have used Activity Theory to analyze a more complex and crucial range of activities. We have done this after first identifying the various dimensions of an emergency.

Owen introduces the concept of emergency-as-activity in her paper 'Analyzing the activity of work in emergency incident management' (Owen 2007). The paper identifies how shared mindfulness and coordinated information flow can be improved in emergency management. It provides an example of high reliability work and highlights dimensions of emergencies. Owen classifies the main dimensions of emergencies as chronology, complexity & interdependence. The chronological (temporal) dimension is important because the emergency will occur in real time. The complexity dimension covers high order thinking as it involves coordination of multiple tasks. Finally the interdependence dimension draws multiple resources to work together. In this chapter we use the results of this paper and extend the dimensions of emergency in the context of the Mumbai terror attacks and then map it to Activity Theory (Owen 2007).

'Lessons of Mumbai' provides a detailed account of the terrorist incident of November 2008 in Mumbai (Rabasa, Blackwill, Chalk, Cragin, Fair, Jackson, Jenkins, Jones, Shestak and Tellis 2008). It clearly analyses the plan of the attack followed by the terrorists and also describes the emergency response operations. It focuses on the failures of the emergency response activities and exposes the weaknesses of Indian security. We draw many arguments of effective and ineffective emergency responses from this article. These responses are categorized into the activity dimensions and are later used to develop the Activity Theory diagrams for the emergency response in this incident.

We also derive important insights from Wybo and Kowalski (1998) in which a model to achieve optimal efficiency of command centers is developed. The classification of actors into perception actors, analysis actors, information actors and communication actors is drawn from this paper. This classification plays a vital role in setting up a command center which is essential for an emergency of this magnitude (Wybo and Kowalski 1998).

MUMBAI TERROR ATTACKS 26/11

The Mumbai terrorist attacks incapacitated the Indian National security apparatus and impaired the Indian response plan. Although it is practically impossible to shield every hotel, café and building in the nation from an attack of this magnitude, it is possible to provide an effective response and rescue operation. The assault on Mumbai widened the scope of terrorism by targeting unguarded and defenseless public locations, by using modern technology to receive real time information from handlers located abroad, by striking multiple sites concurrently and finally by confounding the motive of the attack itself.

The Technology Angle

Although 'the gun and the bomb' technique was used in the Mumbai terrorist attacks, state-of-the-art digital technologies through cyberspace played a crucial role. There were three main technology related trails – cell phone, email & global positioning systems.

The terrorists stayed connected with each other with the use of cell phones and VoIP (voice-over-Internet protocol). The local police with the help of America's Federal Bureau of Investigation checked the logs of cell phones used by the terrorists to stay in touch with each other throughout the attack. The logs indicated that the calls received came from a United States number which made outgoing calls to three Austrian numbers. All this was made possible by using a VoIP service provider based in the United States. The

money to utilize these services was electronically transferred halfway across the world. The global positioning systems or GPS guided the terrorists to target locations. The FBI experts were able to provide evidence and information after analyzing the global positioning systems (Swami 2009).

According to analysts and experts, the emergency response of this incident was inadequate because it lacked a universally accepted comprehensive framework. Considering the analysis of the experts in newspaper articles and press releases for this incident we have put the inadequate and adequate activities in the form of dimensions of emergency which is explained in the next section. Following this we justify that Activity Theory can provide the missing comprehensive framework.

Dimensions of Emergency

In this paper we have identified the dimensions of an emergency and tabulated them in Table 1. This is an extension of the Emergency-as-Activity concept (Owen 2007). The principal dimensions of the Mumbai 26/11 emergency can be broadly categorized as time, communication, coordination and complexity. We have extensively analyzed the subcategories of these four principal dimensions in the context of the Mumbai terror attacks.

Time is the most critical dimension of an emergency. The response operations should be expeditious and effective at the same time. The evaluation of the response is primarily based on this dimension. The subcategories of the time dimension are named as pace and effective response:

"It took the aircraft [carrying the elite NSG commandoes] almost three hours before it touched down at Mumbai airport... The buses took another 40 minutes to reach the designated place in south Mumbai where the commandos were briefed, divided into groups and sent out on their mission... Many lives might have been saved if this delay had not taken place." (Anonymous 2008)

Table 1. Time Dimension of the Mumbai terror attacks

Time dimension	Effective Activity	Ineffective Activity
Pace	- Immediate response by Central government to tackle Government of Maharashtra crisis. (Press Information Bureau 2008) - Quick response by local police contingents including Anti-Terrorism Squad (ATS) (Rabasa, Blackwill, Chalk, Cragin, Fair, Jackson, Jenkins, Jones, Shestak and Tellis 2008)	- Sluggish response (10 hours) by National Security Guard (NSG) to take charge and arrive at the scene. (Anonymous 2008; Rabasa, Blackwill, Chalk, Cragin, Fair, Jackson, Jenkins, Jones, Shestak and Tellis 2008) -Slow response by firemen. (Rabasa, Blackwill, Chalk, Cragin, Fair, Jackson, Jenkins, Jones, Shestak and Tellis 2008)
Effective Response		- Neglect of advance warnings by Indian officials due to absence of clear information. - Lack of equipment and training of local police contingents. (Press Information Bureau 2008; Rabasa, Blackwill, Chalk, Cragin, Fair, Jackson, Jenkins, Jones, Shestak and Tellis 2008)

The Press Information bureau, which is the official information dissemination entity of the federal government, published on the 11th of December 2008 (2 weeks after the incident) that the Central Government authorities acted quickly to reach out to the Government of Maharashtra. The local Army and Navy authorities were requested to provide support immediately (Press Information Bureau 2008). The Anti-Terrorism Squad (ATS) responded quickly but were deficient in training and also lacked equipment. The firemen were slow to respond and were also inadequate in coordination with the other emergency responders. The local police did not have sufficient training to counter the terrorists (Rabasa, Blackwill, Chalk, Cragin, Fair, Jackson, Jenkins, Jones, Shestak and Tellis 2008).

All the above points are classified into effective and ineffective activities of the time dimension and are tabulated below in Table 1.

Communication is the next dimension which plays a key role in an emergency. This dimension is further categorized into internal and external communication. By internal communication, we mean the communication which takes place between the different emergency responders. We have referred to internal communication as collaboration in the rest of the paper. External communication is defined as the communication with entities not involved in the emergency response, such as the media, the general public, and victims. The subcategories of this dimension are explained with regard to the Mumbai attacks in Table 2. There are three categories in the communication dimension – crisis command center, line of succession and the press.

Having a crisis command center, which serves as a single point of contact is imperative for an emergency of this magnitude. Also, the line of succession should be predefined. This can be seen from the following quote.

"..They are supposed to set-up a command centre in complete control as their first priority, instead they arrived and went in guns blazing...It was blind. They didn't have maps of the hotels, yet the terrorists had done enough reconnaissance to use the service facilities to maneuver." (McElroy 2008)

The right amount of information should be given to the people at the right time. This should be done by a designated media spokesperson in charge of informing the press.

"Major criticism was directed at a cabinet minister on the first day of the crisis, after he announced

Table 2. Communication Dimension of the Mumbai terror attacks

Communication dimension	Effective Activity	Ineffective Activity
Crisis command centre		-Failure to set up an operational command center as first priority (McElroy 2008; Rabasa, Blackwill, Chalk, Cragin, Fair, Jackson, Jenkins, Jones, Shestak and Tellis 2008)
Line of succession	- Appointment of new ATS Chief hours after the killing of Hemant Karkare. (Multiple 2008)	
Press/Media	- Deducing the fact that the intention of the attack was not to free all "mujahedeen" after one of the alleged gunmen spoke indecisively to an Indian TV reporter by cell phone. (Moreau and Mazumdar 2008)	- Alerting the terrorists by announcing that 200 NSG Commandos were to be deployed in the area in 2 hours confirmed that no forward operating units had been mobilized yet. (Rabasa, Blackwill, Chalk, Cragin, Fair, Jackson, Jenkins, Jones, Shestak and Tellis 2008) - Forewarning to the terrorists in the form of too much information given to the press by the government itself. (McElroy 2008) -Failure to project an image of control by central government & the security forces failed to project an image of control. (Rabasa, Blackwill, Chalk, Cragin, Fair, Jackson, Jenkins, Jones, Shestak and Tellis 2008)

that 200 NSG commandos were to be deployed in the area in two hours. Not only did this alert the terrorists as to when a hostage rescue mission might occur, it also effectively confirmed that no forward operating units had yet been mobilized". (Rabasa, Blackwill, Chalk, Cragin, Fair, Jackson, Jenkins, Jones, Shestak and Tellis 2008)

The above activities have been categorized as ineffective. Two other important activities have been termed as effective in terms of the communication dimension. These include the immediate appointment of a new ATS Chief after the death of Hemant Karkare and the incident which incorporated the efficient management of misinformation which is later explained in the complexity dimension.

The third dimension is coordination. Emergency responders or first responders are trained personnel who assist at the location(s) of the emergency and are responsible for taking immediate steps. The emergency response team for the Mumbai attacks consisted of the state police, Anti-Terrorist squad (ATS), firemen, paramedics, specialist units including NSG, MARCOS (Marine Commandos), Army Special Operations.

The terror attacks on Mumbai were incessant and tactical and occurred simultaneously at different locations. In order to terminate this kind of an assault, coordination among response teams was imperative. The coordination dimension stresses on the ability to handle concurrent attacks which can be achieved only if the emergency response teams cooperate and work together. Interdependence between emergency response teams was lacking and they were unable to handle concurrent attacks on Mumbai. The importance of coordination can be seen from the following quote.

"Intelligence failure, inadequate counterterrorist training and equipment of local police, delays in the response of NSG commandos, flawed hostage-rescue plans, and poor strategic communications and information management all contributed to a

less-than-optimal response. These gaps suggest the need for improved counterterrorist coordination between national-level and local security agencies and for strengthened counterterrorist capabilities on the part of first responders." (Rabasa, Blackwill, Chalk, Cragin, Fair, Jackson, Jenkins, Jones, Shestak and Tellis 2008)

The ineffective activities are tabulated in Table 3. The coordination dimension has two categories – concurrency and interdependence. Mumbai faced several attacks at the same time in different locations. The local police were unable to handle these multiple concurrent attacks. This occurrence is captured in the concurrency dimension.

The complexity dimension made the 2008 Mumbai terror attack an emergency distinct from other similar incidents in the past. The use of modern technology for communication along with misinformation amplified the complexity of the emergency. The details of the complexity dimension are explained in Table 4. The complexity dimension has two categories – misinformation and technology.

An example of misinformation was an email from the Deccan Mujahideen allegedly taking responsibility for the terrorist attacks. But it was later established that the email was just a diversion and Deccan Mujahideen did not even exist. Even though they were able to ascertain that this was an instance of misinformation it is classified as an ineffective activity of the complexity dimension because it diverted several resources for a good amount of time during the emergency response.

Table 3. Coordination Dimension of Mumbai terror attacks

Coordination dimension	Ineffective Activity
Concurrency	- Inability of the police to cordon concurrent attacks in diverse locations. (Rabasa, Blackwill, Chalk, Cragin, Fair, Jackson, Jenkins, Jones, Shestak and Tellis 2008)
Interdependence	- Lack of requisite synchronization between central security agencies -the Research & Analysis Wing (R&AW), the Intelligence Bureau (IB) and the local police in Bombay (Rabasa, Blackwill, Chalk, Cragin, Fair, Jackson, Jenkins, Jones, Shestak and Tellis 2008) -Failure of firemen to coordinate their actions with local police and national paramilitary forces. (Rabasa, Blackwill, Chalk, Cragin, Fair, Jackson, Jenkins, Jones, Shestak and Tellis 2008) -Unidentified gap in intelligence gathering between human resources and technical resources. (Press Information Bureau 2008)

Table 4. Complexity Dimension of Mumbai terror attacks

Complexity dimension	Ineffective Activity
Misinformation	- Confusion created due to an email claiming responsibility for the Mumbai attack by a hitherto unknown organization called "Deccan Mujahideen" sent to the media. (Multiple 2009)
Technology	- Real time information exchange between terrorists and controllers via mobile phones activated through VOIP platforms. - Monitoring Indian Television channels by terrorist controllers. -Usage of GOS and other technology by the terrorists for the attack. (Multiple 2009) -Absence of night vision equipment, thermal imaging systems and advanced human detection gear by Indian coast guard. (Rabasa, Blackwill, Chalk, Cragin, Fair, Jackson, Jenkins, Jones, Shestak and Tellis 2008)

The technology component increased the complexity of the emergency. A report on the Mumbai 2008 terrorist attack highlights the role of technology:

".. the death they delivered was facilitated by state-of-the-art digital technologies — on ones and zeros flying, as it were, through cyberspace. Mobile phones and voice-over-Internet protocol links connected the Lashkar fidayeen to satellite phones used by their controllers in Pakistan; hacked Internet servers were used to set up fake e-mail addresses; money was electronically transferred halfway across the world; and global positioning systems guided the perpetrators to their targets." (Swami 2009)

ANALYSIS USING ACTIVITY THEORY

Activity Theory recognizes that changing conditions can realign the constituents of an activity. In Activity Theory the unit of analysis is an activity. An activity is comprised of a subject, object, actions, and operations. A subject is a person or a group engaged in an activity. An object is held by the subject and motivates the activity, giving it a specific direction (Nardi 1995).

Transforming the object into an outcome motivates the existence of an activity. An object can be a material thing, but it can also be less tangible (like a plan) or totally intangible (like a common idea) as long as it can be shared for manipulation and transformation by the participants of the activity. A "tool" can be anything which is used in the transformation process, including both material tools and tools for thinking; "rules" cover both explicit and implicit norms, conventions and social relations within a community; "division of labor" refers to the explicit and implicit organization of a community as related to the transformation process of the object into the outcome (Kuutti 1995).

In light of Activity Theory we have analyzed a better coordinated emergency response for the Mumbai terror attacks. The five core activities identified by the authors based on expert reports and prior literature (Wybo and Kowalski 1998; Bigley and Roberts 2001; Department of Homeland Security 2003; Rabasa, Blackwill, Chalk, Cragin, Fair, Jackson, Jenkins, Jones, Shestak and Tellis 2008) are: setting up a crisis command center, assessing real time needs of the crisis, dispatching emergency responders, communication (external) and collaboration (internal). Activity Theory provides us with a conceptual framework to organize these activities. However, the constituents of these activities could change dynamically as the crisis conditions change.

When an emergency of this magnitude occurs, the primary task is to set up a crisis command center. A command centre is a central place for carrying out orders and for supervising tasks (Behera 2009). It includes a group of experts unified to manage the emergency. The roles of different experts (referred to as actors) who form the command center team are explained as follows. The first group is composed of all those who are in charge of data collection. They collect crisis data and process it to be further synthesized into helpful information. They are called perception actors. The second category of actors includes those who are responsible for analyzing the situation and taking decisions. They are called analysis actors. The first-in-command should be in charge of making decisions and should operate from the crisis command center. The third category is in charge of operational and tactical communication with the actors outside the command center. They are called communication actors. The last category of actors are those responsible for informing the persons not directly involved with the management of the emergency and are called information actors (Wybo and Kowalski 1998). Figure 1 shows the tasks in the first activity - setting up a crisis command center and its components.

Figure 1. Activity Theory applied to Setting up a crisis command center

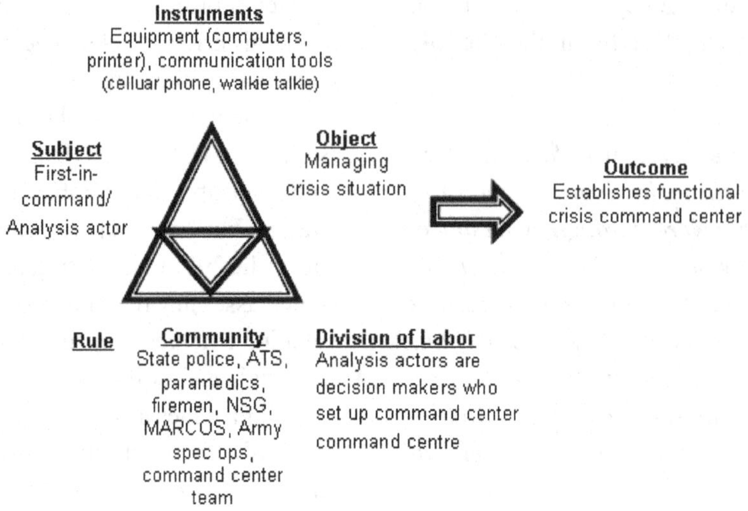

The other four core activities mentioned above can also be represented similarly using the framework illustrated in Figure 1. The detailed descriptions of these core activities are tabulated in Table 5. In the interest of managing the crisis situation, the first-in-command (decision maker(s)) who is also an analysis actor sets up a crisis command center. Office equipment (computers, printer, and photocopier), communications tools (walkie-talkies, cellular phones) serve as tools (instruments) in establishing a functional command center.

Once a functional crisis command center is set up, the next activity is to promptly assess the needs of the crisis from time to time. The needs could be in the form of operations, maintenance, transportation, public relations, legal advice, risk management, human resources, security, environmental health and safety. As shown in Table 5, the analysis actor(s) is the subject who analyses the needs (the object). This results in the decision regarding requisite resources. The inputs/information about the crisis, along with the decision support tools are the instruments which help in the transformation of this activity. The analysis actors are assisted by the perception actors who process the crisis data and convert it to useful information (Wybo and Kowalski 1998). This information helps the analysis actors assess the needs appropriately. Rules guide the subjects about how they should work on the object and hence represent a key component. The Incident Command System (ICS) represents "best practices," and is a standard for emergency management. ICS based organizations appear to be able to structure and restructure themselves on a moment to moment basis. It is highly formalized, characterized by extensive rules, procedures, policies and instructions (Bigley and Roberts 2001).

The subsequent activity is dispatching the emergency responders. The outcome of the second activity was determined as the decision of requisite resources. This is used as an instrument by the first-in-command (analysis actor) to dispatch emergency responders in order to provide an effective response with sufficient resources for the crisis situation. Here the emergency responders are the objects which give the activity specific direction. The analysis actor takes into account resource constraints such as equipment and transport capabilities of the responders. Here again, the perception actors process and keep

Table 5. Application of Activity Theory to Mumbai Terror attacks

Activity	Subject	Object	Instruments	Community	Division of labor	Rule	Outcome
Setting up a crisis command center	First-in-command/ Analysis actor	Managing crisis situation	Equipment (computers, printer), communication tools (celluar phone, walkie talkie)	State police, ATS, paramedics, firemen, NSG, MARCOS, Army spec ops, command center team	Analysis actors are decision makers who set up command center		Establishes functional crisis command center
Accessing real time needs of crisis	Analysis Actor(s)	Operations, maintenance, security, transportation etc needs	Inputs/information about emergency, Decision support tools	State police, ATS, paramedics, firemen, NSG, MARCOS, Army spec ops, command center team	Perception actors process crisis data into information, Analysis actors make decision about requisite resources	Incident command system	Decision regarding requisite resources
Dispatching Emergency Responders	First-in-command/ Analysis actor	Emergency responders	Decision of real time resource assessment, Decision support tools	State police, ATS, paramedics, firemen, NSG, MARCOS, Army spec ops, command center team	Perception actors process & update crisis data into information, analysis actors make decision about requisite resources		Effective response on emergency site
Communication (External)	Information actor/ Designated media spokesperson	Reporting the Crisis	Media, Emergency call center	Command center team, media, victims/ hostages, government executives, family of victims/ hostages, general public	Perception actors process & update crisis data into information, analysis actors make decision about requisite resources	Standard Operating Procedures	Convey appropriate information through proper channels to general public, victims
Collaboration (Internal)	Communication actors	Emergency responders	Cell phone, walkie talkies, internet	State police, ATS, paramedics, firemen, NSG, MARCOS, Army spec ops, command center team	Communication actors are in charge of operational and tactical communication with the actors outside the command center	Incident Command system	Results in an integrated interoperable system

updating the crisis information and the analysis actors decide how many resources to dispatch to the crisis location from time to time.

Effectively communicating to persons not directly involved with the management of the emergency crisis (general public, victims) is the next activity and is referred to as communication (external). It is of utmost importance to deliver clear and consistent messages in response to the

crisis from time to time. For this, it is essential to understand the diversity of the audience. There should be a designated media spokesperson (information actor) who reports the crisis to the general public and victims throughout the crisis. The information actor should be clear and confident and at the same time he/she should release the right amount of information at the right time. The outcome of this activity will be appropriate information conveyed to the general public and victims through proper channels. The media and the emergency call center act as tools which assist to obtain this outcome. To report the crisis, the information actor should follow standard operating procedures which will serve as rules in the entire communication process.

The ultimate goal of all the emergency responders is to provide prompt and effective assistance at the crisis location. These emergency responders exchange information about the crisis, communicate resource requirements amongst themselves (reflective communication) (Chen, Sharman, Chakravarti, R. and Upadhyaya 2008). They must work together as a team to achieve this. This activity is referred to as collaboration (internal communication). The crisis command center serves as a single point of contact where all the emergency response teams report their activities in order to be seamlessly integrated. The communication actors are in charge of this operational and tactical communication. Cell phones, walkie talkies and Internet are used as instruments which form the communication system for emergency responders (Chen, Coles, Lee and Rao 2009). The outcome achieved is an integrated interoperable system which provides a common motive for all emergency responders.

As the above example demonstrates, Activity Theory is an effective method to create the ideal design for emergency response. However, more research is needed to develop the theory so that it can be used to guide the allocation of scarce resources, address inter-organizational procedural and communication barriers and any issues arising from cultural differences. Another current limitation of Activity Theory is that while it is effective at planning the initial response, the information requirements of Activity Theory may be too intensive for the theory to be helpful in responding to the event as it unfolds. Further research is needed to reduce the information requirements to use Activity Theory so that it may also be useful during the event response.

CONCLUSION

The impact of the 2008 Mumbai terror attacks was tremendous. This makes it crucial to comprehend the lessons learned and to avoid the intensity of any future crisis by providing an effective emergency response. In this paper we have clearly identified the key dimensions of the 2008 Mumbai terror attacks and we have discussed them in detail. The importance of setting up a functional command center, communication and collaboration between emergency response teams was demonstrated using Activity Theory. The use of Activity theory also served as a mechanism for evaluation of the crisis and the development of security policies, standards and practices. It gave the analysis a clear structure and distinctly identified significant activities of the emergency response. The paper also identified several concepts to comprehend and interpret emergency response activities hence serving as a guide for future analysis and emergency management.

ACKNOWLEDGMENT

We sincerely thank the referees for their valuable feedback to improve this paper. An early version of this paper was presented at Indo-US Conference & Workshop on Cyber security, Cyber crime & Cyber Forensics at Kochi, India, August 2009. We would like to acknowledge NSF for funding this research under grants IIS-0926371 and IIS-0926376. The usual disclaimer applies.

REFERENCES

Anonymous,. (2008). *Why did NSG take 10 hours to arrive?* Mumbai, India: The Economic Times.

Behera, L. (2009). Force equipped. *Kerala Calling*, 28-29.

Bigley, G. A., & Roberts, K. H. (2001). The Incident Command System: High Reliability Organizing for Complex and volatile task environments. *Academy of Management Journal, 44*(6), 1281–1299. doi:10.2307/3069401

Chen, R., Coles, J., Lee, J., & Rao, H. R. (2009). *Emergency Communication and System Design: The Case of Indian Ocean Tsunami.* ICTD Conference. Doha, Qatar.

Chen, R., Sharman, R., & Chakravarti, N., R. H. R. & S. Upadhyaya. (2008). Emergency Response Information System Interoperability: Development of Chemical Incident Response Data Model. *Journal of the Association for Information Systems, 9*.

Department of Homeland Security (2003). *National Response Plan.*

Engestrom, Y. (1999). *Outline of three generations of activity theory.* Retrieved 05/04/2010, from http://www.bath.ac.uk/research/liw/resources/Models%20and%20principles%20of%20Activity%20Theory.pdf.

Engestrom, Y., Miettinen, R., & Punamaki-Gitai, R.-L. (1999). *Perspectives on activity theory.* Cambridge, UK: Cambridge University Press.

Kuutti, K. (1995). Activity Theory as a potential framework for human computer interaction research. In Nardi, B. A. (Ed.), *Context and consciousness: activity theory and human-computer interaction* (pp. 17–44). Cambridge, MA: Massachussetts Institute of Technology.

McElroy, D. (2008). *Mumbai attacks: foreign governments criticize India's response.* The Telegraph.

Moreau, R., & Mazumdar, S. (2008). The Pakistan Connection. *Newsweek.*

Multiple (2008). Important developments in the Mumbai terror attack. *The Hindu.* Chennai, India.

Multiple (2009). Mumbai Terror attacks - Dossier of evidence. *The Hindu.* Chennai, India.

Nardi, B. A. (1995). Activity Theory and Human-Computer Interaction. In Nardi, B. A. (Ed.), *Context and consciousness: activity theory and human-computer interaction.* Cambridge, MA: Massachussetts Institute of Technology.

Nardi, B. A. (1995). A Comparison of Activity Theory, Situated Action Models, and Distributed Cognition. In Nardi, B. A. (Ed.), *Context and consciousness: activity theory and human-computer interaction* (pp. 69–102). Cambridge, MA: Massachussetts Institute of Technology.

Oh, O., Agrawal, M., & Rao, H. R. (in press). Information Control and Terrorism: Tracking the Mumbai Terrorist Attack through Twitter. *Information Systems Frontiers.*

Owen, C. A. (2007). Analysing the activity of work in emergency incident management. *Activités (Vitry-sur-Seine), 4*(1), 217–225.

Press Information Bureau. (2008). *Home Minister announces measures to enhance security.* New Delhi, India.

Rabasa, A., Blackwill, R. D., Chalk, P., Cragin, K., Fair, C. C., & Jackson, B. A. (2008). *The lessons of Mumbai.* RAND.

Swami, P. (2009). *Mumbai investigators found key clues in cyberspace.* Chennai, India: The Hindu.

Wybo, J. L., & Kowalski, K. M. (1998). Command centers and emergency management support. *Safety Science, 30*(1-2), 131–138. doi:10.1016/S0925-7535(98)00041-1

KEY TERMS AND DEFINITIONS

Activity Theory: A framework in which any task is broken into activities, which are further composed of subjects, objects, instruments, communities, division of labor, rules, and outcomes. These categories can provide a system designer with an understanding of the steps necessary for a user to carry out a task

Emergency Response: An effort by public safety personnel and citizens to mitigate the impact of an incident on human life and property

Incident Command System: A place that is used to provide centralized command to respond to an unforeseen incident.

Chapter 5
Pirates of the Copyright and Cyberspace:
Issues Involved

Charulata Chaudhary
Rajiv Gandhi National University of Law, India

Ishupal Singh Kang
Rajiv Gandhi National University of Law, India

ABSTRACT

The chapter discusses the issues involved in the protection of copyrights of intellectual creation over the Internet. The chapter focuses upon concept of liability and jurisdiction in cyberspace in context of the threat of violation of the rights of copyright holders. The chapter examines the role of technological advancement vis-à-vis the legal scenario make several observations and suggestions in regard.

INTRODUCTION

Not very long ago, fearsome pirates roamed the seas, looting and plundering the merchant ships and creating havoc, before they slowly vanished from the scene with the advancement of technology. Now, the world has seen the revival of pirates in a much more sophisticated, advanced and threatening form, owing to the same technological advancements. Yes, the reference being made here point towards the growing menace of intellectual property theft and piracy. In these early years of the 21st century, we continue to

live in the Information Age -- an age when our economy's greatest assets are not steel and coal, but ideas and their practical applications (Yang and Hoffstadt, 2006, 201). We have been able to exploit this intellectual capital more effectively in large part due to the widespread use of computers, which has enabled businesses to manipulate their intellectual property with greater ease and to buy and sell physical products with greater efficiency over the Internet. Just like various other fields this has also affected the realm of intellectual property rights. Due to technological advancements new avenues in respect of intellectual creation are emerging coupled with new issues

DOI: 10.4018/978-1-60960-123-2.ch005

relating to their protection. The consequences brought about in the content industry as a result of new technologies are already before our eyes (Lucchi, 2006, 11). The recent times, which have seen path-breaking scientific and technological advancement, has revolutionized the world in which we live. This Chapter focuses particularly on problem of copyright piracy in the digital age where it has assumed new dimensions due to its intermingling with the rapid growth of technology. It is quite evident a fact that the problem of piracy and theft of intellectual creations is not of recent origin and is probably as old as human creativity itself, but the point of discussion which will be presented and argued upon is based upon the multiplicity of issues involved which have arisen solely due to this interplay.

The basic working pattern of copyright is to reward the creative and innovative works and individuals to live by their creative efforts and skills. It covers the vivid areas of human creativity and extends to the protection of the contributors such as actors, dancers, singers, musicians and broadcasting organisations who adds value in the presentation of artistic and literary works to the public. The system of copyrights accomplish two goals: Firstly, protecting the creativity and consequently engendering the same by extending some special privileges to the producers of creative works (Ahuja, 2006, 429). The practice of pirating of copyrighted works eats away the very basis of this system. Copyright regimes throughout the world are facing a big challenge of budding technologies. Various digital and information technologies are emerging those have defined the new era of communication. This has led to a twofold effect, at one side they assist the copyright owners in better utilization of their intellectual capital and on the other darker prospect threatening them loss of control even over their own property. The impact of digital technology specially the Internet is such a massive one that, even the basic fundamentals of copyright law are under the threat of revisions and modifications

(Edwards and Walde). Not only has this intensified the occurrence of copyright infringements but has led to such violations of the rights of the copyright holder which, due to their unprecedented nature, are protected poorly in IP regimes of various legal systems around the globe.

OVERVIEW OF THE ISSUES INVOLVED

The fact that computers have now being in existence for over half a century, protection of the intellectual property rights in computer programs has only really become an issue since the advent of microcomputers, a much more recent development (Rowland and Macdonald, 2005, 5). The extent to which the development of new situations and consequences resulting from the intermingling of intellectual property and internet is taking place today is wide and dynamic. This is precisely due to involvement of various factors like the worldwide reach of the Internet, the millions of websites on the World Wide Web, the easy access to and copying of others' intellectual property and famed anonymity of this medium (Ryder, 2002, 1). Two prominent issues involved in the debate of copyright protection over the Internet are who is to be made liable for the violations and what should be the proper and effective forum to adjudicate such a liability. These are the two broad issues under which several complex issues relating to liability and jurisdiction can be assimilated. These concerns regarding finding liability and effective jurisdiction are also important from the point of view of the whole notion of protection of rights of the copyright holders as well as stemming the increasing occurrence of copyright violations.

Who is Liable: Copyright Infringements in the Cyberspace

Fixing of liability for copyright infringements in cyberspace is a very difficult issue. The dynamic and anonymous nature of internet often serves as a haven for the copyright pirates. The liability issue is such an intricate one as the transmission of information content on internet involves several actors and various stages before it reaches the end user. Hence, those involved in copyright infringement, range considerably on the basis of their motives, frequency of infringement and other factors. For instance many of individuals involved in infringement are ignorant that they are committing an offence and simple download material because it is available on the Internet; then there are professional pirates who are involved for profit making and maintain databases and websites of infringing materials; technological advancements like peer to peer file sharing software has given birth to another category of individual who share and mutually distribute copyrighted material.

From a broader point of view there seems no difference between the traditional copyright infringement and the one through the digital medium, as regard the person doing the infringement is concerned. Consequently, it would be a general tendency to impose the liability on the person who is actually copying or storing the copyrighted material (Reed, 2004, 96). Imposing liability on the end users who are actually the main involved in copyright infringement however present its own complications. However, there have been various lawsuits against the individual copyright infringers most notably in the case of music piracy (Martin, 391). But, suing the direct individual infringer, though seem a logical action, does not serve a great role in curbing the menace of piracy. More often than not, the users are ignorant of the copyright laws and unaware of the illegality of their downloads. In consideration of this, the role of the intermediaries becomes more relevant. Intermediaries in the exchange of digital communication on the internet like Internet Service Providers, Web Hosting services and other third party actors are better suited in plugging the hole of rampant piracy of copyrighted materials.

Internet Service Providers (ISPs)

The question concerned here is that whether the ISPs which provide access to the information content on the web can be held liable for infringements by the people whom they have provided access and what should be the extent of such a liability? ISPs are the intermediary companies or businesses which serve as a medium for the public, be it companies, individuals or institutions, to have access to the World Wide Web or the internet. In addition to being the gateway to the information content on the web these ISPs provide several other facilities to their customers (Unni, 2001, 5). This issue is not a very new one and the question of liability of ISPs has been since the times when the internet started to become popular and common (Verma and Mittal, 2004, 147). The chief reason for why this question emerged, in the first place, is the 'inherent difficulties of enforcing copyrights against individual Internet users worldwide' (Ibid.). 'Identifying the individual who posts allegedly infringing material is not an easy task, whereas spotting the ISP is quite simple. Even if the offending individual is caught, there is no guarantee that he will have the resources to pay legal damages. ISPs, on the other hand, are in a position to pay with the profits the ISPs make from the pirates' use of the Internet' (Unni, supra). This clearly suggests that it is basically a sort of protective measure so that the ISPs keep a tighter check of the internet users and thus consequently compliance to the copyright laws. Apart from this, several other factors like, 'ownership of the equipment that stores, makes, and transmits copies of copyrighted material' (Yen, 2000, 1836), the relationship between the ISPs and internet users. Moreover the liability also arises in the cases when the ISP intentionally or knowingly allows the use of its service for the purpose of violation of rights of any copyright holder.

On a global overview there are very few jurisdictions around the world that have been successful in implementing the ISPs' liability for copyright infringement through enacted legislations. For example the Indian Copyright Law does not have any express provision for determining ISP liability and has to be construed within the general meaning of section 51 (a)(ii) of the Copyright Act, 1957 (Verma and Mittal, supra, 148). In fact, there are hardly any judicial precedents or legal principles which discuss the liability of ISPs under this provision. In 2007 case of *Microsoft Corporation* v. *Kiran,* the Delhi High Court only recognized internet piracy as a form of piracy with growing significance without laying down any guidelines or rules. Moreover there was no question involved relating to the liability of ISPs for internet piracy. Further, section 79 of the Indian Information Technology Act, 2000 exempt the ISPs from any kind of liability if it is proved that the infringement occurred without the knowledge of the provider and if such a provider had exercised 'due diligence' in preventing the infringement of a copyright. Thus in Indian scenario, it can easily be seen that the legal provisions through which an ISP can be made liable for a copyright infringement using its services are vague and escapable. In United Kingdom, section 23 of The Copyright, Designs and Patents Act 1988 lays down two 'requirements which need to be satisfied so as to invoke the liability of an ISP. These two requirements are: First possession of infringed copyright material while in course of business and secondly having knowledge that the material held is protected under copyright. 'Furthermore, the Copyright and Related Rights Regulations 2003 provides that an injunction can be sought against an internet service provider where he has actual knowledge of another person using his service to infringe copyright' (Wei, 2006, 532). However, it is the Unites States where the concept of ISP liability is the most developed due to a plethora of case laws and legislative enactments. Especially, the Digital Millennium Copyright Act, 1998 lays down specific provisions for determining the liability of the Internet Service Providers. Based on such provisions and the various cases which

have come before the U.S. courts, the liability for copyright infringement can be categorized in three categories: direct liability, vicarious liability, and contributory liability (Kostyu, 1999, 1243). 'A finding of direct copyright infringement is based on two factors: 1) the plaintiff's ownership of a valid copyright and 2) a defendant's violation of one of the plaintiff's exclusive rights. The 1976 Copyright Act imposes strict liability for direct copyright infringement, but knowledge is relevant to an award of statutory damages' (Salow, 2001). The concept of vicarious liability is born out of the creativity of the judiciary and requisite for this is ISP was in position of stopping the direct infringer and some benefit has accrued from the infringement to the ISP. 'Contributory liability is the third and most likely way in which an ISP might be held liable for subscriber copyright infringement' According to the courts, "one who, with knowledge of the infringing activity, induces, causes or materially contributes to the infringing conduct of another, may be held liable as a 'contributory' infringer" (Yen, supra, 1872).

Web Hosting Providers

A concurrent issue related to ISP liability is the liability of the web hosting services also known as the Internet Host Providers (IHPs), which provide web space to put up website on the internet. The ambit of liability of the ISPs and IHPs is somewhat overlapping as it would be clear by the following discussion.

In context of concepts of contributory and vicarious liability as developed by U.S Courts, the web hosting providers can be considered the most suitable targets for copyright infringements. This is so because in actual sense it is the web hosting providers on whose web space the infringed material is hosted. The person using the service is using it for display and distribution of copyrighted material. In this regard, *Playboy* v *Frena,* one of the earliest case law concerning copyright infringement on internet is important in discussing the liability of the web hosting providers. The court adjudicated upon the liability of an operator of the bulletin board system for displaying the content which was held under copyright by Playboy. In reality, it were the subscribers of the BBS who had uploaded the content and the operator claimed that upload the images onto his bulletin board system and he was unaware of the copyright violation using the BBS owned by him 'until such time as he was served with the summons and complaint in this action, at which time he caused them to be deleted'. The claim of the BBS operator was unsuccessful and the court found that the defendant committed copyright infringement by encouraging the user to use BBS for display of Playboy's copyrighted material (Reed, supra). Though the case does not involve the liability of a web hosting provider as such but the principle involving the liability is very much same. Another case which primarily involved Netcom, an ISP for infringement of Church of Scientology's copyrighted material provides an instance of an ISP acting as IHP (as it hosted the infringing content also) (Martin, supra, 395). The principle of vicarious liability as pronounced in *Playboy* v. *Frena* was not followed in the case as the court acknowledged that no monetary gain accrued to the defendant in the case. However on the question of contributory liability the court observed that Netcom can be made liable if the fact that it had knowledge of the infringement can be proved.

Liability in P2P File Sharing

What is Peer to Peer File Sharing

Peer to peer file sharing is perhaps the most notorious technology as far as copyright infringement on internet is concerned and has threatened the copyright holders more than anything else (Belzley, 2005, 10). P2P file sharing programs are software which enables internet users to swap and share music files, video files and other files. P2P file sharing software establishes a network of all the people using the software and create a database of resources of available material on the users' systems. Anyone using the software has access to this database of resources which can be transferred to his or her own system.

Legal Stand

This is because of the ease of transferring of copyright material such as music, videos, other documents etc. has increased manifold with use of P2P technology. Napster was the first popularly recognized P2P file sharing software. With Napster individual users stored those files that they wanted to share over the internet directly with other users who did the same thing (Verma and Mittal, supra, 136). The important question in this regard is concerning the liability of the providers of such P2P software. The first case regarding legality of P2P sharing involved Napster itself. The decision was against Napster and though there was no direct involvement in the infringement the court held that it was in a position of monitoring the activities of the user and ordered to prevent access to copyrighted material. 'Clearly, centralized P2P networks like Napster are liable for contributory infringement in the United States, because the architecture of their systems allows such networks to both know of infringing files on their servers and materially contribute to illegal file-sharing transactions'. (Tabatabai, 2005, 2341)

The question of liability becomes more complex when the P2P file sharing system is without any centralized networking. The problem here is that contributory liability for copyright infringement of the software provider is hard to prove because the two elements of actual knowledge and contribution cannot be established. But the U.S Supreme Court came up with a landmark decision in the *Grokster case*. The Supreme Court reversed the judgment of the lower courts which acquitted the file sharing company Grokster for copyright infringement by its users. The Court opined that the primary motive of the P2P file sharing system offered by Grokster was aimed at inducing copyright infringement and any person doing so is liable for any copyright infringement done by using that device, irrespective of the argument whether it had actual knowledge of the violation.

Jurisdictional Issues

Introduction

As explained above, the vibrant and anonymous nature of internet is a threat to the copyright owners as to setting liability on different persons and intermediaries, sharing one umbrella in different jurisdictions. The internet has drastically changed the concept of territoriality. For locating liability on anyone, one needs to know the intricacies of the jurisdiction issue. The questions regarding jurisdiction are extremely complex. So starting from the conceptualisation of jurisdiction, in order to maintain the transparency and effectiveness of a judicial system it rests upon some bedrock regulations, which are necessary for defining the functioning aspect of that particular system, principally revolves around jurisdiction. The term 'jurisdiction' defers from the point of view of interpretation. Generally, jurisdiction is the power of a court to adjudicate upon certain issue. In cases involving questions of jurisdiction, the most fundamental rule is that a court must have personal jurisdiction as to make applicable over a particular category of persons, a subject matter over which particular kind of suit can be entertained and a suitable venue for giving the enforceability to judgement. There is a need for focus to be given on establishing a correlation between jurisdiction and internet and the effect of internet over the jurisdictional aspect of a judicial system. On World Wide Web different type of material is posted from different places of globe in order to make it accessible to everyone on earth as to getting information on various subjects, it becomes very difficult to determine work's country of origin. So in this scenario the basic question arises regarding the jurisdiction as to which place a suit can be

filed by an individual with respect to transaction on web. Moreover, an internet transaction may involve parties of more than one jurisdiction so adding a step more towards complexity. So the copyright laws in respect of cyberspace restrict the jurisdiction over a territory only. A relation of the work's country of origin with jurisdiction is determined on the basis of working of choice of law whether the particular work is entitled to get the protection under copyright law and related substantive issues (Solley, 2008, 815). The issue in this regard can be seen from two perspectives. First is the problem of conflict of laws and second, the development of international copyright regimes.

The Approaches

When the problem of conflict of laws arises between the different jurisdictions, the rule of *'lex loci deliciti'* that where the act has occurred the last time is to be taken into consideration. When an act has occurred in more than one country then court will apply the copyright laws of different countries even if the act may be characterised differently in those countries. The practicability of this rule has posed a question in making out the single act done at various places (Ibid.). So a new rule has laid down to counter the problem faced by the beforehand discussed rule namely, *closest relationship test,* where there is a choice between the application of jurisdiction the court should apply that law which has a closest nexus with the litigation (Kamath, 2007, 17). In this regard it can be concluded that despite of emergence of various rules of construction for harmonizing the municipal laws pertaining to copyright protection still there is no definitive solution and instead these have added to confusion of the existing legal standards.

For example, even in the United States, there is a dichotomy in the decisions of the various courts. The question of application of U.S copyright law to acts leading to copyright violation in some other jurisdiction was discussed in '*Subafilms Ltd.* v.

MGM-Pathe Communications Co., by the United States Court of Appeals for the Ninth Circuit. It was held that the copyright laws of United States would not apply to cases involving secondary infringement where authorization of such act was not done in the territorial jurisdiction of U.S. The court in this case adopted a strict and restrictive notion of territoriality. However, in *Itar-Tass Russian News Agency* v. *Russian Kurier, Inc.*, the United States Court of Appeals for the Ninth Circuit took a liberal view and did not considered the national treatment rule as conflict of law principle to be followed (Frohlich, 2009). In the United Kingdom the law regarding the question of conflict of laws has changed considerably. From the practice of narrow application of foreign law the approach has been relaxed and broadened. Important thing to be noted here is that one of the relevant and driving factor in this change has been the enactment of *Private International Law (Miscellaneous Provisions) Act of 1995*. In New Zealand, the present position is highlighted by *Atkinson Footwear* v. *Hodgskin International Services Ltd.* where the assumption of jurisdiction in cases involving foreign copyright infringement was restricted (Austin, 2000).

International Regimes

Due to the global nature of the internet, the infringement of intellectual property rights cannot be restricted to national jurisdiction and it has become essentially a question of international law. World Intellectual Property Organization ("WIPO") Copyright Treaty ("WCT") and WIPO Performances and Recordings Treaty ("WPPT") deserve special mention here. When the Internet era dawned, the WCT and WPPT were adopted to deal with the new issues that were created by this new medium (Gao, 2006, 590). There are four following principles of these treaties. First, the authors of a work, performers, and producers of a sound or video recording shall be granted the right to make and store their works in digital

form, much the same as they enjoy the right of reproduction for conventional works. Second, the copyright owners mentioned above shall possess the right to disseminate digital works to the public so that the digital works can be accessed easily on the Internet. Third, as digitalized work can be easily copied; effective legal remedies against the circumvention of effective technological measures shall be provided. Finally, the protection of electronic management information shall be provided (Ibid.). But, the weak nature of international legislations and lack of any sovereign authorities to oversee their proper implementation act as big obstacle in the effectiveness of these efforts on the international scenario.

ANALYSIS

The Overall Scenario

The problem of piracy is the biggest one faced by industries that heavily depend on intellectual properties. The internet has only added fuel to the fire. What the *World Wide Web* has done is expanded the horizon of copyright infringement and has made the legal provisions concerning copyright law look pathetic and ill-suited to the present needs. The internet has rendered the problem with an ugly global face. Intellectual creations irrespective of their origin are facing continued threat from infringers who are equally diverse in territorial sense. 'Hollywood boasted earnings of $4.2 billion at the U.S. box office in the fall of 2007, but the industry doubts similar future earnings due to copyright infringement' (Martin, supra, 366). According to the USTR, "China's own 2004 data showed that it channeled more than 99 percent of copyright and trademark cases into its administrative systems and turned less than one percent of cases over to the police." The impact on the music industry has been catastrophic. 'Worldwide revenue, which peaked at $45 billion in 1997, was projected to fall to $23 billion by 2009, and approximately half the people employed in the music industry a decade ago have been laid off' (Schleimer, 2008, 140). So the magnitude of the problem of copyright piracy can easily be gauged. Despite various efforts and devices formulated to counter this problem of widespread copyright infringement over internet no serious and definitive impact can be seen. The same internet which was developed and initially used to reap the benefits of superior communication and mass connectivity has been manipulated and misused in the stealing of intellectual property. Not only has this, due to its transnational nature and constant development the World Wide Web has proved to be a headache for the law makers and the administrators of justice. But law has been unable to keep up with the pace of the emergence of issues relating to copyrights and cyberspace due to blinding technological advancement. As it has been seen from the discussion in sections above, most of the national legislations are woefully inadequate to curb the challenge posed by cyber piracy. The United States is probably the only country where some legal principles specific to the question of copyright piracy over internet have evolved and have been tested in realistic circumstances, but even in the American context the law is young, raw and developing and provisions are far from being conclusive.

This point give rise to the argument that how far is it right to use legal provisions and statutory enactments as a shield against the threat of copyright piracy where the changing technology keeps on changing the nature of issues involved. There is no doubt that the evolution of legal principles is a must with the change of times as the opposite case will bring in chaotic and disrupted atmosphere. Still, the nature of problem is quite technical and complex in nature as several issues are purely of technological origin. Hence, calls have been made for stricter technological measures in consonance with these legal provisions so as to fully tackle the problem.

Suggestions

'It is often said that regulating the Internet is impossible because of its chaotic structure, which consists of hundreds of millions of computers connected by cables, radio transmission links, servers and routers'. Despite its unruly nature, there are interconnection points where the Internet bit stream can be monitored, and copy-right infringements can be detected, filtered, and blocked (Ibid.). Hence, efforts need to be made to streamline the internet so that proper vigilance can be exercised to check the transmission of copyrighted material.

Another approach has been to evolve an efficient 'dispute resolution system that is available internationally to enable copyright holders to protect their interests from being infringed on the Internet, whether domestically or internationally. To succeed, such a forum must be economical, efficient, internationally available, and consistent, in order to further the original principles of copyright protection (rewarding creators and benefiting the public) and to support economic and social development' (Solley, supra, 814). Such a system must be strengthened with the concretizing of some basic legal principles which can be universally applied in a multijurisdictional world scenario. Such an approach will save duplication of efforts at domestic and regional level and would streamline and solidify the legal standards required due to conflict of laws.

But implementation of these approaches in practical circumstances also comes with its own set of problems and consequences. For example, the measures of stringent regulation and scrutiny over cyberspace has been met with the concerns relating to privacy of internet users while surfing the cyberspace; and the devising of a proper redressal forum has to have a global consensus which seems unlikely in near future.

CONCLUSION

As a conclusion it is worthwhile to note that in the case of the fearsome pirates discussed at the start of the chapter it was only when they faced a superior mechanism which went beyond the statutory provisions aimed at stopping them, that they were contained and wiped. In the same essence, the pirates of the modern world who have seriously impaired the copyright protection regimes are to be confronted with a comprehensive approach both at the national and the global level. Not only the harmonization of the national laws concerning copyright protection aimed at establishing a uniform pattern of international copyright laws but also need is to coordinate the legal principles with the use of technological measures. But apart from focussing on the challenge at hand, there is also a need to be aware of what lies in the future. This is so because the race here is not for a definite point but it is a continuing one, an unending struggle. It would be too much to expect that the gap is fully diminished but nevertheless efforts should be aimed at keeping the water under the bridge so much so that conflict is under a manageable limit and does become unsustainable.

REFERENCES

Ahuja, V. K. (2006). Importation of Pirated Copyright Articles into India: Powers of Customs Authorities to Confiscate. *E.I.P.R. 2006, 28*(8), 429-432

Austin, G. W. (2000). *Copyright Infringement in New Zealand's Private International Law*, 19 NZULR 1.

Belzley, S. R. (2005).*Grokster and Efficiency in Music*, 10 Va. J.L. & Tech. 10.

Edwards, L., & Waelde, C. (2009). *Law and the Internet* (2nd ed.). Houston, TX: Hart Publications.

Frohlick, A. B. (2009). *Copyright Infringement In The Internet Age--Primetime For Harmonized Conflict-Of-Laws Rules?*, 24 Berkeley Tech. L.J. 851.

Gao, L. (2006). *Intellectual Property Rights In The Internet Era: The New Frontier*, 5 J. *Marshall Rev. Intell. Prop., L*, 589.

Kostyu, J.L. (1999). *Copyright Infringement on the Internet: Determining the liability of Internet Service Provider*, 48 Cath. U. L. Rev. 1237.

Lucchi, N. (2006). *Digital Media & Intellectual Property*. New York: Springer.

Martin, T. S. (n.d.). *Vicarious and Contributory Liability for Internet Host Providers: Combating Copyright Infringement In The United States, Russia, And China*, 27 Wis. Int'l L.J. 363

Nandan, K. (2007). *Law Relating to Computers Internet & E-Commerce* (3rd ed.). New Delhi, India: Universal Law Publishing Co.

Reed, C. (2004). *Internet Law: Text and Materials 96* (2nd ed.). New Delhi, India: Universal Law Publishing Co.

Rowland, D., & Macdonald, E. (2005). *Information Technology Law*. Singapore: Cavendish Publishing Limited.

Ryder, R. D. (2002). *Intellectual Property and the Internet*. New York: Lexis Nexis Butterworths.

Salow, H.P. (2001). *Liability Immunity for Internet Service Providers--How is it working?*, 6 J. Tech. L. & Pol'y 0.

Schleimer, J. D. (2008). *Protecting Copyrights at The "Backbone" Level of the Internet*, 15 UCLA Ent. L. Rev. 139.

Solley, T. (2008).*The Problem and the Solution: Using the Internet to Resolve Internet Copyright Disputes,* 24 Ga. St. U. L. Rev. 815.

Tabatabai, F. (2005). *A Tale of two countries: Canada's Response to the Peer-To-Peer Crisis and What it Means for The United States,* 73 Fordham L. Rev. 2321.

Unni, V.K. (2001).*Internet Service Provider's Liability for Copyright Infringement- How to Clear The Misty Indian Perspective*, 8 Rich. J.L. & Tech. 13.

Verma, S. K., & Mittal, R. (2004). *Legal Dimensions of Cyberspace 147.* New Delhi, India: Indian Law Institute.

Wei, W. (2006). The Liability of Internet Service Providers for Copyright Infringement and Defamation Actions in The United Kingdom and China: A Comparative Study. *E.I.P.R. 2006, 28*(10), 528-534.

Yang, D. W. & Hoffstadt, B. M. (2006). *Countering The Cyber-Crime Threat, 43 Am. Crim. L. Rev. 201.*

Yen, A. C. (2000). *Internet Service Provider Liability for Subscriber Copyright Infringement, Enterprise Liability, And The First Amendment,* 88. *Geological Journal, 1833,* 1836.

Section 2
Cyber-Security:
Technology Review

Chapter 6
Classifying Host Anomalies:
Using Ontology in Information Security Monitoring

Suja Ramachandran
Bhabha Atomic Research Centre, India

R.S. Mundada
Bhabha Atomic Research Centre, India

A.K. Bhattacharjee
Bhabha Atomic Research Centre, India

C.S.R.C. Murthy
Bhabha Atomic Research Centre, India

R. Sharma
Bhabha Atomic Research Centre, India

ABSTRACT

In this chapter, the authors propose an ontology based approach to classify the anomalous events occurring in a number of hosts, thus filtering the interesting or non-trivial events requiring immediate attention from a set of events. An ontology is developed to structure the domain of anomaly detection. It expresses the semantic relationships among the attributes of an anomaly detection system and events collected by it. The system harnesses the reasoning capability of ontology and that of inference engine to make meaningful assumptions about anomaly events. This enables automatic classification of the reported anomalies based on the functionality and significance of the originating host as well as the associated system resource or parameter.

1. INTRODUCTION

Security is a fundamental issue of concern in computing systems. With the recent trends in distributed computing and the emergence of World Wide Web as a universal medium for conducting business, security has become critical in IT architectures.

With the proliferation of computer systems and networks, security problems such as unau-

DOI: 10.4018/978-1-60960-123-2.ch006

thorized access of data, tampering of information systems etc. have turned into a major concern for all organizations. In maintaining secure computer networks, much of the difficulty can be attributed to the lack of proper information management: the amount of information at hand is enormous, much of it changes rapidly, and the relevant information is difficult to identify. The limitations of each security technology combined with the growth of cyber attacks impact the efficiency of information security management and make the network administrator's job tedious. Therefore, there is a need for automated information security monitoring systems that can manage themselves given high-level objectives from administrator.

The focus of modern information systems is moving from data-processing towards concept-processing, that is, the basic unit of processing is becoming more a semantic concept which carries an interpretation and exists in a context with other concepts. (Brank, Grobelnik and Mladenic, 2005). An ontology can be defined as a "formal, explicit specification of a shared conceptualization" (Gruber, 1993). It is a formal representation of a set of concepts within a domain and the relationships between those concepts. Ontological analysis clarifies the structure of knowledge. For a given domain, its ontology acts as a structure that captures and represents the knowledge on that domain. Ontologies are used in artificial intelligence, the Semantic Web, software engineering, biomedical informatics, library science, information architecture etc. as a form of knowledge representation about the world or some part of it.

In this chapter, we are proposing an information security monitoring system which is a combination of an anomaly detection system and an ontology based reasoning mechanism. In a diverse and complex network set-up, it is nearly impossible for the administrator to keep track of the activities and events occurring in each and every servers and devices. In our view, a comprehensive information security monitoring system must not only provide alarms on possible intrusion attempts,

but it should be able to capture all the events of interest occurring in a network, thus providing a complete overview of system security. Such a system should be capable of analyzing the obtained data and presenting meaningful information to the system administrators.

The proposed system looks for anomalous behaviors of a host which might include security breaches, performance bottlenecks, resource misuses or configuration problems. Such a strategy of extensive event collection provides the administrator with a complete picture of what is happening in the network. Also, it improves the possibilities of real time detection of an attack taking place against the network. But, at the same time, this approach leads to a situation where the system administrators are flooded by the torrent of events to be able to understand the significance of each of them. In such cases, the events are usually just stored for future reference without any analysis or correlation; hence intrusion attempts might go unnoticed.

At this point, a matter of prime concern is that the significance/criticality of the reported anomalies varies from each other. Every host has a precise behavior in terms of its system resources and services running on it, hence what is considered normal/ trivial in one host's environment could be different in another. For example, an activity that can be ignored in a web server may be considered crucial when occurred in a mail server.

In this work, we attempt to categorize the obtained anomaly events based on their originating host and associated system resource or parameter, thus essentially filtering and reducing the amount of events requiring further analysis. Our idea is to develop an ontology to express the semantic relationships among attributes of the anomaly events, thus structuring the domain of anomaly detection. The power of ontology is used in expressing relationships between collected data, and its reasoning capability to categorize the events into predefined compartments.

The developed Anomaly Detection ontology acts as a representation or common understanding of the knowledge about the domain of anomaly detection, which constitutes a set of hosts, their salient resources and behavior patterns and the events of interest occurring in them at any point of time. We attempt to explore the utility of ontological reasoning in filtering, correlating and reasoning on the represented domain, thus identifying non-trivial and interesting events from the avalanche of events identified by the system.

This chapter is organized as follows: In section 2, we give an introduction on ontologies and how they have been used in the field of information security. Section 3 gives an overview of the proposed system. It explains the process of detecting anomaly events, role of ontology in anomaly detection and the system design. Section 4 explains the Anomaly Detection Ontology and the classification of anomaly events using the ontological reasoning process. In section 5, we present and discuss the results of ontology development along with a use case scenario with respect to a particular event.

2. BACKGROUND

Ontology

Ontology is a term borrowed from Philosophy. It is the study of the nature of 'being' or 'existence' (Gruber, 1993). In computer science and information science, ontology defines a common vocabulary for researchers who need to share information about a domain. It includes machine-interpretable definitions of basic concepts in the domain and relations among them. It is used to reason about the properties of a domain, and may define the domain.

Ontology technology finds its roots in description logics (Nardi and Brachman, 2002). Formal logic provides two important things used in ontological research: languages for knowledge representation, and functional models for

the implementation of reasoning process. With a proper reasoning mechanism, an ontological specification can be used to infer interesting details about the represented domain, or in other words, deduce properties or relations between concepts that are not explicitly defined.

Noy and McGuinness (2001) puts forward some of the reasons for developing an ontology:

- To share common understanding of the structure of information among people or software agents.
- To enable reuse of domain knowledge.
- To make domain assumptions explicit.
- To separate domain knowledge from the operational knowledge.
- To analyze domain knowledge.

Gruber (1993) advocates the role of ontologies in supporting knowledge sharing activities and presents a set of criteria to guide the development of such ontologies. According to him, ontology is a representational vocabulary in which definitions associate the names of entities in the universe of discourse (e.g., classes, relations, functions, or other objects) with human-readable text describing what the names mean, and formal axioms that constrain the interpretation and well-formed use of these terms.

According to Guarino (1998) every symbolic information system (IS) has its own ontology, since it ascribes meaning to the symbols used according to a particular view of the world. He discusses the peculiar role an ontology plays within an information system. He argues in favor of ontology-driven information systems, where the role of ontology is a central one, and it profitably drives all aspects and components of an IS.

Ontologies in the Context of Information Security

A lot of work has been done in the field of information security and application of ontologies. Donner (2003) recognizes the need for a security ontology.

Far too many terms in security terminology are vaguely defined, which causes confusion among security technologists as well as their customers-he says. He emphasizes that a security ontology would include the concepts of data, secrecy, privacy, availability, integrity, threats, exploits, vulnerabilities, detection, defense, cost, policy, encryption, response, value, owner, authorization, authentication, roles, methods and groups. Such an ontology will help in reporting incidents more effectively, sharing data and information across organizations, and enabling security specialists to communicate more clearly.

Raskin et al (2001) introduce and advocate an ontological semantic approach to information security. They argue that a security ontology could organize and systematize all the security phenomena. The approach pursues the dual goals of inclusion of natural language data sources as an integral part of the overall data sources in information security applications, and formal specification of the information security community know-how for the support of routine and time-efficient measures to prevent and counteract computer attacks.

Tsoumas and Gritzalis (2006) present a security management framework of an arbitrary information system (IS) which builds upon a security ontology (SO). They argue that they employ a structured approach to support the process leading from informal, high-level statements found in policy and requirement analysis documents to deployable technical controls. The outcome is a knowledge-based, ontology-centric security management system, separating the security requirements ('What') from their technical implementations ('How'), which are eventually matched in order to formulate the necessary actions ('Do') to be deployed in the information assets.

Martimiano et al. (2005) propose a security incident ontology to ease and make it possible to correlate different security incidents from different sources, and also to ease the knowledge and information management about security incidents.

The paper defines a unique vocabulary of terms and relations related to the domain. Undercoffer, Joshi and J. Pinkston (2003) state the benefits of using ontologies instead of taxonomies giving case scenarios within a distributed Intrusion Detection system. They have produced an ontology specifying a model of computer attack using the DARPA Agent Markup Language + Ontology Inference Layer, a descriptive logic language. "Because ontologies provide powerful constructs that include machine interpretable definitions of the concepts within a specific domain and the relations between them, they may be utilized not only to provide an IDS with the ability to share a common understanding of the information at issue, but also to further enable the IDS, with an improved capacity, to reason over and analyze instances of data representing an intrusion." (p.122)

Isaza, Castillo and Duque (2009) present an intrusion detection and prevention architecture based on multi-agent systems that represent their knowledge using ontology and semantic models. The attack signatures are represented using an intelligent agent, and an ontological model for reaction rules provides intrusion prevention.

In this work, we are trying to apply ontology to make meaningful assumptions about the wide range of events detected by an anomaly detection system. An ontology is modeled to express the semantic relationships among the attributes of the anomaly events. The system harnesses the reasoning capability of ontology and ontological inference engine to determine the effect of an event on a host and classify the events, thus filtering significant events from the rest.

3. THE PROPOSED SYSTEM

Detecting Anomaly Events

Anomaly detection methodology is based on the notion that attack behavior differs enough from normal user behavior, that it can be detected by cataloging and identifying the differences involved.(Denning,1987). The differentiator of anomaly detection technology resides in the methods for constructing a normal behavior profile, which is the area that attracts the majority of research and development in anomaly detection. Stefan Axelsson (2000) has identified a variety of anomaly detection systems such as statistics-based systems, rule based systems, and artificial neural network (ANN) based systems and systems employing state series modeling.

In the proposed system, we are employing a Specification based approach on anomaly detection. According to Sekar et al. (2002), specification-based techniques are based on manually developed specifications that capture legitimate system behaviors. This avoids the high rate of false alarms caused by legitimate, but, previously-unseen behaviors in the statistical anomaly detection approach.

The system tries to detect anomalies at host-level. From the security point of view, a host-based anomaly detection approach has the potential of detecting abnormal behaviors in a host that might indicate inside attacks as well as bottlenecks/ issues of concern in hosts. A network-based system will not be able to detect such events because they do not generate network traffic. Additionally, what is considered normal in one host's environment could be different in another; hence a distinct model of 'normal behavior' needs to be developed individually for each host. In our system, the anomaly detection process is confined to hosts running in Unix environment.

As stated earlier, our intent was to develop a comprehensive security monitoring system which is capable of capturing all the events of interest occurring in the server setup, thus providing a complete overview of system security. We wish to take a broader perspective in anomaly detection by looking for abnormal behaviors of a host which might include intrusions/attacks as well as non-malicious behavior. The effectiveness of anomaly detection is greatly affected by the aspects of the

system behavior which are learnt. Selecting an appropriate set of features to monitor has proved to be a hard problem. Our system regularly collects monitoring data regarding a wide variety of system parameters (metrics) such as:

1. Performance metrics like CPU utilization, memory utilization, disk statistics, network interface utilization statistics, partition utilization statistics, system load average etc.
2. Security metrics such as open port information, firewall policy, user accounts, suid files etc.
3. Service specific metrics like service configurations, email traffic information, antivirus update status etc...
4. Process metrics giving information regarding processes running on the host such as existing processes, created processes, process count etc

This metric set is a characterization of the state of the protected system, which is both reflective of the system health and sensitivity to attacks. It models the micro-level manners of the system. By monitoring a wide range of parameters, the system employs redundancy to improve attack detection. The redundancy provides a 'safety cushion' against missing some attacks by making a poor choice of characteristics to monitor. Also it becomes much harder to craft evasive attacks, where an attacker attempts to carry out an attack without perturbing the parameters being monitored. Given a set of real time behavior profiles, everything that does not match the specified system state is considered to be a suspicious action. Thus, the system is characterized by very high detection efficiency (it is able to recognize novel attacks).

Role of Ontology

The anomaly events detected by the above mentioned anomaly detection system may include security events of prime concern (such as an unauthorized super-user account), events signifying an undesirable system configuration (e.g. a change in default firewall policy), those denoting a performance bottleneck (e.g., high system load average) or an operational issue in the system(e.g. antivirus program is not updated). The anomaly detection system can only detect an anomaly, but cannot describe what it is. Although obtaining a wide variety of events provides a comprehensive view of the system status, it will lead to a situation where the system administrators are overwhelmed by the avalanche of events to be able to understand the significance of each of them.

In such a situation, the real challenge is to filter the 'interesting' events from the 'non-interesting' ones for further analysis. In the real world, a network administrator uses his knowledge on the environment such as, the system resources crucial for the host, the services running in the host, key metrics indicating the host health, factors pointing to a security hazard in the host etc., to identify the events requiring immediate action. He will also take into consideration the cause-effect relationships existing between events.

If it is possible to express the administrator's knowledge on the domain in a structured manner such that an intelligent system can analyze it and reason on it, the process of event filtering can be automated. In this work, we are attempting to map a conceptual model of the administrator's domain knowledge to an ontological representation. Events have internal attributes having semantic interpretations. By exploiting these semantic relationships among events, we can use ontology capabilities to express the above said knowledge in a systematic fashion, which can be used by a software agent to categorize the anomaly events and solve the problem of too many events reported. Specifically, this work will address the following problems:

- Identify key variables/concepts in the domain of anomaly detection.

- Define relationships between these concepts.
- Define rules to correlate and infer information about event criticality from the existing relations and
- Use ontological reasoning to categorize anomaly events.

System Design Overview

The proposed Information Security Monitoring System (ISMS) comprises of the following components.

Sensory Processors

Inputs to the system are provided via sensors, which monitor the day-to-day status of the environment. The sensors give a real-time account of the activities going on in the hosts, by collecting information using standard system tools, log files, configuration files etc. The data given by the sensors is processed and organized to create a snapshot/ internal representation of the system state at any point of time.

Anomaly Detection Subsystem

A legitimate behavior profile or 'system profile' is constructed for each monitored host, which is a manually developed specification capturing the valid host behaviors. The current state of the environment provided by the sensors is analyzed with respect to this legitimate state. Any discrepancy between the two states will trigger the generation of an anomaly event.

The sensory processors and anomaly detection subsystem together captures the anomalous behaviors occurring in the protected hosts in real time.

Ontological Reasoning Subsystem

An ontology is developed to structure the domain of anomaly detection. It conveys as much as possible the state of the environment by describing pertinent terms in the domain and their relations. By making use of ontological capabilities, the reasoner and inference engine will draw further inferences on the anomalies occurring in the system. This will finally lead to classifying an event based on its type and criticality.

Figure 1 gives an overview of the system design.

4. ANOMALY DETECTION ONTOLOGY

The Anomaly Detection ontology is developed using OWL, the Web Ontology Language. OWL (Dean M et al.,2004) is a language for making ontological statements, developed as a follow-on from Resource Description Framework (RDF) and RDF Schema (RDFS), as well as earlier ontology language projects including OIL (Ontology Inference Layer), DAML (DARPA Agent Markup Language) and DAML+OIL. W3C's Web Ontology Working Group defines OWL as three different sublanguages: OWL-Lite, OWL-DL and OWL-Full. Of these, OWL-DL is based on Description Logics. Description Logics are considered as decidable fragments of First Order Logic. They are known for their expressiveness

and have clearly defined semantics. Several reasoning tasks can be carried out on a knowledge base expressed in DL, such as computing the subsumption relation between two concept expressions, checking whether a certain assertion is logically implied by a knowledge base etc. (Nardi and Brachman, 2002).

The Anomaly Detection ontology is edited using Protégé/OWL. Automated reasoning over the ontology is performed using the Description Logic reasoners, RacerPro and Pellet. Rules in the ontology are written in Semantic Web Rule Language (SWRL) and executed with Jess Rule Engine.

Steps in Building the Ontology

The following steps are involved in building the ontology:

(1) Define purpose, scope and requirements: The proposed ontology is designed to support reasoning for event filtering through the use of OWL-DL. In terms of scope, the ontology will be confined to the events defined during the anomaly detection phase. In this work, we are concerned with the various aspects of events collected by the anomaly detection system such as (a) what are the factors to be considered for classifying events? (b) how does the criticality of an event

Figure 1. System Design

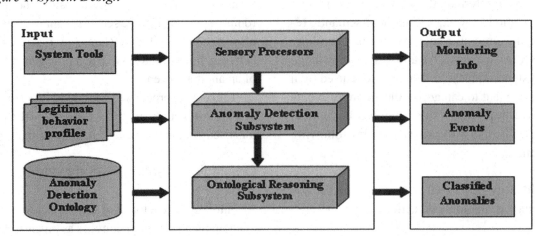

Figure 2. Terminology Identification

vary from host to host? (c) how is the occurrence of one event related to others? and (d)how can we express significant system aberrations in terms of these events?

The key requirement of the ontology is to convey as much as possible the state of the system by describing the events, hosts, metrics and system resources so that the reasoner and inference engine will be able to draw further inferences on the anomalies occurring in the system. This will finally lead to the classification of anomaly events based on their type and criticality.

(2) *Terminology Identification:* Based on the purpose and domain of the ontology, the relevant terms in the domain of interest have to be identified. The core parts of an anomaly detection domain are the hosts monitored by it and the events collected from these hosts. In our system, each defined event is generated as a result of monitoring a particular system metric. Also, there will be a system resource associated with the event (such as cpu/memory/disk/network interface/ service). Due to cause-effect relationships in the network, there can be events that cannot be directly obtained by monitoring the system metrics. Such a macro-event is expressed as a combination of one or more (micro) events. For example, a new super-user account in the system or an unknown port open in the system will signify a macro-event, '*a system backdoor is detected*'.

Keeping these in mind, we have recognized the following concepts that appear to be relevant

in the scenario of anomaly detection: 1) Defined Anomaly Events 2) Hosts in the network 3) Monitored Metrics 4) System Resources 5) Macro events and 6) Category to which an event belongs. Figure 2 depicts these pertinent terms in the domain.

(3) *Identifying Semantic Relationships in the Environment:* We want to identify all possible relationships between variables making up an event, and in that way represent the knowledge we have about the system state. The basic relationships we have recognized in our environment are 1) An event is owned by a host. 2) An event is generated by a metric 3) An event may be associated with a system resource 4) An event may directly/ indirectly act as the cause of another event- For example, if the number of users logged into a host is higher than the defined threshold, it is very likely that the number of processes created over a time period also exceeds the defined value. 5) One or more events may signify a macro-event in the system 6) A host may consider some of its resources as critical ones 7) Information given by some metrics may be of more interest to some hosts.

The above said relations stem from the background knowledge about the domain. In addition to these, we have added a relation that the events have a 'criticality' value associated with them, which is explained later in this chapter. These semantic relationships are shown in Figure 3.

Figure 3. Semantic Relationships in the Anomaly Detection Domain

In the next section, we will describe how the above said terms and relations are modeled in Web Ontology Language (OWL).

Modeling the Ontology in OWL

Any OWL ontology is made up of three components, namely, classes, individuals and properties. Classes are sets containing individuals, described to precisely give the requirements for class membership. (e.g.: Mammal, Person, Company). Individuals represent objects in the domain of interest. They are also referred to as instances of classes. (e.g.: Tom, Italy). A property describes a relationship that exists between Individuals and between Individual and data. (e.g.: hasPart, isInhibitedBy)

Class membership can be explicitly specified using two conditions, namely 'necessary' and 'necessary & sufficient'. Necessary conditions are conditions that must be fulfilled by Individuals to belong to that class. Necessary & Sufficient conditions represent conditions that are not only necessary for class membership, but also sufficient to determine that any Individual that satisfies these conditions can be inferred to be a member of the class in question. Classes with Necessary & sufficient conditions are called **Defined classes** while those with only Necessary conditions are called **Primitive classes**. A defined class gives a complete definition of a particular class while the primitive class gives a partial description of a class.

A developer of an OWL ontology thinks in terms of necessary and sufficient conditions to define a class, building new concepts from existing ones by fitting them together in definitions and determining what conditions sufficiently define something as an instance of a class. A Description Logic reasoner can use the sufficient conditions to infer which classes are subclasses of the defined class.

In the Anomaly Detection ontology, since our aim is to represent how variables and entities are structured through the relationships between them, we positioned the classes in a hierarchy (taxonomy) to reflect these relationships. Ontology enables to specify richer semantic relations between entities apart from the 'is kind of' relations in taxonomies.

In our ontology, the following primitive super-classes exist: 1. Event 2. Metric 3. Host 4. SystemResource 5. Criticality and 6. MacroEvent (see Figure 4).

The Event class represents all the anomaly events defined in the system. Events can be broadly classified into performance events, security events, process events and service events. Hence, the Event class has four sub-classes namely, PerformanceEvent, SecuriyEvent, ServiceEvent and ProcessEvent. The Host class represents all hosts in the network. The Metric class includes all metrics monitored by the system. The SystemResource class represents different system resources such as system partitions, system interfaces, system

Figure 4. Classes in Ontology

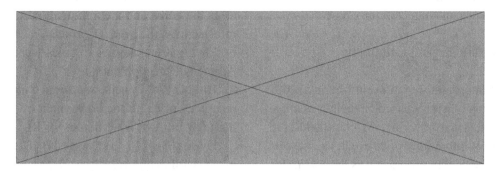

ports, system services etc. The MacroEvent class represents the macro-events defined by the system.

The major reason for developing the ontology is to enable the filtration of events. For this, the ontology must provide some information regarding the criticality of an event. To materialize this, a 'Criticality' class is present in the ontology. The class is modeled as a Value Partition, i.e., the parent quality, 'Criticality' contains sub-qualities for each degree, namely High, Medium and Low; i.e.

Criticality = High *or* Medium *or* Low

Once the classes and individuals are identified, the next step in the implementation is to add the identified relations between classes and individuals. In ontology, relationships are formed along properties. Object properties are binary relations between individuals. A property will have a domain and a range. For example, if a relation is: *"subject-Individual → hasProperty → object-Individual"*, then, the domain is the class of the subject-Individual and the range is the class of the object-Individual. Table 1 lists the object properties which depicts the semantic relationships in our environment. Some of these are having corresponding inverse properties, (denoted by '⇔'), which will link the individuals linked by the original property in the reverse direction.

Towards Classification of Anomaly Events

Once the ontology is fully developed, our aim is to use this ontology to attain our goal of classification of anomaly events. In this work, we achieved the automatic classification of events through two

Table 1. Properties in Ontology

	Property	**Domain**	**Range**
1	isOwnedBy ⇔ owns	Event	Host
2	generatedBy ⇔ generates	Event	Metric
3	hasSystemResource	Event	SystemResource
4	isCritical	SystemResource or Metric	Host
5	isSecurityCritical	SystemResource or Metric	Host
6	mightTrigger ⇔ mayResultFrom	Event	Event
7	isSignifiedBy ⇔ signifys	MacroEvent	Event
8	monitors	Metric	SystemResource
9	hasCriticality	Event or MacroEvent	Criticality

steps: 1. Assign the criticality of events and 2. Classify the events into Defined classes.

(1) Assigning Event Criticality

The most important step in event filtering is the classification of events based on their criticality. We have stated that the 'Criticality' class represents the degree of importance of an event. i.e., we can assign the criticality of an event as *high_critical, medium_critical* or *low_critical* using the 'has-Criticality' property.

Some events by themselves may be of high criticality. For example, a change in number of super-users, change in firewall policy etc. are events of highest concern irrespective of the host and the time in which they occurred. So these events can be explicitly stated in the ontology as having a criticality value of *high_critical.*

But in certain other cases, the criticality may depend on the host from which the event originated and the system resource or metric with which the event is associated. Each host in the network has its own specific role, its own set of critical parameters and its own definition of a 'normal state' of the system. The role of a host in the network plays an important part in deciding whether an event is interesting or not. For example, in a mail server, any event generated by the metric associated with the system service 'sendmail' can be regarded as highly critical. For a web server with web service listening on port 80, any event related to the system port 80 will be of high criticality. Therefore, for achieving event filtering through ontology, it is important to assign the criticality of an event based on system resources crucial for the host, the services running in the host and key metrics indicating the host health.

Assignment of event criticality is accomplished by writing SWRL Rules. SWRL (Semantic Web Rule Language) is intended to be the rule language of the semantic web. It allows users to write rules to reason about OWL individuals and to infer new knowledge about those individuals. A SWRL rule

contains an antecedent part, which is referred to as the body, and a consequent part, which is referred to as the head. (Horrocks, I. et al, 2004) Following are examples of rules written in the Anomaly Detection ontology:

Rule 1: Every event associated with a system resource critical to the host which owns it is of high criticality. It is written in SWRL as:

Event(?e) ^ isOwnedBy(?e,?h) ^ hasSystemResource(?e,?r) ^ isCritical(?r,?h) ^ High(?x) → hasCriticality(?e,?x)

Rule 2: Every event generated by a metric which is critical to the host which owns it is of high criticality. In SWRL,

Event(?e) ^ isOwnedBy(?e,?h) ^ generatedBy(?e,?m) ^ isCritical(?m,?h) ^ High (?x) → hasCriticality(?e, ?x)

Rule 3: Every security event associated with a system resource which is 'security critical' to the host which owns it is of high criticality. In SWRL,

SecurityEvent(?e) ^ isOwnedBy(?e,?h) ^ hasSystemResource(?e,?r) ^ isSecurityCritical(?r,?h) ^ High(?x) → hasCriticality(?e,?x)

Once the rules are executed, new property axioms will be inferred, assigning a criticality value to the concerned events.

(2) Defined Classes in the Ontology

As stated earlier, defined classes are those classes in the ontology with *necessary and sufficient conditions*, which implies, "If something fulfils these conditions then it must be a member of this class". In our ontology, to attain the aim of categorizing the events into different compartments, we have defined some classes using necessary and sufficient conditions. An event may or may not fall into one or more of these classes depending on its type and criticality.

Some of the classes we have defined to categorize the events are:

1. **HighCriticalSecurityEvent**: A security event of high criticality i.e.

   SecurityEvent and (*hasCriticality* some **High**)

2. **HighCriticalServiceEvent**: A service related event of high criticality. i.e.

   ServiceEvent and (*hasCriticality* some **High**)

3. **HighCriticalNWInterfaceEvent**: An event associated with a network interface having a criticality value of 'high'. i.e.

   Event and (*hasSystemResource* some **SystemNetworkInterface**) and (*hasCriticality* some **High**)

4. **HighCriticalPartitionEvent**: A high critical event associated with a system partition or mount point. i.e.

   Event and (*hasSystemResource* some (**SystemPartition** OR **SystemMountPoint**)) and (*hasCriticality* some **High**)

5. **HighCriticalProcessEvent**: A process related event of high criticality. i.e.

   ProcessEvent and (*hasCriticality* some **High**)

6. **TriggerHighCriticalEvent**: An event which acts as a trigger of a high critical event.

   Event and (*mightTrigger* some (**Event** and (*hasCriticality* some **High**)))

7. **SignifysHighCriticalMacroEvent**: An event which signifies a macro-event of high criticality.

   Event and (*signifys* some (**MacroEvent** and (*hasCriticality* some **High**)))

Description Logic reasoners can be used to identify individuals belonging to each of the defined classes. The reasoner does subsumption checking as well as instantiation checking to populate the defined classes with anomaly events. It is possible that an event belongs to more than one of these defined classes.

Figure 5 shows the Event class taxonomy together with the defined classes.

5. RESULTS AND DISCUSSION

Ontology Evaluation Process

Ontology evaluation is the problem of assessing a given ontology from the point of view of a particular criterion or application. There is no single correct way of developing an ontology or modeling a domain. The evaluation process aids the users facing a multitude of ontologies to select the one which best fits their requirements. Also, it helps the ontology developers to evaluate the resulting ontology and thus guide the construction process and any refinement steps. (Brank, Grobelnik and Mladenic, 2005).

The Anomaly Detection ontology is developed using Protégé-OWL. Protégé OWL Plug-in provides a mechanism to execute a configurable list of tests on the ontology being edited. The test framework provided by Protégé-OWL contains various tests programs that basically verify arbitrary conditions specified in the ontology, and in case of failure, return an error message.

Because an OWL-DL ontology can be translated into a Description Logic representation, it is possible to perform automated reasoning over the ontology using a Description Logic reasoner. Description Logic reasoners play an important role in the ontology development life cycle. We used the DL reasoners, Racerpro and Pellet to check the consistency of classes within the ontology and to compute the subsumption relations. Consistency checking is done to ensure that none of

Figure 5. Event Class Taxonomy

the definitions of an ontology element contradicts another. Inconsistent classes in an ontology are those that cannot have any instances. The ontology consistency is verified to avoid the risk of logical problems when the ontology is used in a knowledge base to infer new facts. Subsumption checking arranges the classes in a hierarchy according to the superclass/subclass relationships.

Automatic Event Classification: Use Case Scenario

For putting the developed ontology into practical use, an ontology application is developed, which uses the ontology for solving the real problems in the domain. We can say that an ontology lies at the core of an intelligent application. We have developed the ontology application in Java using the open source Java library, Protégé-OWL API. The application will perform the classification of anomaly events, after executing the ontology rules and invoking the reasoner.

To get a better understanding of the working of the system, here we will discuss the process by which the system detects and classifies an anomaly event. Consider a mail server, '*hostA*' in the monitored network. Suppose the '*sendmail*' process stopped running in the host. As this signifies a deviation from the profile specification for

hostA (i.e., at least one sendmail process should be running), the anomaly detection engine will generate the anomaly event, '*hostA_sendmail_not_running*'.

Now, the event has to be classified according to the knowledge represented in the ontology. For that, the following two steps are involved:

Step 1: *Mapping the Anomaly Event Data:* As a first step in using the ontology for anomaly event classification, a knowledge base on the events defined by the system is developed. The information on the individual anomaly events and their attributes (such as the host owning the event, the system resource/metric associated with the event) are encoded in the ontology. Also, the ontology is loaded with information regarding the critical parameters, services or resources for each host.

In the Anomaly Detection ontology, the data about the above discussed event has to be mapped in accordance with the classes and properties present in it. It is evident that the event '*hostA_sendmail_not_running*' belongs to 'ProcessEvent' class, is owned by the host '*hostA*' and is associated with the system process '*sendmail*'. From the administrator's knowledge on the domain, the information that the *sendmail* process is critical to *hostA* can be represented in the ontology.

Step 2: *Inferencing, Reasoning and Event Classification:* Once the anomaly event is received by the ontology application, the application proceeds to invoke the Jess Rule Engine to execute the SWRL rules. The particular event, *'hostA_sendmail_not_running'* will result in triggering the rule which states "*Every event associated with a system resource critical to the host which owns it is of high criticality*" *[Rule 1]*. Once this rule is executed, the event will be assigned a criticality level 'high', i.e., the property axiom, *hostA_sendmail_not_running* → hasCriticality → *high_critical,* will be inferred by the rule engine.

In the next step, the application invokes the DL reasoner, Pellet to compute the inferred types of the event. As the event satisfies the conditions for membership of the 'HighCriticalProcessEvent' class (ProcessEvent and *hasCriticality* High), it is grouped under that class.

6. CONCLUSION AND FUTURE WORK

In the course of this work, we examined the feasibility of using ontology as a means for supporting filtration of the multitude of events collected by an Anomaly Detection engine. We developed the ontology focusing on our approach of anomaly detection, by mapping the conceptual model of our domain to an ontological representation. The concepts, hierarchy and relationships in our domain were identified and modeled in the ontology. Ontological reasoning capabilities were successfully applied to achieve automatic classification of anomaly events based on their type and criticality.

We believe that the development of an ontology to represent the domain of anomaly detection has offered a great deal of advantages such as:

- With the ontology, the administrator is able to encode his knowledge on the domain in a structured manner, thus enabling knowledge sharing.
- An ontological model provides our security monitoring system a solid structure for

knowledge representation, which provides a complete and accurate modeling of the domain and intelligent reasoning to analyze security alarms.

- The ontology provides valuable insights on the status of the hosts as well as the cause-effect relationships in the environment.
- The ontology makes domain knowledge explicit, i.e., any change in the host/network configuration over time has to be reflected only in the ontology; the application remains unaltered.
- The ontology can be extended to any number of hosts and events as long as the concepts and relations in the anomaly detection domain will remain same.

One theoretical foundation of ontology is logic, more specifically, Description Logic for OWL (Web Ontology Language). That is, the ontology technology belongs to symbolic computation where it brings value to solving problems with automated reasoning and inference. It is not meant to replace various software technologies in the procedural computation category, such as Java, SQL, data mining, statistics, etc. Instead, ontology brings most value when it is used in combination with such procedural technologies. For example, ontology can help make data-mining procedures more efficient, adaptive, and smart by externalizing and organizing domain knowledge used by data-mining algorithms in ontological models.

There is a lot of scope for further research on the suitability of ontologies for effective representation of knowledge intended for different purposes other than knowledge sharing. The Anomaly Detection Ontology can be extended further by adding more concepts, relations and rules. For example, the criticality of an event can be defined based on the day of the week and time of the day in which it occurred. Also, we can think of exploring the inter-connections between different system resources in a machine/ group of machines using ontology, thus realizing the actual significance of an anomaly event.

The ontology developed in this work is based on a specification based approach to anomaly detection. The possibilities of expanding this ontology to include other anomaly detection models, such as, statistics based or rule based, is worth studying.

REFERENCES

Axelsson, S. (2000). Intrusion detection systems: A survey and taxonomy. *Technical Report 99-15*, Department of Computer Engineering, Chalmers University, March 2000.

Brank, J., Grobelnik, M., & Mladenic, D. (2005). A survey of ontology evaluation techniques. In *Proceedings of the Conference on Data Mining and Data Warehouses* (SiKDD05), Ljubljana, Slovenia, 2005.

Dean, M., & Schreiber, G. (2004). OWL Web Ontology Language Reference. *World Wide Web Consortium, Recommendation REC-owl-ref-20040210*, February 2004.

Denning, D. E. (1987). An Intrusion-Detection Model. *IEEE Transactions on Software Engineering, SE-13*(2), 222–232. doi:10.1109/TSE.1987.232894

Donner, M. (2003). Towards a Security Ontology. *IEEE Security and Privacy, 1*(3), 6–7.

Gruber, T. R. (1993). Toward principles for the design of ontologies used for knowledge sharing. In Guarino, N., & Poli, R. (Eds.), *Formal Ontology in Conceptual Analysis and Knowledge Representation*. Amsterdam: Kluwer Academic Publishers.

Guarino, N. (1998). Formal Ontology and Information Systems. In N. Guarino (Ed.), *Proceedings of Formal Ontology and Information Systems* (pp. 3–15), 1998, Trento, Italy. Amsterdam: IOS Press, Amsterdam

Horrocks, I., Patel-Schneider, P. F., Boley, H., Tabet, S., Grosof, B., & Dean, M. (2004). *SWRL: A semantic web rule language combining OWL and RuleML*. Retrieved on May 10, 2010 from http://www.w3.org/Submission/SWRL/

Isaza, G., Castillo, A., & Duque, N. D. (2009). An Intrusion Detection and Prevention Model Based on Intelligent Multi-Agent Systems, Signatures and Reaction Rules Ontologies. In *Advances in Intelligence and Soft Computing - 7th International Conference on Practical Applications of Agents and Multi-Agent Systems (PAAMS 2009)* (pp. 237-245). New York: Springer.

Martimiano, A. F. M., & Moreira, E. S. (2005). An owl-based security incident ontology. In *Proceedings of the Eighth International Protégé Conference* (pp. 43–44) Poster.

Nardi, D., & Brachman, R. J. (2002). An introduction to description logics. In Baader, F., Calvanese, D., McGuinness, D. L., Nardi, D., & Patel-Schneider, P. F. (Eds.), *The Description Logic Handbook: Theory, Implementation and Applications* (pp. 1–40). Cambrdige, UK: Cambridge University Press.

Noy, N., & McGuiness, D. (2001). Ontology Development 101: A Guide to Creating Your First Ontology. *Stanford Knowledge Systems Laboratory Technical Report KSL-01-05*. Retrieved on May 10, 2010 from http://protege.stanford.edu/publications/ontology_development/ontology101-noy-mcguinness.html.

Raskin, V., Hempelmann, C. F., Triezenberg, K. E., & Nirenburg, S. (2001). Ontology in information security: A useful theoretical foundation and methodological tool. In [New York: ACM.]. *Proceedings of, NSPW-2001*, 53–59.

Sekar, R., Gupta, A., Frullo, J., Shanbhag, T., Tiwari, A., Yang, H., & Zhou, S. (2002). Specification Based Anomaly Detection: a New Approach for Detecting Network Intrusions. In *Proceedings of the 9th ACM conference on Computer and communications security* (pp. 265-274). New York: ACM.

Tsoumas, B., & Gritzalis, D. (2006). Towards an Ontology-based Security Management. In *Proceedings of the 20th International Conference on Advanced Information Networking and Applications (AINA'06)* (Vol. 1, pp. 985-992). Washington, DC: IEEE Computer Society.

Undercoffer, J., Joshi, A., & Pinkston, J. (2003). Modeling computer attacks: An ontology for intrusion detection. In *Proceedings of the 6th International Symposium on Recent Advances in Intrusion Detection (RAID'03),* Pittsburgh, PA (LNCS 2820, pp. 113-135).

ADDITIONAL READING

Adaa, M. P. (2007). *Ontology for Host Based Anomaly Detection.* Oslo, Norway: University of Oslo. Retrieved May 10, 2010 from http://research.iu.hio.no/theses/pdf/master2007/maggie.pdf

Borgo, S., Guarino, N., & Masolo, C. (1997). An Ontological Theory of Physical Objects. In L. Ironi (Ed.), *Proceedings of Eleventh International Workshop on Qualitative Reasoning (QR'97)* (pp. 223-231), Cortona, (Italy).

Borst, W. N., Akkermans, J. M., & Top, J. L. (1997). Engineering Ontologies. *International Journal of Human-Computer Studies, 46*(2-3), 365–406. doi:10.1006/ijhc.1996.0096

Calvanese, D., De Giacomo, G., Lenzerini, M., & Nardi, D. (1999). Reasoning in expressive Description Logics. In Robinson, A., & Voronkov, A. (Eds.), *Handbook of Automated Reasoning* (pp. 1581–1634). Amsterdam: Elsevier Science Publishers.

Gennari, J. H., Musen, M. A., Fergerson, R. W., Grosso, W. E., Crubézy, M., & Eriksson, H. (2003). The evolution of Protégé: an environment for knowledge-based systems development. *International Journal of Human-Computer Studies, 58*(1), 89–123. doi:10.1016/S1071-5819(02)00127-1

Guarino, N. (1995). Formal Ontology, Conceptual Analysis and Knowledge Representation. In B.R. Gaines, N. Guarino, & R. Poli (Eds.), *International Journal of Human and Computer Studies, 43*(5-6), 625-640

Horrocks, I., Patel-Schneider, P., McGuinness, D., & Welty, A. (2007). OWL: a Description Logic Based Ontology Language for the Semantic Web. In Baader, F., Calvanese, D., McGuinness, D. L., Nardi, D., & Patel-Schneider, P. F. (Eds.), *The Description Logic Handbook: Theory, Implementation and Applications* (2nd ed., pp. 458–486). Cambridge, UK: Cambridge University Press. doi:10.1017/CBO9780511711787.016

Horrocks, I., Sattler, U., & Tobies, S. (2000). Reasoning with Individuals for the Description Logic SHIQ. In D. MacAllester (Ed.), *Proceedings of the 17th International Conference on Automated Deduction (CADE-17)* (pp. 482-496). London: Springer-Verlag.

Ko, C., Ruschitzka, M., & Levitt, K. (1997). Execution monitoring of security-critical programs in distributed systems: a Specification-based approach. In *Proceedings of the 1997 IEEE Symposium on Security and Privacy* (pp. 175-187).

Lindqvist, U., & Jonsson, E. (1997). How to Systematically Classify Computer Security Intrusions. In *Proceedings of the 1997 IEEE Symposium on Security and Privacy* (pp. 154 – 163), May 1997.

Mizoguchi, R. (2003). Tutorial on ontological engineering part 1: Introduction to ontological engineering. *New Generation Computing, 21*(4), 365–384. doi:10.1007/BF03037311

Mizoguchi, R. (2004). Tutorial on ontological engineering part 2: Ontology development, tools and languages. *New Generation Computing, 22*(1), 61–96. doi:10.1007/BF03037281

Rector, A. L. (2003). Modularisation of domain ontologies implemented in description logics and related formalisms including OWL. *Second International Conference on Knowledge Capture 2003(K-CAP)*, (pp 121-128), Sanibel Island, Florida.

Staab, S., & Maedche, A. (2000). Ontology Engineering beyond the Modeling of Concepts and Relations. In R.V. Benjamins, A. Gomez-Perez, N. Guarino, M. Uschold (Eds.), *14th European Conference on Artificial Intelligence, Workshop on Applications of Ontologies and Problem-Solving Methods*.

Undercoffer, J., Finin, T., Joshi, A., & Pinkston, J. (2005). A target centric ontology for intrusion detection: using DAML+OIL to classify intrusive behaviors. In *Knowledge Engineering Review - Special Issue on Ontologies for Distributed Systems* (pp. 2–22). Cambridge, UK: Cambridge University Press.

Undercoffer, J., & Joshi, A. (2002). On web semantics and data mining: Intrusion detection as a case study. In *Proceedings of the National Science Foundation Workshop on Next Generation Data Mining*.

van Heijst, G., Schreiber, Th., & Wielinga, B. J. (1997). Using explicit ontologies in KBS development. In B.R. Gaines (Ed). *International Journal of Human-Computer Studies, 46,* (2-3) (p. 183 - 292). Duluth, MN: Academic Press, Inc.

Chapter 7
Securing Next Generation Internet Services

Asoke K. Talukder
ABV Indian Institute of Information Technology & Management, India & Geschickten Solutions, India

ABSTRACT

In Next Generation Internet (NGI), internet will graduate from being just a network of networks to network of interoperable services. Security in NGI must cover all 7 layers of the OSI model instead of just 3 bottom layers as in the past. This chapter discusses the security issues in NGI and proposes a methodology for security countermeasures in NGI.

1. INTRODUCTION

First Generation Internet was the data communication protocol for researchers – it was born on 1969 with RFC1 (Crocker S. 1969) which was entitled "Host Software" and dealt with Interface Message Processor (IMP) and Host-to-Host protocols. The IMP was the packet-switching node used to interconnect participant networks to the ARPANET from the late 1960s to 1989. IMP was the first generation of gateways, which are known today as routers. Some literatures state though – Internet was born on 1972 when Larry Roberts and Bob Kahn demonstrated the ARPANET at the International Conference on Computer Com-

munication (ICCC) held in Washington, DC, in October 1972. This generation of Interne was used by the research community. These days, people in the industry were using their own proprietary protocols like System Network Architecture (SNA), DECnet etcetera. Second generation Internet was the generic data communication protocol; it can be timed at 1989 when inter-domain routing was included in the Internet with specifications like Open Shortest Path First (OSPF) protocol (RFC1131), the Border Gateway Protocol (BGP) (RFC1105), with IP Multicasting (RFC1112). These protocols helped quick acceptance of Internet – Australia, Germany, Israel, Italy, Japan, Mexico, Netherlands, New Zealand and the United Kingdom joined the Internet (Internet History 2010). The number of hosts increases from 80,000 in January

DOI: 10.4018/978-1-60960-123-2.ch007

1989 to over 160,000 in November of that year. Then was the emergence of Third Generation Internet with voice being integrated in Internet on 1995. This was through Voice over IP (VoIP) protocols – that made Internet the protocol for generic communication – be it data, voice, image, or multimedia.

By the turn of the century, the domain of Internet started expanding – it graduated from the protocol for communication to a media for services; emergence of Next Generation Internet (NGI) became apparent. In NGI, consumers became the innovators. We saw large software slowly fading out; task based thin services started emerging. Also, applications and services started moving from private data centers and servers to the internet. Services, platforms, infrastructures will be agnostic to each other. Like energy, consumers will not worry where the server is, how to access it – they will get the service as and when they need, on-demand, using any device – be it a desktop computer or a mobile phone. Users will access these solutions or services through simple user-agents on these devices. All these thin services will hide behind the cloud and interoperate to offer a rich set of services and rich user experience. NGI will offer subscription based services that will be dynamically scalable and mobile. As services in the NGI will move from private space (intranet) to a public space (Internet), NGI services will become more vulnerable to security attacks. Therefore, in the NGI security must cover all 7 layers – network security at Layer 1 to 3; Transport and Platform security at layer 4; and, Application security at layer 5 to 7. This chapter will discuss security issues in the Next Generation Internet – how they synergize.

2. NEXT GENERATION INTERNET (NGI)

The current internet – IPv4 has many problems; major ones are,

- **Addressing space:** the current address space of internet is 32 bits. With the growth of internet users this is not sufficient
- **Quality of Service:** it is a major challenge to guarantee quality of service
- **Mobility:** IP inherently does not include mobility by design
- **Security:** IP inherently does not include security by design

According to some researchers NGI is Internet2 (Internet2), according to some thinkers NGI is Internet 3.0 (Jain, 2009); according to many thinkers, IPv6 (Deering, 1998) is the NGI. However, in our analysis, NGI is combination of all of these and many more (Talukder & Prahalad, 2009c) features that can be listed as,

- **Multi-user-agent:** Smartphones and Computers (Portable & Desktops)
- **Multi-service:** Voice (telephony), TV (consumer entertainment), and multimedia (computer communication) over IP
- Multi-access (Wireless, & Wired Broadband)
- Multi-provider
- Multi-protocol networks
- Web 2.0 and Web 3.0
- Services deployed in Cloud-computing paradigm
- Services availability anywhere anytime through universal user-agents
- Trust (Opinion, Emotions, and Intent)
- IPv6 with IPsec
- Support seamless mobility at vehicular state
- Intelligent and programmable networks
- Definable service quality
- Definable security level
- On demand scalability
- API in the network to obtain context information (spatial, environmental, and temporal attributes)

- API in the network to enforce QoS and security

IPv6 address the address issues; it uses 128 bit addressing scheme (approx. 3.4*10**38 IP addresses) (Talukder et al, 2010a). However, IPv6 is not sufficient to address all challenges of future Internet. IPsec addresses the security issues at lower layers. In NGI many applications will be on the cloud – they need to be elastic so that they can scale up and scale down on-demand; they will also be accessed through untrusted and unpredictable networks. Therefore, the application in the NGI must be cloud-aware and security-aware.

3. SECURITY ISSUES IN NEXT GENERATION INTERNET

Security attributes of telecommunication is different from the security attributes in datacommunication. In telecom, security was defined as protection against unavailability of service and protection from making free calls; i.e., security here was to ensure that services are fault-tolerant and the system is equipped to handle metering, charging, billing, and fraud. Sometime telecom also looked at the *anonymity* as a security attribute for securing the identity information. Security attributes of *authentication* and *authorization* were not important in early days of telecommunications; because, starting from the customer premise equipment to the transmission line were private, trusted, and most of the time owned by few providers; also, security in this environment was addressed through physical security. However, over time, multiple providers, virtual providers, interoperability, and advancement in technology and services, made the scenario complex where authentication and authorization become critical. To realize this, networks were made intelligent with security awareness. In telecom networks the user is not authenticated, instead – the device is authenticated. Because, devices can remember strong secrets, a strong authentication system can be built for authentication in these networks.

In telecom authorization is more commonly known as service capabilities or provisioning. A device can access only these services that are provisioned for this device. In telecom, authorization is dependent on the subscription type driven by accounting criteria of the subscriber. In mobile networks, telecom signals and content pass over the air in a wireless environment; here the content are encrypted to ensure confidentiality and integrity. Telecom network uses out-of-band signaling through SS7 network; and, users have access to the traffic channel only – a hacker does not have access to the signal channel. This makes telecom network secured. Spoofing, snooping etc are virtually impossible in telecom networks.

In datacom however, signaling is in-band; data and signal go together through an open channel where any user, be it a genuine user or a hacker have access to. This makes datacom networks highly insecure. It is quite easy to snoof, sniff, and spoof Internet Protocol (IP) traffic. Therefore, in IP, security attributes like *confidentiality, integrity, availability, authentication, authorization, accounting,* and *anonymity* (CI5A) (Talukder & Chaitanya, 2008) are important. IPv6 comes native with security protocol called IP Security (IPsec). IPsec (Kent et al., 2005) will offer Authentication Header (AH) and Encapsulating Security Payload (ESP), specified in RFC4302 and RFC4303 respectively. AH will provide integrity, data origin authentication, and protection against replays. ESP on contrast will offer confidentiality, integrity, authentication, and anti-replay. In NGI, network security will not only cover public network but needs to secure the private networks as well. Network security at private networks will address Vulnerability analysis of each platform in the network – with the patch management. It will analyze the status of the platforms against National Vulnerability Database (NVD). Also, it will use the philosophy of Artificial Hygiene (Talukder & Chaitanya, 2008); as it discovers some hygiene related anomaly, it will communicate with other devices through Application Vulnerability Description Language (AVDL). AVDL (Bialkowski et al. 2004) is a security interoperability standard for creating a uniform method of describing security vulnerability using XML. At network security level – perimeter security will continue to be same as it was in the traditional network to include Firewalls, IPS, IDS, antivirus, malware catchers etc.

Unlike in the telecom, in datacom, a user is authenticated instead of a device – the user can move from device to device and use the same service. As the user is a human who cannot remember strong passcode, strong passcode for challenge and response is not possible here. Authorization here is implemented through role based security – the role of the user in a hierarchy – be it in a organization or in a social setup.

In telecom especially in GSM, the concept of a central database that contains the authentication, authorization, and presence information within the hone network allowed universal roaming and interoperability. This database is central to the GSM network and called Home Location Register (HLR). This database is accessible by other networks to locate the device, authenticate it; and, assess the capabilities of the device. HLR is evolving as Home Subscriber Server (HSS) in IP Multimedia Subsystem (IMS) and will evolve as User Profile Server Function (UPSF) in the future. It is assumed that UPSF will function similar to Federated identity for global identification, authentication and authorization for both telecom networks and data networks. Liberty Alliance (Liberty Alliance) is developing open standards for federated identity management for such converged networks.

NGI will support universal seamless roaming. In universal roaming a device can move from one network to another and continue using the service. However, here the roaming generally happens between networks from same family like GPRS to 3G or from GSM to GPRS. But, in universal seamless roaming, networks can be from different families like EDGE to WiFi. In universal seamless roaming authorization will not only depend on the service provisioning capabilities – but also on service quality parameters like cheaper tariff or better quality of service or higher security etcetera.

In NGI, platform security will cover part of Layer 3 and Layer 4 security. Here the platform attack surface must be minimized. Platform security will not only include the application server but also all database servers. Wherever possible, point-to-point transport layer security like Transport layer Security (TLS) (Dierks et al. 1999) or Secured Socket Layer (SSL), or even SNP (Secured Network Programming (Woo et al. 1994) must be used. Countermeasure against DOS attacks will be managed at this layer.

Majority of attacks in the past were related to network security vulnerabilities. Recent attacks suggest that network security countermeasures have matured and are able to counter most of the network level attacks. However, attacks exploiting security vulnerabilities at the applications are increasing. The convergence of telecom and datacom increases the security risk even further. In NGI, application security will play a significant role. It will offer application level authentication and authorization. If the application needs end-to-end security, it has to be catered by the application to offer confidentiality and integrity. Application security will also have countermeasures against buffer overflow, escalation of privileges attack. For this Security-aware Software Development Life Cycle (Talukder 2009b) can be used. In NGI many services will move to the cloud. In cloud security risks are higher; therefore, cloud security with minimization of the attack surface is absolutely necessary.

In Web 1.0, it was mainly a simplex type of publishing. In Web 2.0 this transformed into interaction and collaboration where a consumer can also become the producer and create contents. Web 3.0 (Web 3.0) is a place where machines can read Web pages, and make a meaning out of that much as we humans read them, Web 3.0 will be a place where search engines and software agents can better troll the Net and find what the users are looking for. In Web 3.0, we will move from *content to intent*. Trust is another criterion that will be addressed by NGI. In social environment trust (Venkatraman J. et al. 2004) is dependent on competence, trustworthyness, consistence, and context. All these properties will be combined with Semantic Web to build trust in the NGI.

4. NEXT GENERATION INTERNET SERVICES

There cannot be any consensus on what is NGI Services; however, we would like to take the Global Information Infrastructure (GII 1998) as the references for definition of NGI Services. We can define NGI services as these computer communication, telecommunication, or consumer entertainment services that are user-agent agnostic, device agnostic, network agnostic, and location agnostic over Internet; and, it is secured, scalable, and interoperate to offer a seamless service of services. Above all, one should be able to use these services as consumables, which means – one need not spend money to buy software or computer/networking hardware to use that application. The user will be able to rent the same function as a service from someone and *pay-as-you-use* basis. And, user should be able to access these service from any device; you should be able to access this service from any network – be it a home network or while you are roaming in a foreign network; you should be able to use the service without bothering whether the data is being stolen by a hacker or not. This means that the data and the application must be somewhere outside your own computer being managed by someone who understand datacenter management and secure your data. According to PEW internet & American Life project (Horrigan 2008), already 69% of online Americans use webmail services, store data

online, or use software programs such as word processing applications whose functionality is located on the web. All these services like Gmail, GoogleApps, facebook, eBay, Salesforce, WebEx, PayPal etcetera store your picture, business data, personal data in one of their data centers and offer you the service you need. Even Microsoft office will soon be available in the Web; you need not have a computer of your own and buy the Microsoft Office; you just pay a fee as and when you want to use MS-Word or MS-PowerPoint. This paradigm of service management is being called the Cloud Computing.

5. CLOUD COMPUTING

Cloud computing is a paradigm of computing with virtualized resources as a service to offer dynamic scalability. In cloud, users use services from *cloud-vendor* who in tern source services from *infrastructure as a service* (IaaS) provider, *platform as a service* (PaaS) provider, and *software as a service* (SaaS) provider. The IaaS service provider offers the physical computing infrastructure like the central processing units (CPU). online *random access memory* (RAM) and the disk storage. The PaaS provider is responsible for supplying and managing all the middleware platforms necessary to enable the software to run over a cloud. Finally, the SaaS provider will offer the software applications that will be used by the end-user (Wikipedia; Cloud Security Alliance 2009; Talukder et al. 2010b). Supply of resources in the cloud increase or decreases on demand; through virtualization – services are platform and infrastructure agnostic. Sometime some of these services could even be over Web Services accessed in *service oriented architecture* (SOA). Users need not have knowledge of, expertise in, or control over the technology infrastructure in the cloud that supports them. Cloud computing services usually provide business applications online that are accessed from a thin client or a web browser, while the software and data are stored on the utility servers – these servers and services may be in *clusters*, *cluster of clusters*, or in *grids*. These grids could well be *processor grids*, *data grids*, or a combination of both. The *cloud stack* is shown in Figure 1.

Benefits from Cloud Computing are,

- Quick and easy to Deploy without any fixed investment
- The infrastructure and platform is supplied on demand and guaranteed to scale up or down
- Users pays on-usage basis like any other utility services
- Pay only for what is used or consumed – move from capital (capex) to operational expense (opex)

- Reduce internal IT cost by reduction in maintenance and support cost of the datacenter
- Latest up to date software and the software is used on rent as pay-per-use
- Data sharing is simpler
- Eco friendly and helps Green computing through shared resource

6. SECURITY CHALLENGES FOR SERVICES IN THE CLOUD

For a long time, data networks were closed – security within these networks were guaranteed through isolation. The trusted private Local Area Network (LAN) was isolated from the untrusted public networks like internet through firewalls to ensure that adversaries and hackers cannot intrude

Figure 1. The Cloud Reference Model (Portions reprinted, with permission, from (Talukder Asoke, Prahalad H.A, Security & Scalability Architecture for Next Generation Internet Services, Proc. International Workshop on Emerging Internet Applications (WEIA2009), 9th December 2009, Bangalore, India) © 2009 IEEE)

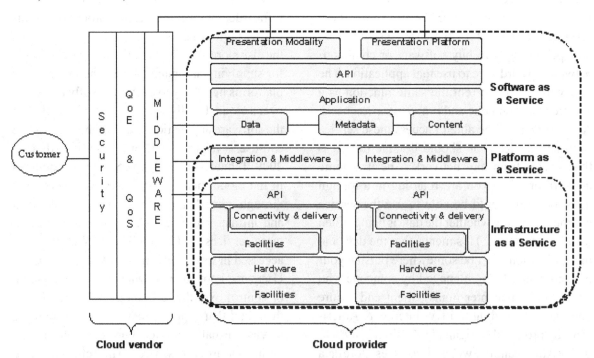

into the private network and steal valuable digital assets or cause harm to the digital assets. Other security mechanisms like Proxies, IDS (Intrusion Detection System), IPS (Intrusion Prevention System), Anti-Virus, Malware catchers etcetera were also installed to secure digital assets. These security measures fall within the domain of network security. The belief was that applications and assets used by the organization can be secured through in-vitro perimeter security – the network security. Therefore, software engineering techniques never looked into security as an important component in Software Develop Life Cycle (SDLC); and, identified security as nonfunctional requirement (Talukder & Chaitanya, 2008).

In mainframe or client-server or even in Web deployment paradigm security was never considered to be a functional requirement during software development life cycle; systems were secured through in-vitro security mechanisms. However, in recent times many applications have moved out of the private network and being deployed as Web Services or mobile agents (Talukder & Chaitanya, 2008). These applications are accessible to genuine users and hackers alike; therefore, security must be part of the application to protect itself from security threats. Application security will however be over and above the perimeter network security. To achieve this, security now need to be treated as functional requirement and must be part of SDLC. Many authors (Talukder & Chaitanya, 2008; Hernan et al. 2006; Swiderski & Snyder, 2004; Schneir, 1999; Moberg, 2000; Diallo at al. 2006; Sindre & Opdahl, 2000; Sindre & Opdahl, 2001a; Sindre & Opdahl, 2001b; Sindre & Opdahl, 2005; Meier et al. 2003) have identified application security as a need and proposed ways to achieve this. All these isolated and independent techniques have been combined together in a thread to form a methodology for *scalability & security-aware software development life cycle* (SaSDLC) (Talukder 2009b). Also, open-source tool Suraksha (Suraksha) was built at National Institute of Technology Karnataka, Surathkal

(http://www.nitk.ac.in) to facilitate design application security.

Along with advantages, there are some challenges in Cloud environment as well – security is the most important one. Many of these security challenges are common to any Internet application. In any of these paradigms, the associations between the runtime instance and network or processor are static. However, in the cloud unlike an Internet environment, due to virtualization, one runtime instance may run on different processor at different point in time. This makes it mandatory that an application security is additionally aware of interface security. Security challenges in public Cloud are higher in magnitude compared to a private network or datacenter or even a private cloud. This is because the major areas of vulnerabilities in Cloud are,

1. Untrusted public network (e.g., internet)
2. Sessionless HTTP protocol
3. Extensive usage of virtualization
4. Often uses SOA architecture
5. Often uses Web Services

Cloud carries higher security risks because the application is deployed on the Internet and is accessible by a hacker with many free hacking tools available for free. Also, Internet applications have many security vulnerabilities starting from session hijacking to SQL injection. Internet applications also increase the security risk because they use HTTP protocol with too many entry and exit points unlike a mainframe or client-server application. Adding virtualization software increases the security risk even further. Bugs in the virtualized middleware can give a local attacker root or local system access to the entire system. Thus, compromises the protection we once had in isolated systems by going virtual. An exploit in one virtualized server can provide unfettered access to all servers, as they are hosted on the same hardware (Farrow, 2009). Deployment using SOA or Web services also increases the security risk as the attack surface in such cases grow substantially.

7. SECURITY REQUIREMENT ANALYSIS FOR CLOUD-READY SERVICES

The open-source Security designers' workbench tool Suraksha (Talukder 2009b; Suraksha) was developed to elicit the security requirement of an application. This is done through 11 steps as follows,

- **Step 1:** Functional Requirements using UML
- **Step 2:** Identification of Assets
- **Step 3:** Separation of Concerns
- **Step 4:** Decision on deployment with Input/Output, Protocols, Interfaces, and API
- **Step 5:** Minimize the Attack Surface
- **Step 6:** Security Requirements
- **Step 7:** Threat and Attack Tree
- **Step 8:** Rating of Risks
- **Step 9:** Decision on In-vivo Versus In-vitro Security
- **Step 10:** Nonfunctional to Functional Requirement
- **Step 11:** Iterate

For cloud-aware application, the requirement elicitation will be different; it will include more steps compared to conventional SDLC model where only functional requirements are considered. To ensure security in the NGI services, both functional and non-functional requirements need to be captured. An NGI service must also be fault tolerant and must be available all the time; also, it must be elastic so that it can scale-up on demand and can scale-down when there is no demand. In a Cloud, the application may run on any virtualized platform; also, the same application instance may run on different platform at different point in time.

This increases the attack surface of a Grid-aware application making it more vulnerable to attacks. Therefore, for Cloud-ready application requirement elicitation is done in 11 steps as follows.

Step 1. Functional Requirements: This is the traditional way of elicitation of requirement. In this step, Functional requirements of the system are analyzed and captured. During this step, Unified Modeling Language (UML) methodology is used (Horrigan, 2008). As part of UML following nine diagram are used to capture the requirements,

- **Use case diagram** shows the functionality provided by a system in terms of actors, their goals represented as use cases, and any dependencies among those use cases.
- **Class diagram** describes the structure of a system by showing the system's classes, their attributes, and the relationships among the classes.
- **Object diagram** shows a complete or partial view of the structure of a modeled system at a specific time.
- **State machine diagram** standardized notation to describe many systems, from computer programs to business processes.
- **Activity diagram** represents the business and operational step-by-step workflows of components in a system. An activity diagram shows the overall flow of control.
- **Sequence diagram** shows how objects communicate with each other in terms of a sequence of messages. Also indicates the lifespan of objects relative to those messages.
- **Collaboration diagram** models the objects and links that are meaningful within an interaction – it shows the roles in the interaction. A classifier role describes an object and an association role describes a role link within a collaboration.
- **Component diagram** depicts how the software system is split up into compo-

nents and shows the dependencies among these components.

- **Deployment diagram** serves to model the hardware used in system implementations, and the execution environments and artifacts deployed on the hardware.

Step 2. Identification of Assets: In any security system you first need to identify what is that you want to secure? To answer this question you must identify all the digital assets that belong to you. You also need to know which assets are handled by you but may not belong to you. Remember, a hacker will try to take away your asset or try to damage your asset. To the hacker it really does not matter whether you own it or someone else owns it. Any digital assets that is being handled in your service must be secured. When an object is found to be valuable to you, it is termed as an asset. Example of asset could be identity information, credit card details, bank password etc. To identify assets you take the object diagram of UML is an input. Objects are taken one after the other and the criticality of an object is assessed.

A brainstorming session is conducted to list all assets; in addition, various existing documents are examined to identify important assets. Assets are then categorized based on their perceived value and impact in case a security attack happens. Security measures depend on state of mobility -- they are either stationary assets or assets in transit (Cloud Security Alliance 2009). In case of Grids, all assets are likely to move around the network; therefore, they are considered to be mobile objects.

To evaluate the value of an asset, an object from the object diagram is taken and viewed from different perspectives i.e. service provider, user, and the attacker. From these perspectives, each asset is assigned a value indicating the importance from STRIDE and CI5A perspective. STRIDE (Talukder et al. 2010b; Cppcheck) is used by Microsoft for threat modeling of their systems – threats are identified by exploring the possibilities of Spoofing Identity, Tampering with Data, Repudiation, Information Disclosure, Denial of Service and Elevation of Privilege in the given case. Threats are also identified with respect of CI5A that deals with Confidentiality, Integrity, Availability, Authentication, Authorization, Accounting, and Anonymity. While assets are being identified following tangible and intangible assets like Identity, Financial, Property or sensitive information, Property & life, Reputation, Privacy & regulatory, Availability guarantees, and Regulatory. Valuations of each asset are added and the asset with highest sum is ranked as the most valuable asset.

Step 3. Separation of Concerns: Separation of concerns is the process of breaking business logic into distinct features so that there is minimum or no overlap in functionality. Separation of Concerns is critical to make the program distributed or parallel. Activity diagrams, Sequence diagrams, Collaboration diagrams, and Component diagrams are examined and reviewed to ensure separation of concerns. Result of this will yield into multiple parallel tasks.

Traditional scalability and Cloud scalability differs in a way – traditional scalability is introduced in the application and remains static; whereas, a Cloud scalable application needs to manage scalability both at a static level and on-demand. In a Cloud, parallelism can be implemented using algorithms like MapReduce (Sindre & Opdahl, 2001a). This will help scalability of the application at the runtime. MapReduce however increases the total entry and exit points of the application increasing the attack surface of the application.

Any application to be scalable should be analyzed for application level dependencies such as one portion of application depending on another for its execution, loop, virtual block, etc so that performance and scalability can be achieved by introducing parallel component structure into the application.

Step 4. Decision on Deployment: Following identification of assets, the Collaboration and Deployment Diagrams is taken. Here it is decided how the system is going to be deployed – it is going to be one single system deployed on a Cluster, Grid, or Cloud. If it is a cluster, how different modules are going to interact with each other. The messages that will be transferred will be identified at this step.

Grid deployment could be over a Public Cloud or a Private Cloud. Also the interactions between objects are identified. If the deployment is over a pubic Cloud, it could be over Web Services. Additional security measures need to be adopted on these objects. Here two types of threats are important to consider. These are Object to Object and Platform to Object. The object-to-object category represents the set of threats in which some agent or an object of another Grid application exploit security weaknesses of an object or launch attacks against other agents. This set of threats includes masquerading, unauthorized access, DoS, and repudiation. Many agent platform components are also agents themselves. These platform agents provide system-level services such as directory services and inter-platform communication services. Some agent platforms allow direct inter-platform agent-to-agent communication, whereas others require all incoming and outgoing messages to go through a platform communication agent. The platform-to-object category represents the set of threats in which platforms compromise the security of an object. This set of threats includes masquerading, DoS, eavesdropping, and alteration.

Step 5. Minimizing the Attack Surface: In computers, only that part of the program will be a target of attack that is accessible to a hacker. A piece of code or part of a program is exposed to the public as an API (application programming interface) that can be the target of attack. The attack surface (Wikipedia) of an application is the union of code, interfaces, services, protocols, and practices exposed to a user (or attacker alike). In security design, therefore, the attempt is always to analyze the attack surface and reduce it. Re-

duction of attach surface is always advisable for any application. For a conventional application where the deployment scenario is static, attack surface is generally reduced through perimeter security; however, for cloud-ready application attack surface reduction will be part of functional requirement. If the attack surface is reduced, the security is automatically increased by reducing the risk of attack. Attack surface reduction focuses on reducing the area of the code accessible to unauthorized users. This is achieved by understanding the system's entry and exit points and the trust level required to access them through authentication and authorization checks and through escalation of privileges.

To reduce the attack surface, one needs to get answers to the following questions (Talukder & Chaitanya, 2008):

- **Question 1.** Is this feature (API) really necessary? Who are the users that need this feature? If this feature is not necessary to a majority of users, can it be hidden?
- **Question 2.** Is it necessary to offer this feature from remote location? If yes, determine from where and what type of access mechanism this feature will be provided. Also, determine the type of networks the feature will be available from.
- **Question 3.** Who are the users that need to access this feature? Determine the legitimate users and a mechanism to validate them so that unauthorized users cannot access this feature.
- **Question 4.** What type of privilege does this feature need to provide the service? If it needs escalated privilege, determine how long it needs the escalated privilege for.
- **Question 5.** What are the interfaces this feature has with other services, interfaces, and protocols? If this feature crashes, what impact it will have on other services or the system as a whole.

Attack surface analysis helps understand the areas that can be target of attack; and, through threat modeling analyze possible threats. Combining these two will guide the action plan to build a secured Cloud-ready application.

Once the instances (worker in MapReduce) in the Cloud are known, the attack surface needs to be evaluated. In computers, only that part of the program can be a target of attack that is accessible to an adversary. A piece of code or part of a program is exposed to the public as an API (application programming interface) that can be the target of attack. The attack surface (Hernan S. et al 2006) of an application can be defined as the union of code, interfaces, services, protocols, and practices exposed to a user (or attacker alike). In security design, therefore, the attempt is always to analyze the attack surface and reduce it. If the attack surface is reduced, the security is automatically increased by reducing the risk of attack.

All entry and exit points of a Grid-aware application need to be secured. Security of entry and exit points will ensure that all data that enter or exit from the application are secured; also, no invalid data enters or exits from the application. For output data, the application security must ensure Confidentiality and Integrity of data. For input data, Confidentiality and Integrirty must be maintained; in addition, the data must be validated to check out-of-range, overflow, or parameter tampering possibilities. The application must also ensure availability, authentication, authorization, accounting, and anonymity. The attack surface area is measured using simple algorithm of,

Attack Surface = $(\sum w_i + \sum w_o)/(m+n)$

For Cloud-ready systems, it is necessary that the attack surface is minimized. For this, we have enhanced Suraksha tool. Suraksha uses UML to elicit requirement. We take the interaction diagram and the deployment diagram of Suraksha to derive the deployment scenario; and, enhance it to evaluate trust boundaries. The trust boundary is then examined to evaluate pathways of interactions to measure the attack surface.

From deployment diagram we need to first determine which modules will never move out of the private cloud or the private datacenter. All other modules and instances will need security treatment as public cloud. It is possible that some runtime instances may run both in private and public cloud; in such case, the security criteria will be similar to public cloud. In a public cloud assumption will be that it can run on any virtual environment where the application may not have any network or perimeter security.

Once the instances in the public cloud are known, entry and exit points in these instances need to be secured. Security of entry and exit points will ensure that all data that enter or exit from the application are secured; also, no invalid data enters or exits from the application. For output data, the application security must ensure Confidentiality and Integrity of data. For input data, Confidentiality and Integrity must be maintained. In addition, the input data must be validated to check out-of-range, overflow, or parameter tampering possibilities. The application must ensure availability, authentication, authorization, accounting, and anonymity. Higher weightage is given to entry point compared to exit points. Higher weightage is used for sensitive out-data. Additional weightage is given for these entry-points where some of the fields can be used as parameters in SQL query and can potentially be vulnerable for SQL injection or used for parameter tampering. The attack surface can be calculated from the equation,

Attack Surface = $(AS)_{Input/Output} + (AS)_{Protocols} + (AS)_{Interface} + (AS)_{API}$

Where $(AS)_{Input/Output} = (\sum w_i + \sum w_o)/(m + n)$,

w_i is the weightage for i^{th} input and can have total m inputs; and, w_o is the oth output parameter that can be maximum n in number. Higher weightage is given to entry point compared to exit points. Higher weightage is used for sensitive out-data. Additional weightage is given for these entry-points where some of the fields can be used as parameters in SQL query and can potentially be vulnerable for SQL injection or parameter tampering.

For each entry-point and exit-point, a Misuse case diagram (Figure 2) is used to assess the possibility of a security attack. Through STRIDE, the possibilities for *spoofing identity*, *tampering with data*, *repudiation*, *information disclosure*, *denial of service*, and *elevation of privilege* are considered; and, through CI5A, confidentiality, integrity, availability, authentication, authorization, accounting, and anonymity in the given case by misactor are explored. This yields a list of possible abstract threats. "A use case generally describes behavior that the system/entity owner wants it to provide. A misuse case is a special kind of use case, describing behavior that the system/ entity owner does not want to occur." A misactor is the inverse of an actor, who does not want the system to function in an expected fashion. A

misactor can also be defined as a special kind of actor (hacker) who initiates misuse case (Sindre & Opdahl, 2001a).

Using the misuse-case diagram as shown in Figure 2, Suraksha helps analyze the entry & exit-points and determine whether there is a possible attack scenario. If yes, refine it during the design and go for information hiding as much as possible. Information hiding will reduce the attack surface. Reduction of attack surface will reduce security risk and in turn increase the security of the application.

Step 6. Security Requirements: For each actor in the Use case, one or more misactors are identified using the Misuse Case diagram (Figure 3). STRIDE with CI5A concepts are applied in connection with each action and assets related to it. Through STRIDE, the possibilities for Spoofing Identity, Tampering with Data, Repudiation, Information Disclosure, Denial of Service, and Elevation of Privilege are considered; and, through CI5A, Confidentiality, Integrity, Availability, Authentication, Authorization, Accounting, and

Figure 2. Misuse Case Analysis (Suraksha)

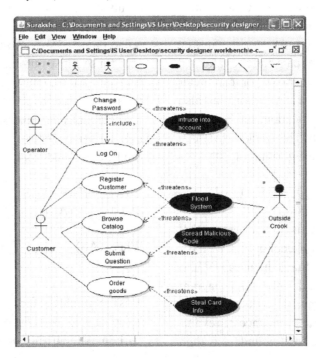

Anonymity in the given case by misactor are explored. This yields a list of possible abstract threats.

Step 7. Threat and Attack Tree: Each abstract threat in the Misuse case diagram is considered as a root node and corresponding attack tree (Sindre & Opdahl, 2005; Meier et al. 2003) is constructed to understand what are the AND and OR relationship in the threat path (Figure 3). Here the user goes through each and every Misuse case (Sindre & Opdahl, 2001b; Talukder et al. 2009b; Suraksha); a node in the attack-tree is an actual threat. In this phase of the analysis and design of the application security, threat modeling of Suraksha is used. In threat modeling, each abstract threat in the Misuse case diagram is considered as a root node and corresponding attack tree (Figure 3) is constructed to understand what are the AND and OR relationship in the threat path. Here the user goes through each and every Misuse case; a node in the attack-tree is an actual threat. In an AND relationship each and every attack path needs to

be successful for a successful attack; whereas, in OR path anyone needs to be successful. Threat model is used to include proper security classes and methods in the application. Once the threat model is known, the attack path is also known. During design, all these attack paths need to be covered. In a non-Cloud environment it may be possible to cover an attack path through network security; but, in Cloud-ready application this must be covered through proper countermeasures within the application through proper security-awareness.

Step 8. Rating of Risks: For each attack type, DREAD (Sindre & Opdahl, 2001a; Wikipedia) is used to rate a threat. This is done by assigning values to each node beginning from leaf nodes using simple formula,

Risk DREAD = (D+ R + E +A + D) / 5

Where,

D = Damage Potential,

R = Reproducibility,

E = Exploitability,

A = Affected Users,

D = Discoverability.

The calculation always produces a number between 0 and 10; the higher the number, higher the risk.

Step 9. Decision on In-vivo Security versus In-vitro Security: After careful examination of each threat rating using DREAD, a threat is ranked as a high risk or moderate risk or low risk threat. These ratings are compared with value of assets as measured in Step 2. All high value assets must be secured. If it is too expensive to secure an asset in-vivo, compared to the cost of the asset, those threats need not be secured in-vitro – a candidate for in-vitro security could be Denial-of-Service attack.

Step 10. Nonfunctional to Functional Requirement: All these threats that are decided to be protected in-vivo through countermeasures now

Figure 3. Threat Model (Suraksha)

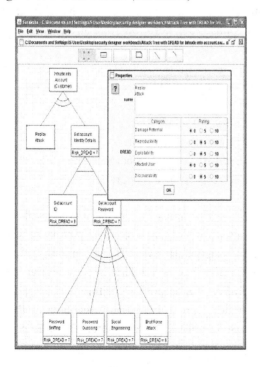

become candidate for functional requirement for a Security-aware application. In other words, all these countermeasures that need to be included in-vivo will move into the software as functional requirements.

Step 11. Iterate: In the last step all misuse cases go through above 7 steps. The security design might force revisit of these 7 steps. Also, there might be necessity for some refinements.

8. SECURITY DESIGN FOR CLOUD-READY SERVICES

Yoder and Barcalow (Yoder & Barcalow, 1997) proposed seven security design patterns for information security that were extended to ten (Talukder & Chaitanya, 2008). These security patterns are,

Single Access Point: Providing a security module and a way to log into the system. This pattern suggests that keep only one way to enter into the system.

1) **Check Point:** Organizing security checks and their repercussions. Authentication and authorization are two basic entity of this pattern.
2) **Roles:** Organizing users with similar security privileges.
3) *Session*: Localizing global information in a multi-user environment.
4) **Full View with Errors:** Provide a full view to users, showing exceptions when needed.
5) **Limited View:** Allowing users to only see what they have access to.
6) **Secure Access Layer:** Integrating application security with low-level security.
7) **Least Privilege:** Privilege state should be shortest lived state.
8) **Journaling:** Keep a complete record of usage of resource.
9) **Exit Gracefully:** Designing systems to fail in a secure manner.

At the end of the design, the attack surface is analyzed. If the attack surface area is high, above process is repeated until the attack surface is reduced to the minimum level.

To make scalability in-vitro, Separation of Concerns patterns can be used as proposed by Noda and Kasha (Noda & Kishi, 2001). Ahluwalia (Ahluwalia, 2007) defined 10 patterns for scalability, which are,

1) **Pattern 1:** Introduce Scalability
2) **Pattern 2:** Optimize Algorithm
3) **Pattern 3:** Add Hardware
4) **Pattern 4:** Introduce Parallelism
5) **Pattern 5:** Optimize Decentralization
6) **Pattern 6:** Control Shared Resources
7) **Pattern 7:** Add Intra-process parallelism
8) **Pattern 8:** Add Inter-process parallelism
9) **Pattern 9:** Add Hybrid parallelism
10) **Pattern 10:** Automate Scalability

Out of these 10 patterns pattern 5 and 6 are handled during requirement analysis in Step 3 of the requirement elicitation. Pattern 2, 7, and 8 are potential candidate for design. If there are patterns but no use-case identified in the requirement phase, the iteration starts from Step 2 of requirement analysis.

During design phase therefore following design patterns are required to be used for scalability,

1) Separation of Concern
2) Optimize Algorithm
3) Add Intra-process parallelism
4) Add Inter-process parallelism

The performance of any parallel algorithm is dependent on problem size, number of processors, and message startup cost (Designing and Building Parallel Programs). However, to analyze the scalability of a parallel algorithm it is important to consider how the algorithm behaves with an increased number of processors. It may be noted that the performance is governed by Amdhal's

Law (Hill & Marty, 2007). To understand this simulation is necessary to examine the scalability of the system using the messages and queues. "One approach to quantifying scalability is to determine how execution time T and efficiency E vary with increasing processor count P for a fixed problem size and machine parameters. This fixed problem analysis allows us to answer questions such as, what is the fastest I can solve problem A on computer X? and What is the greatest number of processors I can utilize if I want to maintain an efficiency of 50 percent? The latter question may be of interest if a computer is shared and there is a charge for each processor used. It is important to consider both E and T when evaluating scalability. While E will generally decrease monotonically with P, T may actually increase if the performance model includes a term proportional to a positive power of P. In such cases, it may not be productive to use more than some maximum number of processors for a particular problem size and choice of machine parameters" (Designing and Building Parallel Programs). Depending on the deployment scenario a decision has to be made on the choice of computing infrastructure.

9. CONSTRUCTION OF NGI SECURED SERVICES

A system can be made secured only against known threats. However, a security-aware application must be able to handle unknown threats as well. Therefore, during construction of the application, safe programming techniques must be adopted. At this state, the application must use all proven security algorithms and protocols for data security starting from data on transit to database security. It is advisable to use a tested libraries and framework where security is already in-vivo. Also, exceptions must be handled properly to channel all unknown exceptions.

Also during coding, proper care must be taken for separation of concerns. A security function always has tendency to become anti-pattern at a later point in time. Therefore, one security function must not embed another security function – each security function must be coded separately. Secure Coding practice is required to ensure that secure coding techniques are adopted. To ensure scalability, proper libraries need to be used either for Shared Memory or Distributed Memory machines. Here care must be taken to avoid racing condition and deadlocks due to lack of synchronization.

10. SECURITY TESTING FOR CLOUD-READY SERVICES

Integrating all tools into Suraksha framework will help a software tester to test the application by using all techniques. Static Testing is used to test the application code and finds security errors that are made in development phase. Different open source tools are available to test different languages. To test the vulnerabilities in C and C++ language we used cppcheck (cppcheck), flawfinder (Flawfinder), and splint (Splint). Vulnerabilities for a program which will find the palindrome of a number can be tested using the tool CheckStyle (Checkstyle).

Application security testing and Fuzz testing are used to find the vulnerabilities at run time. Different tools are used in the Testers' workbench for different kinds of vulnerability testing. WebScarab tool can be used to exploit various vulnerabilities of target web application of system like CRLF injection, XSS attack, it use proxy to observe both HTTP and encrypted HTTPS traffic, by negotiating an SSL connection between WebScarab and the browser and it also automates checks for files that were mistakenly left in web server's root directory. Wikto is a Web Server Assessment Tool. It works by trying to find interesting directories and files on the web site, it looks for sample scripts that can be abused or finds known vulnerabilities in the web server implementation itself.

Fuzz testing is accomplished by attacking all of an application's data interfaces, typically the file system, network, libraries, registry and GUI. In its simplest form, fuzzing is accomplished using randomized data—a jumbled raw network stream for example. Fuzz testing is used to check whether the application crash when it get fuzzed or random data. Tools like JBroFuzz (OWASP JBroFuzz) and SpikeProxy (SpikeProxy) can be used to do fuzz testing on the applications. JBroFuzz is a web application fuzzer for requests being made over HTTP and/or HTTPS. JBroFuzz generates requests, puts them on the wire and records the corresponding responses received back and it is a network protocol fuzzer. There are different kinds of vulnerabilities in a production environment. Different Open-source Tools are available for scanning each kind of vulnerability. These tools will be used to find the vulnerabilities in its specialized category. For finding SQL injection vulnerabilities, we have integrated SQL Map (Sqlmap), BSQLHacker (BSQLHacker), FG-Injector (FG-Injector Framework), Absinthe (Absinthe), and Proxy Strike (ProxyStrike) within the framework. Security auditing and testing can be done for applications in WLAN by using WiFi hopper (WiFiHopper), and Network Stumbler (NetworkStumbler). These will help tester to analyze and categorize the vulnerabilities so that it will be easy at the time of mitigation and reengineering.

Vulnerabilities within the network will be scanned by Nessus (Nessus) tool; this tool helps potential security risks to be identified and also it provides detailed report which helps to mitigate the vulnerabilities that are found. Nessus can automatically detect un-patched remote vulnerabilities as well. Nessus provides an excellent framework that really sets it apart from other scanners with the introduction of the Nessus Attack Scripting Language (NASL, pronounced naz-ul). NASL allows security analysts to quickly create their own plugins for vulnerability checks. The result is that teams can easily add their security

expertise to their Nessus scans by creating custom vulnerability tests.

Suraksha also offers the facility for a user to integrate any customized tool in the workbench and add in the workflow. In addition to the standard tools, we have added Cross Site Scripting tools and a HTTP Attack tool (HTTPattack) which is a Web Stress tool which helps to find various vulnerabilities in a web server and also to simulate DDoS attack. Suraksha provides an environment for ethical hacking where one can simulate the situation of what an attacker will do if one vulnerability exist in the system.

11. SECURED DEPLOYMENT

The deployment security deals with the security of an application at production environment. In traditional Software Development Life Cycle (SDLC), deployment is neither part of SDLC nor is it related to the SDLC; in this model security countermeasures are at layer 1 to 3 through network security and perimeter security. Secure deployment will also have countermeasures at layer 4 through platform security.

In SaSDLC however, security is built at layer 5 to 7 as well. During requirement analysis all security requirements were identified. In Step 10, some security functions have been set-aside to be addressed in-vitro through perimeter security. Therefore, all countermeasures for these vulnerabilities will be moved from application layer to the network layer and will be covered through perimeter security.

Perimeter security is addressed using Border routers, Firewalls, Proxies, Antivirus, IDS, IPS, Malware catcher etc. The concept of Artificial Hygiene (Talukder & Chaitanya, 2008) is implemented here through application-level firewalls, which intercepts the input to the application, and tests them for any malicious data and filters them. This ensures that the application is guarded against the real-time attacks in the production environment.

REFERENCES

Absinthe. (2007). Retrieved from http://www. security-database.com/toolswatch/Absinthe-1-4-1-available.html.

Ahluwalia, K. S. (2007). *Scalability Design Patterns*. In Proceedings of 14th Pattern Languages of Programs (PLoP 2007)

Bialkowski., et al. (2004). *Application Vulnerability Description Language v1.0, OASIS Standard*. Reference from http://www.oasis-open.org

BSQLHacker. (n.d.). Reference from http://labs. portcullis.co.uk/application/bsql-hacker/.

Checkstyle.(2001-2010) Reference from http:// checkstyle.sourceforge.net/.

Cloud Security Alliance. (2009). *Security Guidance for Critical Areas of Focus in Cloud Computing v2.1*. Reference from http://www. cloudsecurityalliance.org/csaguide.pdf.

Cppcheck. (2010). *A tool for static C/C++ code analysis*. Reference from http://cppcheck.wiki. sourceforge.net/.

Crocker, S. (1969). Request for Comments: 1, Host Software, Reference from http://www.faqs. org/rfcs/rfc1.html

Deering., et al. (1998). *Internet Protocol, Version 6 (IPv6) Specification, RFC2460*. Reference from http://www.faqs.org/rfcs/rfc2460.html

Designing and Building Parallel Programs v1.3, An Online Publishing Project of Addison-Wesley Inc., Argonne National Laboratory, and the NSF Center for Research on Parallel Computation.

Diallo at al. (2006). A Comparative Evaluation of Three Approaches to Specifying Security Requirements, presented at 12th Working Conference on Requirements Engineering: Foundation for Software Quality, Luxembourg.

Dierks., et al. (1999). *Request for Comments 2246, The TLS Protocol Version 1.0*. Reference from http://www.faqs.org/rfcs/rfc2246.html

Farrow, R. (2009). musings, LOGIN: VOL. 33, NO. 5, 2. Reference from http://www.usenix. org/publications/login/2009-10/openpdfs/mus-ings0910.pdf.

FG- Injector Framework. (2010). Reference from http://sourceforge.net/projects/injection-fwk/.

Flawfinder.(n.d.). Reference from http://www. dwheeler.com/flawfinder/.

Fredrik, M. (2000). *Security Analysis of an Information System using an Attack tree-based Methodology*. Master's Thesis. Goteborg, Sweden: Chalmers University of Technology.

GII. (1998). *Global Information Infrastructure principles and framework architecture*. ITU-T Recommendation Y.110.

Hernan, S., et al. (2006). *Uncover Security Design Flaws using The STRIDE Approach*. Reference from http://msdn.microsoft.com/en-us/magazine/ cc163519.aspx.

Hill, M. D., & Marty, M. R. (2007). *Amdahl's Law in the Multicore Era*. Reference from http:// www.cs.wisc.edu/multifacet/papers/tr1593_am-dahl_multicore.pdf

Horrigan, J. B. (2008). *Use of Cloud Computing Applications and Services, Data Memo*. The Pew Internet & American Life Project. September 2008, Reference from http://www.pewinternet. org/Reports/2008/Use-of-Cloud-Computing-Applications-and-Services.aspx.

HTTPattack. (2009). *An Open source web stress tool.* Reference from http://isea.nitk.ac.in/HTTPattack/.

Information Security Research Labs. (2009). *Suraksha: A Security Aware Application Developers' Workbench.* Reference from http://isea.nitk.ac.in/suraksha/.

Internet2.(2010). Reference from http://www.internet2.edu/

Internet History. (2010). *Computer History Museum.* Reference from http://www.computerhistory.org/internet_history/internet_history_80s.html

ISO-7498 (1998) - Information processing systems -- Open Systems Interconnection -- Basic Reference Model

Jain, R. (2009). *Internet 3.0: The Next Generation Internet.* Reference from http://www.cse.wustl.edu/~jain/talks/in3_bng.htm

Kent., et al. (2005). *Security Architecture for the Internet Protocol.* Reference from http://www.faqs.org/rfcs/rfc4301.html

Liberty Alliance. (n.d.). Reference from http://www.projectliberty.org

Meier., et al. (2003). *Improving Web Application Security: Threats and Countermeasures.* reference from http://www.msdn.microsoft.com/en-us/library/aa302419.aspx.

Moberg, F. (2000). *Security Analysis of an Information System using an Attack tree-based Methodology.* Master's Thesis. Goteborg, Sweden: Chalmers University of Technology.

Nessus. Network Vulnerability Scanner.(2010) Reference from http://www.nessus.org/nessus/.

NetworkStumbler. (n.d.). Reference from http://www.netstumbler.com/.

Noda, N., & Kishi, T. (2001). *Implementing Design Patterns Using Advanced Separation of Concerns.* Object-Oriented programming, Systems, Languages, and Applications (OOPSLA 2001).

OWASP JBroFuzz. (n.d.). Reference from http://www.owasp.org/index.php/Category:OWASP_JBroFuzz.

ProxyStrike. (2008). Reference from http://www.edge-security.com/proxystrike.php.

Schneir, B. (1999) *Modeling Security Threats.* December 1999. Reference from http://www.schneier.com/paper-attacktrees-ddj-ft.html

Shawn., et al. (2006). *Uncover Security Design Flaws using The STRIDE Approach.* Retrieved from http://msdn.microsoft.com/en-us/magazine/cc163519.aspx.

Sindre, G., & Opdahl, A. L. (2000). Eliciting Security Requirements by Misuse Cases, in Proceedings of 37th Conference on Techniques of Object-Oriented Languages and Systems. *TOOLS Pacific 2000,* 120–131.

Sindre, G., & Opdahl, A. L. (2001a). *Capturing Security Requirements by Misuse Cases.* In Proceedings of 14th Norwegian Informatics Conference (NIK'2001), Troms, Norway.

Sindre, G., & Opdahl, A. L. (2001b). *Templates for Misuse Case Description.* Proceedings of the 7th International Workshop on Requirements Engineering, Foundation for Software Quality (REFSQ'2001), Interlaken, Switzerland.

Sindre, G., & Opdahl, A. L. (2005). Eliciting security requirements with misuse cases. *Requirements Engineering, 10*(1), 34–44. doi:10.1007/s00766-004-0194-4

Spike Proxy. (2004). Reference from http://www.immunitysec.com/resources-freesoftware.shtml.

Splint - Secure Programming Lint. (n.d.). Reference from http://www.splint.org/.

Sqlmap - A SQL Injection Tool. (2010). Reference from http://sqlmap.sourceforge.net/.

Steinberg S. G., Bellheads vs. Netheads (2006), Wired, Issue 4.10, Oct 1996.

Swiderski, F., & Snyder, W. (2004). *Threat Modeling*. Washington: Microsoft Press.

Talukder., et al. (2009b). *Security-aware Software Development Life Cycle (SaSDLC) - Processes and tools*. Proceedings of IEEE Conference on Wireless and Optical Communications Networks, 28-30.

Talukder, (2010a). *Mobile Computing – Technology, Application, and Service Creation* (2nd ed.). New York: McGraw-Hill.

Talukder, (2010bin press). *Cloud Economics: Principles, Costs and Benifits, Cloud Computing: Principles, Systems and Applications*. New York: Springer.

Talukder, A. K. (2009a). *Tutorial on Next Generation Internet through Next Generation Networks*. WOCN2009, Cairo, 28th April, Reference from http://www.geschickten.com/NGI-through-NGN.pdf

Talukder, A. K., & Chaitanya, M. (2008). *Architecting Secure Software Systems*. Amsterdam: Auerbach Publications. doi:10.1201/9781420087857

Talukder, A. K., & Prahalad, H. A. (2009c). *Security & Scalability Architecture for Next Generation Internet Services*. IEEE International Workshop on Emerging Internet Applications (WEIA2009), 9th December 2009, Bangalore, India

Venkatraman, J., et al. (2004). *Trust and Security Realization for Mobile Users in GSM Cellular Networks*. AACC Conference, Kathmandu October 29-31, LNCS 3285 pp-302-309.

Web 3.0. (n.d.). Reference from http://en.wikipedia.org/wiki/Semantic_Web

WiFiHopper. (2006). Reference from http://wifihopper.com/.

Wikipedia, The Free Encyclopedia. (n.d.). reference from http://en.wikipedia.org/.

Woo., et al. (1994). *SNP: An interface for secure network programming*. Proceedings of the USENIX Summer 1994 Technical Conference, Boston, Massachusetts, USA

Yoder, J. W. Barcalow J (1997). *Architectural Patterns for Enabling Application Security*. Proceeding of 4th Conference on Patterns Languages of Programs (PLoP '97) Monticello, Illinois.

Chapter 8
An Examination of Identity Management Models in an Internet Setting

Kenneth J. Giuliani
University of Toronto Mississauga, Canada

V. Kumar Murty
University of Toronto, Canada

ABSTRACT

The purpose of this chapter is to examine the strengths and weaknesses of the most commonly used model for digital identities. It is compared to other models which have preceded it, thus giving a background on its development. The models are measured against a set of criteria which it is desirable for an identity management system to have. The underlying hope is that understanding this model will help improve it or even lead to a different model.

1. INTRODUCTION

As more and more websites arise on the internet every day, users now have an incredible amount of possible activities available to them. However, the sheer volume of these possibilities comes with its share of challenges.

One of the key problems that exists on the internet is that of entity authentication. It is essential that the parties involved in any transaction be sure that the entities they are communicating with are indeed who they say they are. Failure to do so can lead to fraud, disclosure of private information, or many other undesirable consequences.

To solve this problem, many internet sites require a user to log in using a userid and password. While theoretically effective, the proliferation of websites has made this paradigm highly inconvenient.

Quite often, users will choose passwords to be too short, easily-guessed, or will use the same password for multiple sites. This has given rise to the recent phenomenon of password fatigue.

In addition, with the great diversity of transactions that may take place comes varying levels of

DOI: 10.4018/978-1-60960-123-2.ch008

personal information which needs to be transmitted. It is imperative that the information not only gets to its desired destination securely, but that the right kind of information is transmitted.

One solution that has been proposed for this is the use of digital identities. Digital identities allow entities to uniquely identify themselves to other parties on the internet. In this way, they can bypass many of the problems associated with the userid/password paradigm.

In this paper, we examine the current model used for digital identity management in detail. In order to do so, we first examine models previously used, either theoretical or practical, to give a background on how the current model evolved to its present point. We examine its strengths and weaknesses. We also establish a set of criteria which are desirable for an identity management system to have.

2. PRELIMINARIES

The phrase *identity management* can take on many different meanings. Birch and David (2007) gave good introduction into the subject. For the purpose of this paper, however, we will restrict ourselves to the management of digital identities in an internet setting. More formally, we define *identity management* to be the set of processes, protocols, and policies which deal with digital identities. A digital identity consists of a set of elements including an *identifier*, a unique string

which is bound to a specific user and *attributes* associated with that identifier. For example, an e-mail address or a userid can be considered as identifiers. An *identity management system* is the architecture that defines the mechanisms related to the interaction of parties using digital identities.

3. THE TRADITIONAL MODEL

The traditional model for internet transactions involved two parties:

- **A user:** a person who makes use of the services in an online environment,
- **A relying party:** an entity which provides a service on the internet, normally but not restricted to being a website.

The main transaction will occur between the user and relying party. As a practical example, the user may be an individual and the relying party a website such as an online bank or store. In this context, transactions will be initiated by the user. Furthermore, the biggest challenge will be for the relying party to authenticate the user.

We note here that relying party authentication should also be considered since spoofing or phishing attacks or malicious relying parties are also possible.

A typical transaction between the two parties is shown in Figure 1.

Figure 1. Transaction in the traditional model

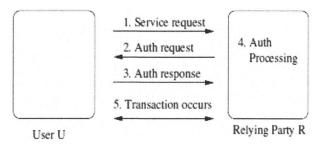

It would typically consist of the following steps:

1. User **U** requests a service from relying party **R**.
2. **R** requests some sort of authentication from either **U**.
3. **U** sends authenticating information to **R**.
4. **R** examines the information from **U** and establishes that **U** is authentic.
5. **U** and **R** carry out their transaction.

Logging on to websites using a username and password may be the most common realization of this model.

There are many inherent problems with this model. Perhaps, the largest problem is that this puts users in charge of their own security. Since many users are not well-briefed on proper security measures, this may present some security problems.

Another problem with this model is the implicit trust that the user has for the relying party. **R** is completely trusted and the onus is on **U** to prove its authenticity.

Finally, we note that **R** must accept the responsibility of managing user's identities. This may be a responsibility it may not be prepared to properly undertake.

4. THE OMNIPRESENT AUTHORITY MODEL

To solve the problems established in the traditional model, one idea would be to introduce an additional entity into the model which will handle all management of identities. In this section, we introduce a model in which this additional entity is given total control over communication. In most cases, this would not be practical, but is useful in examining future models.

The additional party in this model is referred to as:

*   **An omnipresent authority:** an entity which controls all authentication transactions and verifications between users and relying parties which has the prerogative of issuing and revoking identities.

A typical transaction in this model is shown in Figure 2.

It would have the following steps:

1. User **U** sends a request to authority **A** stating that it wishes to perform a transaction with relying party **R**.

Figure 2. Transaction in the omnipresent model

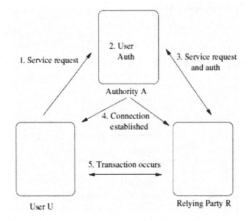

2. **A** decides whether or not to process **U**'s request given authentication information provided by **U**.
3. **A** contacts **R** and authenticates it, informing it that **U** wishes to perform a transaction.
4. **A** puts **U** and **R** in contact with each other.
5. **U** and **R** carry out their transaction (possibly with **A**'s involvement).

The big contribution of this model is the concept of an authority which can be trusted. Clearly, this solves the problems of user's and relying parties dealing with identities since the authority completely handles this.

In many cases, however, it may be impractical to think that one single entity could be responsible for all of the substantial amount of transactions which take place in real time. However, this model's advancement leads to the following refinement.

5. THE CERTIFICATE AUTHORITY MODEL

One of the major problems with the previous model is the overriding involvement of the authority. It would be more practical for an authority to be involved only in the initial setup of the system, but not during the actual transactions. The authority would have to supply some sort of information to users and relying parties so that they can authenticate each other. We will refer to this information as a *certificate* and the authority as a *certificate authority CA*.

Before any transaction takes place, the following must occur:

1. Certificate authority **A** supplies a certificate to each user **U** and to each relying party **R**.

Users and relying parties can now perform transactions as shown in Figure 3.

1. User **U** informs relying party **R** that it wishes to perform a transaction and sends its certificate from **A** and any additional required information to **R**.
2. **R** authenticates **U** by verifying the information provided by **U**.
3. **R** sends its own certificate and information back to **U**.
4. **U** authenticates the information provided by **R**.
5. **U** and **R** carry out their transaction.

Figure 3. Transaction in the certificate authority model

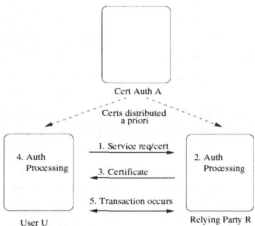

The well-known concept of *public-key infrastructure (PKI)* fits into this model. The idea behind PKI is to send public keys authenticated by the certificate authority to each of the parties involved. This allows all transmissions to be either encrypted or digitally signed or both.

PKI typically suffers from two main problems. The first has to do with the deployment and refreshing of keys. It is a non-trivial task to ensure that each party not only has a key, but that it has one which is up-to-date.

The second problem deals with the *certificate revocation*. Once a certificate has been issued to a particular entity, that entity may use it at any point in the future. However, it is sometimes the case that the authority wishes to disable a particular entity's ability to perform transactions. But how does one prevent a party which has possession of a valid certificate from using it?

The most common solution to this problem is through the use of *certificate revocation lists (CRL's)*. Before accepting a certificate, a particular party must check a list provided by the certificate authority to make sure that it this certificate has not been revoked. Unfortunately, in many cases, this is not practical since this may either require extra cost or even interaction with the certificate authority which is what this model was trying to avoid.

6. THE IDENTITY MANAGEMENT MODEL

One of the main problems with the previous two models is centralization. There is one single authority responsible for all authentication of identities. The internet, though, is very de-centralized, so whatever model we are using should be reflected by this.

One option to deal with this is to have more than one entity with the authority to manage identities. This, of course, would change the authority and functionality of the authenticating party. The

model encompassing these changes is what we refer to as the *identity management model*. We describe it in this section.

In practice, several identity management systems or frameworks exist which fit into this model, such as OpenID, Liberty Alliance, and WS-Trust to name a few (see Ping Identity (2007) for an overview of these and more systems). While each are different in their own way, they have many similarities which we highlight here.

Interaction of parties using digital identities still involves a user and a relying party, but instead of a centralized authority, it uses a different type of entity.

- **An identity provider:** an entity with the authority to create, maintain, verify, and manage digital identities for certain users, relying parties, and/or other identity providers.

There are several difference between an identity provider and the authorities in the previous model. There may be many different identity providers, each with the ability to manage digital identities and perform authentication procedures in different ways. As such, each identity provider will have its own jurisdiction with regards to which users and relying parties it manages. However, user and relying parties using different identity providers may still be able to communicate with each other provided there is sufficient trust between identity providers. A system in which this functionality is allowed is said to be *federated*.

Interaction between the identity providers and other entities can only occur if there is a certain degree of *trust* between the parties, which may not be the case. In the previous models, the authority implicitly had the trust of all other parties.

While scaling back on authority, we allow the identity provider to have more capability during transactions. In particular, we allow the identity provider to be involved somehow within the transaction between the user and relying party.

Let us examine how the authentication of the user takes place. As a pre-condition for this transaction to take place, the user **U** must have a pre-existing relationship with at least one identity provider **I**. By this, we mean that **U** has given **I** the authority to handle its digital identity and gives it access to the certain attributes it needs to carry out transactions.

One may be tempted to say that **R** must also have a pre-existing relationship with **I** and has identified itself to **I** as a service provider. In practice, this is often the case. However, we leave open the possibility that, in certain settings, **I**'s function is to merely store **U**'s attributes and return them to **U** upon request. This may be the case for entities focused on password retrieval.

A simplified transaction in this model is shown in Figure 4. It may have the following form:

1.   User **U** requests a service from relying party **R** and sends **R** its digital identity.
2.   **R** requests some sort of authentication from either **U** or from an agreed upon identity provider **I**.

3.   The identity provider **I** receives **U**'s identity and a request from either **U** or **I** requesting information which will authenticate **U** to **R**.
4.   **I** retrieves attributes for **U** and generates some sort of token which can be used for authentication.
5.   **I** sends these attributes to **R** (possibly by going through **U**).
6.   **R** examines the token from **I** and establishes that **U** is authentic.
7.   **U** and **R** carry out their transaction.

The token referred to in step 4 is sometimes referred to as a *credential*. In practice, it may be as simple as a password for the relying party's website which has been stored by the identity provider. However, more complex credentials such as digital signatures may also be used.

In many cases, all communication between **R** and **I** pass through **U**. This allows **U** to (theoretically) monitor and control personal data transmitted between **R** and **I**. Note that if any communication occurs directly between **R** and **I**, then the two must have a preexisting relationship.

Figure 4. Transaction in the identity management model

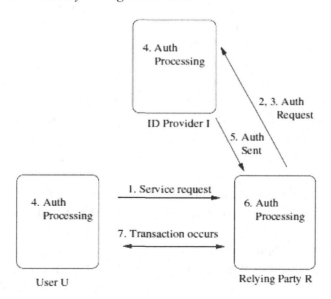

Finally, we note that since the identity provider is involved within the transaction, the issue of revocation is no longer a problem.

7. SECURITY ASPECTS OF THE MODEL

In this section, we annotate some of the security considerations which arise from the above model.

User's Security Burden: In a more direct model, **U** would be forced to ensure his/her own security, something many users are ill-equipped to do. In this model, **I** handles much of this burden on behalf of **U**.

Relying Party's Security Burden: In a normal setting, **R** may be required to develop its own advanced security policy to handle sensitive user information. This model shifts some of this burden to **I**.

Trust: A reliable identity provider can provide some assurance to **U** and **R** that the other party can be trusted. However, since interaction now involves a third party **I**, which has significant authority, a malicious or unreliable identity provider can cause significant damage.

Recovery: Users who lose or forget their identities or personal data can recover it via mechanisms put in place by the identity provider. This eliminates the need for a recovery policy with **R**.

Data Control: On one hand, users are now freed from having to figure out which data is supposed to be sent to which relying parties. However, it is possible that in the course of user authentication, the identity provider sends data to the relying party which the user does not want sent.

Cascading Loss: If the credentials for one site are compromised, then damage would be limited to that site. However, if an identity or identity provider is compromised, then damage can extend to many different sites.

Complexity of the New Model: The new model shown here is more complex than direct user-relying party interaction. As such, it has the

potential to introduce weak points both in the framework of the model and in its implementation.

With regards to the last point, there is a special phishing attack which can work in some implementations of this model. Suppose a user intends to visit a website hosted by relying party **R**, but instead is phished to a fake website hosted by **R** *. This website **R** * can redirect transmission to a fake identity provider **I** *, which can perform the duties that **I** can perform.

This type of attack is particular dangerous when the authentication procedure requires the user to interact with the identity provider by sending sensitive information along. Not only does this have the potential to give away sensitive information, but there is also the possibility that **I*** can also redirect the user back to the original relying party **R** such that neither **U** nor **R** became aware that anything malicious has happened.

Certain versions of OpenID may be particularly vulnerable to this attack (Crowley, Paul 2005).

8. OTHER CONSIDERATIONS FOR THIS MODEL

While security is certainly an important factor in an identity management system, it is not the only one. Many other factors related to functionality and usability can often affect user acceptance far more than security. Some of these factors include:

- **Convenience:** In some implementations, the extra procedures of this authentication procedure may require user interaction at several steps. This may be a bother to some users and cause them to stop using this system. On the other hand, use of an identity management system may also enable certain functionalities such as single sign-on and one-click login which can make for a more convenient user experience.
- **User Control:** As much of the work is performed by the identity provider, the user

inherently loses some control over certain personal information. Possibilities exist that an identity provider may share more personal information with a relying party than is necessary or that the user wishes to reveal.

- **Collaboration:** Any identity management system requires the collaboration of all parties involved. This requires communication setup in advance of the transaction occurring. It cannot be done at the spur of a moment. With an increasingly number of websites appearing every day, this appears to be a massive undertaking.
- **(De)Centralization:** Identity management systems tend to run smoother in centralized environments where there is a central authority. By its very nature, the internet is very decentralized which would appear to be a clash of philosophy. It is definitely a challenge in attempting to place an inherently centralized system into a decentralized environment. While the new model pushes in this direction, it still has its degree of centralization.
- **Operability:** Identity management systems may be required to integrate themselves with technologies which have already been deployed. This is mainly an implementation issue.
- **Portability:** With the growing functionality of cell phones and PDAs and an increasingly mobile society, it will be necessary for an identity management system to be accessible from anywhere and any device. As credentials will typically be stored on the servers of identity providers, this type of system may be conducive to this. However, in many ways, it would still be implementation dependent.
- **Reliability:** As with any system, it should be reliable, even if users access the system from different locations.

9. SUMMARY

On the surface, it would appear as if this model of identity management alleviates many problems users face today. It eases the security burdens on both the user and the relying party. It also makes processes such as user login and information recovery much simpler. In addition, it also has the potential to provide a certain degree of trust and peace-of-mind that the other entity involved in the transaction is legitimate.

Unfortunately, this model also has its share of drawbacks. The new complexities may introduce security complications which may detract from the security of the transaction. It also has the property that leaks in security can cause far more damage than in a traditional situation. It also suffers from the inherent drawback of extensive collaboration with all parties involved. Finally, we note that, in its very nature, this model appears to be centralized ship in a decentralized sea.

In the future, efforts should be made to improve this model and its implementations. The ultimate prize, though, would be to design a new model which can build on the strengths of this one, but minimize its drawbacks. In particular, it would be interesting to design a model which is not as inherently centralized.

REFERENCES

Birch, D. (2007). *Digital Identity Management: technological, Business, and Social Implications*. Aldershot, UK: Gower Publishing.

Crowley, P. (2005). *Phishing Attacks on OpenID*. Available at http://lists.danga.com/pipemail/yadis/2005-June/000470.html

Oasis. (2007). Retrieved from http://docs.oasis-open.org/ws-sx/ws-trust/v1.3/ws-trust.html

Open, I. D. (n.d.). Retrieved from http://www.openid.org.

Ping Identity. (2007). *Internet-Scale Identity Systems: An Overview and Comparison.* White paper, Available at http://www.pingidentity.com/information-library/resourcedetails.cfm?customel_data pageid_1296=1738.

Project Liberty. (n.d.). Retrieved from http://www.projectliberty.org.

Chapter 9
Securing Cloud Environment

N. Harini
Amrita Vishwa Vidyapeetham, India

C. K. Shyamala
Amrita Vishwa Vidyapeetham, India

T. R. Padmanabhan
Amrita Vishwa Vidyapeetham, India

ABSTRACT

Cloud Computing has rapidly emerged as a new computing paradigm that arrays massive numbers of computers in centralized and distributed data centers to deliver web-based applications, application platforms, and services via a utility model. Cloud computing technologies include grid computing, utility computing and virtualization. It is very much essential to make computations of the virtual machines confidential and secured. Challenges that cloud computing currently face, when deployed on a large enterprise scale, include self-healing, multi-tenancy, service-orientation, virtualization, scalability and data management. Undoubtedly, any model which involves data assets residing on equipment not within users' immediate control needs to address security and privacy. Securing the cloud environment encompasses many different things, including standard enterprise security policies on access control, activity monitoring, patch management, etc. This paper focuses on the approaches to secure the cloud environment.

1 INTRODUCTION

Cloud computing offers a utility model for IT, enabling users to access applications, middleware and hardware via the Internet as opposed to owning it themselves. It does not require up-front invest-ments, but instead, as an on-demand service, one pays for capacity as needed.

1.1 The Major Delivery Models of Cloud Computing

The different types of cloud delivery models and their service deployment and consumption modalities are:

DOI: 10.4018/978-1-60960-123-2.ch009

SaaS (Software as a Service): The customer is provided the facility to use the provider's applications running on a cloud infrastructure. This facility can be accessed through a thin client interface. The consumer is not bogged down by the responsibility of managing or controlling the underlying infrastructure.

PaaS (Platform as a Service): The consumer is provided the facility to deploy on to the cloud infrastructure consumer created applications using the provider's programming languages and tools. Here again the consumer does not manage or control the underlying infrastructure, but the consumer has control over the deployed applications and the application hosting environment configurations.

IaaS (Infrastructure as a Service): The consumer is provided the facility to rent fundamental computing resources for executing software's. Here again the consumer does not manage or control the underlying infrastructure, but the consumer has control over the operating systems, storage and deployed applications. He can also select networking components.

Narrowing the scope or specific capabilities and functionality within each of the *aaS offerings or employing the functional coupling of services and capabilities across them may yield derivative classifications. Such as "Storage as a Service" is a specific sub-offering with the IaaS "family," "Database as a Service" may be seen as a derivative of PaaS, etc.

Cloud services can be availed based on the on demand need of providing of computing instances/ computing capacity. Table 1 summarizes the cloud service deployment and consumption modalities regardless of the delivery model utilized (SaaS, PaaS, etc).

The vision for the Cloud is one where applications, platforms and infrastructure can all be consumed as and when required. The ability to rapidly scale-up and scale-down is perceived by many and directly leads to cost savings. Characteristics include on demand self-service, ubiquitous network access, location independent resource pooling, rapid elasticity, and pay per use. Cloud environments deliver softwares, platforms or infrastructures as services. 'Cloud nirvana' is a future where cloud service providers utilize the cloud to deliver dynamic capability enhancements; resources are switched on and off like taps, and users can switch suppliers quickly in order to access the best solution on the market.

Major Companies Offering On Demand Software(SaaS): Salesforce.com (CRM), Google (GOOG), NetSuite (N), Taleo (TLEO) Concur Technologies (CNQR) .

Major Companies offering Active platforms(PaaS): Google (GOOG) - Apps Engine,Amazon.com (AMZN) - EC2, Microsoft (MSFT) - Windows Live,Terremark Worldwide (TMRK) - The Enterprise Cloud, Salesforce.com (CRM) - Force.com, NetSuite (N) - Suiteflex, Mosso - Mosso, a division of Rackspace Metrisoft - Metrisoft SaaS Platform

Major companies offering Infrastructure as service (IaaS): Google (GOOG) - Managed hosting, development environment International Business Machines (IBM) - Managed hosting SAVVIS (SVVS) - Managed hosting,Terremark Worldwide (TMRK) - Managed hosting,Amazon. com (AMZN) - Cloud storage

The chapter discusses in detail the cloud architecture and the computing challenges faced in a cloud environment followed by a discussion on the security challenges with an overview of various approaches to security from different perspectives.

2. ARCHITECTURE

Cloud computing gained prominence in 2007 and is picking up momentum. Consumers of the cloud are concerned with services it can provide rather than the underlying technologies used to achieve the requested function. The advancement of grid computing and web services has substantially facilitated the growth of cloud computing.

Table 1.

Type of cloud	Operations, Security, Compliance., etc Managed By	Infrastructure like Facilities, Compute, Network and Storage Equipment,etc. Owned By	Infrastructured Location – (Both Physical and Relative to an organizations management umbrella)	Accessible and Consumed By
Public- Public Clouds are provided by a designated service provider and may offer either a single dedicated-tenant or multi-shared tenant operating environment	Third Party Provider	Third Party Provider	Off - Premise	Untrusted
Managed - Managed Clouds are provided by a designated service provider and may offer either a single- dedicated tenant or multi- shared tenant operating environment	Third Party Provider	Third Party Provider	On - Premise	Trusted and Untrusted
Private - Private Clouds are provided by an organization or their designated service provider and offer a single dedicated tenant operating environment	Organization/Third Party Provider	Organization/Third Party Provider	On/Off - Premise	Trusted
Hybrid - Hybrid Clouds are a combination of public and private cloud offerings that allow for transitive information exchange and possibly application compatibility and portability across disparate Cloud service offerings and providers utilizing standard or proprietary methodologies regardless of ownership or location.	Organization and Third Party Provider	Organization and Third Party Provider	On and Off - Premise	Trusted and Untrusted

Other net-centric computing paradigm like utility computing, ubiquitous computing or on-demand-computing also promote cloud computing. The success of cloud computing largely depends on the effective implementation of its architecture (White Paper, 2009 June). In cloud computing, architecture is not just based on how the application will work with the intended users. Cloud computing requires an intricate interaction with the hardware which is very essential to ensure uptime of the application. Cloud computing technologies include those cited in Table 2.

The architecture of the cloud consists of three layers, namely cluster, infrastructure for cloud computing platform, and data processing applica-tion layer. The cluster layer provides the hardware and storage devices for large scale data process-ing, co-ordination and management. The applica-tion layer provides the services to users, where users can develop their own applications, such as Web data analysis, language processing, cluster and classification, etc. (Figure 1).

3. CLOUD COMPUTING CHALLENGES

The acceptance and adoption of cloud services will vary across enterprises and users. The data storage and computation capability are the major factors

Table 2.

Technology	Features
Grid Computing	A form of distributed, parallel computing where-in processes are divided to leverage the available computing power of multiple CPU's acting in concert. Grids tend to be more loosely coupled, heterogeneous, and geographically dispersed.
Utility Computing	A model of purchasing computing capacity – such as CPU, storage and bandwidth from an IT service provider and paying for it based on consumption i.e. Offers computing resources as a metered service. The burden of maintaining and administering the system falls to the utility computing company, allowing the client to concentrate on other tasks.
Virtualization	Virtual servers and VPNs with the ability to quickly reconfigure available resources on demand and provide the necessary security assurance.

of the cloud computing platform, which determine how well the infrastructure can provide services to end users. Challenges that cloud computing currently faces, when deployed on a large enterprise scale, include self-healing, multi-tenancy, service-orientation, virtualization, scalability and data management. Undoubtedly, any model which involves data assets residing on equipment not within users' immediate control needs to address security and privacy. In cloud environments this will only become more acute, and potentially more challenging. As data leaves organizations' local area networks there may be a strong feeling that cloud computing is not secure enough.

3.1 Security Challenges

Cloud computing is a convergence of many technologies having their own standards and presentation states. This convergence combined with massively scaled deployments represents leap-ahead capabilities. In cloud environment there is the danger that sensitive data could fall into the wrong hands, either as a result of people having more privileges than required to do the job or by accidental or intentional misuse of the privileges they were assigned to do their job. Since the Cloud Service consumer has no visibility inside the cloud, the only option is to trust the environ-

Figure 1. Infrastructure of Cloud

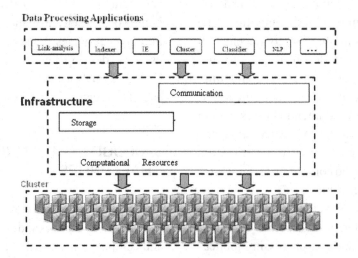

ment. Customers should trust their providers, and at the same time verify the security claims made by them. Cloud computing providers that can prove the trustworthiness of their resources will differentiate themselves from their competitors. To do this, they must have a way for customers to independently verify the security of the cloud service. To trust the security of a cloud provider, customers should be able to:

- Verify the integrity of the machines at the cloud provider
- Verify the identity of those machines as well as users, administrators and cloud customers
- Verify what kind of network security measures are being used

Virtualization technology (Marcia Savage (Ed.),2009) presents new vulnerabilities that must be managed. In addition, there are a vast number of configuration options that security and systems administrators need to understand, with an added layer of complexity that has to be managed by operations teams. Virtualization technologies connect to network infrastructure and storage networks. At the foreground careful planning with regard to access controls, user permissions, and security controls are essential.

Specific issues to security include:

- Provider Security In a cloud environment, all security depends on the security of the cloud provider who controls the hardware and the hypervisors on which data is stored and applications are run.
- Customer Attacks In an environment shared among customers, barriers between customers may be broken down providing access to another customer's data and paving way and means to interfere with their applications.
- Availability and Reliability Cloud is only usable through the Internet so Internet reli-

ability and availability is essential. Outages do occur and is a issue.
- Legal and Regulatory The virtual, international nature of cloud computing raises many legal and regulatory issues: export of data, jurisdiction's rules, who is liable for security breaches? These issues must be addressed for any sensitive applications of cloud computing.
- Integrating Provider and Customer Security Systems Cloud providers must integrate with the customer's security systems.

A secure cloud environment requires greater infrastructure security, reduction in certification and accreditation activities, simplified compliance analysis, low-cost disaster recovery and rapid reconstitution of services. Other security challenges (White Paper, 2009 August) include conflicts with existing data dispersal, service guarantees, securing virtual machines, handling of massive outages and encryption needs.

4. SECURE ARCHITECTURE MODEL

Cloud computing is redefining the way organizations access applications, middleware and hardware. With its distributed nature the cloud poses an acute need for a security model to protect assets of organizations as now they can be accessed by an intruder from anywhere in the Internet. The Figure 2 shows a security model for the cloud environment. The important entities involved in the data flow are end users, developers, system architects, third party auditors and the cloud itself. A brief discussion of the entities and their security needs follows:

End-users: End Users need to access certain resources in the cloud and should be aware of access agreements. Signatures may be used to confirm the same. It is also essential for the client organization to run mechanisms to detect vulnerable code or protocols at entry points such as

Figure 2. Security Model

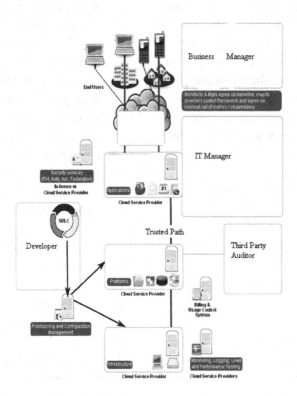

firewalls, servers, or mobile devices and upload patches on the local systems as soon as they are found. A cloud should include a denial of service protection to be secure from any user with malicious intent that may attempt to gain access to information or shut down a service. Integrity can be ensured using secure socket layer (SSL) or transport layer security (TLS) to ensure that the sessions are not being altered by a man in the middle attack. At a lower level, the network can be made secure by the use of secure internet protocol (IPsec).

System Architects: System architects are employed with writing the policies that pertain to the installation and configuration of hardware components such as firewalls, servers, routers, and software such as operating systems, thin clients, etc. They designate control protocols to direct the information flow within the cloud such as router update/queuing protocols, proxy server configurations or encrypted tunnels.

Developers: Developers building an application in the cloud need to access the infrastructure where the development environment is located. They also need to access some configuration server that allows them to test applications from various views. Software monitoring may be done by monitoring API calls for server requests. As far as security patches for the software go, updating a patch is easily done in the cloud and shared with everyone effortlessly, rather than finding every machine that has the software installed locally.

Third Party Auditors: Third party auditors are used by clients and providers alike to determine the security of the cloud implementation. Depending on the level of commitment to security and usefulness in obtaining a competitive edge, a cloud vendor may choose to submit itself to regular security assessments in an attempt to obtain accreditation.

Cloud computing promises to change the economics of the data center, but before sensitive and regulated data move into the public cloud, issues of security standards and compatibility must be addressed. All are elements of a secure identity, information and infrastructure model, and are applicable to private and public clouds as well as to IAAS, PAAS and SAAS services (Table 3).

4.1. Security Approaches

End Users: The data need to be encrypted as it is to be protected from being observed by any unauthorized user. Strong authentication (White paper, 2001 December) between application components should exist to ensure that data is transmitted only to known parties. Keen attention should be given to cryptography and how algorithms are cracked and are replaced by new ones over time. The rapid growth of information technology has resulted in significant advances in protecting the integrity and confidentiality of data is astounding. Public key cryptography has become the main stay for secured communications over the Internet and throughout many other forms of communications. It provides the foundation for both key management and digital signatures. For the past 20 years, Internet communications have been secured by the first generation of public key cryptographic algorithms (Wenbo, M., 2003) developed in the mid-1970. In the recent past, new techniques have been developed which offer both better performance and higher security than these first generation public key techniques. New public key techniques built on the arithmetic of elliptic curves are at the forefront in assuring security. As one scales security upwards over time to meet the evolving threat posed by eavesdroppers and hackers with access to greater computing resources, elliptic curves begin to offer dramatic savings over the old, first generation techniques. Elliptic curve cryptosystems require less computational power. The primary reason for the attractiveness of ECC over RSA and discrete log (DL) public-key systems is that the best algorithm known for solving the underlying hard mathematical problem in ECC (the elliptic curve discrete logarithm problem, ECDLP) takes fully exponential time. On the other hand, the best algorithms known for solving the underlying hard mathematical problems in RSA and DL systems (the integer factorization problem, and the discrete logarithm problem) take sub-exponential time. The algorithms for solving the ECDLP become infeasible much more rapidly as the problem size increases than those algorithms for the integer factorization and discrete logarithm problems. For this reason, ECC (Alan, G., Konheim, 2007) offers security equivalent to that of RSA and DL systems, while using significantly smaller key sizes. Table 4 shows the comparison of these public curve cryptosystems.

System Architects: Traditional network monitoring and security measures such as switches, routers, firewalls, intrusion detection, sniffers and analyzers are not able to see or control the growing volume of inter-VM traffic. A virtual firewall (stateful packet filtering) can provide visibility and control of inter-VM traffic and reduce

Table 3.

Entity	IaaS	SaaS	PaaS
End User: Business owners	N/A	Occasional users	N/A
End User: Business user	N/A	Main users- perform simple configuration tasks and use add-ons	N/A
System architect: IT administrator	Deploy images of existing software	Administration use	N/A
Developer	Deploy software	To browse and find existing services to reuse and add-ons	Main users

Table 4.

Public – Key System	Examples	Mathematical Problem / Running time	Benefits	Drawbacks
Integer Factorization	RSA, Rabin-Williams	Given a number n, find its prime factors / Sub Exponential	RSA can be used both for encryption as well as for digital signatures Trapdoor in RSA is in knowing value of n but not knowing the primes that are factors of n	If any one of p, q, m, d is known, then the other values can be calculated. So secrecy is important To protect the encryption, the minimum number of bits in n should be 2048
Discrete Logrrithm	Diffie-Hellman(DH), DSA, Elgamal	Given a prime n and numbers g and h find x such that $h = g^x$ mod n / Sub Exponential	The security factors with respect to the fact that solving the discrete logarithm is very challenging. The shared key (i.e. the secret) is never itself transmitted over the channel.	Expensive exponential operations involved. The algorithm cannot be used to encrypt messages - it can be used for establishing a secret key only. Lack of authentication.
Elliptic curve Discrete Logarithm	ECDH, ECDSA	Given an elliptic curve E and points P and Q on E, find x such that $Q = xP$ / Fully Exponential	ECC devices require less storage, less power, less memory, and less bandwidth than other systems. This allows you to implement cryptography in platforms that are constrained, such as wireless devices, handheld computers, smart cards, and thin-clients. It also provides a big win in situations where efficiency is important.	Hyper-elliptic cryptosystems offer even smaller key sizes. ECC is mathematically more subtle than RSA difficult to explain/justify to the client.

the risks of viruses, worms, Trojans, and inappropriate use in a virtual environment. VFS provides an interactive web-based user interface for managing numerous firewalls from one system, while maintaining the look-and-feel of a standard firewall. This makes it favorable for users transitioning from a traditional firewall solution to VFS (Virtual Firewall System). VFS also provides the capability of adding and deleting security domains.

Benefits of Virtual Firewalls include:

Ease of Deployment: Virtual Firewall reduces the requirement to procuring one box that will connect to the external Internet one end, and to multiple networks providing for several subscriber networks on the other, each with the security of a separate firewall.

Ease of Management: A service provider with multiple subscribers will need to host one instance of a virtual firewall for all subscribers of a network, governed by one set of policies. For a second subscriber network, there will be another instance of a Virtual Firewall with its set of policies, and so on. Here, the Service provider has multiple logical firewalls for multiple networks, but needs to manage only one system.

Lower Costs: The capital equipment cost of one system providing multiple firewalls for multiple networks is far less than the compounded costs of purchasing and maintaining a separate simple firewall system for each subscriber network. The direct cost benefits include

- Savings on hardware purchases
- Savings on administration and maintenance costs

Developers: Applications must be secure by design, with interfaces that present only the appropriate data to authorized users. During implementation, developers must take care to avoid coding practices that could result in vulnerability to techniques such as buffer overflow or SQL injection. Common practices include escaping single quotes, limiting the input character length, and filtering the exception messages. Despite these suggestions, vulnerabilities continue to surface in applications, implying the need for a different approach. New database IDS/IPS can be used to proactively validate the messages as they flow from the client to the server.

Intrusion detection, intrusion prevention and log analysis systems can be critical to identifying trouble areas and potential security breaches. Intrusion detection (ID) is a type of security management system for computers and networks. An ID system gathers and analyzes information from various areas within a computer or a network to identify possible security breaches, which include both intrusions (attacks from outside the organization) and misuse (attacks from within the organization). ID uses vulnerability assessment, which is a technology developed to assess the security of a computer system or network. Intrusion prevention is a preemptive approach to network security used to identify potential threats and respond to them swiftly. In a cloud it becomes necessary to isolate customer data networks from each other and from any management networks. This can be accomplished in both a secure and scalable way by employing either physical or virtual appliance IDS/IPS to provide powerful security between networks.

Third Party Auditors: They are to conduct audits on their infrastructure, platforms, personnel, applications and data. They describe the threats to the organization, conduct risk assessments and implement mitigation strategies.

CONCLUSION

While cloud computing provides compelling benefits, it is highly distributed. It is essential to have a security model that can be implemented in the distributed cloud infrastructure. Protective zones around servers, applications and even individual pieces of data must extend beyond the physical control of the in-house corporate network. It is also equally important to understand how the cloud computing provider builds its services and manages the data because it can mean the difference between real cost savings and false economy. This paper is an overview of security architecture and approaches that make the cloud environment more secured. We have planned to implement a fully functional prototype based on our architecture & suggested approaches. It is to be followed by a performance evaluation process.

REFERENCES

Alan, G., & Konheim (2007). *Computer Security and Cryptography*. New York: John Wiley and Sons.

Savage, M. (Ed.). (2009). Security challenges with cloud computing services. *Information Security magazine*.

Wenbo, M. (2003). *Modern Cryptography theory and Practice*. Upper Saddle River, NJ: Prentice Hall PTR.

White Paper. (2009, June). *Introduction to Cloud Computing architecture. 1st Edition*.

White Paper. (2009, August) *Cloud Computing Security*. A Trend Micro White Paper.

White paper (2001, December). Impact of Electronic Signatures on Security Practices for Electronic Documents. *A National Electronic Commerce Coordinating Council White Paper*.

Chapter 10
DoS Attacks in MANETs:
Detection and Countermeasures

Rajbir Kaur
Malaviya National Institute of Technology, India

M. S. Gaur
Malaviya National Institute of Technology, India

Lalith Suresh
Malaviya National Institute of Technology, India

V. Laxmi
Malaviya National Institute of Technology, India

ABSTRACT

A mobile ad hoc network (MANET) is a collection of mobile devices that communicate with each other without any fixed infrastructure or centralized administration. The characteristics specific to MANET (1) dynamic network topology, (2) limited bandwidth, (3) limited computational resources, and (4) limited battery power pose challenges in achieving goals of security and availability. MANETs are vulnerable to Denial of Service (DoS) attacks that can adversely affect performance of MANET. In this chapter the authors present a survey of DoS attacks at various layers, their detection and respective countermeasure.

INTRODUCTION

With the widespread use of lightweight devices like laptops, PDAs, wireless telephones and sensors, the importance of wireless computing and particularly mobile ad hoc networking have come to the fore. Continued reduction in cost has resulted in diverse fields where deployment of such networks is being conceived. In mobile networks, there are some applications, which cannot rely on the presence of any fixed infrastructure. Examples of such applications are: emergency disaster relief in a damaged area after a storm or an earthquake; a set of digital sensors positioned to take measurements in a region unreachable by humans; military tanks and planes in a battlefield; and finally, students (or researchers) sharing

DOI: 10.4018/978-1-60960-123-2.ch010

information during a lecture. This infrastructure independence leads to the concept of mobile networks namely, ad hoc networks.

A mobile ad hoc network (MANET) is a collection of mobile devices that communicate with each other without any fixed infrastructure or centralized administration. The mobile hosts in MANET establish their own network as and when required. It is for this reason that MANET is characterized by having a dynamic, continuously changing network topology due to mobility of nodes.

In MANET the nodes can communicate directly if they are within each other's transmission range. If the source node is outside the destination node's wireless range, it needs to rely on intermediate hosts to relay its packets. This is referred to as a multi hop scenario. Each node in MANET functions as a source, destination or an intermediate router. Another characteristic of MANET is that mobile hosts have limited resources (CPU, storage, energy, etc.), the wireless channels are unreliable and have limited bandwidth.

These very characteristics of MANET make it vulnerable to a wide variety of attacks. Like any other network, ad hoc networks must also provide some security services to protect resources and information from attack. An effective security architecture must ensure (1) Availability, (2) Authentication, (3) Data confidentiality, (4) Integrity and (5) Non-repudiation. With all other security services in place, MANET is not achieving its objective if the services provided by it are not **available** to authorized users when they need it. This non-availability of resources to authorized users is known as Denial of Service (DoS).

This chapter surveys DoS attacks and it's countermeasures based on protocol stack, in MANETS. The rest of the chapter is organized as follows: In Section 1, an overview of DoS is presented followed by taxonomy of DoS attacks in MANET. In section 2 we discuss DoS attacks and its countermeasures in the physical layer, followed by attacks and countermeasures at MAC

layer in section 3. A general description of two protocols - DSR and AODV - largely adopted by (IETF's MANET working group, n.d.) can be found in Section 4. This is subsequently followed by a discussion on attacks and detection schemes in the network layer in section 5. Section 6 concludes the chapter.

1. DENIAL OF SERVICE (DOS)

A DoS can be characterized as an attack with the purpose of preventing the legitimate users from using a victim computing system or a network resource. A DoS attack usually has the following properties:

(a) **Malicious:** Intentional act of harming a node so as to cause a failure.
(b) **Disruptive:** Degradation or disruption of some capability or service.
(c) **Asymmetric:** The property of prevention/ detection measure effort of an attack being greater that the effort required mounting it. For example, buffer overflow attacks are easy to execute but the effect may crash the server.
(d) **Remote:** Attacks are usually carried out over the network using a spoofed IP to escape traceback.

DoS attacks are thus proving to be a serious and permanent threat to users, organizations and network resources.

Figure 1 outlines the taxonomy of DoS attacks at the lower three layers of the wireless protocol stack. In this chapter, we analyze attacks in terms of IEEE 802.11 standard, which covers physical and MAC layer. The standard currently defines a single MAC that interacts with three PHYs (running at 1 or 2 Mbit/s). We also survey attacks and defense mechanisms in the routing layer. In the remaining sections we discuss these attacks.

Figure 1. Taxonomy of DoS attacks in MANET

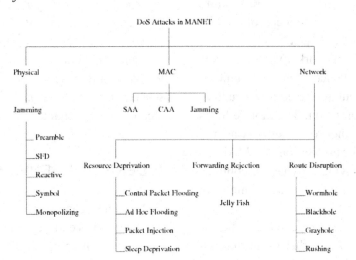

2. PHYSICAL LAYER

Note: We only highlight those parts of 802.11 standard, which present malicious users with opportunities to exploit secure, fair, and efficient protocol operation.

All 802.11 frames have the following components (Table 1).

The Preamble and PLCP (Physical Layer Convergence Procedure) Header are PHY dependent.

As illustrated in Figure 2, 802.11 MAC frames are encapsulated by the PLCP header. The PLCP preamble is composed of a SYNC field and a Start Frame Delimiter (SFD). The SYNC field is not only used for synchronization between sender and receiver, it also triggers the energy detection circuitry that differentiates noise and/or interference from a valid frame transmission. An SFD

Table 1. 802.11 Frame

Preamble	PLCP Header	MAC Data	CRC

(Start Frame delimiter) field indicates the actual start of PLCP header. The PLCP header follows the preamble and comprises of - a length field that represents the number of bytes contained in the packet, a signal field that contains the rate information, and a frame check sequence for error detection.

2.1. DoS Attacks in 802.11 Physical Layer

Physical layer DoS attacks are generally known as "*jamming*". Jamming aims to prevent a node from successfully transmitting or receiving frames in the physical layer so that frames cannot be passed on to higher layers. DoS attacks on the physical layer may be launched by targeting either the complete frame preamble or by manipulating certain parts of the frame preamble. The attack can be continuous, periodic, random or reactive. The attacker may have the same resources as the other nodes in the network. He may also have unlimited energy resources. Based on these attributes, the physical layer DoS attacks can be classified as:

Figure 2. PLCP Frame

PLCP Preamble		PLCP Header			
SYNC 128 bits	SFD 16 bits	SIGNAL 8 bits	SERVICE 8 bits	LENGTH 16 bits	CRC 16 bits

2.1.1. Resource Unlimited Attack (RUA)

An attacker (jammer) having virtually unlimited resources (i.e., energy, power, and bandwidth) can maintain a high level of signal strength at any receiver continuously for a wide frequency range. This blocks all wireless devices in the effective range and jams the bandwidth as long as the attack continues. A receiver can be interrupted even if the jamming signal is much weaker than the signal strength of a legitimate frame transmission. Such attacks are described below.

2.1.2. Preamble Attack

A SYNC frame is used to synchronize between the sender and the receiver. A jammer continuously transmits a SYNC pattern. Thus a receiver station is prevented from synchronizing to any other station's transmissions (Gummadi, Wetherall, Greenstein, & Seshan, 2007). There can be significant frame losses even when the received power of the jammer is three orders of magnitude less than the power of a legitimate frame transmission. This attack prevents the nodes to communicate with each other. This decreases the network availability.

2.1.3. SFD Attack

The end of the preamble is signaled by the SFD pattern. It also marks the beginning of the frame. When the receiver sees the SFD pattern it starts to process the incoming frame following the SFD pattern. If the receiver receives the SFD pattern transmitted by the jammer before the SFD pattern of the transmitter, it starts to process the

incoming bits with wrong ordering. This results in errors both at the PLCP header and the MAC frame (Gummadi et al., 2007). This deteriorates the performance of the network to a great extent.

2.1.4. Reactive Attack

In this kind of attack the jammer node aims to disrupt the ongoing communication. The jammer monitors the channel continuously. When it senses a frame transmission, it starts sending interfering signals to corrupt the ongoing transmission. This saves the energy resources of the jammer (Xu, Ma, Trappe, & Zhang, 2006), as it is not jamming continuously i.e., when the nodes are not communicating. These attacks are more effective in jamming and denying access to the channel.

2.1.5. Symbol Attack

Forward Error Correction (FEC) schemes are not included in 802.11 and 802.11b frames. Thus, the whole frame can be rendered useless by creating an error in a single symbol. A jammer can result in destroying the whole frame during an ongoing transmission by transmitting a strong signal for the duration of a single symbol.

2.1.6. Monopolizing Attack

An attacker may try to monopolize the wireless channel by sending a short frame in every SIFS period. However, it is shown in (Bellardo & Savage, 2003) that the number of frames that is needed for a full disruption is huge (50,000 packets/s are needed for the SIFS period of 20 μs).

2.2. Countering DoS Attacks in the Physical Layer

The first and essential step to counter a DoS attack in the physical layer is to detect the jamming station itself. Two parameters that assist this are: (a) Signal Strength Consistency and (b) Location Consistency (Xu et al., 2006). If the packet delivery ratio (PDR) between two nodes communicating between each other is low, it could either mean congestion of the network or presence of a jamming station in the vicinity.

If the two stations enjoy a high level of average input signal strength, low PDR implies presence of a jamming station. In the Signal Strength Consistency approach, the signal strength level is used to estimate the quality of the transmitting channel (the average input signal strength) and in the Location Consistency method; the physical distance between the two nodes is used as the metric. Once the active jamming station is detected, the remaining nodes in the network can perform rapid frequency hopping in order to mitigate the effect of jamming (Gummadi et al., 2007).

According to (Xu, trappe, Zhang, & Wood, 2005) signal strength distribution is affected by the presence of a jammer. Network devices may gather noise level measurements during a time interval prior to jamming and build a statistical model to describe normal energy level in the network to discriminate jamming from normal traffic.

2.2.1. Survivability Techniques Against Jamming

(Virendra, Upadhyaya, Kumar, & Anand, 2005) propose survivability scheme against AP failure in wireless LANs. To recover from the AP failure and reconnect to the network, the nodes under a failed AP form an ad hoc network with the surviving neighboring AP. This scheme is called an infrastructure for ad hoc migration scheme (IAMS). It has three major components:

(a) **Leader Selection Criteria:** A node can be selected as a leader using either a trust based model or a region based (proximity to the bridge nodes) model.

(b) **Topology Graphs:** These are built by the AP's working normally in the infrastructure mode and periodically distributed to the leaders under it. These graphs are used to determine the routes in case of AP failure.

(c) **Switching Methodology**: When the nodes stop receiving beacon messages from the AP, they wait for a certain threshold period. The leader sends control messages to the nodes giving details of the new route.

The upper panel illustrates the timing and order of handshake frames. The lower frame illustrates the virtual carrier sensing targeted via the handshake. The sender's RTS frame silences the stations (disks with darker filling) in its transmit range (indicated by the large circle). The destination's CTS frame silences the stations in its transmit range. During the DATA and ACK frame exchanges stations within the transmit ranges of the sender and receiver do not attempt channel access until their NAV expire.

3. MEDIA ACCESS CONTROL LAYER

Any mobile station gets access to the channel by executing a contention-based mechanism similar to the IEEE 802.11 Standard.

3.1. IEEE 802.11 MAC Protocol

The 802.11 Distributed Coordination Function (DCF) standards (Anonymous, 1999) combines Carrier Sense Multiple Access/Collision Avoidance (CSMA/CA) with a Request to Send/Clear to Send (RTS/CTS) handshake to avoid collisions. A node can only transmit when no carrier of a transmitting node is sensed in the vicinity. Otherwise, it has to defer its own transmission until the channel is determined to be idle. The node, then, requests the channel by sending an RTS to the receiver that, in turn, replies with CTS. The nodes in the vicinity overhearing the RTS or CTS defer their own transmission for a period that is long enough for the subsequent DATA/ACK exchange. When the RTS/CTS handshake is completed, the sender commences data transmission. The receiver acknowledges the data with an ACK. If no CTS or ACK is received, the sender exponentially backs off, and retransmits the RTS or DATA. The binary exponential scheme (Anonymous, 1999) favors the last winner among the contending nodes.

To prioritize access to the radio medium three time windows are defined. Short Inter frame Space (SIFS) is used for ACK, CTS and poll response frames. Distributed Coordination Function Inter frame Space (DIFS) and Extended Inter frame Space (EIFS) are used as the minimum delay for asynchronous frames contending for access. Before transmitting the next data each node must waits for a period of DIFS/EIFS duration to determine the channel status. If a collision does occur, the sender uses a random exponential back off algorithm before retransmitting.

Each 802.11 frame carries a duration field indicating the time in microseconds for which the channel is reserved. This value is used to program the Network Allocation Vector (NAV) in each node. During the RTS/CTS handshake the sender first sends a small RTS frame containing the time needed to complete the CTS, data and ACK frames. Each neighbor of the sender and receiver updates the NAV field and defer their transmission for the duration of the future transaction for this time. Figure 3 depicts the channel access mechanisms.

3.2. DoS Attacks in 802.11 MAC Layer

802.11 nodes are identified at the MAC layer with globally unique 12-byte address. A field in the MAC frame holds both the source and the destination address. This allows the attacker to spoof other nodes and request MAC-layer services on their behalf. DoS attacks at this layer can be broadly classified in two typical approaches (Zhou, Wu, & Nettles, 2004):

Figure 3. 802.11 channel access mechanisms

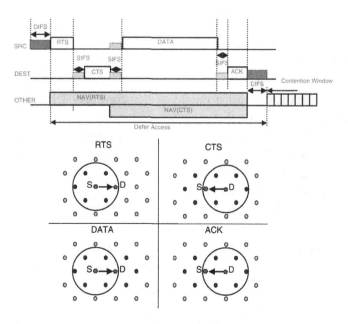

(a) **Single adversary attack (SAA):** Only one malicious node participates in attack.

(b) **Colluding adversaries attack (CAA):** As the name suggests, two or more nodes collude to launch an attack. Severity of the attack depends on number of adversaries.

A simple attack that may involve one or more attacking nodes is Jamming. This attack disrupts message signals through transmission of high intensity noise by attacking nodes. Following paragraphs describe these attacks in detail.

3.2.1. Single Adversary Attack

By leveraging unauthorized data transmission in 802.11, a single adversary can intrude into a network, send enormous flows to legitimate nodes, and hence drain the energy of legitimate nodes as well as substantially reduce the available channel capacity for legitimate communications. In MANET, all the participating nodes should receive or forward packets unconditionally. This feature provides the adversaries a perfect opportunity to launch SAA attacks. A malicious node may keep sending CTS messages in response to a source node's RTS messages. The source node has to wait for the duration indicated in the CTS frame before it can receive data from other neighbor (s). The services of this node are denied to all the neighboring nodes. The binary exponential scheme favors the last winner amongst the contending nodes. This leads to what is called the capture effect (Li & Zeng, 2006). Nodes that are heavily loaded capture the channel by continually transmitting data, thereby causing lightly loaded neighbors to back off endlessly. A malicious node takes advantage of this vulnerability and prevents legitimate nodes from sending data on the channel.

3.2.2. Colluding Adversary Attack (CAA)

By leveraging unfairness present in 802.11, two colluding adversaries may send enormous data flows directly to each other, and hence deplete the channel capacity in their vicinity. This unfairness is caused by two basic mechanisms in the 802.11 MAC protocol: The DIFS/EIFS timing scheme and the exponential backoff mechanism. In CAA attacks, the concept of Attacking Region (AR) is used. AR is associated with the traffic flow of a node. If another traffic flow moves into AR of the first node and commences transmission with enormous amount of traffic, throughput of the first node will be suppressed. Two colluding adversaries may move into the attacking region of either the sender or the receiver and send enormous traffic directly to each other. This exhausts the channel capacity leading to denial of service to other nodes. The colluding adversaries may also cause data packet dropping at the intermediate nodes. Not only is the traffic suppressed, but the energy of forwarding the packets is also wasted.

3.2.3. Jamming

An attacker corrupts those frames for which their exact transmission times are known: CTS/RTS frames, ACK frames, and DATA frames. The distributed operation of the CSMA/CA protocols ensures that a node being jammed defers the transmission of its next frame following the multiplicative decrease algorithm. A terminal undergoing a few successive jams would virtually stop transmission. There are two types of jamming:

(a) p-random jamming in which the jammer corrupts CTS frame with certain probability p and

(b) Misbehavior jamming, when one of the terminals in the network deliberately selects a different window size from that specified by the protocol in order to gain unfair access to the network.

3.3. Countering DoS Attacks in the MAC Layer

To counter SAA attacks; a packet-by-packet authentication scheme is used that is based on key shared among legitimate nodes. Data transmission requests from unauthenticated adversaries may thus be rejected.

To mitigate CAA attacks FairMAC protocol (Gupta, Krishnamurthy, & Faloutsous, 2002) can be used. Another protecting traffic flow can be triggered in the vicinity of adversaries and distance between sender and receiver is reduced to reduce the AR.

(Toledo & Wang, 2008) propose that jamming in a CSMA/CA network can be detected based on calculating the probability that the collisions in the network can be explained by simple observation of the events in the network. The distribution of the explainability of the collisions is an excellent indicator of the presence of jammers and misbehaving nodes in the network. The traffic is then rerouted in order to avoid compromised areas.

4. NETWORK LAYER

The Network Layer is responsible for end-to-end (source to destination) packet delivery including routing through intermediate hosts.

4.1. Routing Protocols in MANET

The goal of routing is to discover the most recent topology of a continuously changing network to find a correct route to a specific node. Routing protocols in MANET can be classified as either being reactive (e.g. AODV, DSR) or proactive (e.g. OLSR, TBRPF). An on-demand (or reactive) routing protocol is one in which a node attempts to discover some destination only when it has a packet to send to that destination. On the other hand, in periodic (or proactive) routing protocols, nodes periodical exchange topology information. Hence nodes can obtain route information any time they must send data. We discuss DoS issues related to reactive protocols. We discuss AODV and DSR in the following sub sections.

4.1.1. AODV (Ad Hoc On Demand Distance Vector)

In AODV (Perkins, Royer, & Das, 2003), when a source node S wishes to send a data packet to a destination node D and does not have a route to D, it initiates route discovery by broadcasting a route request (RREQ) to its neighbors. The intermediate neighbors who receive this RREQ in turn broadcast the same RREQ to their neighbors until the RREQ reaches the destination node. Upon receiving the first arrived RREQ, the destination sends the route reply (RREP) to the source node through the reverse path where the RREQ arrived.

Figure 4 depicts the protocol for sending message in AODV.

4.1.2. DSR (Dynamic Source Routing) Protocol

In DSR (Johnson, Maltz, & Hu, 2007) a node (initiator) that has a packet to send to some destination and does not currently have a route to it in its *Route Cache*, initiates Route Discovery to find a route. The initiator transmits a ROUTE REQUEST packet as a local broadcast, specifying the target and a unique identifier. Each node receiving the ROUTE REQUEST discards the packet if it has recently seen this request identifier from the initiator. Otherwise, it appends its own node address to a list in the REQUEST and rebroadcasts the REQUEST. When the ROUTE REQUEST reaches its target node, the target sends a ROUTE REPLY back to the initiator of the REQUEST, including a copy of the accumulated list of addresses from the REQUEST. When the REPLY reaches the initiator, it caches the new route in its Route Cache. DSR is based on *source routing*: when sending a packet, the originator lists in the header of the packet the complete sequence of nodes through which the packet is to be forwarded.

In an environment where mobile nodes may join or leave a domain freely, there is no guarantee that path between two nodes will be devoid of

Figure 4. Messaging in AODV Protocol

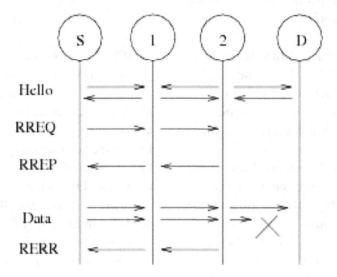

malicious nodes. These nodes may not comply with the protocol operation. These malicious nodes may impose excessive transmission overhead and harm the network operation in various ways. Thus, there has been an emphasis on developing secure versions of the routing protocols to combat misbehaving nodes and safeguard transmitted information. The routing protocols AODV and DSR, which we have discussed in this chapter, do not provide any type of security. We discuss some of the secure versions of AODV and DSR in the following sections.

4.1.3. Secure Versions of AODV

The nodes of an ad hoc network cooperate to prevent selfish behavior. Collaborative reputation mechanism is used to detect misbehaving nodes. CORE (Michiardi & Molva, 2002) consists of three entities: mobile nodes, Reputation Table (RT) at each node and a Watchdog (WD) mechanism. RT and WD form the basis of the collaborative reputation mechanism that allows individual entities to observe the participating nodes involved in request/reply process.

Another protocol proposed to secure AODV is SAODV (Zapata & Asokan, 2002). SAODV de-

signs single signature extensions (SSE) to AODV. Signature based mechanism is used by a node to authenticate fields of RREQ and RREP when forwarding. Hash Chains are used to authenticate hop count as it is the only mutable field. This prevents certain impersonation attacks.

Security Aware Ad-Hoc Routing (SAR) (Yi, Naldurg, & Kravets, 2001) protocol uses trust level to discover a path through nodes with desired security attributes. A node that initiates route discovery sets the required minimal trust level for the participating nodes. Nodes having this trust level share symmetric keys. So only nodes with the required key can read the header and forward the packet.

Authenticated Routing for Ad hoc Networks (ARAN) (Sanzgiri, Levine, Shields, Dahill, 2002), detects and protects against malicious actions by third parties and peers by making use of cryptographic certificates. The routing messages are authenticated at each hop from source to the destination and back.

Secure Position Aided Ad hoc Routing (Carter & Yasinsac, 2002) (SPAAR) uses geographical information to make forwarding decisions in order to improve the efficiency and security of mobile ad hoc networks. Asymmetric cryptography is used for end-to-end as well as hop-to-hop communication.

4.1.4. Secure Versions of DSR

ARIADNE (Hu, Perrig, & Johnson, 2005) extends DSR and provides security using symmetric cryptography. Three schemes are suggested: shared secrets between each pair of nodes, shared secrets between communication nodes combined with broadcast authentication, or digital signatures. The target verifies the authenticity and integrity of the ROUTE REQUEST using a message authentication code (MAC) computed with a shared key. The ROUTE REPLY messages are authenticated using a Tesla key. A one-way hash function is applied for per-hop hashing by intermediate nodes. This is used to avoid removal of nodes from ROUTEREQUEST list.

CONFIDANT (Cooperation Of Nodes: Fairness In Dynamic Ad hoc Networks) (Bucheggar & Boudec, 2002) is also provided as a security extension for DSR, but it can also be applied to other source routing protocols. Reputation based system is used to isolate and exclude misbehaving nodes from route discoveries. CONFIDANT consists of four elements: monitor, trust manager, reputation system, and path manager. The monitor ensures that the next node in the forwarding chain forwards the message correctly. If an anomaly is observed, the reputation system is triggered to take action based on the tables of ratings that it maintains. Trust manager warns other nodes about malicious nodes and the path manager manages the path such that the malicious nodes are avoided in route discovery.

4.2. DoS Attacks in Network Layer

These are also termed as "Routing Attacks". DoS attacks on the network layer take the advantage of the vulnerabilities of the network layer protocol. On the basis of consequences of the attack, these can be classified into three types

(a)   Resource Deprivation Attacks
(b)   Forwarding Rejection Attacks
(c)   Route Disruption Attacks

4.2.1. Resource Deprivation Attack

In a resource deprivation attack, malicious nodes inject extra control or data packets into the network. In such attacks a malicious node keeps sending fake messages to its neighbors at a high rate. The attacker may also change the sequence numbers or destination addresses of the messages. It is difficult for the neighboring nodes to discriminate between fake and new messages. They also forward these messages to their neighbors. The neighbors have to spend many resources, such as bandwidth, CPU cycles, and battery energy, to handle these fake messages. Some of the resource consumption attacks are discussed in following paragraphs.

4.2.1.1. Control Packet Flooding Attack

In a flooding based route discovery process in protocols such as AODV, each RREQ initiated by a node results in n broadcasts in the MANET, where n is the number of nodes in the MANET. As the mobility and load of the network increases, the control packets used for route discoveries may consume more bandwidth than the data packets. When the network is saturated, increasing the offered load causes rapid decrease in achieved throughput due to *false* route breaks. In a false route break, the sender assumes the next hop does not exist though it is still within the radio range of the sender but did not respond owing to busy wireless channel (Desilva & Boppana, 2004). This creates a vicious circle.

False route-breaks cause sending nodes to initiate frequent route discoveries and wasting wireless channel bandwidth. Since a broken route disrupts data flow, control packets are given higher priority over data packets in transmitting in order to repair broken routes as quickly as possible. So at high loads, the wireless channel usage can be completely dominated by the control packets used for route discoveries. An attacker (a malicious node) may keep initiating route discovery requests at a lower rate but ignoring any reply to them, thus exhausting the bandwidth.

Mitigating Control Packet Flooding Attack: One way to mitigate Control Packet Flooding Attack is to use broadcast management techniques (Williams & Camp, 2002) that reduce transmission rate for network wide floods. These techniques use passive hearing to reduce redundant broadcasts and keep track of neighbors. One of such techniques is the random assessment delay (RAD). RAD requires keeping track of redundant RREQ packets over a short period. If these redundant packets exceed a certain threshold then RREQ is not relayed.

The other proposed technique (Desilva & Boppana, 2005) uses statistical analysis to detect misbehaving nodes. Each node maintains a count of RREQs received for each RREQ sender during a preset time period. At the end of the time period, the node computes the rate at which it has been receiving route requests from each sender and computes smoothed average. Average rate of RREQs per sender and its smoothed average is also computed. If the smoothed average of certain sender falls below a certain Cut Off Rate, it is treated as malicious.

4.2.1.2. Ad Hoc Flooding Attack

This attack is used against on-demand routing protocols, such as AODV and DSR, for mobile ad hoc networks. To exhaust the communication bandwidth and node resources, the intruder or the attacker broadcasts a lot of Route Request packets for node ID who is not in networks so as to congest in links.

Flooding RREQ packets in the whole network can lead to congestion and consumption of network resources. To reduce congestion in a network, the AODV protocol limits RREQ packets. A node cannot originate more than RREQ_RATELIMIT RREQ messages per second. After broadcasting a

RREQ, a node waits for a RREP. The broadcasting node waits for some time (in milliseconds) for RREP. If a route is not received within this time, the node may try again to discover a route by broadcasting another RREQ, up to a maximum of retry times at the maximum TTL (time-to-live) value in the IP headers. Repeated attempts by a source node at route discovery for a single destination must utilize a binary exponential backoff.

In ad hoc flooding attack, the attack node violates the above rules to exhaust the network resource. The attacker selects many IP addresses, which are not in the network. As no node can answer RREP packets for these RREQ, the reverse route in the route table of node will be conserved for longer. The attacker successively originates mass RREQ messages for these void IP addresses. The attacker tries to send excessive RREQ without keeping RREQ_RATELIMIT within per second; TTL of RREQ is set up to a maximum without using expanding ring search method. The whole network becomes full of RREQ packets generated by the attacker. These flooded RREQ packets exhaust the communication bandwidth and the other resources of the nodes. For example, the mass RREQ will exhaust the storage of the route table. So the node will be unable to receive new RREQ packet. As a result, the legitimate nodes cannot set up paths to send data.

Prevention of Ad Hoc Flooding Attack: The technique of neighbor suppression (Yi et al., 2005) is used to prevent ad hoc flooding attack. This technique works by modifying the first in first out (FIFO) rule for processing RREQ packets to the rule of priority. FIFO rule forbids a node to receive subsequent RREQ packets unless the packets that have arrived earlier (may be from the attacker) are processed. To counter this attack each node sets a processing priority and threshold for its neighbor nodes. The priority of a node is in inverse proportion to the frequency of originating RREQ. The threshold is set to the maximum of originating RREQs in a particular time period. If the frequency of RREQs originated by a node (say *A*) exceeds the threshold, its neighbor denies further packets from *A*. Thus the flooding attack is prevented by its neighbor nodes.

4.2.1.3. Packet Injecting Attack

In this attack (Gu, Liu, Zhu, & Chu, 2005) a malicious node injects a large number of junk data packets into the route to consume the resource of intermediate routing nodes. Packet injection attacks can be launched either by a malicious node or a compromised node. The attacker may use spoofed ID as the source of the injected packets.

Detection and Prevention of Packet Injection Attacks: (Gu et al., 2005) have proposed a hop by hop source authentication forwarding (SAF) protocol that filters out injected junk packets with high probability or exposes the true identity of the injector. The attack is prevented in three steps: First, the source sets up pairwise keys with the en route nodes. Then the source node authenticates its packets for each en route node using these keys and lastly, all en route nodes verify data packets upon receiving them. Authentic packets are forwarded while others are discarded. Attributes such as source Id, packet count and an authentication token (which is a keyed-hash of packet count and the packet size) are used in authentication header that is attached to each data packet. To inject junk packets, the attacker needs to provide a valid authentication token. The probability of guessing the token is very small; SAF filters out junk packets.

4.2.1.4. Sleep Deprivation Attack

The aim of this attack is to drain the limited resources like battery powers in mobile ad hoc nodes. Once the attacker node launches itself into the route, it can flood any node by sending a large number of route request (RREQ), route replies (RREP) or route error (RRER) packets to the target node. As a result, the target is always busy processing the unnecessary packets. This drains the resources of the target node and is rendered unreachable by other nodes in the network. These attacks can be categorized into

(a) **Service Request Power Attacks:** in which the valid service requests like ssh, telnet are made repeatedly in order to exhaust the battery capacity.

(b) **Benign Power Attacks:** energy hungry tasks are executed immediately such as displaying a hidden animated gif.

(c) **Malignant Power Attacks:** similar to viruses and Trojan horses.

Countermeasures: To detect power drain DoS attacks, (Bu, Norden, & Woo, n.d.) propose Architecture for Wireless Attack Resistance (AWARE). The attack is detected in three steps.

(a) Determine the normal traffic characteristics and power consumption of mobiles in the network. This is used to determine the normal Energy Efficiency Ratio (EERs) of each mobile.

(b) This is compared with EERs under normal operating conditions. If the values deviate from the threshold the wireless network is considered to be under attack.

(c) The attack is countered by using functions like blacklisting.

(Martin, Hsiao, Ha, & Krishnaswami, 2004) propose a power secure architecture to thwart power attacks by employing multi level authentication and energy signatures. The goal of the architecture is to provide some guaranteed fraction of the systems expected battery life. The multi level authentication is designed to prevent energy loss from service request attacks by making sure that all trusted services rendered consume less than a certain amount of energy. The energy signature monitor is designed to catch intrusions entering the system via dynamic validation of the dynamic energy signature against known energy signatures for the device and application.

4.3. Forwarding Rejection Attacks

Compared with the resource deprivation and route disruption attack, malicious nodes launching forwarding rejection attacks may comply with all routing procedures. A malicious node launching such attacks may keep active in both route discovering and packet forwarding in order to prevent it from detection and diagnosis, but the malicious node can attack the traffic via itself by reordering packets, dropping packets periodically, or increasing jitters. One of the forward rejection attacks is the JellyFish attack.

4.3.1 JellyFish Attack

*JellyFish (*JF) (Aad, Hubaux, & Knightly, 2004)) attack is a new and general class of *protocol compliant* denial-of-service attacks. Previously studied attackers *disobey* protocol rules; on the contrary, JellyFish conforms to all routing and forwarding protocol specifications, and moreover, as implied by the name, are passive and difficult to detect until after the "sting". JellyFish target *closed-loop* flows that are responsive to network conditions such as delay and loss. The goal of JF nodes is to reduce the goodput of all traversing flows to near-zero while dropping zero or a small fraction of packets. In particular, JF nodes employ one of three mechanisms.

(a) First JF variant is a packet reordering attack. TCP has a well-known vulnerability to reordered packets due to factors such as route changes or the use of multi-path routing. However, *no* TCP variant is robust to *malicious* and persistent reordering as employed by the JF misordering attack.

(b) Second JF mechanism is periodic dropping at relay nodes according to a maliciously chosen period (timeout phase). A JF periodic-dropping node can drop no more packets than neighboring congested nodes, but in-

flict near-zero throughput on all TCP flows traversing it.

(c) Third JF attack is a delay-variance attack in which the attacker delays packets (preserving order) in order to thwart TCP's timers and congestion inferences.

5. ROUTE DISRUPTION ATTACK

A Route Disruption Attack causes legitimate route data packets to be routed in a dysfunctional way. Some typical attacks in this category are

(a) Wormhole Attack
(b) Black Hole Attack
(c) GrayHole Attack
(d) Rushing Attacks

5.1. Worm Hole Attack

In protocols like AODV a concept of tunneling is used. In tunneling, two remote nodes collaborate to encapsulate and exchange messages between them through existing data routes giving an impression of adjacent nodes. This is a useful service in connection the network efficiently.

In a *wormhole attack* (Hu, Perrig, & Johnson, 2005), an attacker receives packets at one point in the network, tunnels them to another point in the network, and then replays them into the network from that point. For tunneled distances longer than the normal wireless transmission range of a single hop, it is simple for the attacker to make the tunneled packet arrive sooner than other packets transmitted over a normal multi hop route, for example through use of a single long-range directional wireless link or through a direct wired link to a colluding attacker. This attack can be mounted against an on-demand routing protocol such as DSR or AODV, by tunneling each RREQ packet directly to the destination target node of the RREQ. When the destination node's neighbors hear this RREQ packet, they will follow normal routing protocol processing to rebroadcast that copy of the RREQ and then discard without processing all other received RREQ packets originating from this same Route Discovery. This attack thus prevents any routes other than through the wormhole from being discovered. To exploit the wormhole, the attacker discards rather than forward all data packets, creating a permanent Denial-of-Service attack or selectively discard or modify certain data packets. Figure 5 illustrates a scenario of wormhole attack.

5.1.1. Techniques for Detecting Wormhole Attack

In (Song, Qian, & Li, 2005), the performance of mutipath routing under wormhole attack is studied. To detect this attack and to identify malicious nodes a scheme called Statistical Analysis of Multipath (SAM) has been proposed. The main idea of this scheme is based on the observation that certain statistics of the routes discovered by routing protocols change dramatically under wormhole attack. This chapter considers two statistics to detect the wormhole attack. First, the maximum relative frequency of link appearing in the set of all obtained routes (p^{max}) and second, the difference between the most frequently appeared and the second most frequently appeared link in the set of all route obtained routes from the route discovery. The chapter demonstrated that both

these statistics are much higher under wormhole attack that in the normal system.

Hu et al. (2003) introduce the notion of a packet leash as a general mechanism for detecting and defending against a wormhole attack. They have used the concept of geographical and temporal leash to restrict the maximum transmission distance of a packet. A temporal leash restricts the maximum travel distance by ensuring that the packet has an upper bound on its lifetime. To use temporal leash the sender includes the packet expiration time in the packet as an offset of the time at which it sends the packet. The packet expiration time is based on the allowed maximum transmission distance and the speed of light. The receiving node processes the packet to check if the temporal leash has expired in which case it drops the packet. The packet expiration time is authenticated to prevent an attacker from authenticating it. Protocol called TIK (Tesla with Instant Key disclosure) provides instant authentication of received packets.

Marianne, Azer, Sherif, Kassas, Hassan and Soudani (2008) have proposed a decentralized Intrusion Detection (ID) scheme using the concept of diffusion of innovations. Network monitors (NMs) monitor the suspected routing parameters for the wormhole attacks. These NMs are cooperative and exchange their local data through secure channels. The ID scheme is called persuasion and has two main phases. In the first phase called observations the NM attempts to form its own observation based on routing parameters and marks suspected nodes. In the second phase called the judgment these suspicious nodes are checked with the suspicious nodes in the other NMs list. Malicious nodes are marked with global consensus.

In the method described in (Wang & Wong, 2007), the sender estimates the shortest path between the sender and receiver using the Euclidean distance estimation model in terms of hopcounts (h_e) and compares it with the hopcount value (h_r) received in the ROUTE REPLY packet sent by the receiver. There is a huge probability that there is a wormhole if $h_r < h_e$. After the detection of a

Figure 5. WormHole Attack

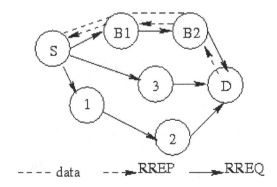

---- data   ----▶ RREP   ____▶ RREQ

wormhole a TRAINING procedure is launched by the source to identify the endpoints of a wormhole and the other nodes notified of malicious node.

5.2. Black Hole Attack

A Black Hole attack by Aad et al. (2004) is a kind of denial of service where a malicious node can attract all packets by falsely claiming a fresh route to the destination and then absorb them without forwarding them to the destination. Co-operative Black hole means the malicious nodes act in a group. When the source node wishes to transmit a data packet to the destination, it first sends out the RREQ packet to the neighboring nodes. The malicious nodes being part of the network, also receive the RREQ. Since the Black hole nodes have the characteristic of responding first to any RREQ, it immediately sends out the RREP. The RREP from the Black hole node reaches the source node, well ahead of the other RREPs. On receiving the RREP from BlackHole node, the source starts transmitting the data packets. On the receipt of data packets, the malicious node simply drops them, instead of forwarding to the destination (Figure 6). Thus the data packets get lost and never reach the intended destination.

5.2.1. Techniques for Detecting Blackhole Attack

In the method described by Raj and Swadas (2009), the node that receives RREP packet, compares the RREP_Seq_no with a dynamically updated threshold value, to detect a malicious node. The node then sends an ALARM packet to its neighboring node, so that the malicious node is isolated from the network.

(Shurman, Yoo, & Park, 2004) proposed two different approaches to solve blackhole attack. In first proposal the sender node needs to verify the authenticity of the node that initiates the RREP packet by utilizing network redundancy. The idea of this solution is to wait for the RREP packet to

arrive from more than two nodes. During this time the sender node buffers its packets until a safe route are identified. Once a safe route is identified, these buffered packets will be transmitted. But the main drawback of this algorithm is time delay. In the second proposal every node stores the last sent packet sequence number and last received packet sequence number. When a node receives a RREP from another node it checks the last sent packet sequence number and received packet sequence number. If there is any mismatch then it generates an alarm indicating the existence of a blackhole node.

Sun, Guan, Chen and Pooch (2003) used two additional control packets for collecting the neighborhood information for detecting blackhole node. The formats of these packets are

RQNS{Scr_addr,Dest_Addr,Request_neighbor_seq#,Next_hop}

and

RPNS{Scr_Addr,Dest_Addr,Request_neighbor_seq#,Neighbor_Set}

The basic idea of this approach is that the neighbor set difference of one node at different time instance is less than or equal to one, and the probability that the neighbor set difference of two nodes at same time instance is very small. After

Figure 6. BlackHole Attack

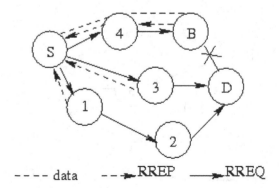

getting RREP from more than one node the sender sends the RQNS packet. After receiving more than one RPNS packet the sender node compare the received neighbor set, if the difference is larger than some predefined threshold value then the current network is affected by blackhole attack.

Yu, Kuang, Wu, Heng, Cheng and Chang (2007) proposed a distributed and cooperative procedure to detect blackhole node. Each node collects information through overhearing packets to evaluate if there is any suspicious node in its neighborhood. On finding one, the detecting node initiates local detection procedure to analyze whether the suspicious one is a malicious black hole node. Subsequently, cooperative detection procedure is initiated by the initial detection node, which proceeds by first broadcasting and notifying all the one-hop neighbors of the possible suspicious node to cooperatively participate in the decision process confirming that the node in question is indeed a malicious one. Voting scheme is used to identify a blackhole node.

Kurosawa, Nakayama, Kato, Jamalipour and Nemoto (2007) use an anomaly detection scheme using dynamic training method where the training data is updated at regular time intervals. To express state of the network at each node, multidimensional feature vector is defined. The feature vector contain {Number of sent RREQ messages, Number of received RREP messages, The average of difference of Dst Seq in each time slot between the sequence number of RREP message and the one held in the list}. Mean vector is calculated. The distance between the mean vector and input data sample is compared. If the difference is greater than some threshold value then there is an attack.

Deng, Li and Agrawal (2002) propose a solution for single blackhole node detection. Intermediate nodes send next hop information along with RREP. When the source node receives the reply message, it does not send the data packets right away, but extracts the next hop information from the reply packet and then sends a Further-Request to the next hop to verify that it has a

route to the intermediate node who sends back the Further reply message, and that it has a route to the destination node.

Ramaswamy, Fu, Sreekantaradhya, Dixon and Nygard (2003) proposed a method for identifying multiple black hole nodes. They are the first to propose a solution to cooperative or group black hole attack. The methodology works with slightly modified AODV protocol by introducing Data Routing Information (DRI) Table and Cross Checking. DRI table contains {Node ID, From, Through}. Every node maintains this table. They rely on reliable nodes (nodes through which the source node has routed data) to transfer data packets. When an intermediate node sends a RREP to a given source node, the Next Hop Node (NHN) and DRI entry of NHN should also be sent together. The Source node will then use the information together with its own DRI table to check whether the Intermediate Node (IN) is a reliable node. If it is not reliable, then it sends a Further Route Request to IN and queries NHN as to

(a) Weather IN has routed data packets through NHN
(b) Who is the current NHN's next hop to destination and
(c) Weather the current NHN routed data through its own next hop.

The NHN in turn responds with Further Route Reply message including

(a) DRI entry for IN
(b) The next hop node of current NHN, and
(c) The DRI entry for the current NHN's next hop.

Based on the Further Route Reply message from NHN, source node checks whether NHN is a reliable node or not.

5.3. GrayHole Attack

The Gray Hole attack is a kind of Denial of Service (DoS) attacks. In this attack, an adversary first exhibits behavior equivalent to an honest node during the route discovery process, and then silently drops some or all of the data packets sent to it for further forwarding even when no congestion occurs. The malicious node thus degrades the network performance and disturbs route discovery process.

5.3.1. Detection of GrayHole Attack

Xiaopeng and Wei (2007) propose three algorithms to detect gray hole attack:

(a)   The creating proof algorithm
(b)   The checkup and
(c)   The diagnosis algorithm

In the creating proof algorithm, all nodes involved in a session stores some proof based on aggregate signature algorithm on forwarded messages. The sender checks intermediate nodes after the detection of abnormal packet dropping and invokes the Checkup algorithm. The sender sends the Checkup Request (CREQ) message to which the intermediate nodes reply by Checkup Reply (CREP) message. By using the public keys of intermediate nodes, the message is verified and malicious nodes marked. In the diagnosis phase, the value of malicious node is increased if it fails to pass verification and when it reaches a predefined threshold, the node is accused of being malicious.

Marti, Giuli, Lai and Baker (2000) propose to trace malicious nodes by using watchdog/pathrater scheme. This scheme consists of two related algorithms

(a)   The watchdog algorithm and
(b)   The pathrater algorithm.

In the watchdog algorithm, the node's watchdog verifies that the next node forwards the packet forwarded by it by entering into a promiscuous mode. The next node will be suspected as malicious if it does not forward the packet in certain time interval. This node is accused of being malicious to the sender if its tally exceeds a predefined threshold. In the pathrater algorithm, the source node selects the path that will deliver packets with high probability, according to the reports provided by watchdogs equipped with each node in the network.

Awerbuch, Holmer, Rotaru and Rubens (2002) propose to detect malicious nodes by using acknowledgments sent by destination node. This scheme consists of three related algorithms

(a)   The route discovery with fault avoidance in which the source node discovers routes that is most likely to deliver packets by employing flooding, cryptography algorithms and weight list
(b)   The Byzantine fault detection in which the source node detects malicious nodes with Byzantine behavior using binary search technique and the input path
(c)   The link weight management algorithm updates the link weight

Just, Kranakis and Wan (2003) propose to detect malicious nodes by using probe technique which consists of three related algorithms

(a)   The probing path selection algorithm selects the probing paths
(b)   The probing algorithm detects possible malicious nodes in the probing path and
(c)   The diagnosis algorithm tests the possible malicious nodes by using the property of bi-directional communication link.

Huang, Avramopoulos, Kobayashi and Liu (2005) propose to detect malicious nodes based on one-way hash chain and one-time hash tag commitment. Each packet sent by the source node includes an element in the one-way hash chain, a one-way hash tag commitment of the destination node, and a commitment of the next packet. Each intermediate node verifies the previous one-way hash chain element with the current one-way hash chain element, and one-way hash tag commitment with the response provided by the destination node. Intermediate nodes also monitor the behavior of its succeeding node, and report the link state to the source node in an encrypted manner.

Shila and Anjali (2008) formulate a non-cooperative, non zero sum two player Markov game to detect a gray hole attack. There are two players in this game: the sender (player1) and the attacker (player 2). The objective of each player is to optimize the individual performance in terms of the packet delivery ratio. Each player chooses a strategy that gives it maximum returns in terms of utilities (or rewards). The attacker selects the strategy that maximizes the packet loss. The authors show that as the dropping probability of the attacker increases, the utility of the sender decreases. To counteract this situation, the player1 (sender) switches to a high cost secure path with high probability.

5.4. Detection of Cooperative Black and Gray Hole Attacks

Agrawal and Ghosh (2008) propose a protocol in which nodes with high computing power and radio range (strong nodes) maintain a backbone network to monitor traffic in ad hoc network and determine malicious nodes. The algorithm consists of two phases

(a) Core formation and maintenance phase in which the backbone network is formed
(b) Detection phase in which malicious nodes are detected

In the first phase, a new node entering the network becomes a regular node (RN), a backbone node (BN) or a backbone capable node (BCN). A coordination protocol is initialized between BN's to compute the best location of BCN, one that serves the highest number of RNs. In the detection phase the data packets are sent in small equal sized blocks. After every block of data, the source and destination node carry out an end-to-end checking with the assistance of backbone network to ensure that destination has received the data packets. If the check fails, the grayhole removal process starts. The first suspect is the node that sent the RREP packet. Based on the voting system by neighboring nodes, the suspect is confirmed malicious and dropped.

In (Deb, 2008), a two-phase cooperative detection mechanism is proposed. In the first phase, a malicious node is detected by taking the difference between the sequence number stored in the sequence table (SnT) and the *destination_seq_no* of RREP packet received at a node. If this difference is greater than a threshold, then the sender of RREP is marked as malicious and a notification is sent to the source node. In the second phase the mobile node cooperates to detect the blackhole node from the list of malicious nodes, by sending a test packet (TP) through the malicious node. The black hole will not forward the TP and is thus detected.

In (Banerjee, 2008), the neighbors forward the traffic flow of the nodes in the route. The source node elects the malicious nodes from the responses of monitoring nodes based on a voting process. Monitoring nodes check whether the monitored nodes forward packets to next node in the route. If the id of the next node is NULL, monitored node is marked as malicious. This node is avoided by searching for alternative secure path.

Tamilselvan and Sankaranarayanan (2008) propose use of a "Fidelity Table", where every node in the route is assigned a fidelity level that determines the reliability of that node. The unfaithful participation of the participating node decrements its fidelity level and this node is considered a black hole if this level reaches zero.

Alarm packets are sent to intimate other participating nodes to eliminate the black hole.

5.5. Rushing Attack

The rushing attack Hu, Perrig and Johnson (2003) acts as an effective denial-of-service attack against all currently proposed on-demand ad hoc network routing protocols. In an on-demand protocol, each node typically forwards only one ROUTE REQUEST that first arrives from each Route Discovery. In the rushing attack, the attacker exploits this property of the operation of Route Discovery by making sure that the ROUTE REQUESTs forwarded by it are the first to reach each neighbor of the target. Thus any route discovered includes a hop through the attacker. When a neighbor of the target receives the rushed REQUEST from the attacker, it forwards that REQUEST, and will not forward any further REQUESTS from this Route Discovery. When non-attacking REQUESTS arrive later at these nodes, they will discard those legitimate REQUESTS. As a result, the initiator is unable to discover any route that does not include the attacker containing at least two hops (three nodes). Thus all the data packets will pass through the attacker node that may choose to drop them. Hence the data packets never reach the destination. A misbehaving node that discards any packets passing through it can result in repeated retransmissions, which in turn cause network congestion.

5.5.1 Detection of Rushing Attack

Hu et al. (2003) propose a secure route discovery component called Rushing Attack Prevention [RAP] containing three mechanisms that prevent against rushing attack - Secure Neighbor Detection, Secure Route Delegation and Randomized ROUTE REQUEST forwarding. Secure Neighbor Detection protocol ensures that the sender and receiver of a ROUTE REQUEST are within communication range by using a mutual authentication protocol. The measured delay between the Neighbor Solicitation packet transmitted by the sender and Authenticated Neighbor Reply packet received by it from the responder provides an upper bound on the distance of the neighbor. The responder uses a similar approach to verify the sender. Secure Route Delegation mechanism is used to enable adjacent pair of nodes to verify that all the secure neighbor detection protocols were executed and that both neighbors believe that they are within transmission range. To thwart a rushing attack, the technique of randomized message forwarding is used in which nodes buffers REQUESTS and then forwards them at random.

5.6. Secure Wireless LAN Architecture

It is evident from the previous sections that MANETs are susceptible to a variety of security attacks that compromise its effective operation. Nodes may misbehave either because they are malicious, or because they are selfish and wish to conserve their own limited resources such as power, or for other reasons. Virendra and Upadhyaya (2005) propose a secure wireless LAN architecture (SWAN) that addresses the problem pertaining to malicious node behavior. The main components of SWAN are

(a)   The admission controller (AC) and

(b)   Global monitor (GM)

AC decides whether a new node should be included into the wireless network. This decision is based on the intent query scheme between the AC and the node to determine the trust level of the node. GM is responsible for proper functioning of the network.

6. CONCLUSION

In this chapter we have described Denial of Service attacks and countermeasures in the physical layer, link layer and network layer in MANETS. In particular, we have surveyed attacks and its available countermeasures in the network of the routing layer. The main routing protocols in use are AODV and DSR. In this chapter we have surveyed the techniques for detecting route disruption attacks. Some of these techniques detect attacks based on authenticating techniques viz. use of public private key pair. Others suggest making changes to the underlying routing protocol. Other techniques rely on the information exchanged between the neighboring nodes for the detection of malicious nodes.

In the wireless networks DoS attacks can be launched with very little effort but they can have huge impact. The effort to launch attacks reduces further with the availability of automated tools to carry out the attacks. Though it is difficult to detect and isolate the source of the attack, available countermeasures must be utilized to lower the risk of these attacks.

REFERENCES

Aad, I., Hubaux, J.-P., & Knightly, E. W. (2004). *Denial of service resilience in ad hoc networks.* Proc. Of ACM MobiCom '04, 202- 215.

Agrawal, P., & Ghosh, R. K. (2008). *Cooperative black and gray hole attacks in mobile ad hoc networks.* Proceedings of the 2nd International Conference on Ubiquitous Information Management and Communication, 310 – 314.

AL-Shurman, M., Yoo, S. M., & Park, S. (2004). *Black hole attack in mobile ad hoc networks.* AC-MSE'04, 96 - 97.

Anonymous. (1999). Draft international standard ISO/IEC 8802-11 IEEE P802.11/D10. *LAN MAN Standards Committee of IEEE Computer Society.*

Anonymous,. (1999). *Wireless LAN medium access control and physical layer specifications. IEEE 802.11 Standards.* IEEE Computer Society LAN MAN Standards Committee.

Awerbuch, B., Holmer, D., Nita-Rotaru, C., & Rubens, H. (2002). *An on-demand secure routing protocol resilient to byzantine failures.* ACM Workshop on Wireless Security (WiSe), 21 - 30.

Azer, M. A., El-Kassas, S. M., Hassan, A. W. F., Magdy S., & El-Soudani. (2008). *Intrusion detection for wormhole attacks in ad hoc networks: A survey and a proposed decentralized scheme.* The Third International Conference on Availability, Reliability and Security, 636-641.

Banerjee, S. (2008). *Detection/removal of cooperative black and gray hole attack in mobile ad-hoc networks.* Proceedings of the World Congress on Engineering and Computer Science, 337-342.

Bellardo, J., & Savage, S. (2003). *802.11 Denial-of-service attacks: Real vulnerabilities and practical solutions.* Proceedings of The 12th Conference on USENIX Security Symposium, 15 – 28.

Bu, T., Norden, S., & Woo, T. M. (n.d.). *Detection of power-drain denial-of-service attacks in wireless networks.* European Patent: EP1708538.

Buchegger, S., & Le Boudec, J. (2002). *Performance analysis of the CONFIDANT protocol: Cooperation of nodes - Fairness in dynamic ad-hoc networks.* Proceedings of the 3rd ACM International Symposium on Mobile Ad hoc Networking and Computing (MobiHoc,) 226-236.

Carter, S., & Yasinsac, A. (2002). *Secure position aided ad hoc routing.* Proceedings of the IASTED International Conference on Communications and Computer Networks.

Chang, W. Y., Wu, T.-K., Cheng, R. H., & Chang, S. C. (2007). *A distributed and cooperative black hole node detection and elimination mechanism for ad hoc network. Emerging Technologies in Knowledge Discovery and Data Mining* (pp. 538–549). New York: Springer-Verlag.

Deb, M. (2008). *A cooperative blackhole node detection mechanism for ad hoc networks.* Proceedings of the World Congress on Engineering and Computer Science, (pp. 343 – 347).

Deng, H., Li, W., & Agrawal, D. P. (2002). Routing security in wireless ad-hoc network. *IEEE Communications Magazine, 40*, 70–75. doi:10.1109/MCOM.2002.1039859

Desilva, S., & Boppana, R. (2004). On the impact of noise sensitivity on performance in 802.11 based ad hoc networks. *Proceeding of International Conference on Communications 7*, 4372- 4376.

Desilva, S., & Boppana, R. V. (2005). Mitigating malicious control packet floods in ad hoc networks. *Proceedings of IEEE WCNC, 05*, 2112–2117.

Gu, Q., Liu, P., Zhu, S., & Chu, C. H. (2005). Defending against packet injection in unreliable ad hoc networks. *Proc. of IEEE GLOBECOM '05, 3*, 1837 - 1841.

Gummadi, R., Wetherall, D., Greenstein, B., & Seshan, S. (2007). *Understanding and mitigating the impact of RF interference on 802.11 networks.* Proceedings of the ACM SIGCOMM, 385–396.

Gupta, V., Krishnamurthy, S., & Faloutsous, M. (2002). *Denial of service attacks at the MAC layer in wireless ad hoc networks.* Proceedings of MILCOM. http://www.ietf.org/html.charters/manet-charter.html

Hu, Y., Perrig, A., & Johnson, D.B. (2005). Ariadne: A secure on-demand routing protocol for ad hoc networks. *Wireless Networks, 11(1 – 2)*, 21 – 38.

Hu, Y. C., Perrig, A., & Johnson, D. B. (2003). Packet leashes: A defense against wormhole attacks in wireless networks. *Proc. of IEEE INFOCOM '03, 3*, 1976 - 1986.

Hu, Y. C., Perrig, A., & Johnson, D. B. (2003). Rushing attacks and defense in wireless ad hoc network routing protocols. *Proc. of ACM WiSe*, 30 - 40.

Huang, Q., Avramopoulos, I. C., Kobayashi, H., & Liu, B. (2005). Secure data forwarding in wireless ad hoc networks. *IEEE International Conference on Communications, ICC 2005, 5*, 3525-3531.

Johnson, D. B., Maltz, D. A., & Hu, Y. (2007). The dynamic source routing protocol for mobile ad hoc networks. *IETF RFC 4728.*

Just, M., Kranakis, E., & Wan, T. (2003). *Resisting malicious packet dropping in wireless ad hoc networks.* Ad – Hoc, Mobile, and Wireless Networks, 2865. Berlin: Springer Berlin/Heidelberg, 151-163.

Kurosawa, S., Nakayama, H., Kato, N., Jamalipour, A., & Nemoto, Y. (2007). Detecting blackhole attack on AODV-based mobile ad hoc networks by dynamic learning method. *International Journal of Network Security, 5(3)*, 338–346.

Marti, S., Giuli, T. J., Lai, K., & Baker, M. (2000). *Mitigating routing misbehavior in mobile ad hoc networks.* Proceedings of the Sixth Annual ACM/IEEE International Conference on Mobile Computing and Networking (MOBICOM 2000), 255 - 265.

Martin, T., Hsiao, M., Ha, D., & Krishnaswami, J. (2004). *Denial-of-service attacks on battery-powered mobile computers.* Proceedings of the Second IEEE Annual Conference on Pervasive Computing and Communications, 309.

Michiardi, P., & Molva, R. (2002). CORE: A collaborative reputation mechanism to enforce node cooperation in mobile ad hoc networks. *IFIP-Communication and Multimedia Security Conference*, 107 – 121.

Perkins, C., Belding-Royer, E., & Das, S. (2003). Ad hoc on-demand distance vector routing. *IETF RFC 3561.*

Raj, P. N., & Swadas, P. B. (2009). DPRAODV: A dynamic learning system against blackhole attack in AODV based manet. *IJCSI International Journal of Computer Science Issues, 2*, 54–59.

Ramaswamy, S., Fu, H., Sreekantaradhya, M., Dixon, J., & Nygard, K. (2003). *Prevention of cooperative black hole attack in wireless ad hoc networks.* Proceedings of International Conference on Wireless Network.

Sanzgiri, K., Levine, N., Shields, C., Dahill, B., & Belding-Royer, E. M. (2002). *A secure routing protocol for ad hoc networks*. ICNP, Proceedings of the 10th IEEE International Conference on Network Protocols, 78 – 89.

Shila, D. M., & Anjali, T. (2008). Game theoretic approach to gray hole attacks in wireless mesh networks. *IEEE Military Communications Conference,* 1 – 7.

Song, N., Qian, L., & Li, X. (2005). *Wormhole attacks detection in wireless ad hoc networks: A statistical analysis approach.* 19th IEEE International Parallel and Distributed Processing Symposium (IPDPS'05) Workshop. 289a.

Sun, B., Guan, Y., Chen, J., & Pooch, U. W. (2003). Detecting black-hole attack in mobile ad hoc network. *5th European Personal Mobile Communications Conference,* 490 - 495.

Tamilselvan, L., & Sankaranarayanan, V. (2008). Prevention of co-operative black hole attack in MANET. *Journal of Networks, 3*(5), 13–20. doi:10.4304/jnw.3.5.13-20

Toledo, A. L., & Wang, X. (2008). Robust detection of MAC layer denial-of-service attacks in CSMA/CA wireless networks. *IEEE Transactions on Information Forensics and Security, 3*(3), 347–358. doi:10.1109/TIFS.2008.926098

Virendra, M., & Upadhyaya, S. (2004). SWAN: A secure wireless LAN architecture. *Proceedings of the 29th Annual IEEE International Conference on Local Computer Networks,* 216 – 223.

Virendra, M., Upadhyaya, S., Kumar, V., & Anand, V. (2005). SAWAN: A survivable architecture for wireless LANs. *Proceedings of the Third IEEE International Workshop on Information Assurance,* 71 – 82.

Wang, X., & Wong, J. (2007). An end-to-end detection of wormhole attack in wireless ad-hoc networks. *31st Annual International Computer Software and Applications Conference, 1,* 39-48.

Williams, B., & Camp, T. (2002). Comparison of broadcasting techniques for mobile ad hoc networks. *Proceedings of the 3rd ACM International Symposium on Mobile Ad hoc Networking and Computing,* pp. 194-205. New York: ACM Press.

Xiaolong, L., & Zeng, Q. (2006). Capture effect in the IEEE 802.11 WLANs with rayleigh fading, shadowing, and path loss. *IEEE International Conference on Wireless and Mobile Computing, Networking and Communications,* 110-115.

Xiaopeng, G., & Wei, C. (2007). A novel gray hole detection scheme for mobile ad hoc networks. *IFIP international Conference on Network and Parallel Computing,* 209 - 214.

Xu, W., Ma, K., Trappe, W., & Zhang, Y. (2006). Jamming in sensor networks: attack and defense strategies. *IEEE Network, 20*(3), 41–47. doi:10.1109/MNET.2006.1637931

Xu, W., Trappe, W., Zhang, Y., & Wood, T. (2005). The feasibility of launching and detecting jamming attacks in wireless networks. *MobiHoc, 05,* 46–57.

Yi, P., Dai, Z., Zhong, Y., & Zhang, S. (2005). Resisting flooding attacks in ad hoc networks. *Proceedings of the International Conference on Information Technology: Coding and Computing, II,* 657–662.

Yi, S. Naldurg, & P. Kravets, R. (2001). Security aware routing protocol for wireless ad hoc networks. *Proceedings of ACM International Symposium on Mobile Ad Hoc Networking and Computing.*

Zapata, M. G., & Asokan, N. (2002). Securing ad hoc routing protocols. *Proc. ACM Workshop on Wireless Security* (WiSe), 1 – 10.

Zhou, Y., Wu, D., & Nettles, S. (2004). Analyzing and preventing MAC-layer denial of service attacks for stock 802.11 systems. *Workshop on BWSA, BROADNETS.*

Chapter 11

Detecting Cheating Aggregators and Report Dropping Attacks in Wireless Sensor Networks

Mohit Virendra
State University of New York at Buffalo, USA

Qi Duan
State University of New York at Buffalo, USA

Shambhu Upadhyaya
State University of New York at Buffalo, USA

ABSTRACT

This chapter focuses on an important, challenging and yet largely unaddressed problem in Wireless Sensor Networks (WSN) data communication: detecting cheating aggregators and malicious/selfish discarding of data reports en route to the Base Stations (BSs). If undetected, such attacks can significantly affect the performance of applications. The goal is to make the aggregation process tamper-resistant so that the aggregator cannot report arbitrary values, and to ensure that silent discarding of data reports by intermediate en-route nodes is detected in a bounded fashion. In our model, individual node readings are aggregated into data reports by Aggregator Nodes or Cluster Heads and forwarded to the BS. BS performs a two-stage analysis on these reports: (a) Verification through attached proofs, (b) Comparison with Proxy Reports for ensuring arrival accuracy. Proofs are non-interactive verifiers sent with reports to attest correctness of reported values. Proxy Reports are periodically sent along alternate paths by non-aggregator nodes, piggybacked on data reports from other nodes. The model is intended as a guide for implementing security in real sensor network applications. It is simple and comprehensive, covering a variety of data formats and aggregation models: numeric and non-numeric data and aggregators located across one or multiple hops. Security analysis shows that the reports, both primary and proxy, cannot be forged by any outsiders and the contents of the reports are held confidential and the scheme is robust against collusion attacks. Lightweight design aims at minimal additional control and energy overhead. Simulation results show its fault tolerance against random and patterned node failures.

DOI: 10.4018/978-1-60960-123-2.ch011

INTRODUCTION

Wireless Sensor Networks (WSNs) are finding increased application in data collection operations, especially in hostile terrains, wartime operations and in emergency responder systems. Aerial scattering or similar quick and infrastructure-less installation of sensor nodes and strategic positioning of Base Stations (BSs) allows rapid network deployment. Individual sensor readings are aggregated into data reports by Aggregator Nodes (ANs) or Cluster Heads (CHs) and forwarded to the BSs. Data collected at the BS in such scenarios may be critical for decision making (e.g., tracking moving enemy targets). Any en route data tampering or data loss will result in inaccurate collection at the BS and significantly affect the underlying decision making process besides depleting the nodes' battery power (Karlof & Wagner, 2003). Admissible robustness and dependability in data reporting are thus desirable.

Wireless channel constraints, computational capability of sensor nodes and battery power issues are inhibitors to attaining these goals. Adverse ambient deployment conditions may additionally magnify the impact of any attacks or Byzantine failures in the network, enhancing the success-probability for an adversary.

1.1 Threat Model and Problem Definition

WSN security research has chiefly concentrated on key management, secure broadcast, Sybil attacks and false data injection attacks (Zhu et al, 2004) (Chan et al, 2003)(Chan, 2005)(Newsome, 2004). Even though these schemes assume data reports to be end-to-end encrypted between aggregators and BS, the reports may still be:

- *Misaggregated* in the first place by cheating aggregators (Wu,2006) or compromised aggregators (Perrig, 2003) and this

may go undetected if aggregation occurs across multiple hops, or
- Selectively dropped by malicious aggregators or other intermediate nodes along the path to the BS

Such miasggregation and discarding are very simple exploits which abuse the basic open-air property of the wireless channel. It would be very hard to distinguish genuine data-aggregation, in-network-processing and passive-participation operations[1] from malicious altering or arbitrary discarding of data reports. These hard-to-detect attacks constitute the system-centric threat model of our chapter.

For better understanding, we formally define *Misaggregation* and *Report Dropping* Attacks as follows:

- **Misaggregation:** ANs/CHs deliberately send incorrect values in the data reports to the BS. This attack is especially relevant when the aggregation occurs across more than one wireless hops (large clusters); not all the nodes in the aggregation group or cluster can "hear back" and verify the reports forwarded to the BS by the aggregator.
- **Report Dropping:** Intermediate nodes en route to the BS deliberately and unnecessarily drop data reports to skew/adversely-affect the data collection process at the BS.

The BS should be able to detect in a determinate fashion if node readings are deviant (indicating anomalies in the aggregation process, possibly due to aggregators reporting incorrect values). It should be able to pinpoint cheating/misreporting aggregators and be able to detect any malicious extraneous/superfluous/unnecessary dropping or discarding of reports as well. Both these problems are considered collectively because their solution achieves the same end goal: reducing incorrect data collection at the BS (It is seen eventually that the solution of latter problem is achieved as a design by-product of achieving the former goal).

Existing security schemes cannot detect these attacks (Sec. 2.1) and neither can the communication reliability schemes (e.g., TCP (http://www.faqs.org/rfcs/rfc793.html)) be effective against them (Sec. 2.2). These attacks can be extremely impacting with limited effort from an adversary. It is thus necessary to develop efficient solutions for detecting them. Such solutions if used in conjunction with schemes to prevent false data injection (Zhu et al, 2004)(Chan & Perrig,2005), could result in enhancing the dependability and achieving enhanced reliability in sensor networks data communication.

1.2 Summary of Contributions

This chapter adopts cryptographic techniques to address the following security problems in the WSN domain: detecting cheating aggregators and arbitrary report dropping by the nodes. A comprehensive, yet simple and practical solution methodology encompassing different data formats and aggregation models is presented: numeric and non-numeric data; and aggregators located across one or multiple hops. The salient attributes can be summarized as:

- Specific report verification techniques at BS for different data types and aggregation models built on mathematical analysis of cluster size and aggregator area coverage.
- Design of **non-interactive***verifiers/proofs* sent with data reports to BS for assuring the accuracy of values reported by the aggregator. These proofs bound the error margins of reported values; values outside bounds confirm cheating. This is in contrast to previously proposed interactive proofs (Perrig, Przydatek & Song, 2003)which are not practical for sensor networks.

- Design of a *Proxy Reports* scheme for additional robustness. Proxy reports are periodically generated by non-aggregator nodes within the aggregation group/cluster and sent along alternate paths to BS. Comparison with them builds further confidence on the correctness of received data reports. Thorough analysis and mathematical techniques for comparison and cheating detection are developed.
- Analytical security evaluation that includes attacks against the model and collusion detection.

Thus, individual node readings are aggregated into data reports and a two-stage analysis of received data reports occurs at the BS: (a) Verification through attached proofs, (b) Comparison with Proxy Reports for ensuring arrival accuracy. Proxy Reports are piggybacked on data reports from other aggregators to reduce communication overhead. All this is achieved in **a single round of communication**.

1.3 Advances over Exiting Techniques

Our model utilizes two existing techniques in WSN security literature as its base and makes significant advances over them. These two techniques are stated below for better understanding of our work and to put our contributions in perspective:

- In Secure Information Aggregation (SIA) (Perrig, Przydatek & Song, 2003), Perrig et al. first utilized Sampling Theory and statistical techniques to ensure data authentication and to detect cheating/tampering in WSNs. Their "aggregate-commit-prove" approach mandated that an aggregator "commit" to the aggregated data before sending it to the BS (commitment enables non-repudiation and cheating detection at BS). The aggregator then "proves" the accuracy of the reported data to the BS through *interactive* proofs. This enables the BS to evaluate whether these reported quantities were within a good approximation of the individual sensor readings. The paper detailed proofs for some commonly reported numeric functions (MIN, MAX and MEDIAN).

The model claimed *sub-linear* communication overhead for proving accuracy of the *committed data* to the BS. However the overhead is sub-linear *in terms of number of reporting nodes*, simply implying that the model performs better than sending each node's individual data (i.e., no aggregation). The interactive nature of the *aggregator-BS proofs* may require multiple rounds of aggregator-BS communication to attest correctness of each reported value. Clearly the associated communication overhead would make such a technique impractical for WSN applications.

SIA model is important in that it is the only body of work to address aggregator cheating (see Sec. 2.1), but a model with constant or linear communication overhead *in terms of number of reports sent to the BS* is more desirable and practically realizable. Though Wu et al (2006) proposed some improvements over the base SIA model, their Secure Aggregation Tree (SAT) scheme heavily relied on child node monitoring parent node and the child and parent together forming a non-malicious clique. The assumption that at least one of parent or child nodes is always non-malicious is restrictive and not always practically realizable, and will not work for scenarios where a parent and child are non malicious but a series of upstream nodes towards BS are malicious.

Additionally, SIA did not consider any aggregation model, topologies or report formats: i.e., how data would be received by an aggregator, which subsets of nodes can the aggregator hear from, which nodes' data it would report to BS and

how would it construct a report and send it to BS. Our model addresses both these issues. Designing non-interactive proofs append-capable with the reports (one proof per report) is a non-trivial task.

- Zhu et al. proposed the first secure WSN cluster data aggregation model (Zhu et al, 2004). The topology assumptions in their model were stringent and restrictive and it only considered clusters with a fixed number of nodes (say p) where all nodes are within one hop of each other. Additionally, the CH was assumed to be non-malicious and the model did not consider cheating aggregators and report dropping attacks. We utilize their baseline secure-aggregation model, relax both these assumptions and incorporate large clusters and aggregation across multiple hops.

1.4 Chapter Organization

The rest of this chapter is organized as follows: Section 2 reviews additional related work, discusses the network and security assumptions and gives the conceptual description of our scheme. Section 3 describes the design considerations for various report formats and aggregation topologies. Section 4 details report verification and consistency-check techniques at the BS along with the special cases of area coverage for large clusters. Section 5 elaborates the construction of proofs for representative functions. In Section 6, we give techniques on how the BS detects cheating, i.e., we give the error bounds of some key representative functions. In Section 7 we analyze the key security features of our scheme. Section 8 presents experimental results. Finally, Section 9 concludes the chapter by analyzing the current status and future direction of this research in terms of applications and summarizes its contributions.

2 RELATED WORK, ASSUMPTIONS, TECHNIQUE OVERVIEW

2.1 Prior Work in Reliable Data Delivery and Security in the WSN Domain

We briefly review relevant literature on data delivery robustness in WSN domain before analyzing the existing security schemes.

Reliable Data Delivery in Sensor Networks: Akyldiz et al. (2003) consider the problem of reliable downstream point-to-multipoint data delivery, from the sink to the sensors. Wan et al. (2002) propose the first *reliable* transport protocol for wireless sensor networks by "pumping data at slow pace" in networks with light traffic. Deb et al. (2003) provide schemes for differential Quality of Service in Sensor Networks. SPROID (Scalable Protocol for Robust Information Dissemination) (Hari, 2004), tags data generated with a unique identifier and provides reliable data delivery to all the sensor nodes in the network. Dunkels et al.(2004) provide data caching techniques for interfacing WSNs with overlay TCP-based networks. Though these schemes aim at "admissible data reliability", they don't assume the presence of an adversary that maliciously disrupts the network functioning. These schemes will fail under our threat model described in Sec. IA. Next, we discuss the literature on key management followed by specific attacks on WSNs.

Encryption and Authentication: Zhu et al. (2003) and Ning et al.(2003) describe key establishment and management schemes for sensor networks. In TESLA Perrig et al. (2002) present schemes for secure authentication in multicast communication. SPINS (2001) enhances this scheme to include SNEP (data confidentiality, two-party data authentication, and evidence of data freshness) and μTESLA (authenticated broadcast for severely resource-constrained environments). Further improvements are provided

through a Random Key Pre-distribution scheme (Chan, 2003). Another low-overhead variant is a symmetric key distribution protocol for large scale sensor networks (Chan, 2005) which uses en-route sensor nodes as trusted intermediaries to facilitate key establishment. All these schemes are focused on data confidentiality and integrity through encryption. Our model assumes the presence of such schemes to ensure that if the data is encrypted by a non-malicious node, it will not be compromised. However, our model has tougher assumptions/requirement in that it considers that the encrypting node (aggregator or CH) can be malicious and the goal is to detect such maliciousness without repeatedly querying the nodes (scheme should be feasible for resource-constrained sensor networks).

Attacks and Detection: Zhu et al. (2004) present an interleaved hop-by-hop authentication scheme for filtering of injected false data in sensor networks. As described in Sec. IC, this scheme is very restrictive in the topology model it considers. Shukla and Qiao (2007) enhance this model to distinguish data transience from falsely injected data. Perrig et al. (2004) present a scheme to deal with Sybil attacks (node illegitimately assumes the identities of multiple nodes) on sensor networks. They broaden the attack model in "Distributed Detection of Node Replication Attacks in Sensor Networks" (Parno et al, 2007). Key distribution problems in environments with a partially present, passive adversary are discussed by Anderson et al. (2004); a node wishing to communicate securely with other nodes simply generates a symmetric key and sends it in the clear to its neighbors. These schemes patch important vulnerabilities in the WSN domain; our model assumes that they secure the network from the attacks mentioned above. Lastly, two bodies of work with threat models closest to ours are discussed below.

DDMA and SIA: Two possibilities for malicious aggregators/forwarding-nodes to stage Denial-of-Service attacks on BS-node communication by exploiting the wireless channel properties are: (i) Suppress/misrepresent BS broadcasts to the nodes (BS→Node communication), or (ii) Suppress/misrepresent data sent to the BS (Node→BS communication). "Detection of Denial-of-Message Attacks on Sensor Network Broadcasts" (DDMA) (McCune, 2005) presents a game theory based Secure Implicit Sampling (SIS) scheme for BS to probabilistically determine nodes' failure to receive its broadcasts. This is directed towards the first category of attacks. SIA (Perrig et al, 2003), on the other hand, is the only prior work focusing on the second problem.

As is evident from the review, no single existing scheme is able to provide a comprehensive and feasible solution for aggregators and forwarding nodes misrepresenting or suppressing information sent by sensors to the BS, especially when aggregation may occur across several hops. This chapter attempts to address this deficiency in the literature by offering a simple unified solution.

2.2 Assumptions

Network Model: We consider a cluster-based sensor network model with each cluster having a unique ID. The nodes within a cluster forward their data to the CH which aggregates and sends this data to the BS in the form of data reports (equivalently, a tree based aggregation model could be considered where the leaf nodes gather data and aggregation can occur at one or more levels in the tree, with the BS being the root of the tree). We assume the network to comprise of current generation of sensor motes, e.g., the Berkeley MICA/MICA2 Motes (Perrig et al, 2001)(Hill et al, 2000)(http://www.xbow.com/Products/)(http://www-bsac.eecs.berkeley.edu/projects/cotsbots)(Zhang et al, 2005)(http://www.ieee802.org/15/pub/TG4.html). Cluster organization is static, but the role of the CH may rotate according to some popular protocols (Heinzelman, 2000)(Lindsey & Raghavendra, 2002)(Kulik et al, 1999). All links are bi-directional, though the cost of sending data may be different from CHs to BS than from BS to CHs (Stann & Heidemann, 2003)(Karlof & Wagner, 2003). Data forwarding/routing is performed using well known schemes (Stann & Heidemann, 2005) and route updates and path repair (after node failures) can be performed on-the-fly. Route computation, route maintenance and routing protocols are addressed extensively in the literature (Krishnamachari et al, 2002)(Braginsky & Estrin, 2002)(Schurgers & Srivastava, 2001)(Xu et al, 2001)(Khalil et al, 2005) and hence details are omitted here.

Security Model: The aggregated data reports from CH to the BS are end-to-end encrypted; they cannot be tampered or forged by any en-route node from CH to BS without detection. Well known network key management schemes (Zhu et al, 2003)(Liu, 2003))(Liu, 2003) are present: nodes are pre-loaded with keying material, they can establish and update keys on-the-fly. New keys can be established and managed as and when old nodes are removed from the network. Nodes in a cluster share a common group key with the BS which is used for encrypting the cluster's reports. Nodes also share pair-wise keys with their one-hop neighbors and can establish pair-wise keys with other nodes as required. Thus, non-malicious nodes have a way of securely communicating with each other (by renewing keys) even when malicious nodes are detected in the network. Finally, the BS is never compromised.

2.3 Technique Overview

The nodes within a cluster that monitor certain events and generate data are known as aggregation nodes. One of the nodes in a cluster, called Cluster Head (CH) or Aggregator Node (AN) is tasked to generate a primary data report based on the data monitored by the aggregation nodes. An aggregation node periodically creates a proxy (backup) report utilizing data from nodes that are within one-hop distance from it. It can then send this proxy report to the BS on a route *mostly dif-*

ferent from the data report's route[2]. This report will work as a periodic consistency-checker for the data reports. Overhead can be minimized by piggybacking the proxy reports with the data reports from other clusters, enabling efficient path and channel reuse. The BS may thus receive two versions of data reports (data and proxy) from the sensor suite and may perform a two stage analysis: (a) Verify the data reports through information included in them, (b) Check for consistency by comparing the data and proxy reports. This is in addition to inbuilt checks in the reports (like Error Correcting Codes) to detect any transmission/channel errors or any tampering by non-aggregator en-route nodes. The specific verification techniques and the data-proxy consistency-check depend on the nature/contents of the data reports and the cluster size or aggregation model.

Two aggregation models are considered: (a) the aggregator is no more than 1-hop from all aggregation nodes (or CH is within 1-hop of all cluster nodes), and (b) when aggregator may be more than 1-hop from some aggregation nodes (not all cluster nodes are within radio-range of the CH). Besides, two different report types are considered: numeric values (e.g., temperature readings), or non-numeric data-string format.

For small cluster sizes, reports sent to the BS contain *XMAC* values for verification. An XMAC value (Zhu, 2004) is the XOR combination of encrypted message authentication codes (HMAC or encrypted-MAC of messages) sent by individual sensors. For large clusters with numeric report formats, Merkle hash tree (Merkle, 1989) (Merkle, 1980) based non-interactive function-specific proofs are sent to the BS along with the reports for verification. Finally, for large clusters with string data format, the reports sent to the BS contain the HMAC values with some compression function applied to the reports. The BS uses the XMAC values or the non-interactive proofs enclosed in the data reports to ensure that the data reports have been received accurately without any errors or en-route tampering. The BS compares

the data and proxy reports and verifies whether they are within certain error margins.

3 REPORT FORMATS: DESIGN CONSIDERATIONS

There are four different cases pertaining to small and large sized clusters and number and string format reports, each having different security and reliability implications. Below, we first present the notations used in the remainder of this chapter to describe the reports.

3.1 Report Format: Notations

- C is the id of the cluster.
- CH is the id of the cluster head.
- K_{BC} is the pairwise key between the base station and cluster head CH.
- K_{Bp} is the pairwise key between the base station and backup node P.
- K_{Bi} is the pairwise key between the base station and sensor node i.
- $R_1, R_2, ..., R_n$ are the data collected by node 1, 2, ..., n, respectively.
- $id_1, id_2, ..., id_n$ are the ids of node 1, 2, ..., n, respectively.
- Seq is the sequence number of the report.
- $Nonce$ is the random number used only for the report to guarantee message freshness.
- $E_K(M)$ is the symmetric encryption of message M with key K.
- $HMAC_K(M)$ is the encrypted message authentication code of message M with key K.
- $H(M)$ is the hash function of message M.

3.2 Report Format and Cluster Size: Different Cases

(1)   Small Cluster Size: String Format Report

Data Report:

$Seq, Nonce, CH, C, E_{K_w}$

$((R_1, id_1) \| \cdots \| (R_n, id_n)) \|$

$XMAC \| Seq \| Nonce \| CH \| C)$

where $XMAC = HMAC_{K_{B1}}(R_1, id_1) \, XOR \ldots$

$XOR \quad HMAC_{K_{Bn}}(R_n, id_n)$

Proxy Report:

$Seq, Nonce, id_p, C, E_{K_w}((R_1', id_1') \| \cdots \|$

$(R_k', id_k') \| XMAC \| Seq \| Nonce \| id_p \| C)$

where

$XMAC = HMAC_{K_{n_1}'}(R_1', id_1') \, XOR$

$\cdots XOR \quad HMAC_{K_{m}'}(R_k', id_k')$

$id_1', \ldots, id_k'$ are the ids of the nodes whose data was received by the backup node P; $R_1', \ldots, R_k'$ are the data values received from those nodes; $K_{B1}', \cdots, K_{Bk}'$ are the corresponding pair-wise keys between those nodes and BS. To reduce the size of the transmitted reports, the concatenation operator $\|$ in $Seq\|Nonce\|CH\|C$ in the encrypted part can be replaced by the XOR operator. It is important to mention that a data report and its corresponding proxy report would use the same sequence number *Seq*. However, the *Nonce* used would be unique for each report.

(2)   Small Cluster Size: Numeric Format Report

This is identical to (1) above.

(3)   Large Cluster Size, Numeric Format Report

This scenario uses Merkle hash trees. In a Merkle hash tree, every parent is the hash of the concatenation of its two children, and the root of the tree is the commitment of all leaf nodes. Fig.

1 shows the Merkle hash tree of eight nodes. To authenticate a specific leaf node, (e.g., $R_4 id_4 S_4$) the prover needs to provide only the remaining non-generate values from the leaf to the root (r_{32}, r_{20}, r_{11}, r_0) (Perrig et al, 2003). Merkle hash trees also have the following properties which would make them especially suited for this WSN model:

- Given the root of the Merkle hash tree, it is not possible to recover any of the non-root nodes, including the leaf-nodes. This ensures security.
- Changing the root of the Merkle hash tree will lead to failure in future commitment verification. This ensures cheating detection.
- A single message can be the commitment of multiple messages. This ensures reduced communication overhead for WSNs

Data Report:

$Seq, Nonce, CH, C, E_{K_w}$

$(f(R_1, \cdots, R_n) \| r_0 \| proof \| Seq \| Nonce \| CH \| C)$

where f is the function to be computed over collected data in the cluster (e.g., *min* or *max*); r_0 is the root of the Merkle hash tree of the collected data; *proof* is the proof for the BS to verify the correctness of the report, which will be discussed in Section V.

The leaves of the Merkle hash tree are in the format (R_i, id_i, S_i), where $S_i = HMAC_{K_{Bi}}(R_i, id_i)$.

Proxy Report:

$Seq, Nonce, id_p, C, E_{K_w}(f(R_1', \cdots, R_k')$

$\| r_0 \| proof \| Seq \| Nonce \| id_p \| C)$

Again, a data report and its corresponding proxy report would use the same sequence num-

Figure 1. Eight-Node Merkel Hash Tree

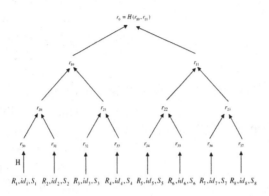

ber *Seq,* but the *Nonce* used would be unique for each report. Also, the root of the Merkle Hash tree would be different in the data and proxy reports.

The construction of *proof* will be dependent on the specific function that is being computed. The details of constructing non-interactive proofs for two of the most common representative functions, *median* and *min (max)* are presented in Section V.

(4) Large Cluster Size, String Format Report

Data Report:

$Seq, Nonce, CH, C, E_{K_{BC}}$

$(Comp \ (R_1 \| \cdots \| R_n) \| XMAC \| Seq \| Nonce \| CH \| C)$

where *Comp* is some lightweight compression function and

$$XMAC = HMAC_{K_{B1}} (R_1, id_1) XOR ... XOR$$
$$HMAC_{K_{Bn}} R_n, id_n)$$

Proxy Report:

$Seq, Nonce, id_p, C, E_{K_{Bp}}$

$(Comp(R_1' \| \cdots \| R_k') \| XMAC \| Seq \| Nonce \| id_p \| C)$

where $XMAC = HMAC_{K_{B1}}$ $(R_1', id_1') XOR...$ $XOR \ HMAC_{K_{Bk}}$ (R_k', id_k') and other notations have the same meaning as in case (1).

Again, the concatenation operator $\|$ in $Seq\|Nonce\|CH\|C$ in the encrypted part can be replaced by the XOR operator for size reduction. The next three sections present the details of report verification and consistency checks for cheating detection that need to be performed at the Base Station to validate each received data report.

4 REPORT VERIFICATION AT BS

We first describe how the BS manages each report-format/cluster-size scenario described above. Small cluster size implies that each node in a cluster is within every other node's radio range, implying that under most circumstances, the data and the proxy reports would be almost identical (or a close approximation of each other). This would make the consistency-check relatively straightforward, a direct comparison of the two reports. Additional checks are required for large clusters with string and numeric format data reports, taking into consideration the area coverage of the backup nodes. This is discussed next.

The design of Merkle hash tree based non-interactive proofs for representative functions for large-size clusters with numeric format data reports are elaborated in Sec. V.

4.1 Report Formats and Cluster Sizes: Computation at BS

(1)   Small Cluster Size: String Format Report

To verify the validity of a report (either data or proxy), the BS needs to investigate the following:

*   The sequence number, nonce and ids of cluster and CH (or backup node) in the plaintext part of the report are the same as that in the encrypted part.
*   The nonce is fresh; it has not been used previously.
*   The XMAC is correct. Since the BS has all the pairwise keys, it can independently compute the XMAC after receiving the report.

To check for consistency between the data report and proxy report, the BS needs to ascertain the following:

*   The sequence number and ids of the cluster in the two reports should be the same.
*   The data values reported by the proxy report should be a subset of the values reported in the data report.
    (2)   Small Cluster Size: Numeric Format Report

This is identical to (1) above.

(3)   Large Cluster Size, Numeric Format Report

Report validation by the BS is similar to the first case. In addition, the legitimacy of the *proof* part inside a report needs to be ascertained, i.e., the BS needs to verify that the *proof* inside the report is an accurate representation of the reported data values. Details of *proof*s for representative functions are presented in Sec. V.

Besides, the BS cannot directly check if the reported data values in the proxy report are a subset of the values in the data report. However, the BS can ascertain this (with some probability) by performing some additional function-specific consistency-checks for the two reports. This is discussed in Sec. VI.

(4)   Large Cluster Size, String Format Report

The BS performs the same checks as in the first case, but it needs one more step to decompress the compressed part in both reports.

4.2 Special Verification for Large Size Clusters: Area Coverage Analysis

For simplicity, we assume that the cluster is a circle. Suppose the radio range of a single sensor node is r, the radius of the cluster is R, the distance between the backup node and the center of the cluster is u. Then the backup node can cover area:

$$A = r^2 \arccos\left(\frac{r^2 + u^2 - R^2}{2ru}\right) + R^2 \arccos\left(\frac{R^2 + u^2 - r^2}{2Ru}\right) - 2\sqrt{s(s-u)(s-r)(s-R)}$$

where $s = \dfrac{R + r + u}{2}$.

The area that is not covered by the backup node is $\emptyset = \pi R^2 - A$.

If $R=1$ and r is fixed, then the expected area *not covered* by a random backup node with random distribution in the cluster is:

$$\emptyset_R = \int_0^1 (1 - A/\pi)du$$

For $R=1$ and $r=1$, the expected area not covered by the backup node is 0.9786. This accounts for about 31.15% of the entire cluster area. In the worst case, if the backup node is located near the edge of the cluster, the backup node will cover about 39.1% of the area, which means the backup node will receive data from about 39.1% of the nodes in the cluster. Figure 2 represents the values for $[1 - A/\pi]$ for different p and r, if we assume $R=1$. This is the percentage of the cluster area not covered by the backup node. From the figure it is clear that the proportion of area not covered by the backup node is almost inversely proportional to the radio range of a single node, and as long as the distance between the backup node and the CH is less than 0.8 times the cluster radius, the proportion of area not covered by backup node will be less than one half.

5 PROOFS

This section details construction of non-interactive proofs that are attached with the data reports. The *proof* in a report is specific to the function f being computed; proofs for two most common representative functions, *median* and *min/max* are detailed here.

The main idea behind non-interactive proofs is that the prover itself generates some random bits. For example, one method to obtain the seed of the public random function can be from the clock in the sensor nodes. These random bits are equivalent to the random bits or challenge bits sent by the verifier in interactive proofs. The prover then sends all answers to multiple queries in one string back to the verifier. It is important to guarantee that the random bits generated by the prover must be truly random. Else, the prover may use some non-random bits to cheat or to increase the success probability of cheating.

We present a few possible techniques that sufficiently demonstrate extraction of information for constructing non-interactive proofs and are adequate for understanding our scheme. There exist other techniques which are not so relevant for this chapter and hence are omitted. SIA describes uniform sampling of $O(\log n/\varepsilon)$ elements, where n is the number of sensors in one cluster and ε is the approximation error which represents the tolerable error margin in reporting data. We suggest performing uniform sampling through some public random functions. Our construction of the *proof* part requires some random bits to be used as seed for some pseudorandom functions. To guarantee safety, we must ensure that the CH and the backup node cannot control or predict the random bits. To achieve this, one of the following methods can be chosen.

- The first method is to install some tamper-proof hardware to generate random bits in the sensor nodes. Tamper-proof hardware can be used in some scenarios where security is critical and any compromised nodes should be excluded from the protocol. This approach has no communication overhead but is expensive if the number of sensor nodes is very large.

- Another method is to use the current time as the random seed. This requires the sensor nodes to have precise time synchronization (time synchronization in sensor networks is a well researched problem). If the nature of the network requires time synchronization then this technique entails no additional overhead in terms of communication or hardware costs. Otherwise this technique would not be useful, especially when data aggregation needs to be performed frequently, resulting in frequent time synchronization requirements.

- The third method is to use the delayed verification technique. In this scheme, the attached *proof* part in a data packet is the evidence of validity of the data sent in the previous data packet (or several previous data packets). The random bits are includ-

Figure 2. Percentage of cluster area

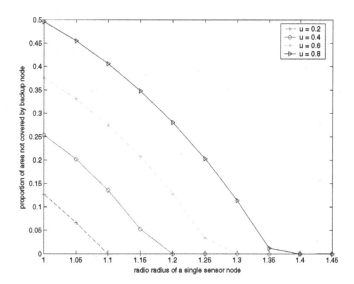

ed in the *Ack* packet sent by the BS before this round of data aggregation. In this approach, the CH or backup node needs to cache the data of the previous round or several previous rounds (depending on the frequency of *Ack* packets). Alternately, several sets of random bits can be included in the *Ack* packet sent by the BS. These sets of bits can be used for the next successive packets until the next *Ack* arrives.

5.1 The Proof for Median Function

The *proof* part for the data and proxy reports are similar; the only difference is that the backup node may only collect data from $n_l \leq n$ nodes. Thus the sampling is done only over these l elements.

According to the following theorem [25], the median of l elements should be close to the median of n data points with high probability if l is not too smaller than n.

Theorem: The median of uniform sample of l out of n elements $a_1, a_2, ..., a_n$ with probability at least $1 - (2 / e^{2l\varepsilon^2})$ yields an element whose position in the sorted sequence $a_1, a_2, ..., a_n$ is within εn of $n/2$ (here ε is the approximation error).

Remarks: If the backup node can receive data from all the nodes in the cluster, then the median reported by the backup node should be identical to the median reported by the CH. For large clusters, the scenario that the backup node receives only a subset of data elements is considered (as any inter-cluster communication scheme to send all data to the backup node would be too resource consuming).

Verification at BS: In the event that the data report is lost and only the proxy report is received, the BS can still obtain and check the median from the proxy report (though the value may be inaccurate if the backup node does not receive enough data). If the BS receives both the data and proxy reports, it checks the difference between the two medians reported by the CH and the backup node. If the difference between the two medians is located more than $(1 - k)n/2$ positions apart in the sorted sequence of elements in the data report, then the BS detects that one of the two nodes (CH or backup) is cheating. Here k is the percentage of the cluster nodes covered by the backup node.

Proof Construction by CH: The CH computes the minimum value of k and includes in the *proof* the two boundary values that are located more than $(1 - k)n/2$ positions apart from its reported median (along with corresponding values in the Merkle hash tree). The BS compares these two values with the median reported by the backup node. If the median reported by the backup node does not lie between the two boundary values, then one of the CH and backup node must have cheated, and the BS can adopt some mechanism to cope with this.

5.2 The Proof for Min/Max Function

For the min/max function, we propose two approaches for constructing the *proof*.

Approach 1

We enhance the data propagation scheme for min/max function in SIA. First a spanning tree is constructed such that the root of the tree holds the minimum (maximum) element, and then it is checked if the tree was constructed properly.

Proof Construction by CH: If we make the same assumption as in SIA that uncorrupted sensors form a connected component, then both CH and backup node can receive the min/max value. The backup node may not receive authenticated states from all nodes in the cluster while CH can receive all of them. The CH constructs the *proof* part as described in SIA, containing $O(1/\varepsilon)$ random samples of nodes and their corresponding paths to the root of the tree.

Proof Construction by Backup Node: Since the backup node receives the authenticated states only from some of the nodes in the cluster, it cannot construct the *proof* part in the same manner as the CH does.

Assume that each sensor node i maintains a tuple of state variables (p_i, v_i, id_i) where p_i, v_i and id_i are the parent of the node in the tree being constructed, received min/max value, and identity of the node i, respectively. Now, suppose the backup node receives the min/max value from k neighboring nodes $(n_1, n_2, ..., n_k)$ and the final state of node

i is (p_i, v_i, id_i), for $i = 1,2, ...,k$. Then the backup node can construct the *proof* through t random samples of nodes from $n_1, n_2, ..., n_k$, where every sample of node i is the concatenation of (p_i, v_i, id_i) and the MAC of (p_i, v_i, id_i), computed using the shared key between node i and the BS.

Theorem 5.1 If no more than ε fraction of the sensors are corrupted, and the backup node reports a false min (max) value, then the BS will detect the false value with probability at least $1 - \varepsilon^t$.

Proof: For every sample node i, no node except i can forge the authenticated code of (p_i, v_i, id_i). The backup node cannot cheat on this unless the node i is corrupted. Node i is corrupted with probability ε, since no more than ε fraction of the sensors are corrupted. For t random samples, the BS will detect the false value with probability at least $1 - \varepsilon^t$.

Approach 2

The scheme to find min/max in SIA requires d steps of broadcasting in the cluster, where d is the diameter (in terms of radio range) of the cluster. This scheme is still too expensive for practical sensor networks. If the data commitment (root of the Merkle hash tree in the aggregate-commit-prove approach) is constructed from the sorted leaf elements and random sampling is used to construct the *proof* part directly, then a simpler and admissibly secure *proof* is obtained.

In this case, the *proof* (in both the data and proxy report) contains the random sample of $1/\varepsilon$ leaf elements and their corresponding hash in the Merkle hash tree. It is evident that if the CH (or backup node) chooses an element whose position is more than εn elements away from the true minimum (or maximum) in the sorted data list, the following condition evaluates to true:

- Considering both reports together, the probability that one of the sampled elements (in either data or proxy report) is smaller than the reported minimum (or greater the reported maximum) is $1 - (1 - \varepsilon)^{2\varepsilon} > 1 - e^{-2}$. This probability can be further improved if we consider that the "sorted list" property will be violated if the CH or backup node reports a non-min-imum (or non-maximum) element.

6 ERROR BOUNDS FOR SOME REPRESENTATIVE FUNCTIONS: CHEATING DETECTION AT BS

This section details how the BS detects cheat-ing. It provides error bounds for the proofs of representative functions described in the previous section. Any values lying outside of the bounds computed below will confirm cheating.

Lemma 1 (min/max value) If the cluster has n nodes, the data value of these nodes are randomly distributed, and the backup node receives data from m nodes ($m<n$), then with probability $e^{-km/n}$, the min or max value reported by the backup node will be more than k ($k<n$) nodes away from the true min or max value.

Proof: If the reported min/max value of backup node is more than k nodes away from true min/max value, then none of the values received from the backup node is in the set of the k nearest nodes of the min/max node. This will happen with prob-ability $(1 - k/n)^m$, which is $e^{-km/n}$, when n is large.

Lemma 2 (median value) If the cluster has n nodes, the data value of these nodes are randomly distributed, and the backup node receives data from m nodes ($m<n$), then with probability $e^{-km/n}$, the median value reported by the backup node will be more than $k/2$ ($k<n/2$) nodes away from the true min or max value.

Proof: If the reported median value of backup node is more than $k/2$ nodes away from the true median value, then none of the values received from the backup node is in the set of the k nearest nodes of the min (or max) node. This will happen with probability $(1 - k/n)^m$, which is $e^{-km/n}$, when n is large.

The analysis for average value is difficult, since the average value greatly depends on the distribution of the values reported from the cluster nodes. If the underlying distribution is estimable through some technique, then we can evaluate some bound for the difference in average reported by the CH and the backup node:

Lemma 3 (average value) If the cluster has n nodes, the backup receives data from m nodes and the distribution of the data values reported from the cluster nodes have mean μ (this is the average value reported by the CH) and variance σ^2, then we have the following result:

$$\Pr(\mid \mu' - \mu \mid > \lambda) < \frac{\sigma^2}{m\lambda^2}$$

Proof: We can consider the m data values received by the backup node as a sampling of a random variable with mean μ and variance σ^2. This sampling will have a distribution of mean μ and variance σ^2/m, then the above result follows directly from the Chebyshev inequality (Planet Math (n.d.).).

7 SECURITY ANALYSIS

This section analyzes several key security features of our scheme and evaluates their impact. We first present some security considerations as regards the actual implementation of our scheme. We then show that the reports (both data and proxy) cannot be forged by any outsiders and the contents of the reports are confidential. By proving the NP-hardness of the minimum cost blocking problem, we demonstrate that it is difficult for any adversary to determine within an optimal cost, the subset of nodes to compromise such that the traffic from certain specific clusters can be completely blocked from reaching the BS. This is further reinforced by simulation results in the next section.

7.1 Security Considerations

There are some important security considerations which need to be followed in the actual implementation of our scheme. The role of the CH/Aggregator should rotate frequently to prevent a malicious CH from repeatedly affecting the aggregation process. Existing CH election schemes (Heinzelman, 2000)(Lindsey& Raghavendra, 2002)(Kulik et al, 1999) can be used for implementing this. A careful selection of backup nodes for every cluster is also in order. Backup nodes should be different from the CH, should not have sent more than a certain number of contiguous proxy reports to the BS in the immediate past, and their choice should be non-trivial to an adversary. This is to avoid malicious backup nodes repeatedly discrediting the primary data reports. The remaining battery power for the candidates should be greater than a certain threshold. Possible backup node selection techniques are:

Random Selection: Nodes randomly elect to be backup nodes. The advantage of this scheme is its simplicity; however, a malicious node can repeatedly elect to be the backup node.

Static Selection: Candidate nodes are arranged in an ordered set and sequentially assigned to be backup nodes. This can be done in a fashion such that the nodes are able to uniquely determine their order without exchanging any information (Virendra et al, 2005). The advantage over random selection is that a single malicious node cannot continually discredit the primary report at the BS.

Evaluation-based: Here a simple metric N is evaluated for each candidate node, where N can be a function of amount of traffic sent by the node, the remaining power, and the percentage area of the cluster covered by that particular node. This is more complex but a fine-grained selection of nodes is achievable.

7.2 Outsider Attacks

It is evident that if the pairwise key between the CH and BS is not compromised, then the contents of the data values in the reports cannot be decrypted by any outsiders. Also, no outsider can launch a replay attack since we use nonces and sequence numbers. False data injection attacks can also be prevented since all public parts in the reports (those items that are not encrypted in the report, such as sequence number, nonce, cluster id and node id) can be verified in the encrypted parts. Thus our scheme ensures safety against attacks by an outside adversary.

7.3 Hardness of Minimum Cost Blocking Problem

Suppose there are m clusters: C_1, C_2, ..., C_m. Every cluster C_i uses a primary path P_i and backup paths $P_{i1}, P_{i2}, \cdots, P_{ik}$ in k different rounds. One of the adversary's goals is to block the primary path and all backup paths in k rounds for some clusters, so no report from these clusters can reach the BS in these k rounds. Suppose the total number of sensor nodes is $N = nm$, where n is the number of nodes in one cluster. Every node has an associated cost c_i ($i = 1,2,..., N$) to be compromised. The adversary's goal translates to finding the subset of nodes with minimum total cost such that blocking (or compromising) this subset of nodes can block all traffic between a subset of clusters and BS in all k rounds. We demonstrate below that finding such a subset of nodes is NP-hard.

Theorem 7.1 It is NP-hard to find a subset of nodes with minimum total cost such that blocking (or compromising) this subset of nodes blocks traffic between a subset of clusters and BS in all k rounds for some k.

Proof: It is evident that the problem is equivalent to finding a subset of nodes with minimum total cost to block all primary paths and backup paths in k rounds for the specified clusters. If we regard each path under consideration as an element, every node as a set contains some elements. If a node is in a path, then the path is contained in the set corresponding to the node. The problem becomes the weighted set cover problem (Gandhi et al, (n.d.).), which is the generalization of set cover problem and is NP-hard.

7.4 Collusion Detection

Collusion is very difficult to prevent or detect in most protocols. In our protocol, if the CH and some of the cluster nodes collude, e.g., both of them drop some data values of some other nodes, then the BS may detect this in some later round of data aggregation since the backup node will be rotated and as long as some backup nodes are honest, the BS will detect the cheating in some subsequent rounds (as long as the backup nodes are truly randomly selected). If collusion inside a cluster is detected, the BS may declare the whole cluster as compromised and take some further actions.

Lemma 4: If the cluster head and a backup node both drop the data of another cluster node, then after k rounds of data aggregation, the collusion of cheating will be detected by the BS with probability $1 - e^{-km/n}$, where n is the number of nodes in the cluster and m is the minimum number of nodes that is one hop range of a cluster node.

Proof: In our protocol, the backup node rotates in every round of data aggregation. If in some round, the BS and backup node both drop data from a cluster node, then in a later round, the new backup node will receive data from this cluster node with probability m/n, and the probability that after k rounds, the collusion will be detected with probability $1 - (1 - k/n)^m$, which is $1 - e^{-km/n}$ for large n.

8 EXPERIMENTAL RESULTS

Though a qualitative approach is adequate for the security analysis, simulations are necessary to study the effectiveness of this scheme in detecting report dropping and to evaluate the probability of reports reaching the BS under varied node-failure/ report-dropping scenarios; the BS's decision making ability is dependent on whether or not it receives either of the reports (data or proxy) from a cluster.

We have tested our schemes in a randomly generated network topology. In the simulation, we have considered a total of 100 clusters where every cluster has 10 nodes. The simulation topology is a 1000 meter by 1000 meter square region which is divided into 100 small squares (every square has size 100 meter by 100 meter). Every cluster is located inside a small square, and all nodes belonging to a cluster are randomly distributed inside the small square. CH of every cluster is randomly chosen. We assume that all nodes are homogenous and the radio range of every node is 100 meters. When two nodes are in each other's radio range, we say that they are connected. The BS is located in a corner of the square region, and all routing is based on the criteria that the routes with the smallest number of hops will be selected. If any tie exists, then one of the routes will be randomly chosen.

Report dropping is simulated through node failures: we have tested the performance of our scheme in the presence of two kinds of node failures: single node failures and patterned node failures. In case of single node failures, every node is assigned a probability of it being compromised. In case of patterned failures, all nodes within a selected square region will be compromised. The center of this compromised square region is randomly assigned in the entire topology. We use MATLAB in our tests and all data points are the average of 100 runs.

Figure 3 is the probability of the reports reaching the BS with some nodes compromised

Figure 3. Probability of reports reaching the BS

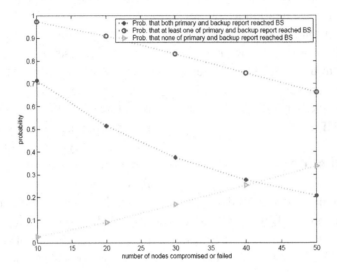

Figure 4. 40m X 40m patterned node failure: no reports reach BS

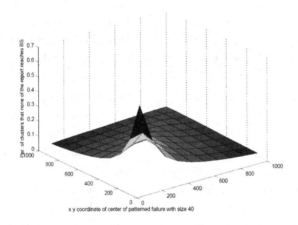

Figure 5. 40m X 40m patterned node failure: one report reaches BS

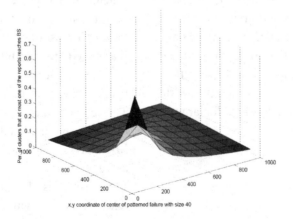

Figure 6. 80m X 80m patterned node failure: no reports reach BS

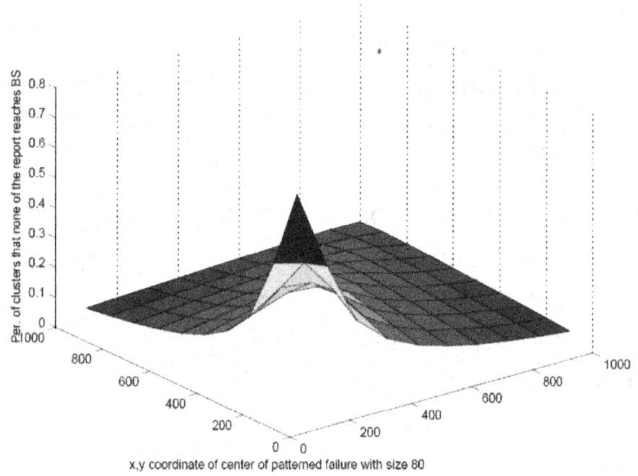

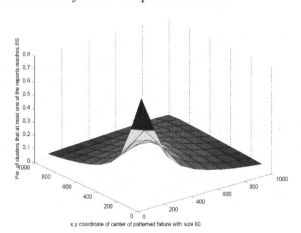

or failed (these nodes are evenly distributed over the network). From Figure 3 we see that when the number of compromised nodes increases, the probability that both reports reach BS decreases almost linearly. The probability that at least one of the reports reaches the BS also decreases almost linearly.

Figure 4 shows the percentage of clusters from which neither the data nor the proxy report reaches the BS when there is a 40m by 40m square patterned failure centered at a certain point. Figure 5 represents the percentage of clusters from which only one of the data or proxy reports reaches the BS when there is a 40m by 40m pat-

terned failure centered at a certain point. Figure 6 is the percentage of clusters from which neither the data or proxy report reaches the BS when there is an 80m by 80m patterned failure centered at a certain point. Figure 7 represents the percentage of clusters from which only one of the data or proxy reports reaches the BS when there is an 80m by 80m patterned failure centered at a certain point.

From Figures 4, 5, and 6 we can see that there is a sharp increase in number of affected clusters when the affected area is near the BS and when the affected area is near the diagonal (with the BS as one end-point) of the entire square simulation

Figure 7. 80m X 80m patterned node failure: 1 report reaches BS

topology region. The trend of increase in the number of affected clusters is similar for clusters losing one report and clusters losing both reports when the affected area is close to the BS and the diagonal. As expected, larger failure area has increased effect.

In reality, sometimes it may be either easier or more difficult for an adversary to compromise the nodes closer to the BS (depending on the ambient conditions). However, our experiments underline the fact that nodes near the BS need more protection as it would be easier for an adversary to have a large impact on the network by compromising fewer nodes proximal to the BS. This conforms to reasoning since nodes closer to the BS will have more paths from other clusters converging on them, than nodes that are further downstream. Failure or compromise of a node close to the BS would thus result in failure of all the cluster paths passing through it.

CONCLUSION

This chapter is one of the first attempts to adopt cryptographic techniques to detect cheating aggregators and arbitrary report dropping attacks in WSNs. It develops a secure aggregation model encompassing different data and aggregation formats. This model is intended as a guide for implementing security in real WSN applications, keeping into consideration the possible adverse deployment conditions for such a network: hostile terrains, wartime operations and in emergency responder systems. Unlike conventional reliability and security schemes, this model is tunable to obtain a desired tradeoff between control overhead and the accuracy of detection. Thus, the degree of reliability in receiving data reports can be governed by the particular application. Using this model in conjunction with other security schemes can result in an end-to-end, semi-reliable data delivery paradigm for WSN applications.

REFERENCES

Adam Dunkels & Thiemo Voigt. "Distributed TCP Caching for wireless sensor networks", Third Annual Mediterranean Ad Hoc Networking Workshop (MedHocNet 2004), June 2004.

Anderson, R., Chan, H., & Perrig, A. (n.d.). *Key Infection: Smart Trust for Smart Dust*. 12th IEEE International Conference on Network Protocols (ICNP'04), pp. 206-215.

Berkeley, U. C. The EECS department.(n.d.). *Cotsbots: The mobile mote-based robots*. Retrieved from http://www-bsac.eecs.berkeley.edu/projects/cotsbots/

Braginsky, D., & Estrin, D. (2002). Rumor Routing Algorithm for Sensor Networks.In the Proceedings of the First Workshop on Sensor Networks and Applications (WSNA), Atlanta, GA, October 2002.

H. Chan, A. Perrig,(2005). *PIKE: Peer Intermediaries for Key Establishment in Sensor Networks*. Infocom 2005.

Chan, H., Perrig, A., & Song, D. (2003). *Random Key Predistribution Schemes for Sensor Networks*. IEEE Symposium on Security and Privacy 2003.

Chieh-Yih Wan. Andrew T. Campbell, Lakshman Krishnamurthy. (2002). *PSFQ: A Reliable Transport Protocol for Wireless Sensor Networks*. WSNA 2002, Atlanta, GA.

CROSSBOWTECHNOLOGY INC. (n.d.). *Wireless sensor networks*.Retrieved from http://www.xbow.com/Products/Wireless Sensor Networks.htm.

Curtmola, R., & Nita-Rotaru, C. (2007). *BSMR: Byzantine-Resilient Secure Multicast Routing in Multi-hop Wireless Networks*.IEEE SECON 2007, June 2007, San Diego, CA.

Budha Deb, Sudeept Bhatnagar, & Badri Nath,(2003). *REinform: reliable information forwarding using multiple paths in sensor networks*LCN 2003.

Deb, B. (2003). Information assurance in sensor networks. In *WSNA 2003*. San Diego, CA: Sudeept Bhatnagar & Badri Nath. doi:10.1145/941350.941373

Detection of Denial-of-Message Attacks on Sensor Network Broadcasts. IEEE Symposium on Security and Privacy 2005.

Ergun, F., Kannan, S., Kumar, S. R., Rubinfeld, R., & Viswanathan, M. (1998). *Spot-checkers*. JCSS, 60:717-751. Preliminary version in Proc. STOC'98.

Ergun, F., Kumar, R., & Rubinfeld, R. (1999). *Fast approximate PCPs*. In Proc. 31st STOC, pp. 41-50.

R. Gandhi, S. Khuller, A. Srinivasan, (n.d.). *Approximation Algorithms for Partial Covering Problems*. Lecture Notes in Computer Science, Springer-Verlag GmbH, (Vol. 2076, pp. 225-236).

Ganesan, D., Govindan, R., Shenker, S., & Estrin, D. (2002). Highly-Resilient, Energy-Efficient Multipath Routing in Wireless Sensor Networks. *Mobile Computing and Communications Review, 1*(2), 2002.

Hari Rangarajan, J. J. Garcia-Luna-Aceves,(2004). *Reliable Data Delivery in Event-Driven Wireless Sensor Networks*. The Ninth IEEE Symposium on Computers and Communications (ISCC2004).

Heinzelman, W. (2000).*Application-specific protocol architectures for wireless networks*. PhD Thesis, Massachusetts Institute of Technology.

Hill, J., Szewczyk, R., Woo, A., Hollar, S., Culler, D., & Pister, K. (2000). *System Architecture Directions for Networked sensors*. ASPLOS IX.

IEEE. 802. (2003). Retrieved from http://www.ieee802.org/15/pub/TG4.html

Jonathan, M. (2005). *McCune, Elaine Shi Adrian, Perrig Michael K*. Reiter.

Karlof, C., & Wagner, D. (2003). *Secure Routing in Wireless Sensor Networks: Attacks and Countermeasures.Ad Hoc Networks, 1, (2—3) (Special Issue on Sensor Network Applications and Protocols)* (pp. 293–315). Amsterdam: Elsevier.

Khalil, I., Bagchi, S., & Nina-Rotaru, C. (2005). *DICAS: Detection, Diagnosis and Isolation of Control Attacks in Sensor Networks*. In the IEEE Conference on Security and Privacy for Emerging Areas in Communication Networks (SecureComm). Athens, Greece from 5 - 9 September, 2005.

B. Krishnamachari, D. Estrin & S. Wicker,(2002). *Modelling Data-Centric Routing in Wireless Sensor Networks*.IEEE INFOCOM 2002.

Kulik, J., Rabiner, W., & Balakrishnan, H. (1999). Adaptive Protocols for Information Dissemination in Wireless Sensor Networks. 5th ACM/IEEE Mobicom Conference, Seattle, WA, August 1999.

Lindsey, S., & Raghavendra, C. S. (2002). *PEGASIS: Power Efficient GAthering in Sensor Information Systems*. 2002 IEEE Aerospace Conference, March 2002, pp. 1-6.

Liu, D., & Ning, P. (2003). *Establishing pairwise keys in distributed sensor networks*.ACM Conference on Computer and Communications Security 2003, pp. 52-61.

Liu, D., Ning, P., & Sun, K. (2003). *Efficient self-healing group key distribution with revocation capability*. ACM Conference on Computer and Communications Security 2003, pp. 231-240.

Math, P. http://planetmath.org/encyclopedia/ChebyshevsInequality.html

Newsome, J., Shi, E., Song, D., & Perrig, A. (2004). *The Sybil Attack in Sensor Networks: Analysis and Defenses*. Third International Symposium on Information Processing in Sensor Networks (IPSN 2004).

Parno, B., Perrig, A., & Gligor, V. (2005). *Distributed Detection of Node Replication Attacks in Sensor Networks*. IEEE Symposium on Security and Privacy 2005.

Adrian Perrig, Ran Canetti, J. D. Tygar, Dawn Song,(2002). *The TESLA Broadcast Authentication Protocol*. RSA Cryptobytes, Summer 2002.

A. Perrig, B. Przydatek, D. Song,(2003). *SIA: Secure Information Aggregation in Sensor Networks*.ACM SenSys 2003.

Perrig, A., Szewczyk, R., Wen, V., Culler, D., & Tygar, J. (2001). *SPINS: Security Protocols for Sensor Networks*Seventh Annual ACM International Conference on Mobile Computing and Networks (Mobicom 2001), Rome Italy.

Ralph, C. Merkle.(1980). *Protocols for public key cryptosystems*. In Proceedings of the IEEE Symposium on Research in Security and Privacy, pages 122-134.

Ralph, C. (1989). A certified digital signature. In *Proc. Crypto'89* (pp. 218–238). Merkle.

Retrieved from http://www.faqs.org/rfcs/rfc793.html

Sankarasubramaniam, Y., Akan, O. B., & Akyildiz, I. F. (2003). *ESRT: Event-to-Sink Reliable Transport in Wireless Sensor Networks*.Proc. of the ACM MobiHoc Conference, Annapolis, Maryland, June 2003.

Schurgers, C., & Srivastava, M. B. (2001) Energy efficient routing in wireless sensor networks.In the MILCOM Proceedings on Communications for Network-Centric Operations: Creating the Information Force, McLean, VA.

Stann, F., & Heidemann, J. (2003). *RMST: Reliable Data Transport in Sensor Networks*. 1st IEEE International Workshop on Sensor Net Protocols and Applications (SNPA). Anchorage, AK, May 2003.

Stann, F., & Heidemann, J. (2005). *BARD: Bayesian-Assisted Resource Discovery In Sensor Networks*.IEEE Infocom, Miami, FL, March 2005.

Vinod Shukla and Daji Qiao Distinguishing Data Transience from False Injection in Sensor Networks. In *Proc*. IEEE SECON'2007, San Diego, CA, June 18~21, 2007

Virendra, M., Upadhyaya, S., Kumar, V., & Anand, V. (2005). *SAWAN: A Survivable Architecture for Wilreless LANs*.3rd IEEE International Workshop on Information Assurance (IWIA'05), Mar 2005.

W. Zhang, H. Song, S. Zhu, G. Cao,(2005). Least Privilege and Privilege Deprivation: Towards Tolerating Mobile Sink Compromises in Wireless Sensor Networks ACM Mobihoc'05, UIUC, May 2005.

Wu, K., Dreef, D., Sun, B., & Xiao, Y. "Secure data aggregation without persistent cryptographic operations in wireless sensor networks", 25th IEEE International Performance, Computing, and Communications Conference, (IPCCC) 2006 Phoenix, AZ

Xu, Y., Heidemann, J., & Estrin, D. (2001). *Geography-informed Energy Conservation for Ad-hoc Routing*. In Proceedings of the Seventh Annual ACM/IEEE International Conference on Mobile Computing and Networking 2001, pp. 70-84.

Zhu, S., Setia, S., & Jajodia, S. (2003). *LEAP: efficient security mechanisms for large-scale distributed sensor networks* (pp. 62–72). Washington, DC: ACM CCS.

Zhu, S., Setia, S., Jajodia, S., & Ning, P. (2004). *An Interleaved Hop-by-Hop Authentication Scheme for Filtering of Injected False Data in Sensor Networks*. IEEE Symposium on Security and Privacy 2004, pp. 259-271.

ENDNOTES

[1]   Standard terms for (a) aggregator node collecting data from several nodes and then sending selective data values to the BS as a report after due processing, (b) a node suppressing its transmission if it overhears a neighbor transmitting the same data, and (c) a forwarding node discarding some reports if it receives multiple similar reports in a short time period to be forwarded to the BS.

[2]   The controlling of frequency of proxy report generation for desired level of reliability and sending proxy reports along routes *mostly different* from the data reports' route can be achieved through simple extensions of existing schemes (Akyldiz et al., 2003; Dunkels et al., 2004). Proxy reports can be sent once per aggregation level. When a node knows that its parent is an aggregator then it may/ may not send a proxy report with a certain probability (Curtmola et al., 2007).

Chapter 12
Extended Time Machine Design using Reconfigurable Computing for Efficient Recording and Retrieval of Gigabit Network Traffic

S. Sajan Kumar
Amrita Vishwa Vidyapeetham, India

M. Hari Krishna Prasad
Amrita Vishwa Vidyapeetham, India

Suresh Raju Pilli
Amrita Vishwa Vidyapeetham, India

ABSTRACT

Till date there are no systems which promise to efficiently store and retrieve high volume network traffic. Like Time Machine, this efficiently records and retrieves high volume network traffic. The bottleneck of such systems has been to capture packets at such a high speed without dropping and to write a large amount of data to a disk quickly and sufficiently, without impact on the integrity of the captured data (Ref. Cooke.E., Myrick.A., Rusek.D., & Jahanian.F(2006)). Certain hardware and software parts of the operating system (like drivers, input/output interfaces) cannot cope with such a high volume of data from a network, which may cause loss of data. Based on such experiences the authors have come up with a redesigned implementation of the system which have specialized capture hardware with its own Application Programming Interface for overcoming loss of data and improving efficiency in recording mechanisms.

DOI: 10.4018/978-1-60960-123-2.ch012

1. INTRODUCTION

While investigating security incidents or trouble shooting performance problems, network packet traces especially those with full payload content can prove invaluable. Yet in many operational environments, wholesale recording and retention of entire data streams is infeasible. Even keeping small subsets for extended time periods has grown increasingly difficult due to ever-increasing traffic volumes. Passive monitoring (Deri, L. & Netikos S.P.A2003)) involves tapping the link on which data needs to be collected, and recording to disk either complete packets, or just packet headers and timestamps indicating their arrival time. Packet switching (Ref. Switching, Circuit switching vs. Packet switching) technology provides flexible and easy management in current Internet routing system comparing with circuit-switch (Ref. Switching, Circuit switching vs. Packet switching) technology. However, packet loss is still a major issue that hurdles high-speed network utilization and performance, and affects quality of real time network services. At transport layer, transmission protocols use packet loss as congestion signal to prevent further packet loss. Where in network layer, routers delay (queue) and drop packets to overcome congestion or to ensure high priority packets passing through the router as fast as possible. Dropping packets seems a necessary entity in current network infrastructure. GPU based snort implementation, Gnort and GPU based software Router (Ref. Han,S., Jang.K., Moon.S. & Park,K. (2010)) also having bottlenecks at packet capturing (Ref. Vasiliadis,G.,Antonatos,S., & Polychronakis, M. (2008)). A better solution to control transmission rate and to ensure high-priority services on networks is to determine what is the available network bandwidth, and sends packets for applications at or below the available bandwidth (Ref. Aurrecoechea, C., Campbell, A.T., & Hauw,L. (1998)). The recording system consists of the following components (Figure 1). Generally the packet capture module receives network packets from the interface to the operating system instead in the system we designed we have a specialized capture hardware that delivers the packets to the classification module (Ref. Malomsoky. S., Molnar.S., Veeres. A. & Szabo G (2010)). Classification allows for different treatment of packets as they are associated with a certain class of packets according to defined properties. The storage containers handle the incoming packets and store them in memory, on disk and evict them later, according to the storage policy defined by their respective class. Indexing provides mechanisms for quick access to subsets of packets that are stored anywhere in the system. The query module accepts queries for stored data, retrieves it from the storage containers and returns it. Finally there is a module that communicates with its environment to offer the functionality of configuration and queries; this is the user interface to the system.

2. TRAFFIC CAPTURE

In general, a capture system has to run on a computer with a network interface to the network from which data has to be cached. Such a computer system is called a packet capture system or sniffer. The sniffer's network interface card (NIC) that is connected to the network to observe is put in a special operation mode by the operating system, such that all packets that are observed by that NIC are accessible by the packet capture application (i.e. recording system) (Dreger, H., Feldmann, A., Paxson, V., & Sommer, R. (2004), Kornexl,S. (2005)). The NIC's connection to the measurement network is called tap. The sniffer's operating system provides a high-level interface to the packet capture mechanisms in the operating system's kernel. On UNIX systems, on which we developed and tested implementations of this design, the libpcap library is such an application programming interface (API) for use by packet capture applications. Of course, there are other

Figure 1. Extended time machine design

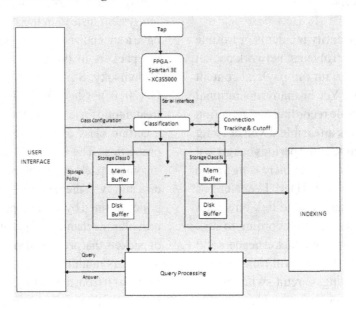

possible ways for the packet flow from the physical network to the application. For example, there is specialized hardware like the Endace DAG card (Ref. Endace DAG Card), which is designed for packet capture purposes only (as opposed to ordinary network interface cards). The DAG card can be accessed by libpcap (Ref. Libpcap) or by a DAG specific library (Ref. Endace DAG API (Libtrace)). Essentially the functionality of packet capture interfaces (APIs) is to deliver all packets received at the NIC to the application. Every packet is completed with additional Meta information, including a timestamp value that indicates the time the packet arrived at the NIC. Other such Meta information on a packet is its total length and the length that was captured from the network (which may be less than the total length if it was cut in the middle due to capture length configuration). The format of the Meta information as passed to the application depends on the packet capture API that is used. Libpcap has its own packet header format. The Endace DAG API, on the other hand, uses the Extensible Record Format (ERF) (Ref. Endace DAG Card, Endace DAG API (Libtrace)). In both cases, the packet data itself is given to the

capture application in raw format (byte string), beginning with the link layer header. The capture module passes the Meta information in the capture API's format and the packet data in raw format on to the classification module.

At this point in the system, performance problems may impact the integrity of the captured data. If an application using a capture API is not able to process packets as quickly as they are delivered by it, the capture API buffers the packets from the network until they can be dispatched to the application. If this packet buffer runs out of free space, further packets arriving on the network will be dropped. This is a situation that clearly is to avoid, since lost packets may mean that relevant information our system aims to save is lost. Using ordinary NICs and libpcap, the packet timestamps are of limited accuracy. Due to the interaction of NIC hardware buffers, the computer hardware and the operating system, the timestamp value given by libpcap is not exactly the time the packet arrived at the NIC's network connection. Specialized hardware like the DAG card can give the timestamp of packets much more accurately because they implement special hardware timers that yield the timestamp information for single packets. Instead in our proposed system we deploy a Spartan 3E XC3S5000 as our capturing device from the network tap. A dedicated FPGA as the capturing interface could greatly reduce the burden of high speed

networks on the recording system. The design of the circuit on the FPGA is based on the ideas taken from a specific network interface called NetFPGA (Ref. NetFPGA). NetFPGA is a special network interface card designed for Gbps network link speeds. The design of the MAC core on Spartan 3E FPGA kit is shown in Figure 2.

Features of this specially designed Capture Interface:

1. Capture interface supports data rates up to 12.5Gbps with full back to back Frame transfer support.
2. Unicast, Broadcast and Multicast Ethernet Frames supported in both transmit and receive.
3. Dynamically programmable MAC address with promiscuous mode option

4. Multicast addresses filtering with 64-bit hash code lookup table on receive reducing processing load on higher layers.
5. Automatic discard of error received frames, for example frames with preamble, length or type error.
6. Programmable frame maximum length providing support for any frame (e.g. Jumbo Frame or any tagged Frame).
7. Fully programmable FIFOs providing rate and clock decoupling on the interface to the user application. In-System programmable FIFO threshold settings for system level performance optimization.
8. Frame padding, preamble and SFD (Start of Frame Delimiter) / insertion and deletion.

3. EXTENDED TIME MACHINE DESIGN

In this section we give an overview of the design of the Extended TMs internals, and its query and remote-control interface, which enables coupling the TM with a real-time NIDS Snort. What we

Figure 2. 10G Ethernet MAC Core on Spartan 3E FPGA kit

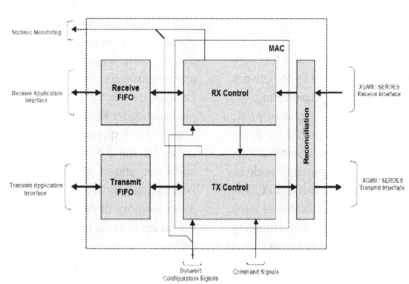

present is a complete reworking of the original approach framed in (Ref. Maier, G., Sommer, R., Dreger, H., Paxson, V., Berkeley,I.U., & Schneider, F. (2005)), which, with experience, we found significantly lacking in High Speed Gbps environments.

3.1 Architecture

In some ways the Time Machine (Ref. Kornexl,S., Paxson, V., Dreger, H., Feldmann,A., & Sommer, R. (2005)) can be viewed as a database, yet it differs from conventional databases in that:

(i)   Data continually streams into the system and out of it.

(ii) It suffices to support a limited query language rather than full SQL, and

(iii) It needs to observe real-time constraints in order to avoid failing to adequately process the incoming stream.

(iv) It cannot handle speed of order of Gbps. Consequently, we base the TM on the multi-threaded architecture shown in Figure 1. This structure can leverage multiple CPU cores to separate recording and indexing operations as well as external control interactions. The FPGA kit receives traffic from the network tap and passes the packets to the capture module.

The Capture Thread is responsible for: capturing packets of the Spartan 3E FPGA network interface; classifying packets; monitoring the cutoff; and assigning packets to the appropriate storage class. Index Threads maintain the index data to provide the Query Threads with the ability to efficiently locate and retrieve buffered packets, whether they reside in memory or on disk. The Index Aggregation Thread does additional book keeping on index files stored on disk (merging smaller index files into larger ones), and User Interface Threads handle interaction between the TM and users or remote applications like a NIDS.

Packet Capture: The Capture Thread uses libpcap to access the packets on the monitored link and potentially pre-filters them. It passes on to Classification.

Classification: The classification stage maps packets to connections by maintaining a table of all currently active flows, as identified by the usual 5-tuple. For each connection, the TM stores the number of bytes already seen. Leveraging these counters, the classification component enforces the cutoff by discarding all further packets once a connection has reached its limit. In addition to cutoff management, the classification assigns every connection to a storage class. A storage class defines which T M parameters (cutoff limit and budgets of in-memory and on-disk buffers) apply to the connections data.

Storage Classes: Each storage class consists of two buffers organized as FIFOs. One buffer is located within the main memory; the other is located on disk. The TM fills the memory buffer first. Once it becomes full, the TM migrates the oldest packets to the disk buffer. Buffering packets in main memory first allows the TM to tolerate bandwidth peaks by absorbing them in memory before writing data to disk, and to rapidly access the most recent packets for short-term queries, as we demonstrate in Figure 3.

Indexing: The TM builds indexes of buffered packets to facilitate quick access to them. However, rather than referencing individual packets, the TM indexes all time intervals in which the associated index key has been seen on the network. Indexes can be configured for any sub set of a packets header field, depending on what kinds of queries are required. For example, setting up an index for the 2-tuple of source and destination addresses allows efficient queries for all traffic between two hosts. Indexes are stored in either main memory or on disk, depending on whether the indexed data has already been migrated to disk.

The Extended TM provides three different types of interfaces that support both queries

Figure 3. Example control and query commands

Interactive console interface queries

An example query. Results
are stored in a file.
*query to_ *file "trace.pcap" index ip "1.2.3.4"*

Dynamic class. All traffic of IP 5.6.7.8 is assigned to class
alarm
*set_ *dy_ *class 5.6.7.8 alarm*

Command Line Queries for Common Line Queries

An example query to select all packets associated with a particular ip
address.
tm-query –ip 1.2.3.4 localhost host.pcap –time 12h

requesting retrieval of stored packets matching certain criteria, and control of the TMs operation by changing parameters like the cutoff limit. For interactive usage, it provides a command line console into which an operator can directly type queries and commands. For interaction with other applications, the TM communicates via remote network connections, accepting statements in its language and returning query results. Finally, combining the two, we developed a stand-alone client-program that allows users to issue the most common kinds of queries (e.g., all traffic of a given host) by specifying them in higher-level terms. Processing of queries proceeds as follows: Queries must relate to one of the indexes that the TM maintains. The system then looks up the query key in the appropriate index, retrieves the corresponding packet data, and delivers it to the querying application. Our system supports two delivery methods: writing requested packets to an output file and sending them via a network connection to the requester. In both cases, the TM returns the data in libpcap format. By default, queries span all data managed by the system, which can be quite time-consuming if the referenced packets reside on disk. The query interface thus also supports queries confine d to either specific time intervals or memory-only (no disk search).

In addition to supporting queries for already-captured packets, the query issuer can also express interest in receiving future packets matching the search criteria (for example because the query was issued in the middle of a connection for which the remainder of the connection has now become interesting too). To handle these situations, the Extended TM supports query subscriptions, which are implemented at a per-connection granularity. Queries and control commands are both specified in the syntax of the TMs interaction language; Figure. 3 shows several examples. The first query requests packets for the TCP connection between the specified endpoints, found using the connection four-tuple index conn4. The TM sends the packet stream to the receiving system nids-61367-0 (feed), and includes with each packet the opaque tag t35654 so that the recipient knows with which query to associate the packets. Finally, subscribe indicates that this query is a subscription for future packets relating to this connection, too. The next example asks for all packets associated with the IP address 1.2.3.4 that reside in memory, instructing the TM to copy them to the local file x.pcap. The time interval is restricted via the start and end options. The final example changes the traffic class for any activity involving 5.6.7.8 to now be in the alarm class.

4. PERFORMANCE EVALUATION

4.1 Packet Drop Avoidance

Our experiments demonstrate that to avoid packet delay and loss, the basic concept is not to refine kernel level logic with ring buffers during packet transmission to the application. A number of factors need to be considered in packet drop avoidance (PDA) based transmission protocol design. (i) Do not fully (100%) utilize networks, especially on ultra high-speed networks. This will avoid filling up the interface buffers.(ii) Develop and deploy mechanisms to avoid buffer overflow when queue is filling up.(iii) Selectively drop obsolete real-time data as soon as possible and preferably drop these packets at transmission hosts. All these factors are directly or indirectly related to router queues, which are used for surge protection. Transmission protocol design that tries to use router queues as flow cushion is improper use of router queues. For example, sending a large packet burst at or above the bottleneck router capacity to cause the router queue partial burst (bunch) and letting the router pace this queued burst out is extremely poor transmission methodology as bunched packets can cause queue overflow and overwhelm further slow links. We addressed basic mechanisms to avoid packet loss, and two main components are in PDA:

(i) Rate pacing is based on network available bandwidth transmitting data at or below the available bandwidth to avoid router queuing.

(ii) Transmitting burst size is preferably smaller than one quarter of bottleneck router queue size avoiding router queue overflow in case that network surge happens Knowing available bandwidth is the mechanism

To avoid filling up the queue at a bottleneck router, and transmitting bursts in proper size is the key to avoid queue overflow in case the bottleneck router queue is filling up due traffic surge.

4.2 Querying

As we plan to couple the TM with other applications, e.g., an intrusion detection system Snort that automatically generates queries it is important to understand how much load the TM can handle. Accordingly, we now examine the query performance of the TM with respect to the number of queries it can handle, and the latency between issuing queries and receiving the corresponding replies. We ran the TM on a system for experimentation. For all experiments, we configured the TM with a memory buffer of 150MB and a cutoff of 15KB. We focus our experiments on in-memory queries, since according to our experience these are the ones that are is-sued both at high rates and with the timeliness requirements for delivering the replies. In contrast, the execution of disk-based queries is heavily dominated by the I/O time it takes to scan the disk. They can take seconds to minutes to complete and therefore need to be limited to a very small number in any setup.

Load: We first examine the number of queries the TM can support. To t his end, we measure the TMs ability to respond to queries that a simple benchmark client issues at increasing rates. All queries request connections for which the TM has data, so it can extract the appropriate packets and send them back in the same way as it would for an actual application.

To facilitate reproducible results, we add an offline mode to the TM: rather than reading live input, we preload the TM with a previously captured trace. In this mode, the TM processes the packets in the trace just as if it had seen them live, i.e., it builds up all of its internal data structures in the same manner. Once it finishes reading the trace, it only has to respond to the queries. Thus, its performance in this scenario may exceed its performance in a live setting during which it continues to capture data thus increasing its head-room for queries. (We verified that a TM operating on live traffic has head-room to sustain a reasonable query load in realistic settings).

On the TM, we log the number of queries processed per second. As long as the TM can keep up, this matches the clients query rate. Figure 4 plots the outcome of the experiment. Triangles show the rate at which queries were issued, and circles reflect the rate at which the TM responded, including sending the packets back to the client. We see that the TM can sustain about 120 queries/secs. Above that point, it fails to keep up. Overall, we find that the TM can handle a high query rate. Moreover, according to our experience the TMs performance suffices to cope with the number of automated queries generated by applications such as those discussed.

Latency: Our next experiment examines query latency, i.e., the time between when a client issues a query and its reception of the first packet of the TMs reply. Naturally, we wish to keep the latency low, both to provide timely responses and to ensure accessibility of the data (i.e., to avoid that the TM has expunged the data from its in-memory buffer).

To assess query latency in a realistic setting, we use the following measurement with live traffic. We configure a benchmark client (the Snort NIDS) on a separate system to request packets from one of every n fully-established TCP connections. For each query, we log when the client sends it and when it receives the first packet in response. We run this setup for about 100 minutes in the early afternoon of a work-day. During this period the TM processes 73GB of network traffic of which 5.5GB are buffered on disk at termination. The TM does not report any dropped packets.

We choose n = 100, which results in an average of 1.3 connections being requested per second (= 0.47). Figure 5 shows the probability density of the observed query latencies. The mean latency is 125 ms, with = 51 ms and a maximum of 539 ms (median 143 ms). Of the 7881 queries, 1205 are answered within less than 100 ms, leading to the notable peak (a). We speculate that these queries are most likely processed while the TMs capture thread is not performing any significant disk I/O (indeed, most of them occur during the initial ramp-up phase when the TM is still able to buffer the network data completely in memory). The second peak (b) would then indicate typical query latencies during times of disk I/O once the TM has reached a steady-state. Overall, we conclude that the query interface is sufficiently responsive to support automatic Time Travel applications.

5. CONCLUSION

In this work we have explored the significant capabilities attainable by extending the already

Figure 4.

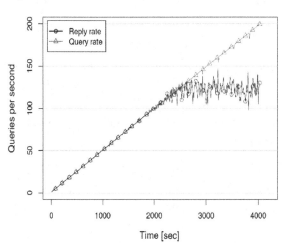

Figure 5. Latency between queries and replies

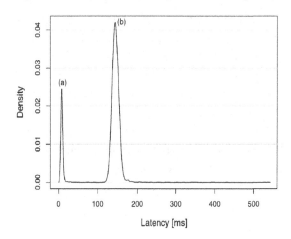

existing Time Machine. This will further improve the ability to quickly access past network traffic for network analysis and security forensics. Using an FPGA as network interface instead of a normal system network interface will greatly reduce the packet drops. Also it is useful for quick storage and retrieval. This approach is particularly powerful when recording traffic at high speeds of the order of 10 Gbps and also integrating traffic from the past with a real-time NIDSs analysis. We support Time Travel via the Time Machine (TM) system, which stores network traffic in its most detailed form, i.e., as packets. To reduce the amount of traffic stored, the TM leverages a simple but effective cutoff heuristic: it only stores the first N bytes of each connection (typically, N = 1020 KB). This approach leverages the heavy-tailed nature of network traffic to capture the great majority of connections in their entirety, while omitting storage of the vast majority of the bytes in a traffic stream.

To further improve performance in high-volume environments, we plan to develop a version of the system that implements cutoff processing in dedicated hardware (such as the Shunt FPGA (Ref. Gonzalez, J.M., Paxson, V., & Weaver, N. (2008))) or in the kernel, in order to reduce the traffic volume as early as possible. Using ideas from (Ref. Vasiliadis,G., Antonatos,S., & Polychronakis, M. (2008)), we also plan to further extend the period we can travel back in time by aggregating packet data into higher level representations (e.g., flows) once evicted from the TMs buffers. Overall, we have found that retrospective analysis requires a great deal of experience with a TM/NIDS setup in operational environments to identify the most useful applications, especially considering the trade-offs discussed in (Ref. Cooke.E., Myrick.A., Rusek.D., & Jahanian.F. (2006)). Now that we have the TM/NIDS hybrid in place, the next step is to pursue a study of these possibilities.

REFERENCES

Aurrecoechea, C., Campbell, A. T., & Hauw, L. (1998). A survey of QoS architectures. *Multimedia Systems*, 138–151. doi:10.1007/s005300050083

CoMo. (n.d.). *Design the fundamental building block of a network monitoring infrastructure.* Retrieved from http://como.sourceforge.net.

Cooke, E., Myrick, A., Rusek, D., & Jahanian, F. (2006). Resource-aware multi-format network security data storage. *In Proceedings of the 2006 SIGCOMM workshop on Large -scale attack defense - LSAD '06*, 177-184.

Deri, L., & Netikos, S. P. A. (2003). Passively Monitoring Networks at Gigabit Speeds Using Commodity Hardware and Open Source Software. *In Passive and Active Measurement Workshop.*

Dreger, H., Feldmann, A., Paxson, V., & Sommer, R. (2004). Operational experiences with high-volume network intrusion detection. *In Proceedings of the 11th ACM conference on Computer and communications security - CCS '04*, 2. Kornexl, S. (2005). *High-Performance Packet Recording for Network Intrusion Detection.* Master Thesis.

Endace, D. A. G. Card. (n.d.). Retrieved from http://www.endace.com/endace-dag-high-speed-packet-capture-cards.html

Endace, D. A. G. API (libtrace). (n.d.). Retrieved from http://researchwand.net.nz/software/libtrace.php

Gonzalez, J. M., Paxson, V., & Weaver, N. (2008). *Shunting: A Hardware / Software Architecture for Flexible, High-Performance Network Intrusion Prevention.* In Proceedings of 14th Annual ACM Computer and Communication Security Conference, 139-149

Han, S. Jang. K., Moon. S. & Park, K. (2010). Packet Shader: A GPU-Accelerated Software Router, *In Proceedings of 10th ACM SIGCOMM Conference.*

Kornexl, S., Paxson, V., Dreger, H., Feldmann, A., & Sommer, R. (2005). *Building a time machine for efficient recording and retrieval of high-volume network traffic*. In Proceedings of the 5th ACM SIGCOMM conference on Internet measurement - IMC '05.

Libpcap, a system-independent interface for user-level packet capture. Retrieved from www.tcpdump.org/

Maier, G., Sommer, R., Dreger, H., Paxson, V., Berkeley, I. U., & Schneider, F. (2005). Enriching Network Security Analysis with Time Travel. *ACM SIGCOMM Computer Communication Review, 38*(4), 183–194. doi:10.1145/1402946.1402980

Malomsoky.S., Molnar.S., Veeres.A. & Szabo G (2010). Traffic Classification over Gbit Speed with Commodity Hardware. *Journal of Communications Software and Systems.*

NetFPGA(n.d.). *A line-rate, flexible, and open platform for research*. Retrieved from http://netfpga.org/

Network Instruments. (2007), Network Security Forensics, *white paper.*

Oh, J., Kim, B., Yoon, S., & Jang, J. (2008). A Novel Architecture and Mechanism for High Performance Real-Time Intrusion Detection and Response System. *Journal of Computer Science, 8*, 155–162.

Sniffer, S. D. K. (n.d.). *Packet Sniffer SDK*. Retrieved from http://www.microolap.com/products/network/pssdk/

Switching, Circuit switching vs. Packet switching. (n.d.). Retrieved from http://voip.about.com/od/voipbasics/a/switchingtypes.htm

Vasiliadis, G., Antonatos, S., & Polychronakis, M. (2008) Gnort: High Performance Network Intrusion Detection Using Graphics Processors. *In Proceedings of the 11th international symposium on Recent Advances in Intrusion Detection,* 116-134.

Chapter 13
Metamorphic Malware Analysis and Detection Methods

Vinod P.
Malaviya National Institute of Technology, India

V. Laxmi
Malaviya National Institute of Technology, India

M.S.Gaur
Malaviya National Institute of Technology, India

ABSTRACT

The term 'malware' is collectively used for any program which accesses the system through surreptitious (often unauthorized) means, with malicious intent, resulting in data loss and/or corruption. Some examples are viruses, worms, trojans, botnets etc. Malware is becoming a world-wide epidemic as one infected computer system may compromise all networked systems. Millions of computers connected to the Internet exchange useful data and information and are exposed to malware threats. Malware programs may apply different techniques for unauthorized access, but all of them compromise the system in one way or another. In order to protect from the threats imposed by the malware, we need to understand the techniques used by them in exploiting system vulnerabilities and build an effective detection system. This contribution chapter surveys various malware types, infection mechanisms, detection techniques and metamorphic viruses. This chapter also presents a Longest Common Subsequence (LCS) based methodology for metamorphic malware detection.

Malware or malicious code is software causing some unwanted and unauthorized activities on the system in a stealthy manner without the knowledge of the user. Malware activation makes the system vulnerable to malicious activities of the attacker. Malware makes its way to the system because of the lack of security awareness amongst users. It spreads through network vulnerabilities such as email attachments. Malware can be classified as viruses, Trojans, botnets, adware, spyware, rootkits etc. Some of the activities of notable malware are follows:

- Deletes important files from the system.
- Logs every keyboard input and sends this information to outside computer system.

DOI: 10.4018/978-1-60960-123-2.ch013

- Steals sensitive information by spying on various user activities.
- Brings down the performance of the machine by slowing down its speed.
- Sends storms of spam mails and implements many backdoors to leak user information.

Virus writers target limitations of anti-virus products to create new variants. The traditional method used by the Anti-virus products (AV) is signature based detection. Signature is a binary pattern that uniquely identifies a virus. This method imposes some problems as (a) it fails to detect encrypted code (b) lacks knowledge of the program semantics (c) the size of signature repository increases with time and (d) fails to detect obfuscated malware.

This chapter discusses various types of malware, infection mechanisms, detection and complex obfuscation techniques. The organization of the chapter is as follows: Section 1 presents a brief history of computer viruses followed by malware evolution in Section 2. In Section 3, infection mechanisms are presented. Section 4 discusses anatomy of metamorphic viruses. Section 5 covers Metamorphism techniques. Section 6 details existing malware detection techniques. Section 7 introduces metamorphic malware detection methods. Section 8 highlights our proposed method. Finally, concluding remarks and future work are discussed.

1. EARLY MALWARE

Computer viruses were the earliest malware. A virus spreads by attaching itself to a host program. A typical virus consists of three parts – *infection mechanism, triggering mechanism* and *payload insertion*. Pseudo code of a virus illustrating these three components is shown in Figure 1(a). The virus first searches for infectable data/device on the victim machine. If trigger returns 'true', payload is delivered. The malicious payload performs intentional or unintentional damage to the host application or machine.

1. 1 Boot-Sector Infector

When the machine is powered on, ROM based BIOS performs *"power on self test"* and searches for boot device. Once the boot device is identified, BIOS reads boot block(s) and transfers control to the code in the boot block code. This step is called the *primary boot*. The primary boot loads secondary boot code which understands the file system structure. This secondary boot code is responsible for loading the operating system kernel.

A boot sector infector (BSI) virus infects the boot block. BSI relocates the original boot block to a specific location and the boot block is replaced by the virus code. After infection, control is transferred to the boot block so as to avoid any suspicion of infection. Choosing a specific location

Figure 1.(a) Pseudo code of computer virus and (b) infection mechanism of the virus

```
def virus():
        infect()
        if trigger() is true:

                payload()
```

(a) Pseudo code of computer virus

```
def infect() :
        repeat k times :
        target = select_target ()
        if no target
                return
        infect_code (target)
```

(b) Infection Mechanism

for relocating boot block can pose problems as the same location can be selected by other viruses.

1. 2 File-Infectors

A *file infector* infects the executable files. Following are the locations in the host program where the file infector inserts the viral code.

- **Beginning of File:** The file infector copies the viral code at the beginning of the host program. Whenever the file is loaded, the virus code is executed after execution of the actual program. Each time the virus infects an executable file, it inserts markers at specific locations. This helps the virus from ignoring previously infected files. Such viruses are also called as *prepending viruses* (Aycock, 2006).
- **End of the file:** A virus that attaches itself to the end of a file is called *appending virus* (Aycock, 2006). The file header contain the entry point of the program. The virus modifies this entry point with a jump to the virus code. After execution of viral code, control is transferred to the original code.
- **Over write file:** Viruses which add code to a host program can be detected by monitoring the file size of uninfected code. To escape detection, virus inserts code in either (a) repeated contents or (b) unallocated space created by file system of the host program. Some overwriting file viruses compress part of file and insert the viral code along with the decompression module. These viruses do not have space overheads like appending and prepending viruses.
- **Inserted inside the file:** Some viruses interweave their code inside the target program. After the insertion, the data locations, branch targets and linker relocation information are also updated.

1. 3 Companion Virus

A companion virus is a *'self replicating'* virus. These viruses infect the host file without modifying its contents. Instead, such viruses share the same name as the target file and place themselves in the search path of the target file. In this way, the virus is executed before the target file. If the target file to be located is *abc. exe*, the operating system would search for *abc. com, abc. exe, abc. bat* in that order. If virus creates a file with same name having. *com* extension, it is executed before the original file.

1. 4 Macro Viruses

Macros are small programs to perform a set of user-defined tasks especially in event-driven applications such as Microsoft Office. Macro codes are embedded in user files and/or document templates. Macros, unlike functions, are expanded at run time, generally after an event such as mouse click. Macro viruses corrupt macro code affecting the document template and corrupt the file once it is opened.

2 MALWARE EVOLUTION

The simple boot and file infector viruses developed for DOS have evolved into complex codes to avoid detection and infect more complicated and sophisticated operating systems. The first polymorphic DOS virus evolved in 1996 and dominated until 32 bit Windows started to dominate the market. Following few paragraphs examine the evolution of computer malware.

2. 1 Encrypted Virus

The simplest way to hide the virus functionality is to hide the viral code in encrypted form.

This was implemented in the early DOS virus *Cascade*. The virus contained a decryptor followed by encrypted virus body. Detection was possible as the virus used same decryptor code for subsequent generations. Detection searched for a constant pattern of decryptor body. Figure 2a shows encryption and Figure 2b shows the decryption module used by the viruses.

2. 2 Oligomophic Virus

Oligomophic viruses, unlike the encrypted counterparts, change their decryptor every generation. Detection of Oligomophic virus is based on run time execution of the virus. *Olivia* was first Oligomophic virus that was reported (Sz¨or, 1997). It infects COM, EXE files. Following are the Hex patterns in files and memory.

Hex Pattern in Files:

```
C08E D8FF 3600 00FF 3602 0068
??? 8F06 0000 8C0E 0200
```

Hex Pattern in Memory:

```
CD16 E800 0033 C0CD 110B C075
04B4 4CCD 2144
```

2. 3 Polymorphic Virus

Polymorphism is a method of code evolution in which a virus generates multiple decryptors for encrypted virus program. These viruses contain a polymorphic engine capable of generating new encryption and keys. The virus body is encrypted in different manners in successive generations. Each encrypted virus code consists of a unique decryptor. Most virus scanners employ code emulation techniques for detecting polymorphic viruses. Virus detections could be made even more difficult by hiding the program's entry point and encrypting the virus body using multiple encryption methods.

1. Detection of Polymorphic Viruses
   (i) The program to be monitored is executed in an emulator.
   (ii) The detector waits until the decryption is complete.
   (iii) All decrypted code would appear similar.
   (iv) Finally, signature scanning is employed on identical copies of the code obtained in the previous step.
2. Challenges
   (i) The scanner has to wait until the code is decrypted.
   (ii) Long waiting period can adversely affect the performance of scanning.
   (iii) Emulation based detection would be defeated if virus can detect presence of emulator.
3. Bypassing emulators
   (i) Virus inserts many NOP instructions prior to the entry point of the program.

Figure 2. Encrypted and decrypted virus module

```
count=number of bytes of the virus code
repeat
  {
     tempByte=fetch next byte
     tempByte=encrypt(tempByte,key)
     count=count−1
  } until(count<0);
```

(a) Encryption Code

```
count=number of encrypted bytes
  repeat
  {
     tempByte=fetch next byte
     tempByte=decrypt(tempByte,key)
     count=count−1
  }until(count>0);
```

(b) Decryption Code

(ii) When the emulator encounters strings of NOPs, it skips scanning of the suspected code, considering it as benign.

2. 4 Metamorphic Virus

Metamorphic malware has the capability to transform its entire code. Metamorphic malware evolved from its polymorphic counterparts. These types of viruses consist of source code having large number of junk instructions. *Apparition Virus* (Win 32) looks for installed compilers in UNIX system and replaces the junk instructions with new ones. In this way, each mutant will have different binary pattern. Every metamorphic malware is equipped with a mutation engine consisting of (a) Disassembler (b) Shrinker (c) Permutator (d) Expander and (e) Assembler (Anonymous 2001). Disassembling module reverse engineers malware code to generate its assembly code equivalent. The mutation engine mutates the code and generates new variants structurally different from its original archetype code. Metamorphic engine employs following mutation techniques.

- Swapping of equivalent code constructs.
- Code transposition, i. e., reordering code.
- Junk insertion by adding junk code in the virus source or its compiled binary.
- Register reassignment by replacing some registers with unused registers.

3 INFECTION MECHANISMS

(i) **Code Patching:** Malware modifies API by overwriting few lines with JUMP instruction. This JUMP instruction transfers control to malicious code. First, the malware copies initial lines of the hooked function and control is transferred to viral code. When the viral code completes its execution, it patches instructions of the hooked functions. The complete step could be summarized using the following code snippet.

Hooked Function:

```
JMP NEW FUNCTION
<rest of the original code>
NEW FUNCTION ()
{
  Process Arguments ();
  Restore First Bytes (Hooked Function);
  Hooked Function ();
  Alter Data ();
  Patch First Bytes (Hooked Function);
}
```

This method has some limitations as patching is prone to application crash and the method also requires restoration of original code before the hook is called. To overcome these limitations, malware writers copy the entire code.

(ii) **DLL Injection:** Malware writers can make use of API CreateRemoteThread. This API starts a thread in the address space of the process specified in the parameter *hprocess*. Parameter *lpStartAddress* points to the remote thread. To load all DLLs in the address space of the process, they make a call to API *LoadLibrary*. If *lpStartAddress* is made to point to *LoadLibrary*(*Malicious. dll*). As a result, *Malicious. dll* is loaded and initialized by DLL linker creating a hook.

(iii) **Import Address Table Modification:** In Portable Executable format (PE), dynamic symbols are loaded making use of indirect addresses.

Any call to an external function A requires that the address of A is first populated in a table called *Import Address Table (IAT)*. Using address in IAT, actual call to the function A is completed. Whenever the operating system loads an executable, it fills up addresses of all external references to function call. The malware hooks the IAT and modifies one of the addresses, diverting respective call to the malicious routine. The following Figure 3a shows PE EXE before IAT patching and Figure 3b shows PE EXE after IAT patching.

(iv) **Modification of Entry point:** The antivirus software would not normally scan the entire

Figure 3. Import address table modification

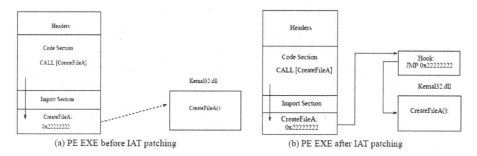

(a) PE EXE before IAT patching   (b) PE EXE after IAT patching

file for extracting sequence of bytes for comparing it with the signature repository. Instead, it checks the entry point or file size for monitoring malicious activities. PE file Infectors modify the entry-point of the infected application and change it to point to the virus body. If the new entry point is written below the last section, the antivirus can easily locate it. The malware writers interweave entry point obscuring code inside the original program code. An example below illustrates the change of the entry point.

Malware employs following steps to change the entry point of the host program:

a) The virus searches for a specific type of file, for e. g. Portable Executable (PE).
b) It tries to locate empty code sections, represented by byte sequence 0x0000 in the disassembled code.
c) It pushes the old entry point on the stack.

d) It inserts jump instruction to transfer control to the new entry point.

Box 1 shows the assembly code sample for entry point modification.

(v) **Direct Modification of Memory:** Any code can be directly injected in the running process using *VirtualAllocEx()* and *WriteProcessMemory()* functions. The main difference is that former function allows us to specify a process while the latter function allocates within the address space of the calling process. With the help *WriteProcessMemory()* function, the malicious code can be inserted in the address space of the required process. The copied code can be started with *CreateRemoteThread()*.

(vi) **Registry Entry Modification:** Registry is an important component in the Windows operating system. Whenever a new application is added or removed, modifications take place in the

Box 1.

```
push ebp
mov ebp, esp          //Standard    StackFrame is build
sub esp, 4            //Make enough space to insert byte
push 0x0050A84        //Push the old entry point on the
                      //stack
mov eax, virus. <new entry point     //New Entry point
jmp eax
```

registry. Windows registry consists of information such as user profiles, applications installed on the computer, icons and folder settings and information about the hardware and ports. Any unwanted modifications in the system registry can damage the system or degrade its performance. In most cases, the system will not boot and a fresh installation will be required. The following are some key registry entries that need to be monitored to protect it from malware threats:

- Shell association keys HKCR\exefile\ shell\open\command. If the default value is changed to filename. exe, it is suspected as an abnormal entry.
- The registry key HKCU\Software\ Microsoft\Command Processor has a value *Autorun*. This is responsible for automatically executing certain commands each time *cmd. exe* is run. The malware program could run under the cover of *cmd. exe* by setting the path to its executable file.
- Some registry entry modifications lead to browser hijack. The following registry entry loads *abc. reg* each time the system is booted:

```
HKEYLOCAL_MACHINE\ SOFTWARE\Micro-
soft\ Windows\CurrentVersion\ URL\
Prefixes:
```

www = http://www.abc.com/cgi-bin?

Similarly, the default page can be modified by changing *default* parameter and the search page can be modified through:

Search Page=http://www.anypage.com.

(vii) **Modification in Interrupt Vector Table (IVT):** The virus alters the standard interrupts used by BIOS (Basic Input Output System) and operating system. It can trap key stroke or disk interrupts or even the CTRL-ALT-DEL reboot command.

Whenever an interrupt occurs, the operating system calls the routine by reading its address IVT. This table contains a pointer to handler routines stored in the resident portion of the memory or ROM. The virus modifies IVT and the viral code residing in memory is executed whenever interrupt handler is invoked. The memory resident virus may modify the IVT in the following two ways:

- It hooks the interrupt by re-directing it to its own code:
  Original Int 21 entry in IVT 0A1D:0273
- The virus follows the IVT entry and patches the code of the routine pointed by the pointer. Firstvirus code is executed and afterwards the control is returned to the original code.

Uninfected system:

```
Original Int 21 entry in IVT 0A1D:0273
Original code at 0A1D:0273 9012CD002090
```

When infected by virus:

```
Original Int 21 entry in IVT 0A1D:0273
Patched code at 0A1D:0273 90EFCD0020AB
```

4 ANATOMY OF METAMORPHIC VIRUSES

Metamorphic malware consists of a mutation engine for generating variants. The mutation engine (refer Figure 4) is composed of the following module (Anonymous 2001).

(i) **Locate own variants:** The metamorphic engine should be capable of locating new variants generated by it. This is required to check if a file is infected by an earlier variant and the new variant is different from its predecessors. Mutation results in variants which are similar in functionality but differ

Figure 4. Anatomy of a metamorphic engine showing major phases used during mutation

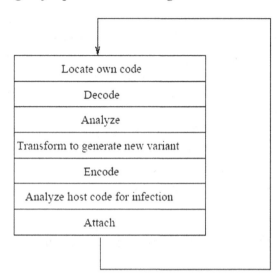

syntactically. The metamorphic malware can be added at fixed locations or locations can be changed to avoid detection. One of the simplest way of doing this could be to add metamorphic malware at the entry point of the executable host program. Alternatively, viruses insert markers at specific locations such as code segments. Scanners can identify such locations easily. The metamorphic engine should randomly select positions in the code to thwart detection.

(ii) **Decode:** The metamorphic engine should be capable of identifying the infected code. In order to identify infected code, the metamorphic engine marks the infected program using certain flags, bit vectors, markers etc. The metamorphic malware encodes useful information about the malware in certain locations of the program executable. In order to obfuscate the program, the metamorphic engine disassembles the program. The disassembly is usually performed using the linear sweep algorithm. The simplicity in the disassembling approach of this algorithm makes easy detection of malware possible by the scanners. In order to add complexity

to linear sweep method, certain locations in the assembled code can be written with jump instructions which transfer the control to certain junk code. After executing the junk code, it returns back to the original code. To complicate anti-disassembling, the engine may employ recursive sweep or knowledge based method.

(iii) **Analyze:** In order to apply the transformation rules, engine should preserve the semantics of existing program. For example, registers are reassigned by checking for register liveness information obtained by "def-use" analysis. Control flow graphs (CFG) for program can be constructed to check if the program semantics is modified by applying transformation rules. It can be used in situations when the program flow needs to be corrected after initial block of the program has been moved during the transformation. CFG is needed to add transformations that can shrink or expand the code.

(iv) **Transform:** This module transforms a given piece of code into its equivalent code. The transformed code is functionally similar to the original code.

(v) **Attach:** The malware needs to attach itself to the uninfected host programs. The metamorphic engine should also contain a feedback module which notifies the engine of the newly generated variant. The engine makes use of the newly generated variants for creation of variants in future generation.

(vi) **Encoding:** The metamorphic malware engine encodes certain data so that the scanners cannot easily decode target locations of jump or call. The metamorphic engine may construct CFG for the code, transform CFG and generate encoding for the new CFG.

A possible encoding could be how the jump targets are implemented. The jump or call could be implemented using the direct or indirect addressing. In direct addressing, the targets of jumps statements are specified directly with branch operands or call instructions. In indirect addressing, target addresses are specified as the contents of memory or register or computed from these contents. It is statically difficult to locate the target address in case of indirect jumps.

5 METAMORPHIC TECHNIQUES

Metamorphic malwares can be broadly classified into (a) closed-world and (b) open-world malware. The closed world malware is self contained whereas the open world malware extends its capability by downloading certain plug-in interpreter from the Internet. Detecting open world malware poses challenges as binary form of malware may be some intermediate representation known only to the malware creator. This is converted to machine language by the plug-in through application of some pre defined rules.

The design space of metamorphic malware is the collections of goals, actions and constraints, and their implications or trade-offs (Walenstein, Mathur, Chouchane M.R, & Lakhotia A, 2007). The design space is seldom conceptualized and viewed in similar fashion by the malware authors and virus scanners. The primary intention of any malware writer is to create malware which the scanners fail to detect. Metamorphism in malware is achieved through obfuscation techniques; basic idea of obfuscating the program is to generate multiple program variants without changing its behavior. Following are some metamorphic techniques used by viruses to create new mutants. It is worth noting that metamorphism can be used as an advantage to protect against malware. Software can be protected from modifications through obfuscation (Collberg, Thomborson, & Low.,1997) embedded in software and known to trusted OS.

5. 1 Garbage Code Insertion

Inserting of garbage/junk code does not change the functionality of the program. It is added by metamorphic engine in order to defeat pattern based scanning. Metamorphic engine of *Win32/Evol* virus had capability to run on any Win32 platform. Box 2 is the piece of code in early generation of Win32 virus, and the piece of code in later generation.

As indicated, the code contains garbage code having no effect on the functionality of the code snippet.

5.2 Insertion of Jump Instructions

Another method used to create metamorphic malware is by insertion of jump instructions within the code. *Win95/Zperm* is an example of this technique (Sz̈or, 2000). This virus adds jump instruction and garbage code in each mutant. Since the virus body is not constant, string based detection is not possible. Consider the following piece of code without any jump instructions.

```
instruction 1 ; entry point
instruction 2
instruction 2
.
.
instruction n
```

In later generation the virus body is modified by the engine by inserting jump instructions at random positions shown below.

```
instruction 2
jump 3
instruction 4
jump n
instruction 1 ; entry point
```

Box 2.

```
C7060F000055            mov dword ptr [esi], 5500000Fh
C746048BEC5151          mov dword ptr [esi+0004], 5151EC8Bh


   The piece of code in later generation is:

BF0F000055       mov edi, 5500000Fh
 893E            mov [esi],edi
 5F              pop edi                 ;garbage
 52              push edx                ;garbage
 B640            mov dh, 40              ;garbage
 BA8BEC5151      mov edx, 5151EC8Bh
 53              push ebx                ;garbage
 8BDA            mov ebx,edx
 895E04          mov [esi+0004], ebx
```

```
jump 2
instruction 3
jump 4
.
.
.
instruction        n
```

5.3 Equivalent Code Replacement

Metamorphic engine of the virus may replace an instruction or block of instructions with an equivalent set of instructions. In assembly language programming, many instructions are semantically equivalent. Some examples are

```
xor reg, reg   ≡   mov reg, 0
  inc eax      ≡   add eax, 1
  mov reg, imm ≡   push imm; pop reg
```

5. 4 Transposition

Transposition or instruction permutation, modifies the instruction execution order if they are not inter-dependent. Consider two instructions op R1, R2 followed by op R3, R4. These two instructions can be swapped provided R1, R2, R3, R4 are different registers. For example, the instructions mov eax, imm and inc eax are not inter-dependent hence they can be swapped.

```
. . .                          . . .
mov ecx, imm      ≡            inc eax
inc eax                       mov ecx, imm
. . .                          . . .
```

5.5 Host Code Mutation

Win95/Bistro mutates its body as well as the host program every generation. The variants are created by engine through random morphing of the code. The host program cannot be recovered as the virus changes (obscures) the entry point of the host application. Replacement of single instruction as well as pair of instructions with equivalent code is easy compared to replacing block of code with another code. For example, the instructions of the form push eax; mov eax, ebx can be substituted as push eax; push ebx; pop eax.

5. 6 Backdoor Installation

Win32/Smorph trojan implements *semi metamorphism*. It installs a backdoor to the system. The executable and its PE header are regenerated during the installation of Trojan, which includes new section names and section sizes. The actual entry point of the code is also obscured. The Trojan uses API calls to its own import address table (IAT) which contain references to essential as well as non-essential API imports.

5. 7 Register Swap

RegSwap virus, created by Vecna (Sz"or, 2000), implements metamorphism through register exchange as illustrated in the following code.

Old generation

```
pop edx
mov edi, 0004h
mov esi, ebp
mov eax, 000Ch
add edx, 0088h
mov ebx, [edx]
mov [esi+eax*4+00001118], ebx
```

New generation

```
pop eax
mov ebx, 0004h
mov edx, ebp
mov edi, 000Ch
add eax, 0088h
mov esi, [edx]
mov[edx+edi*4+00001118],esi
```

Figure 5. Subroutine Inlining and Subroutine Outlining

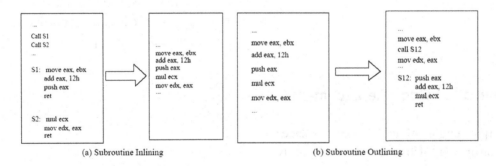

(a) Subroutine Inlining   (b) Subroutine Outlining

Figure 6. Subroutine permutation

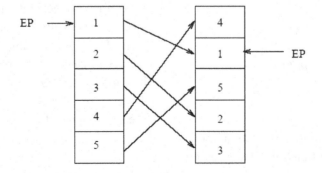

5.8 Subroutine Inlining and Subroutine Outlining

Subroutine inlining is a method in which the call to subroutine is replaced by its definition. It is a form of program obfuscation which replaces some/all calls to the subroutine with their codes.

Code outlining divides a block of code into subroutine(s) and adds subroutine call for the newly created subroutine(s). Figure 5a shows an example of subroutine inlining for two subroutine call S1() and S2(); Figure 5b illustrates outlining of code to create a new subroutine S12().

5.9 Subroutine Permutation

Some metamorphic viruses make use of permutation of subroutines. If a virus code consists of *n* subroutines, it is possible to have *n* generations by reordering subroutines.

Figure 6 shows one possible permutation of the virus code consisting of five subroutines.

6 MALWARE DETECTION METHODS

The malware detection method is based on pattern matching, i. e. scanning for known binary code patterns or *signature*. The scanners based on such techniques would fail to detect malicious codes which change their forms by changing their code in each variant. Two broad categories of malware detection methods are (1) static analysis and (2) dynamic analysis. Static analyzers are fast but more prone to false alarm.

6. 1 Static Analysis

In this technique, analysis is based on structural characteristics of malware. Suspicious binary code is analyzed without executing it. The first step is to disassemble the code. Disassembled code is parsed to collect information pushed onto the stack, stored in processor registers or memory, system calls/APIs and dynamic link libraries. The static detection methods (Sz¨or & Ferrie,2001) include:

- Scanning of unique binary signature of virus.
- Identifying generic finger print for known malicious act.
- The scanner parses the code stripping all non essential code like *nop*. The residual code is used for detailed analysis.

Malware normalization prior to static analysis enhances the detection of obfuscated malware (Christodorescu, Kinder, Jha, Katzenbeisser, Veith,,2005). The use of the normalizer yielded better detection rates than commercial scanners. Normalization of instruction substitution metamorphic malware, based on standard instruction set was proposed in (Jin, Wei, Yang, & Wang, 2007). The method involves two steps. The input is first written using standard instructions. Then, the order of instructions is changed on the basis of the data dependency graph.

In their work (Walenstein, Chouchane & Lakhotia, 2007) proposed a model of probabilistic engine to predict the expected distribution of instruction forms in different generation of variants. These distributions form a type of statistical signature. A classifier program computes the distance of observed and predicted instruction forms using *Euclidean distance* method to determine presence of the malware.

SAVE (Static Analyzer for Vicious Executable) (Sung, Xu, & Mukkamala, 2004) is a strong signature-based malware detection tool capable of detecting obfuscated malware. A signature for a virus is represented by sequence of Windows API calls where each API call is represented by a 32 bit number. The most significant 16 bits correspond to the API call and the least significant 16 bits correspond to specific API position in a vector of APIs. *Euclidean distance* between the known signatures and the sequence of API call in the suspected program is used as discriminant.

In "An Evaluation of API Call Hooking Performance" (Marhusin, Larkin, Lokan, & Cornforth, 2008) API hooking was evaluated for malware detection on three benchmark systems (1) plain computer system without any anti-virus (2) computer with anti-virus and (3) computer with API hooking program. Similarly, authors (Sathyanarayan, Kohli, & Bruhadeshwar, 2008) proposed using critical APIs as the base signature of malware. Difference between the malware program and benign program was measured using *'Chi Square Test'*. If O_i is the observed frequency and E_i is expected frequency of critical API (s), a high value of Chi Square $X_i^2 = (O_i - E_i)^2/E_i$ $i = 1, ..., n$ indicates deviation from normal behaviour and possibly malicious code.

In their proposed system, the authors (Jeong & Lee, 2008) analyze the system call sequences in PE binaries and demonstrate the result in the form of a topological graph called as the code graph. The main objective of the proposed work is that even if the goal of system call is unknown, the system call pattern can help in determining the malevolence by comparing with predefined behavioral pattern. The authors (Xu, Sung, Chavez, & Mukkamala., 2004) also used API call sequence as malware signature in portable executable format. The API call sequence is compared with the sequence call of known malware and thresholding is applied. This signature is saved as a new signature suspecting the API sequence as malicious.

In their static analysis approach, (Karnik, Goswami, & Guha, 2007) focus on instruction frequencies rather than operand frequencies. Instances of suspected programs are disassembled and represented as vector of instruction frequencies within the executable. Similarity between the vectors *A* and *B* of two programs P_a and P_b indicate if they are obfuscated versions of each other. A similarity measure θ determines the angle between two vectors as shown below:

$$A = \{x_1, x_2, x_n\}$$

$$B = \{y_1, y_2, y_n\}$$

$$\cos(\theta) = \sum(x_i \times y_i) / \sqrt{((\sum(x_i^2 \times y_i^2)))}$$

The average similarity measures is computed and if this exceeds a threshold value, then the two programs are marked as similar and obfuscated versions of each other. (Bergeron, Debbabi, Erhioui & Ktari, 1999) presented static analysis based on static slicing of the disassembled code and higher level representation is abstracted.

Worms are malicious programs capable of spreading by exploiting vulnerabilities of the number of hosts connected in the network. Proposed work of (Kruegel, Kirda, Mutz, Robertson, & Vigna,2005) is based on structural analysis of binary code to identify structural similarities between different worms. The main contribution of the work is novel fingerprinting technique based on control flow graph and improvement of the past fingerprinting methods based on the graph coloring methods. The developed prototype was able to identify code modifications carried by the worm.

Data mining approach (Reddy & Pujari, 2006) is based on byte sequences or n–grams. Features are selected on basis of classwise document frequency, classified through multiple classifiers and Dempster Shafer Theory of Evidence is used for combining classifier output optimally. The limitation of n–gram approach is that it lacks semantics awareness.

To evade malware detection, most of the malware writers use packers or crypters to compress the executables and uncompress them while executing. Normally, the anti-virus scanners extract the file-header to find the Original Entry Point (OEP) to search for the malicious code following it. Various unpacking methods have been presented in (Richard Ford and Michael Howard, 2007).

In the work by (Choi, kim, Oh, & Ryou, 2008), the packed file detection based on PE header analysis is proposed. The tool, called PHAD, utilizes the differences between the packed executable and normal files. To present the different features of packed and unpacked executables, the characterization vectors (CV) are defined. Euclidean distance is calculated to differentiate between the packed or unpacked executable. The characteristic values are selected via heuristic analysis of the values of each field in normal and packed PE files.

A heuristic approach for static analysis of obfuscated malware is presented by Treadwell and Zhou (2009). Static characteristics such as (a) Number of non-standard section names (b) Flagged section names (c) Obfuscated entry point (d) Thread Local Storage section check and (e) Import function table check are monitored and a risk score is calculated. If the risk score is below the threshold the binary is assumed to be benign, otherwise, detailed analysis is performed.

6. 2 Dynamic Analysis

In dynamic analysis, the program is allowed to execute and the analyzer checks the strains left by the code in the memory, system registry, processor registers etc. During dynamic analysis, the detector checks for malware and the way it evades detection. There is a potential problem with this approach. The program might destroy all information of the system beyond repair. Dynamic analysis is conducted in sandbox environment such as emulated or virtualized environment.

The main advantage of dynamic analysis is that it can expose what the obfuscated malicious system calls could perform. The following could act as a behavioral signature (Skoudis & Zeltser, 2003).

- Frequently searching for a specific type of file.
- Opening an executable file with read and write permissions.
- Extracting portions of file-header consisting of entry point.
- Modifying the entry point.
- Seeking the end of file.
- Appending data at the end of file.

McBoost is an abbreviation for Malware collection Booster (Lanzi & Lee, 2008). The proposed system consists of three modules (a) A classifier capable of detecting packed code (b) Universal unpacker capable of unpacking the packed code and (c) a second classifier module capable of classifying whether the program is malicious or benign. The tool makes use of (a) Heuristics and (b) *N*-gram analysis based classifiers. The output of classifiers is combined to determine if the executable contains packed code. The hidden code is extracted by the unpacker module using QEMU emulator. The tool uses hybrid - a combination of static and dynamic analysis technique.

Modern malware makes use of stealthy techniques to detect or subvert malware detection mechanisms. Most of the malware scanners are implemented inside the host machine making them vulnerable to such detection. To address these limitations, (Jiang, Wang, & Xu, 2007) implemented malware detection outside the virtual machine (VM), saving the semantics of the host (e. g. files, processes, and kernel modules). The paper introduces a stealthy detection method capable of (1) Comparison based detection, involving comparison of VM's semantics, inside and outside the VM, (2) Out-of-box detection capable of monitoring and detecting malware, such that, it could be used with heterogeneous operating systems. The model was implemented on Linux and Windows platform and was evaluated for kernel level rootkits on both operating systems.

Many dynamic analysis tools are capable of monitoring the execution of single program. Modern malware activates malicious actions under specific circumstances (e. g. on a particular day, when a certain file is present, or when a certain command is received). (Moser, Kruegel, & Kirda, 2008) proposed a technique which explores multiple execution paths to identify malicious actions executed when certain conditions are met. In (Williams, Holz, & Freiling., 2007), the design and implementation of tool CWSandbox is proposed. This tool fulfills three design criteria: correctness, effectiveness and automation. CWSandbox tool allows analysts to trace and monitor system calls and generates an automated readable report consisting of:

- Files created and modified by the malware.
- Modification performed on the Windows registry.
- New DLLs loaded by the malware during execution.
- Network connections opened and information transmitted through the connections.
- Services installed.

7 METAMORPHIC MALWARE DETECTION

The primary concern of malware researchers is metamorphic malware which morphs its code in each generation and challenges intensive static analysis. They can also defeat dynamic analysis techniques as and when they detect the presence of emulated environment (Lakhotia, Kapoor, & Kumar, 2004). This section describes some techniques for detecting metamorphic viruses.

7. 1 Using Engine Signatures to Detect Metamorphic Malware

This technique was proposed by Chouchane and Lakhotia (2006). For a given suspicious program, the metamorphic engine that generated the code is determined. If more than 50% of instructions of the program can be transformed by the engine, the instructions are termed as having *engine friendliness*. The engine is written in such a manner that high engine friendliness applies to all variants of the malware. This method can be useful for detecting unknown malware that make use of known metamorphic engines. Generic metamorphic engine uses the rule set of the metamorphic engine of the Win32/Evol virus. This method can discriminate the engine output from any other

code making use of the scoring function. It can also determine the measure of similarity of the variants in successive generations.

7. 2 Analysis Based on System Calls

The proposed work (Kruegel, Kirda, Mutz, Robertson, & Vigna, 2007) presents a new approach for recognizing metamorphic malware. The approach is based on static analysis of executables to compare program semantics, based primarily on the pattern of system call or library functions which are called. A prototype model was created and was evaluated on three different executables (a) metamorphic variants of malware (b) programs which are not related (c) program variations and code reuse. The model accepts an executable and generates a pattern from the system call sequence and library functions. The output of pattern matching is a score having a value between 0 and 1, where 1 indicates identical functionality.

In order to generate the pattern, the executable is disassembled and control flow is obtained through static analysis. The result of such analysis is the set of basic blocks and transfer of control between these basic blocks. The next step is the data flow analysis which identifies the values in the memory or processor register. The main target in this work is to monitor the target of call instructions. Following the data flow analysis, a sub-pattern is generated. This intermediate representation consists of operation type, the operands and the operand addressing modes.

The next phase, after generation of the pattern, is to compare these sub-patterns. The main requirements of defining a pattern is that (a) the pattern of one malware should be different from that of another malware family and (b) patterns of variants of same metamorphic malware family should be very close to each other. A maximum weighted matching is one that maximizes the sum of the similarity scores of the pairs of sub-patterns.

7. 3 Control Flow Graph Matching

The detection of metamorphic viruses based on control flow graph was proposed by Bruschi, Martignoni and Monga (2007). In this method, an executable program P is disassembled to obtain a normalized program P' by removing redundant instructions without altering the control flow of execution. Normalized program is used for constructing the CFG which is compared with CFG of known malware. The detection process comprises of two components: code normalizer and code comparator.

Code Normalizer: This module is responsible for converting a program into its canonical form so that the detection rate of the scanner is improved. During normalization of the program, care is taken so that the instructions are substituted with their semantic equivalents. The code normalizer performs the following tasks:

- Disassembled code is translated into static single assignment form (SSL).
- Control and data flow analysis is performed on the disassembled code and a CFG is constructed.
- CFG is transformed into static single assignment form.

Code Comparator: This module is responsible for determining if a program P is part of a malicious program M or contains part of it. Distances between the two code fragments are found using the *Euclidean distance*. Higher values indicate differences between the code and values nearing 0 indicate closeness to the program. Two programs are compared based on the following metric:

- Number of nodes in CFG
- Number of edges in CFG
- Number of direct calls
- Number of indirect jumps
- Number of direct jumps
- Number of conditional jumps

Metamorphic malware detection based on only syntactic analysis is generally inefficient. Hence, the detector should consider semantics of the program. To address the issue, morphological detection of metamorphic malware was proposed by Bonfante, Kaczmarek and Marion (2008). This method is based on syntactic and semantic analysis of CFG. This approach represents the program in the form of tree automata which represents CFG as trees with pointers to represent back edges and cross edges. To reduce the size of signature, a minimal automaton is constructed.

Essam, Ahid and Adaan (2009) proposed metamorphic malware detection using arbitrary length of CFGs and node alignment. In (Bonfante, Kaczmarek, & Marion, 2007), authors propose a detection strategy based on *Control Flow Graphs* as signatures. This method is semantics based approach for detection. A CFG has six types of nodes namely jmp, jcc, call, ret, inst and end which correspond to the control flow structure. A graph reduction method is also presented. Nodes of kind inst or jmp are removed from the graph by linking its predecessor and successor nodes. CFGs are automatically extracted from malware, constituting the signature and false positive ratios are evaluated.

7. 4 New Approaches to Malware Detection Some of the New Approaches to Malware Detection, Still In Nascent Stage, Are Discussed In Following Paragraphs

7. 4. 1 Formal Methods

Formal method is mathematical way of specification for the development of any software or hardware. A formal method for detection of metamorphic viruses was proposed by Webster and

Malcolm (2006). In this method, the semantics of programming language IA-32 was specified using OBJ – a formal notation for algebraic specification and theorem proving. This specification can be used to prove the semi-equivalence and equivalence of sequences of IA-32 instructions. The authors termed syntactically different generations of same metamorphic malware as *allomorphs*. This technique was applied on allomorphic code fragments of two metamorphic computer viruses: *Win95/Bistro* and *Win9x. Zmorph. A.* Using the semantics specified in OBJ, reduction can be used to find the effects of instruction sequence on any variable.

It was found that two allomorphs of Win32/Bistro were equivalent with respect to the state of the stack. As a result, only the values of *ebp* register and the value of the stack needs to be verified. The following example from (Webster & Malcolm, 2006) shows the effect of variables using OBJ reduction.

Step 1: Define two store operators x and y.

ops x y: Store ⇒ Store

Step 2: Define the instruction sequence corresponding to x and y

eq x(S)= S ; push ebp ; mov ebp, esp

eq y(S)= S ; push ebp ; push esp ;pop ebp

Step 3: Reductions are applied for checking equivalence with respect to contents of stack and ebp register and non equivalence w. r. t IP instruction pointer.

```
OBJ>  reduce x(S)[[stack]] is y(S)
[[stack]].
result Bool:  true
OBJ>  reduce x(S)[[ebp]] is y(S) [[ebp]].
result Bool:  true
reduce in IA-32:x(S)[[ip]] is y(S)
```

```
[[ip]].
result Bool:  false
```

7. 4. 2 Hidden Markov Models

A method for detecting computer viruses using Hidden Markov Model (HMM) was implemented by Wong and Stamp (2006). HMM is a Markov model in which the states cannot be observed (hence called the hidden states) but the symbols produced or consumed by/from states are observable. A HMM is defined by the tuple < s, H, W, E, A> where s is the start state, S is the set of states, H is the set of observation symbols, E is the observation probability and A is the state transition probability. The key idea of HMM is that it is a finite model which describes the probability over infinite number of observation sequences and the next state is dependent on the current state, which is not observable. An HMM can be trained to represent a set of observation sequences. The transition and observation probabilities are the statistical properties of these features. If score of observation sequence with HMM is high, it can be inferred that input data is similar to the trained data. Hidden Markov model could be used to solve the following three problems:

- **Evaluation Problem:** Given the observation sequence $O = O_1O_2O_3.. O_n$ and model $\lambda = (A, B, \pi)$, we can compute $P(O|\lambda)$ i. e., probability of observation sequence given the model. This can be solved using the forward approach.
- **Hidden State Determination:** Given the observation sequence $O=O_1O_2O_3.. O_n$ and model $\lambda = (A, B, \pi)$, how do we choose $Q = a_1a_2a_3.. a_n$, i. e., finding the state which generated the observation sequence. This can be solved using the *Viterbi Algorithm*.
- **Learning:** How do we adjust the model parameter $\lambda = (A, B, \pi)$ in order to maxi-

mize $P(O|\lambda)$. This can be solved using the *Baum-Welch Algorithm* for learning.

The basic assumption underlying this work is that the metamorphic malware have some features in common if they belong to the same family and hence, a virus can be modelled using an HMM. This model can find the metamorphic viruses with high accuracy if the suspected code has a similar score as that of the trained data. In order to develop an HMM for modelling viruses, states are the features and the opcodes act as observation sequences.

8 STATIC CODE ANALYSIS USING LONGEST COMMON SUBSEQUENCE

Our proposed method (Vinod, V. Laxmi, Gaur, Phani Kumar, & Chundawat, 2009) is based on block analysis of CFG. The executable code suspected to be malicious is disassembled and is further normalized. Control flow graph is created from normalized code. In our analysis, we try to determine similarity match between blocks of given code with those of known malicious code. This similarity is computed on basis of longest common subsequences (LCS) of the basic blocks under consideration and a LCS score is generated. Results are generated with obfuscated variants of each virus and some benign program. Initial results demonstrate effectiveness of our proposed methodology.

The problem statement is: Given a program *P*, consisting of an instruction sequence *s*, obfuscated using a transformation function *O(P)*, to produce variants *V* with instruction sequence *s'*. It is required to find out whether *s'* is equivalent to *s*. Intel x86 instruction set consists of numerous instructions. From this large instruction set, few instructions are used in malicious programs. For this, we categorized instructions into following classes:

(i) **Sequential Instructions**: These instructions do not alter the flow of control. These types include mov, add, sub, push, pop etc.

(ii) **Procedure call instruction**: Instructions used to call a specific procedure or system call. For example if test is a procedure in the program it is called using the statement call test.

(iii) **Return Instruction:** The ret instruction takes the control of the program to the immediate statement following the call instruction or to the end of the program if no statement follows the call instruction.

(iv) **Branch Instruction:** This class of instruction includes unconditional as well as conditional instrutions. These instructions alter the flow of execution. For example, few branch instructions are jmp, ja, jb, jc, jnc, jz etc.

A program consists of sequential statements and control flow statements. During the program execution, sequential statements are followed by next statements in the program, whereas, the statement following the control flow statements is selected by conditional jump. The order of statement during the control flow is described by control flow graph. Basic block is a maximal sequence of instructions $(i_1, i_2, \ldots, i_n)$ that contains, at the most, one control flow instruction. The flow of execution within the basic block is sequential until a call or branch instruction is encountered. Instructions are represented as nodes or basic blocks of CFG. Each sequential instruction is represented by instruction type 'T'. All branch instructions are represented by instruction type 'J'. Procedure calls are represented by instruction type 'C', and return statements are represented by instruction type 'R'.

CFG is a directed graph $G = (V, E, s, e)$, V is the set of nodes called the basic blocks, E is the set of edges, s is the start node and e is called the terminating node(s). All redundant instructions are removed from the CFG and a normalized code is obtained. Edges of basic block are represented as E_D for direct edge or E_I for indirect edge. Consider two nodes '*A*' and '*B*' of a CFG. Node '*A*' is connected to node '*B*' by a direct edge, with edge labelled as E_D. If '*A*' is a branch or call instruction and the target node is '*B*', the edge type is E_D. Otherwise, node '*A*' is connected to node '*B*' through an indirect edge labelled with E_I. C language structure of a node is shown below:

```
struct list{
    char mnoic[6];
    char operand[50];
    char I type;
    char label[25];
    int block no;
    char f, c;
    char s c;
    struct list * first;
    struct list * second;
}*start;
```

where the members of structure has following meaning:

Mnoic: mnemonic of the instruction.
Operand: operand of the instruction.
I type: instruction type $\in$ S, C, J, R.
Label: label of instruction.
Blockno: block number of instruction.
Edgetype1: branch for 'true' condition.
Edgetype2: branch for 'false' condition.

Consider the sample code with the following instructions:

```
L1:
    movl %eax, %esp
    addl $15, %eax
    jmp L2
    subl 12%esp
    jz L2
    shrl %eax
L2:
```

```
    xorl %eax, %eax
    ret
```

Step 1: Create a graph which consists of nodes for each instruction of above code (virus. s). The nodes are connected by either indirect edge or direct edge. In the Figure 7a, dotted lines represent indirect edges and solid lines represent direct edges.

Step 2: The normalized code is obtained after removing junk statements, equivalent statements and unconditional jump instructions from the graph obtained in step1. Figure 7b shows the graph representing the normalized code.

Step 3: Control flow graph consisting of basic blocks is obtained by merging all nodes of graph obtained in Figure 8 until a branch or call statement is encountered. All instructions in a single basic block contain the same value of 'blockno' variable. Block signatures are formed by concatenating all instructions corresponding to the block. Figure 8 shows CFG for a sample virus code. The dotted boxes depict blocks of CFG and block signatures generated are as follows:

```
B1: movl%eax, %espaddl$15, %eax-
subl$12, %esp
B2: jzL2
B3: xorl%eax, %eaxret
B4: shrl%eax
```

Similarity Analysis of Malware Variants: In the proposed method, instructions of basic blocks of original virus sample are compared with that of its variants. The comparison of instructions of basic blocks is performed using longest common subsequence (LCS) (Corman, Leiserson, Rivest, & Stein, 1990). The subsequence of two strings in the instruction occurs in the same order, but may not be consecutive. The problem of finding the longest common subsequence can be framed by aligning the instructions of each block of the original with that of the variants. Instructions in a block are aligned in a manner so as to maximize

Figure 7. Graph consisting of nodes for each instruction of virus

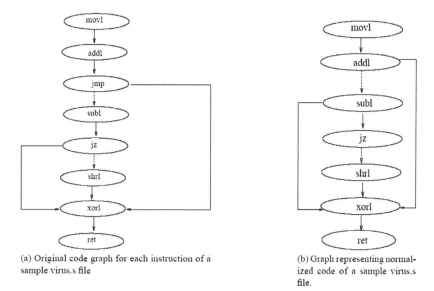

(a) Original code graph for each instruction of a sample virus.s file

(b) Graph representing normalized code of a sample virus.s file.

the number of characters with that of the instructions of variants.

Suppose, the original metamorphic virus has m block signatures and its variants have n block signatures. Then, each block B_i where $i = 1, 2, ..., m$ of original virus sample is compared with n blocks of its variants. The longest common subsequence (LCS) gives maximum number of matching characters at blocks of original virus with that of its variants. Then percentage match of instructions at two blocks B_i and B_j is calculated as:

$$\text{Match}(B_i, B_j) = \text{LCS}(B_i, B_j)/\text{total no. of characters in } B_j * 100$$

This percentage match of instruction of two blocks is stored in table of size $m \times n$, where cells of the table represents percentage match of instruction at block B_i, B_j for any two programs P_a & P_b. Consider block signatures of original virus shown below:

B1: pushl%espmovl$LC4, 4(%esp) popl %espleal-264(%ebp), %eaxmovl%eax,(%esp)
B2: jzL1
B3: pushl%espmovl$LC4, 4(%esp) popl %espleal-264(%ebp), %eaxmovl%eax,(%esp)
B4: movl$LC5, (%esp)
B5: call L2

Figure 8. Control flow graph for sample virus (s file)

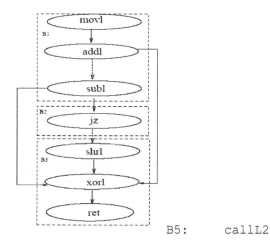

B5:   callL2

also consider block signatures of its variant presented here:

B1: `pushl%esp`

B2: `popl%espmovl$LC4, 4(%esp)ret`

B3: `pushl%eaxmovl$LC4, 4(%esp)`
`popl%espmovl%eax, (%esp)`

B4: `movl$LC5, (%esp)`

The percentage match between two programs (original and variant) is shown in Table 1. Each cell of the Table 3 shows the percentage match in instruction at basic blocks for two different programs.

We have analyzed some viruses that were collected from VX heavens (n.d.), and a number of variants were generated after obfuscating the code. Table 4 shows the comparison matrix of 'black wolf virus I' consisting of 7 blocks with its variant consisting of same number of blocks. The diagonal elements of comparison matrix represents percentage match of instructions between the blocks of two programs.

From the comparison matrix LCS score is computed as follows:

Table 1.

Original Executable	Infected Executable
Entry-Point 0x2000(. code section)	Entry-Point 0x8000(. reloc section)

Table 2. The percentage match of instruction in blocks of original program with that of its variants

O\V	1	2	3	4	5
1	10	24	49	16	5
2	1	1	2	2	2
3	10	24	49	16	5
4	6	15	16	17	3
5	2	3	4	3	7

$$score = 2 \times \sum max(R_{ij}) /(m + n)$$

For example, LCS score computed for the values taken from Table 1 is 24.8 which means that the two programs are dissimilar and have only few instructions in common. From the experiment that was conducted following observation could be made.

- Equal number of blocks was obtained in original virus and its variants.
- If the number of blocks in two programs differs by substantial amount, it can be concluded that the two programs are dissimilar. This can be used to find whether the sample is the variant of a virus.
- If the number of blocks of two programs is similar, LCS score could be used to find whether a program is a variant of original sample of virus. If the LCS score is below 100%, it is concluded that the program is not a variant of the original sample.
- The maximum matching instructions can be found by looking up in the diagonal elements of comparison matrix.

In order to prove the effectiveness of the proposed work, LCS score was computed between samples of virus and certain benign programs. The LCS score obtained after this experiment was substantially less. Refer Table 3 for comparison of

Table 3. The table shows comparison of 7 blocks of original sample of 'Black Wolf 1' virus with that of its variant

O/V	1	2	3	4	5	6	7
1	100	66	93	63	66	65	62
2	1	100	6	2	66	1	1
3	6	33	100	8	50	6	7
4	46	66	93	100	83	49	63
5	1	66	13	2	100	1	2
6	64	50	86	66	50	100	91
7	49	33	80	67	66	73	100

Table 4. Comparison of 20 blocks of screen freeze virus with that of 20 blocks of benign program (student record)

O\V	1	2	3	4	5	6	7	8	9	10	11	12	13	14	15	16	17	18	19	20
1	89	50	55	89	60	79	89	33	79	87	33	63	87	50	86	93	47	84	100	100
2	2	50	2	3	20	3	4	16	3	9	16	1	9	16	3	5	36	3	15	7
3	62	50	35	56	40	57	65	33	56	77	33	33	77	50	55	72	42	61	92	100
4	69	50	44	77	60	65	84	50	65	80	33	46	80	66	68	83	36	84	100	100
5	1	83	1	2	80	2	4	66	2	6	66	1	6	66	2	4	15	4	15	7
6	10	33	6	10	40	14	15	33	13	38	33	6	38	33	10	16	21	14	69	42
7	10	33	6	10	40	13	14	33	12	35	33	6	35	33	10	15	15	14	61	42
8	1	66	1	1	80	1	3	66	1	6	66	1	6	66	2	2	10	3	15	7
9	76	50	59	94	60	81	87	50	79	83	50	63	83	50	83	91	63	90	84	100
10	1	66	1	1	100	2	3	66	1	6	66	1	6	66	2	2	10	2	15	7
11	63	50	45	77	60	73	79	33	73	87	33	44	87	50	71	88	47	79	100	100
12	10	33	6	10	40	13	14	33	12	35	33	6	35	33	10	15	15	14	61	42
13	1	66	1	1	100	2	3	66	1	6	66	1	6	66	2	2	10	2	15	7
14	72	50	57	92	60	80	90	50	78	83	33	60	83	66	82	93	57	88	100	100
15	1	50	0	1	60	1	2	50	2	6	50	0	6	50	2	2	5	1	7	0
16	98	100	94	97	100	96	100	83	97	100	83	94	100	100	98	100	78	97	92	92
17	32	50	25	40	40	42	56	50	41	74	50	23	74	50	38	56	31	45	84	92
18	2	83	2	2	80	3	6	66	3	9	66	1	9	83	3	5	15	4	15	7
19	42	50	26	53	40	45	60	33	45	74	33	25	74	33	46	73	42	56	76	92
20	23	50	15	28	40	31	42	33	31	70	33	14	70	33	26	44	31	34	76	85

20 blocks of Screen Freeze virus with that of 20 blocks of benign program (student record). Table 4 depicts the LCS score calculated between certain virus programs, its variants and benign programs.

9 CONCLUDING REMARKS

Adleman (1988) proved that malware detection is undecidable problem. (Filliol, 1997) "A malware can act in 10 minutes but not malware detection software". Malware detection is crucial in today's world of computers as it has assumed multiple forms. It is exceedingly difficult to detect new variants as traditional signature based techniques do not scale well and can not handle unknown threats. Signature is binary form of a malware. Searching signature of a malicious code in its binary form, these methods are suitable for small size malware and hence can work efficiently only with limited sized signature repository. Malware creators have started using obfuscation techniques and/or encryption to escape detection resulting in metamorphic and polymorphic variants. The idea is to create structurally different malware variants with same functionality so as to avoid signature based detection and prevention. With ever-increasing number of malware strains and sophistication in the modes of infection, signature based detection techniques are increasingly proving inadequate.

Anomaly and specification based detection techniques improved alternative for signature based method. Anomaly based technique can deal with unknown threats but need storage to

Table 5. LCS score computed between original virus with that of some variants and benign program

Original Virus Sample	Variants	No. of blocks	LCS Score
Screen Freeze	Screen Freeze1	20	100%
	Screen Freeze2	20	100%
	Benign(Students Record)	20	83. 9%
Wonder	Wonder variant1	38	100%
	Wonder variant2	38	100%
	Benign(Binary Search)	38	74. 26%
Black Wolf II	Wolf variant1	38	100%
	Wolf variant2	38	100%
	Benign(Binary Search)	38	73. 42%

accumulate information about normal behaviour so that any statistically significant deviation from available information can be regarded as a potential threat and can subsequently isolated till analysis proves it otherwise. For a user machine, this technique is computational resource intensive and may slow down the user machine. This solution can be installed only in a dedicated network host machine set aside for this. The need is to come up with a generic solution to detect malware thereby minimizing false alarms.

The chapter introduces various types of malware. How these malware infect computer systems by looking at system vulnerabilities. The chapter highlights metamorphic malware and its detection mechanisms. State of art research work related to static & dynamic malware analysis and detection methods is also covered. We have also explained our proposed method of malware analysis and shown that block signatures could also be used for detecting malware. Thus, the need is to develop a hybrid tool which has the ability to detect malware using anomaly and specification based techniques. Such a tool should be capable of analyzing code before it executes and discover packed, obfuscated and self modifying code at runtime.

REFERENCES

Adleman, L. M. (1988). An abstract theory of computer viruses. *Crypto '88, Advances in Cryptography*, Lecture Notes. In *Computer Science*. New York: Springer.

Aycock, J. (2006). *Computer viruses and malware*. New York: Springer Science.

Bergeron, J., Debbabi, M., Erhioui, M. M., & Ktari, B. (1999). *Static analysis of binary code to isolate malicious behaviors* (pp. 184–189). DC, USA: IEEE Computer Society Washington.

Bonfante, G., Kaczmarek, M., Marion, J.Y., (2007). *Control flow graphs as malware signatures*.

Bonfante, G., Kaczmarek, M., & Marion, J. Y. (2008). *Morphological detection of malware* (pp. 1–8). DC, USA: IEEE Computer Society Washington.

Bruschi, D., Martignoni, L., & Monga, M. (2007). Code normalization for self-mutating malware. *IEEE Security and Privacy*, 5(2), 46–54. doi:10.1109/MSP.2007.31

Choi, Y. S., Kim, I. K., Oh, J. T., & Ryou, J. C. (2008). PE File Header analysis-based packed PE file detection technique (PHAD). *International Symposium on Computer Science and its Applications*.

Chouchane, M. R. Lakhotia, A.(2006). *Using engine signature to detect metamorphic* .

Christodorescu, M., Kinder, J., Jha, S., Katzenbeisser, S., Veith, H.,(2005). Malware

Collberg, C., Thomborson, C., & Low, D. (1997). *A taxonomy of obfuscating transformations*. Technical Report 148.

Corman, T. H., Leiserson, C. E., Rivest, R. L., & Stein, C. (1990). *Introduction to algorithms*. Cambridge, MA: MITPress.

Essam, Al.D., Ahid, Al.S., Adaan, M.A.(2009). Detecting metamophic viruses by using arbitrary length of control flow graphs and nodes alignment. *Ubiquitous Computing and Communication Journal, 4*(3),628-633.

Filiol, E.(2007). Concepts and future trends in computer virology. *20th CISE Plenary Talk*.

Ford, R., Howard, M.(2007). Revealing packed malware. *Proceedings of Security & Privacy*. IEEE Computer Society.

Heavens, V. X. http://vx. netlux. org/lib.

Jeong, K., & Lee, H. (2008). Code graph for malware detection. *International conference on Information Networking, ICOIN*, 1–5.

Jiang, X., Wang, X., & Xu, D. (2007). Stealthy malware detection through VMM-based "Out-of-the-box" semantic view reconstruction.*Proceedings of the 14th ACM conference on Computer and communications security*, pp.128–138, New York.

Jin, R., Wei, Q., Yang, P., & Wang, Q. (2007). Normalization towards instruction substitution metamorphism based on standard instruction set. *IEEE, International Conference on Computer Intelligence and Security (CIS) Workshop*.

Karnik, A., Goswami, S., & Guha, R. (2007). Detecting obfuscated viruses using cosine similarity analysis. *IEEE AMS '07: Proceedings of the First Asia International Conference on Modelling & Simulation*, pp.165–170, Washington, DC, USA.

Kruegel, C., Kirda, E., Mutz, D., Robertson, W., & Vigna, G. (2005). Polymorphic worm detection using structural information of executables. *RAID*, 207–226, New York: Springer-Verlag.

Kruegel, C., Kirda, E., Mutz, D., Robertson, W., & Vigna, G. (2007). Metaaware: Identifying metamorphic malware. *Twenty-Third Annual IEEE Conference Proceeding on Computer Security Applications Conference, ACSAC*.

Lakhotia, A., Kapoor, A. Uday Kumar,E. (2004). *Are metamorphic computer viruses really invisible?* Part 1.

Marhusin, M. F., Larkin, H., Lokan, C., Cornforth, D. (2008). An evaluation of API calls hooking performance. *CIS '08: Proceedings of the 2008 International Conference on Computational Intelligence and Security*, pp. 315–319. Washington, DC: IEEE Computer Society. Metamorphism in practice or How I made Metaphor and What I've Learnt. http://vx. netlux. org/lib, February 2002.

Moser, A., Kruegel, C., & Kirda, E. (2007). Exploring multiple execution paths for malware analysis. *Security and Privacy, SP '07. IEEE Symposium on*, 231–245. MSDN library. http:// msdn. microsoft. com/en-us/library. normalization. Technische Universitt Mnchen.

Perdisci, R., Lanzi, A., & Lee, W. (2008). McBoost: Boosting scalability in malware collection and analysis using statistical classification of executables.*Annual Computer Security* Applications Conference, ACSAC.

Reddy, D. K. S., & Pujari, A. K. (2006). *N-gram analysis for computer virus detection* (pp. 231–239).

Sathyanarayan, V. S., Kohli, P., & Bruhadeshwar, B. (2008) Signature generation and detection of malware families. *ACISP '08: Proceedings of the 13th Australasian conference on Information Security and Privacy*, 336–349, Berlin: Springer-Verlag.

Skoudis, E., & Zeltser, L. (2003). *Malware: Fighting malicious code*. Upper Saddle River, NJ: Prentice Hall.

Sung, A. H., & Xu, J. Chavez, P., Mukkamala, S.(2004). Static analyzer of vicious executables (SAVE). *20th Annual Computer Security Applications Conference ACSAC'04*, 2004.

Sz¨or, P. (1997). *Virus Analysis 3*. Oxford, UK: Virus Bulletin.

Sz¨or, P. (2000). *The new 32-bit Medusa*. Oxford, UK: Virus Bulletin.

Sz¨or, P., & Ferrie, P. (2001). *Hunting for metamorphic* (pp. 123–144). Oxford, UK: Virus Bulletin.

Treadwell, S., & Zhou, M. (2009). *A Heuristic approach for detection of obfuscated malware*. IEEE Xplore.

Vinod, P., Laxmi, V., & Gaur, M. S. Phani Kumar, GVSS., Chundawat, Y.S.(2009). Metamorphic virus detections through static code analysis. *Indo-US Workshop and Conference on Cyber Security, Cyber Crime and Cyber Forensics*.

Walenstein, A., Chouchane, M.R., Lakhotia, A.(2007). Statistical signature for fast filtering of instruction-substituting metamorphic malware. *Proceedings of Worm'07*.

Walenstein, A., Mathur, R., Chouchane, M. R., & Lakhotia, A. (2007). The Design space of metamorphic malware. *2nd International Conference on Information Warfare*.

Webster, M., & Malcolm, G. (2006). Detection of metamorphic computer viruses using algebraic specification. *Journal in Computer Virology, 2*(3), 149–161. doi:10.1007/s11416-006-0023-z

Williams, C., Holz, T., & Freiling, F. (2007). Toward automated dynamic malware analysis using CWSandbox. *Security & Privacy, IEEE, 5*(2), 32–39. doi:10.1109/MSP.2007.45

Wong, W., & Stamp, M. (2006). Hunting for metamorphic engines. *Journal in Computer Virology, 2*(3), 211–229. doi:10.1007/s11416-006-0028-7

Xu, J.-Y., Sung, A. H., Chavez, P., & Mukkamala, S. (2004). Polymorphic malicious executable scanner by API sequence analysis. *The Fourth International Conference on Hybrid Intelligent Systems*, pp. 378–383. Washington, DC: IEEE Computer Society.

Section 3
Cyber–Security:
Methods and Algorithms

Chapter 14
Towards Checking Tampering of Software

N.V. Narendra Kumar
Tata Institute of Fundamental Research, India

Harshit Shah[1]
Amrita Vishwa Vidyapeetham, India

R.K. Shyamasundar
Tata Institute of Fundamental Research, India

ABSTRACT

Assuring integrity of software is a very challenging issue. Different manifestations of tampering exist such as intentional attack with the aim of harming the user (through some kind of a malware; Baker, 1995) or the user himself tampers with the software to gain features he is not authorized with (Baxter, Yahin, Moura, Sant'Anna, & Bier, 1998). In this chapter, the authors make a survey of various strategies used to assure the integrity of software such as trusted computing platform, software attestation, software similarity, software watermark, software birthmark etc. Subsequently, the authors present a novel method for malware detection from a semantic approach that can be adapted for checking the integrity of software. They shall discuss some of the initial experimental results in this direction.

1 INTRODUCTION

Measuring integrity of software after deployment is important to ensure that software is not tampered with. Software tampering problem manifests itself in different ways: (i) done by an attacker to harm the user/system (e.g., infection by virus), and (ii) done by the user himself to use the software in ways that the creator of software did not intend/permit (e.g., tamper the software

to bypass checks for subscription). In either case, software tampering can result in a great loss to resources, reputation, etc. and is a serious problem that demands robust solutions.

Software providers would want to measure integrity of their software and also the environment in which it executes. This would help to ensure that the user does not tamper with the software so as to use it in unintended ways. For example, unlocking certain restricted features in a demo version. In Kosar, Christodorescu, & Iverson (2003), authors present a mechanism to bypass license checks us-

DOI: 10.4018/978-1-60960-123-2.ch014

ing a binary instrumentation tool. These activities could result in tremendous financial loss to the software provider. Worldwide, the economic losses associated with cracked software are estimated to be tens of billions of dollars[2]. Besides, the cracked software is not trusted and may contain spyware, adware, etc. Inadequate measures to curb piracy, like Sony BMG CD copy protection scandal[3], have also proved damaging. A detailed study of the disc copy protection mechanism revealed that it contained a number of flaws that exposed users to serious security and privacy risks (Halderman, & Felten, 2006).

Further, the impact of malicious programs on the integrity of software is also an important aspect to be considered. Although according to the 2007 malware report on the economic impact of viruses, spyware, adware, botnets, and other malicious code (www.computereconomics.com), the direct damages incurred in 2006 shows a decline in direct damages since 2004, this decline is attributed to a shift in the focus of malware writers from creating damaging malware to creating stealthy, fast-spreading malware so that infected machines can be used for sending spam, stealing credit-card numbers, displaying advertisements or opening a backdoor to an organization's network.

The above issues call for a holistic approach to detection of software tampering. A lot of research has been done in this area. In the forthcoming sections, we will present several approaches to detect tempering. We will also present a promising new approach to detect tampering and analyze its effectiveness in tackling the problem through our initial experimental results.

The chapter is organized as follows: in section 2, we give an overview of different techniques to detect software tampering. In section 3, we present a novel approach to capture program behaviour based birthmark together with a preliminary experimental evaluation. Our experiments suggest that this approach is robust against semantics preserving transformations to which most known approaches are vulnerable.

2 TECHNIQUES FOR DETECTING SOFTWARE TAMPERING

In this section we survey some techniques proposed in the literature for detecting tampering of software. We classify them into three categories:

- Techniques based on trusted computing platform
- Software based techniques for attestation
- Techniques based on program similarity measures

In the following subsections we describe each of the above in detail.

2.1 Trusted Computing Platform and Related Approaches

Trusted Computing Group (TCG)[4] has laid down architectural specification for a Trusted Computing Platform (TCP) that uses a Trusted Platform Module (TPM). TPM is a tamper-proof hardware device that stores certificates, cryptographic keys and integrity measurements. When the machine is turned on, the integrity measurements are started from a trusted component in BIOS. Every executable that is loaded is measured before execution and the measurements are stored in TPM. Thus, starting from a trusted component, the trust boundary extends transitively to include every executable running on the system. This process is shown in Figure 1. The integrity measurements can then be used by other systems on the network to determine whether the execution environment on that machine can be trusted.

Measurements consist of two classes of data: 1) measured values - a representation of embedded data or program code, and 2) measurement digests - a hash of measured values. Data is scanned by the measurement kernel, which generates a message digest – a snapshot of the machine's operational state. The two data elements (measured values and measurement digest) can be stored

Figure 1. Transitive flow of trust

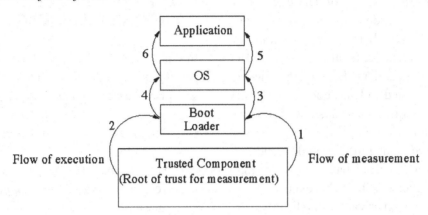

separately. Measurement data describe properties and characteristics of the measured component. It is the responsibility of the measurement kernel implementer to understand the syntax and semantics of measured fields in sufficient detail to produce an encoding suitable for measurement event consumers. The TPM contains a set of registers, called Platform Configuration Registers (PCR) containing measurement digests. Algebraically, updates to a PCR follows as: $PCR[n] \leftarrow SHA\text{-}1(PCR[n] + \text{measured data})$. PCR values are temporal and are reset at system reboot. Verification of measurement events requires recreation of the measurement digest and a simple comparison of digest values (using the PCR value as one of the comparators).

TPM stores Attestation Identity Keys (AIKs) that are used to attest the authenticity of stored integrity values. These keys are generated using an Endorsement Key that comes embedded with TPM. The attestation protocol consists of the following steps: (i) a challenger requests PCR values from a platform, (ii) TPM signs PCR values using AIK and retrieves the stored log of measurement values, (iii) platform collects credentials that vouch for the TPM, signed PCR values, stored log values and sends them to the challenger, (iv) the challenger evaluates the platform credentials and computes the measurement digest and checks it against PCR value.

An implementation of TCG specifications for Linux platform is presented in Sailer, Zhang, Jaeger, & van Doorn (2004).

Other TCP Related Approaches

Next Generation Secure Computing Base (NG-SCB)[5] is a software architecture proposed by Microsoft. NGSCB relies on hardware design proposed by members of TCG. It involves a component called "Nexus" which forms the kernel of an isolated software stack running alongside the existing OS. Nexus aware systems would offer the following security features: (i) Strong process isolation - an application could hide its pages so that other applications (including OS itself) would not be able to view them, (ii) Sealed storage – data could be stored by an application in such a way that it would be accessible only to itself and a set of other components that are cryptographically identifiable, (iii) Secure path from peripheral devices to applications, and (iv) Attestation – to authenticate a combination of software and hardware to a remote system.

In Garfinkel, Pfaff, Chow, Rosenblum, & Boneh (2003), authors present a Virtual Machine (VM) platform for trusted computing. A Trusted Virtual Machine Monitor (TVMM) provides isolation to applications. Each VM is either provided open-box semantics (i.e., general purpose hardware platform) or closed-box semantics (special purpose platform that protects privacy and integrity of its contents). TVMM also acts as a trusted party to allow closed-box VMs to identify software they run to remote parties.

NexusOS (Shieh, Williams, GünSirer, & Schneider, 2005) is an operating system for trustworthy computing that provides microkernel architecture designed to reduce the size of Trusted Computing Base (TCB)[6] by moving drivers and other system services outside the kernel. Even secondary storage devices are not part of TCB. Nexus offers mechanisms to attest to application-specific, run-time properties about programs. This helps formulation of rich access control policies. Secure memory regions provide applications with integrity and confidentiality. This enables a range of trustworthy computing services and applications like implementing linear or limited-number-of-reuse capability. For example, a media player can stipulate that certain protected media can be played only 5 times. In this regard, Nexus is different from other approaches that only compute hash of executables and hence cannot attest to expressive properties of programs.

In Lie, Thekkath, & Horowitz (2003), authors use the XOM architecture (Lie et al., 2000) to enable trustworthy computing. Use of secure processor removes the need to place trust in the OS. XOM architecture has been formally verified to guarantee that even if the OS is malicious, it can only extract limited information about programs. XOM processor encrypts the values in memory and also stores the hash of these values in memory. Since virtual addresses are also used in computing hash, this approach offers copy protection. Programs are prevented from interfering with each other by placing them in separate compartments. These compartments are implemented through cryptography and data tagging in hardware. However, due to performance issues, this approach has not found acceptance in the industry.

Limitations

TCG based approaches rely on tamper proof hardware to store and report integrity measurements. Apart from some isolation to trusted components, these approaches do not guarantee freedom from tampering due to malware. A malware infection would only be detected during attestation when unexpected hash values would show up. Also, since entire programs are hashed to generate integrity measurements, minor modifications to programs (like using a different compiler or optimizing the program for performance) would require that the new versions be certified first. This limits the flexibility of the system. To summarize, these approaches offer protection against user induced tampering by enforcing hardware requirements on the system. However, they reduce its flexibility and provide no protection against external malicious attacks.

2.2 Software Based Techniques for Attestation

These techniques rely on computing checksums of memory locations to detect tampering. In order to prevent pre-compute and replay attacks, randomly generated challenges are used and memory locations are selected randomly. In Kennell, & Jamieson (2003), authors propose to use sufficient architectural meta-information that is produced in a modern CPU to generate a sequence of memory locations whose checksum is to be computed. The authors use memory subsystem information like cache hits and misses, TLB hits and misses as a source of architectural information. This will significantly slow down an adversary who tries to simulate the CPU.

In Seshadri, Perrig, van Doorn, & Khosla (2004), authors present SWATT (SoftWare based ATTestation), an external, software based attestation mechanism to verify memory contents of embedded devices like sensor motes, networked printers, etc. SWATT can detect memory changes with high probability and it does not rely on tamper-proof hardware. SWATT relies on a challenge-response protocol wherein an external verifier sends a challenge to the embedded device. The embedded device computes the response using a verification procedure that is either pre-installed or downloaded before verification. Since the verifier knows the memory layout of the embedded device, it can compute the response locally and verify it. The verification procedure is designed in such a way that even if an attacker changes a single byte in the memory, the response would either be incorrect or there would be a noticeable delay in generating the response. The verification procedure performs a pseudo-random memory traversal using a pseudo random number generator (seeded with randomly generated challenge provided by the verifier) and computes a checksum over the contents. Since the attacker cannot predict the sequence, if the verification procedure touches upon an altered location, the load has to be redirected to the location containing the original content. This introduces a significant delay since the attacker has to check each randomly generated memory location to see if it has been modified. Probability of successful detection can be increased by increasing the number of iterations in the part of verification procedure that selects memory locations and computes checksum.

Pioneer (Seshadri, Luk, Shi, Perrig, van Doorn, & Khosla, 2005) is a technique for verifying code integrity and untampered execution that does not require secure co-processor or hardware extensions. Pioneer relies on a challenge response protocol between the dispatcher and untrusted platform. After successful invocation of Pioneer, the dispatcher obtains assurance that: (i) the executable on the target is unmodified, (ii) unmodified executable is executed on the platform, and (iii) the executable is not tampered with during execution. These assurances hold even in the presence of malware on the target system. The challenge-response protocol proceeds as follows:

1. Challenge - the dispatcher issues a random challenge to the verification function.
2. Compute checksum - the verification function uses random challenge to compute checksum of its entire code (this procedure is similar to the one used in SWATT).
3. Send Checksum - verification function sends the checksum back to the dispatcher. If the checksum is incorrect or it does not arrive within a pre-specified limit, dispatcher exits with error.
4. Hash - verification function then computes hash of the executable and sends it to the dispatcher.
5. Dispatcher verifies the hash of the executable.
6. Verification function invokes the executable.

Thus, the verification function provides a dynamic root of trust that can be used to establish safe execution of untampered executable. As in the case of SWATT, any effort to hide tampering will either result in incorrect checksum or delay the response. Some of the restrictions imposed in order to achieve the desired property are: executable should not invoke other software on untrusted platform, executable should be able to run at highest privilege level with interrupts disabled, CPU should not be over-clocked and should not support Symmetric Multi Threading (SMT).

Limitations

Above approaches have an advantage that they do not rely on secure, tamper-proof hardware. This makes them suitable for embedded devices and legacy systems. However, the detection of tampering is only probabilistic. In order to exploit the timing related characteristics of the verification function, the verifier and the untrusted platform should be connected by a network link where the delays could be bound. If the maximum delay in the network is greater than the extra time needed for an attacker to compute the checksum correctly, then the above techniques can be subverted. Also,

Pioneer imposes constraints on the system (e.g., no support for SMT, ability to execute at the highest privilege level without being interrupted, etc.) that may hamper its performance.

2.3 Program Similarity Based Techniques

We can broadly classify the work in this area into two categories: *code clone detection* and *software birthmark*.

Code Clone Detection

Code clone detection is a technique to find the duplicate code ("clones") in large software. It was traditionally used to decrease code size and facilitate maintenance and debugging. Clone detection can also be used for detecting software plagiarism and software tampering to a limited extent.

In Baker (1995), the author presents an approach to find maximal sections of code over a threshold length that are either exactly same (exact match), or the same except for a global substitution of names of parameters such as variables and constants (parameterized match). This approach is text-based and line-based with comments and white spaces ignored.

Another approach (Kontogiannis, Galler, & DeMori, 1995) describes techniques to localize patterns of code that implement a particular plan or algorithm. Code-to-code matching is achieved by using a dynamic programming based pattern matcher that calculates the best alignment between two code fragments at the statement level. The distance between code fragments takes into account insertion and deletion costs to achieve the alignment. Abstract-description-to-code matching approach is based on abstract pattern languages (typically abstract syntax trees) that are used to describe programming plans. Markov models are used to guide the matching process and a Viterbi algorithm computes the best match between an abstract plan description and a code fragment.

Similarity distances are given in terms of the probability that a given abstract statement can generate a particular code fragment.

In Baxter et al. (1998), the authors present simple and practical methods for detecting exact and near miss clones over arbitrary program fragments in program source code by using abstract syntax trees. This approach is based on variations of methods for compiler common-subexpression elimination using hashing. The method is easy to implement, using standard parsing technology, detects clones in arbitrary language constructs, and computes macros that allow removal of the clones without affecting the operation of the program.

Another interesting approach using web services is presented in Prechelt, Malpohl, & Philippsen (2002) where the authors present an architecture and a comparison algorithm of JPlag, that is a web service that finds pairs of similar programs among a given set of programs. JPlag takes as input a set of programs, compares these programs pairwise computing for each pair a total similarity value and a set of similarity regions. To do this JPlag converts each program into a string of canonical tokens. For the comparison of two programs, JPlag then covers one such token string by substrings taken from the other where possible. JPlag's comparison algorithm is based on Greedy String Tiling. By pointing out the regions that are different, JPlag can be used as a program-differencing engine. Compared to a character-based difference, a JPlag difference ignores much detail and hence produces much smaller differences.

In Kamiya, Kusumoto, & Inoue (2002), the authors propose a tool for clone detection technique CCFinder, which consists of the transformation of input source text and a token-by-token comparison. CCFinder makes a token sequence from the input code though a lexical analyzer and applies the rule-based transformation to the sequence. Representing a source code as a token sequence enables to detect clones with different line structures, this cannot be detected by line-by-line algorithm. Then they use a suffix-tree matching algorithm to compute matching, in which the clone location information is represented as a tree with sharing nodes for leading identical subsequences and the clone detection is performed by searching the leading nodes on the tree. They have also proposed several metrics to select interesting clones.

A class of local document finger-printing algorithms is presented in Schleimer, Wilkerson, & Aiken (2003), which capture an essential property of any fingerprinting technique guaranteed to detect copies. They also present an efficient local finger-printing algorithm called winnowing that guarantees that matches of a certain length are detected.

In Krinke (2001), the author presents an approach to identify similar code in programs based on finding similar subgraphs in attributed directed graphs. This approach is based on program dependence graphs and therefore considers not only the syntactic structure of programs but also the data flow within as an abstraction of the semantics. Identified similar subgraphs can then be mapped onto the program code.

A plagiarism detection tool called GPlag, is presented in Liu, Chen, Han, & Yu (2006), which detects plagiarism by mining program dependence graphs (PDGs). A PDG is a graphic representation of the data and control dependencies within a procedure. In order to make GPlag scalable to large programs the authors propose a statistical lossy filter to prune the plagiarism search space.

Code clone detection techniques have several drawbacks to be used for detecting software tampering. First, all these approaches need access to source code. Also, because all these approaches are syntactic in nature, they are easily beaten by the various semantics preserving obfuscation transformations (see Collberg, Thomborson, & Low, 1997).

Software Watermark

The software watermarking problem is to embed a structure W into a program P such that: W can be reliably located and extracted from P even after P has been subjected to code transformations such as translation, optimization and obfuscation; W is stealthy; W has a high data rate; embedding W into P does not adversely affect the performance of P; and W has a mathematical property that allows us to argue that its presence in P is the result of deliberate actions. Software watermarking is an important tool for combating software piracy.

In Collberg & Thomborson (1999), the authors construct taxonomy of software watermarking techniques based on how watermarks are embedded, retrieved and attacked. They also provided a fundamental formalization of software watermarking. One of the main contributions of the chapter was a family of watermarking techniques in which marks are embedded within in the topology of dynamic heap data structures.

Path-based watermarking is introduced in Collberg et al. (2004) as a new approach to software watermarking based on the dynamic branching behaviour of programs. The idea comes with the intuition that the branches executed by a program are an essential aspect of its computation and part of what makes the program unique. This technique has the advantage that error-correcting and tamper-proofing techniques can be used to make path-based watermarks resilient against a wide variety of known obfuscation attacks. Since branches are ubiquitous in real programs, path-based watermarks are less susceptible to statistical attacks.

Software Birthmark

A new kind of software protection technique called software birthmark has been recently proposed. A software birthmark is a unique characteristic that a program possesses and can be used to identify the program. Software birthmarks can be classified into:

- static source code based birthmark
- static executable code based birthmark
- dynamic whole program path based birthmark
- dynamic API call based birthmark
- dynamic behaviour based birthmark

In Tamada, Nakamura, & Monden (2004), the authors presented four types of static birthmarks to provide an evidence of theft of Java class files: constant values in field variables birthmark (CVFV), sequence of method calls birthmark (SMC), inheritance structure birthmark (IS) and used classes birthmark (UC). Although birthmarks are easily computable, they provide weaker evidence than the watermarks. Tamada's birthmark is vulnerable to obfuscation techniques and also need access to source code.

An opcode-level k-gram based static birthmark has been introduced in Myles & Collberg (2005). Opcode sequences of length k are extracted from a program and k-gram techniques which were used to detect similarity of documents are used for opcode sequences. Although this birthmark is more robust than Tamada's, it is vulnerable to some obfuscations.

In Myles & Collberg (2004), whole program path (WPP) based dynamic birthmark has been introduced. WPP is originally used to represent the dynamic control flow of a program. WPP birthmark is robust to some control flow based obfuscations, but is vulnerable to many other kinds of obfuscations such as loop unwinding. WPP birthmarks are not suitable for large programs due to its large size.

Tamada, Okamoto, Nakamura, Monden, & Matsumoto (2004, 2007) introduced two types of dynamic birthmarks for Windows applications: sequence of API function calls birthmark (EXESEQ) and frequency of API function calls birthmark (EXEFREQ). In EXESEQ, the sequence of Windows API calls is recorded during the execution of a program. These sequences are directly compared to check similarity. In EXEFREQ, the frequency of each Windows API calls is recorded during the execution of a program. The frequency distribution is used as the birthmark.

A dynamic birthmark for Java has been proposed in Schuler, Dallmeier, & Lindig (2007). The call sequences to Java standard API are recorded and the short sequences at object level are used as a birthmark. They also showed that API birthmarks are more robust to obfuscation than the WPP birthmarks.

In Wang, Jhi, Zhu, & Liu (2009), the authors propose a system call dependence graph based software birthmark called SCDG birthmark, and evaluate how well it reflects unique behavioural characteristics of a program. They also identified five features highly desirable of a software birthmark:

1. resiliency to semantics preserving obfuscation techniques
2. capability to detect theft of components which may only be a small part of the whole program
3. scalability to detect large-scale commercial software theft
4. applicability to binary executables because the source code is often unavailable
5. independence to platforms such as operating systems and programming languages

Behaviour characteristics have been widely used to identify and separate malware from benign programs (Christodorescu, Jha, & Kruegel, 2007; Kirda, Kruegel, Banks, Vigna, & Kemmerer, 2006). The concept of a Dynamic Dependence Graph (DDG) of a program run is presented in Zhang, Tallam, & Gupta (2006). System Call Dependence Graph (SCDG, obtained from DDG) is a graph representation of the behaviours of a program, where system calls represent the vertices, and data and control dependencies between system calls are represented by edges. A SCDG shows the interaction between a program and its operating system and the interaction is an essential behavioural characteristic of the program. SCDG's are quite resilient to obfuscation transformations. SCDG birthmark satisfies the above mentioned properties.

Their algorithm can be summarized as follows:

- perform automated dynamic analysis on the original program and the suspected program to record system call traces and dependence relation between system calls
- filter out noises from the system call traces
- construct SCDG birthmarks for both the original and the suspected program
- compare the SCDG birthmarks using graph isomorphism algorithms

They have demonstrated through experiments that SCDG birthmarks are resilient to various kinds of semantic preserving transformations like compiler optimization levels, using different compilers and program obfuscators.

3 CAPTURING PROGRAM CHARACTERISTICS THROUGH BIRTHMARKS

A program can execute on a hardware platform that has the relevant software environment, typically an operating system. Operating system acts as an interface between the user applications and the hardware (note that there are a lot of intermediate steps). By an environment, we mean the OS and its configurations and the associated software and hardware. When a program executes in an environment the following are observable by the system: input and output, the filesystem, trace of the execution (in terms of the process tree created and system calls invoked by each process) etc.

By behaviour of a program executing in an environment we mean the process tree created

and the associated sequence/trace of system calls it makes during execution. The interaction between an application executing in an environment and the environment itself can be viewed as that of requester and service provider. We want the environment to protect itself from being damaged by an application executing in it. To this end, we enrich the environment with a monitor, which records all the observable parameters when a program is executing in the environment. Some of the observable parameters are the effective CPU time used by the program, the amount of memory used by the program, the side effects program caused to the environment like changing the environment variables etc. Note that all the information that a monitor wants can be obtained by monitoring the system calls that the program makes for its execution. System call is the interface through which a program accesses low level system resources.

We now define external behaviour of a reactive program; it is used in the sense, that the program reacts on receiving an input rather than interpreted in the real-time domain.

Definition 1: *Let Σ be a non-empty finite set of signatures that represent interactive operations between the user and the system. The set of possible external behaviours of a program p is then given by $B_p = \{t \mid t \in \Sigma^+, t$ is a properly terminating sequence representing a valid transaction of p}*

Note that B_p is in general infinite. However, for reactive transactional systems it will be finite ignoring the data. For example, for a vending machine there are only finite ways in which a user can interact with the machine. place-coin ^ choose-item ^ receive-item denotes one possible interaction. As another example, we can consider the possible interaction patterns of a text editor. Open-file ^ (insert+delete+modify)$^+$ ^ save-file ^ exit is a typical interaction pattern.

During execution of a program p with external behaviour t, a process may spawn child processes internally (not necessarily observable to the user) for modularly achieving/computing the final result. Thus the total (internal + external) behaviour can be denoted by a tree with processes, data operations etc denoted as nodes and directed edges. Each node in the tree corresponds to a process and there is a directed edge from node r to node s if process s is the child of process r. We call this the process tree and formally define it below.

Definition 2: *Process tree of a reactive program p w.r.t external behaviour t is defined as PTree(p,t)=(V,E) where V is the set of processes created during execution of p from initialization and E⊆V×V such that (v_1,v_2)∈E iff process v_2 is the child of the process v_1.*

We can now define the system behaviour/ internal behaviour of a program as the process tree generated during execution together with the associated system calls made by each process (vertex/node) in the tree. Let *seq* denotes the set of all finite sequences of system calls.

Definition 3: *System behaviour of a reactive program p w.r.t external behaviour t is denoted by systrace(p,t)=(T,L) where T=PTree(p,t)=(V,E) and L: V → seq, L is a labelling function that associates a sequence of system calls (including input and output) with every vertex in the tree.*

Note that alternately system behaviour of a program could be defined as a set of sequences of system calls, where each sequence corresponds to

the concatenation of calls made along some path from root to a leaf in the tree.

Intuitively, for checking whether the behaviours of two programs are the same or not, we check whether the process trees generated by them are same and then check that the sequences of system calls associated with corresponding nodes are closely related.

First, we illustrate some simple methods of comparison using examples.

Experiments with Text Editor *nano*

We have collected the system behaviour of *nano* for the external behaviour create-file-example. txt ˆ write-hello ˆ save ˆ exit. We infected *nano* with a virus v. Behaviour of the infected *nano* at a high level is as follows:

1. creates backdoor to a remote server (address is hardcoded)
2. Infects a randomly selected executable file (by prepending itself to the program)
3. extracts the *nano* program and executes it

We then collected the system behaviour of infected *nano* for the same external behaviour. Genuine *nano* program creates no child processes, whereas the infected *nano* creates a process tree with 5 nodes. Process trees of genuine *nano* and infected *nano* are given in Figure 2.

Figure 2: Process trees of nano and its infected version

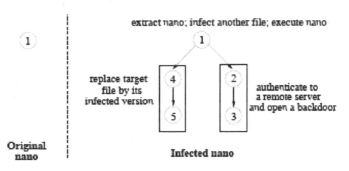

213

From the process trees generated we can immediately conclude that *nano* program has been infected.

Experiments with *ssh*

We have collected the system behaviour of genuine *ssh* and an infected *ssh* for the external behaviour start-sshd ˆ login ˆ logout. We have observed that the process trees generated by both the programs are the same (i.e., there is a one-to-one correspondence between them). Then, we matched the system calls associated with corresponding nodes in the process trees. We observed that during authentication phase the genuine *ssh* program used PAM (Pluggable Authentication Module), whereas the infected version implemented its own mechanism. From this difference we can conclude that the *ssh* program is infected.

We now try to establish these intuitions formally.

Definition 4: *Two tress $T_1=(V_1,E_1)$ and $T_2=(V_2,E_2)$ are said to be isomorphic iff there is a function $h:V_1 \rightarrow V_2$ such that both the following conditions are satisfied*

1. h is a bijection
2. $\forall p, q \in V_1$ $[(p, q) \in E_1$ iff $(h(p),h(q)) \in E_2]$

Definition 5: *Behaviours $B_1=((V_1,E_1),L_1)$ and $B_2=((V_2,E_2),L_2)$ are said to be similar, denoted $B_1 \sim B_2$ iff there is a function $h:V_1 \rightarrow V_2$ such that the following conditions are satisfied*

1. h is a bijection
2. $\forall p, q \in V_1$ $[(p,q) \in E_1$ iff $(h(p),h(q)) \in E_2]$
3. $\forall p \in V_1$ $L_1(p) = L_2(h(p))$

Definition 6: *Programs p and q are said to be equivalent w.r.t external behaviour t iff systrace(p, t)~systrace(q, t)*

Let us say that we have an installation of program p (say p'), which we suspect to have been tampered. We want to verify if it is indeed the case that p' is tampered. We will do so by observing the system behaviour of p' for external behaviour t and comparing it with its intended behaviour. For all frequently used programs we assume access to their intended behaviour in the database D.

Having both the intended behaviour and the observed system behaviour, we can now arrive at various ways of checking for behaviour equivalence. Some of the techniques used are bisimulation (Park, 1981), model checking the behaviours for given properties (Kinder, Katzenbeisser, Schallhart, & Veith, 2005), syntactic matching, trace equivalence of behaviours etc.

Definition 7: *An installation of program p (call it p') is said to be tampered w.r.t external behaviour t iff $D(p, t) \nsim systrace(p',t)$.*

3.1 Experimental Results

We have performed a lot of experiments and obtained encouraging results. We present some of the experiments and our observations in this section. We performed our experiments on a machine with Linux (Ubuntu distribution) OS. We monitored (unobtrusive) the sequence of system calls made (using strace tool), when the genuine text editor *nano* is used to edit a file. Note that system calls act as an interface between the application and the underlying hardware devices (can be thought of as services). We have also noted the % of time spent in various system calls, the number of processes created during execution, total running time, CPU and other resources used during this operation. We have collected similar information for the genuine *ssh* program starting from the time the service is started to the time the user logged in and completed the session.

We executed an infected version of *nano* program and collected the observable information during its execution. We then compared it with its intended behaviour and we easily concluded from the observations made that the version of *nano* we executed is infected. Moreover we were also able to identify the instructions added due to infection to the program.

We used strace to observe the behaviour of *nano* and its infected version (including the processes spawned by each). We assume that the strace program and the components it relies on were not tampered with and hence, traces generated actually corresponded to the true program behaviour.

Traces of System Calls

System call traces of each version (including any spawned processes) were generated and the analyzed. Figure 3 shows the structure of the infected program.

Summary of differences in the system call profiles of the genuine *nano* vs. the infected *nano*:

1. original program made 18 different system calls whereas the infected version made 48
2. infected program made network related system calls like socket, connect, etc. whereas the original program made none
3. infected program spawned 3 processes whereas the original program did not spawn any process
4. there is a huge difference in the number of read and write system calls
5. we observed a difference in the timing information provided by strace summary (when both the versions were run only for a few seconds). Original program spent around 88% on execve system call and 12% on stat64 whereas the infected version spent 74.17% on waitpid, 10.98% on write, 6.28% on read, 4.27% on execve and negligible time on stat64. This indicates that the infected program spent more time waiting on children

Figure 3: Structure of the infected program

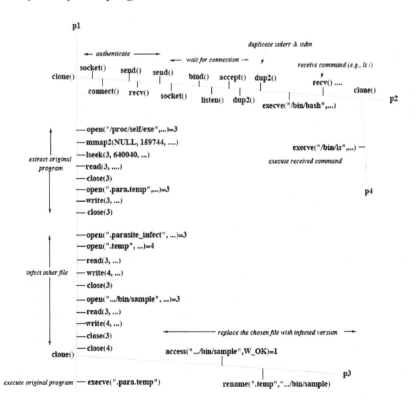

than in execution. This increased percentage of time spent on writing and reading by infected program indicates malfunction.

We executed an infected *ssh* program and collected the observable information during its execution. We then compared it with its intended behaviour and found that infected program modified the authentication module of the *ssh* program. Infected *ssh* would enable an attacker to successfully login to our host using a valid username with a magic-pass. In this case, the infection has removed certain instructions from the program. At a high level we can describe the expected behavior of *ssh* as follows:

1. start sshd service
2. wait for a connection and accept a connection
3. authenticate the user
4. prepare and provide a console with appropriate environment
5. manage user interaction and logout
6. stop sshd

Summary of differences in behavior between genuine *ssh* and the infected *ssh*:

1. start sshd service
   ◦ Genuine *ssh* uses the keys and config files from /etc/ssh whereas the infected *ssh* obtains these from a local installation directory
2. authenticate the user
   ◦ Genuine *ssh* used *kerberos*, *crypto* utilities and *pam* modules which the infected *ssh* does not use
   ◦ The infected *ssh* uses the config and sniff files (local/untrusted resources) which the genuine *ssh* does not use

To test the resilience of our approach to the simple syntactic transformations, that the virus writers are resorting to evade detection, we have compiled the virus responsible for infection un-der various levels of optimization. *gcc* compiler performs several simple syntactic transformations like loop unrolling, function inlining, register reassignment etc. We have executed the infected programs *nano* (similarly *ssh*) compiled under different optimization levels and collected the observable information during execution. What we observed was that barring very minor changes these programs produced the same traces of system calls. One difference we observed was the way in which contents of a file were buffered into and out of memory. Optimized program read in chunks of size 4096 whereas lower level of optimization resulted in reading chunks of a smaller size. These experiments demonstrate that the various obfuscators would have little impact on our approach and we will be able to catch tampering.

To summarize, we have presented an approach in which:

• we benchmark the intended behaviours of trusted programs in an execution environment (we can select the crucial paths of execution),
• whenever we want to validate whether the installation of the trusted program in a similar environment is tampered, we collect the observable information during runtime w.r.t. to the paths benchmarked,
• compare the behaviour with its intended behaviour
• if there is a significant difference between the two, then we say that the program is tampered

Further, we have also shown that the method is resilient to obfuscation. We are conducting experiments to see the effect of polymorphic and metamorphic viruses on our approach. Note that the method, we presented will also be very useful for validating the embedded systems because typically the software and the hardware configurations of an embedded system are very few.

In our study so far, the above approach seems to be very fruitful for checking un-tampering of devices of network communication and automobile software (Seshadri, Luk, Perrig, van Doorn, & Khosla, 2006). In fact, our study shows that our above approach does not need the constraints imposed in Seshadri et al. (2006) or their related works on Pioneer and SWATT protocols. In fact, testing random memory cells as per SWATT protocol can as well be subsumed in our framework above.

4 CONCLUSION

In this chapter, we have surveyed issues, strategies and techniques that have been used to check tampering of software. In addition, we have shown how the semantic malware detection approach (Shyamasundar, Shah, & Kumar, 2010) can be effectively applied to arrive at notions of birthmark. Our experimental results show that it is indeed viable. Our experiments give us the confidence that one can consider the system behaviour of a program p with respect to external behaviour t as its birthmark. More study and experiments are needed to arrive at finer notions of birthmark particularly with the choice of reactions/paths and refining the notion of significant difference or similarity of behaviour.

REFERENCES

Baker, B. S. (1995). *On finding duplication and near-duplication in large software systems.* In WCRE '95: Proceedings of the Second Working Conference on Reverse Engineering, page 86. Washington, DC, USA, Washington, DC: IEEE Computer Society.

Baxter, I. D., Yahin, A., Moura, L., Sant'Anna, M., & Bier, L. (1998) *Clone detection using abstract syntax trees.* In Software Maintenance, 1998. Proceedings. International Conference on, pp. 368–377.

Christodorescu, M., Jha, S., & Kruegel, C. (2007). *Mining specifications of malicious behavior.* In ESEC-FSE '07: Proceedings of the the 6thjoint meeting of the European software engineering conference and the ACM SIGSOFT symposium on The foundations of software engineering, pp. 5–14, New York:ACM.

Collberg, C., Carter, E., Debray, S., Huntwork, A., Kececioglu, J., Linn, C., & Stepp, M. (2004). *Dynamic path-based software watermarking.* In PLDI '04: Proceedings of the ACM SIGPLAN 2004 conference on Programming language design and implementation, PP. 107–118, New York:ACM.

Collberg, C., & Thomborson, C. (1999). *Software watermarking: models and dynamic embeddings.* In POPL '99: Proceedings of the 26th ACM SIGPLAN-SIGACT symposium on Principles of programming languages, pp. 311–324, New York:ACM.

Collberg, C., Thomborson, C., & Low, D. (1997). *A taxonomy of obfuscating transformations.* Technical Report 148, Department of Computer Science, University of Auckland.http://www.cs.auckland. ac.nz/~collberg/Research/Publications/Collberg ThomborsonLow 97a/index.html.

Computer Economics. *(2010).2007 Malware report: The economic impact of viruses, spyware, adware, botnets, and other malicious code.* Retrieved from http://www.computer economics. com/ page.cfm?name =Malware% 20Report

Garfinkel, T., Pfaff, B., Chow, J., Rosenblum, M., & Boneh, D. Terra (2003). *A virtual machine-based platform for trusted computing.* In SOSP '03: Proceedings of the nineteenth ACM symposium on Operating systems principles, pp. 193–206, New York:ACM.

Halderman, J. A., & Felten, E. W. (2006). *Lessons from the Sony CD DRM episode.* In USENIX-SS'06: Proceedings of the 15th conference on USE-NIX Security Symposium, Berkeley, CA:USENIX Association.

Kamiya, T., Kusumoto, S., & Inoue, K. (2002). Ccfinder: a multilinguistic token-based code clone detection system for large scale source code. *Software Engineering. IEEE Transactions on, 28*(7), 654–670.

Kennell, R., & Jamieson, L. H. (2003). *Establishing the genuinity of remote computer systems.* In SSYM'03: Proceedings of the 12th conference on USENIX Security Symposium, pp. 21–21, Berkeley:USENIX Association.

Kinder, J., Katzenbeisser, S., Schallhart, C., & Veith, H. (2005). Detecting malicious code by model checking. In Klaus Julisch & Christopher Krügel (eds).*DIMVA*, (Vol. 3548 LNCS,pp.174–187). New York: Springer.

Kirda, E., Kruegel, C., Banks, G., Vigna, G., & Kemmerer, R. A. (2006). *Behavior-based spyware detection.* In USENIXSS'06: Proceedings of the15th conference on USENIX Security Symposium. Berkeley, CA:USENIX Association.

Kontogiannis, K., Galler, M., & DeMori, R. (1995). *Detecting code similarity using patterns.* In Working Notes of the Third Workshop on AI and Software Engineering: Breaking the Toy Mold (AISE),pp. 68–73.

Kosar, T., Christodorescu, M., & Iverson, R. (2003). *Opening pandora's box: Using binary code rewrite to bypass license checks.* Technical Report 1479, University of Wisconsin, Madison.

Krinke, J. (2001). *Identifying similar code with program dependence graphs.* In WCRE '01: Proceedings of the Eighth Working Conference on Reverse Engineering (WCRE'01), page 301, Washington, DC:IEEE Computer Society.

Lie, D., Thekkath, C., & Horowitz, M. (2003). *Implementing an untrusted operating system on trusted hardware.* In SOSP '03: Proceedings of the nineteenth ACM symposium on Operating systems principles,pp.178–192. New York:ACM.

Lie, D., Thekkath, C., Mitchell, M., Lincoln, P., Boneh, D., Mitchell, J., & Horowitz, M. (2000). Architectural support for copy and tamper resistant software. *SIGPLAN Not., 35*(11), 168–177. doi:10.1145/356989.357005

Liu, C., Chen, C., Han, J., & Yu, P. S. Gplag (2006). *Detection of software plagiarism by program dependence graph analysis.* In KDD '06: Proceedings of the 12th ACM SIGKDD international conference on Knowledge discovery and data mining, pp.872–881, NewYork:ACM.

Myles, G., & Collberg, C. S. (2004). *Detecting software theft via whole program path birthmarks.* In Kan Zhang and Yuliang Zheng, editors, ISC, volume 3225 of Lecture Notes in Computer Science, pp. 404–415. New York: Springer.

Myles, G., & Collberg, C. S. (2005). K-gram based software birthmarks. In Haddad, H., Liebrock, L. M., Omicini, A., & Wainwright, R. L. (Eds.), *SAC* (pp. 314–318). New York: ACM.

Park, D. (1981). *Concurrency and automata on infinite sequences.* In Proceedings of the 5th GI-Conference on Theoretical Computer Science, pp. 167–183, London: Springer-Verlag.

Prechelt, L., Malpohl, G., & Philippsen, M. (2002). Finding plagiarisms among a set of programs with jplag. *J. UCS, 8*(11), 1016.

Sailer, R., Zhang, X., Jaeger, T., & van Doorn, L. (2004). *Design and implementation of a tcg-based integrity measurement architecture.* In USENIX Security Symposium, pp. 223–238. USENIX.

Schleimer, S., Wilkerson, D. S., & Aiken, A. (2003). *Winnowing: local algorithms for document fingerprinting.* In SIGMOD '03: Proceedings of the 2003 ACM SIGMOD international conference on Management of data, pp. 76–85. New York: ACM.

Schuler, D., Dallmeier, V., & Lindig, C. (2007). *A dynamic birthmark for Java*. In ASE '07: Proceedings of the twenty-second IEEE/ACM international conference on Automated software engineering, pp. 274– 283. New York: ACM.

Seshadri, A., Luk, M., Perrig, A., van Doorn, L., & Khosla, P. (2006). Externally verifiable code execution. *CACM, 49*(9), 45–49.

Seshadri, A., Luk, M., Shi, E., Perrig, A., van Doorn, L., & Khosla, P. (2005). Pioneer: verifying code integrity and enforcing untampered code execution on legacy systems. In Herbert, A., & Birman, K. P. (Eds.), *SOSP* (pp. 1–16). New York: ACM.

Seshadri, A., Perrig, A., van Doorn, L., & Khosla, P. (2004). *Swatt: Software-based attestation for embedded devices*. In IEEE Symposium on Security and Privacy, p. 272. Washington, DC: IEEE Computer Society.

Shieh, A., & Williams, D. GünSirer, E., & Schneider, F. B.(2005). *Nexus: a new operating system for trustworthy computing*. In SOSP '05: Proceedings of the twentieth ACM symposium on Operating systems principles, pp. 1–9, New York: ACM.

Shyamasundar, R. K., Shah, H., & Narendra Kumar, N. V. (2010) *Malware: From modelling to practical detection*. In Proc: International Conference on Distributed Computing and Internet Technology, to appear, Lecture Notes in Computer Science. New York: Springer.

Tamada, H., Nakamura, M., & Monden, A. (2004). *Design and evaluation of birthmarks for detecting theft of java programs*. In M. H. Hamza, (ed). IASTED Conf. on Software Engineering, pp.569–574. IASTED/ACTA Press.

Tamada, H., Okamoto, K., Nakamura, M., Monden, A., & Matsumoto, K. (2004). *Dynamic software birthmarks to detect the theft of windows applications*. In Proc: International Symposium on Future Software Technology.

Tamada, H., Okamoto, K., Nakamura, M., Monden, A., & Matsumoto, K. (2007). *Design and evaluation of dynamic software birthmarks based on API calls*. Technical report, Nara Institute of Science andTechnology.

Wang, X., Jhi, Y., Zhu, S., & Liu, P. (2009*). Behavior based software theft detection*. In CCS '09: Proceedings of the 16th ACM conference on Computer and communications security,pp. 280–290. New York: ACM.

Zhang, X., Tallam, S., & Gupta, R. (2006). *Dynamic slicing long running programs through execution fast forwarding*. In SIGSOFT '06/FSE-14: Proceedings of the 14th ACM SIGSOFT international symposium on Foundations of software engineering, pp. 81–91.New York:ACM.

ENDNOTES

[1] Harshit Shah is a PhD candidate at Amrita Vishwa Vidyapeetham, and is supported under Indo-Trento Promotion for Advanced Research at TIFR, Mumbai

[2] http://www.spa.org/ index.php?option =com_content &view=article &id=172:aboutap &catid=162:anti-piracy-articles &Itemid=130

[3] http://en.wikipedia.org/wiki/Sony BMG CD copy protection scandal

[4] http://www.trusted computing group.org/

[5] http://www.microsoft.com/resources/ngscb/default.mspx

[6] TCB is the set of components that have to be trusted to operate without flaws.

Chapter 15
Complexity Measures of Cryptographically Secure Boolean Functions

Chungath Srinivasan
Amrita Vishwa Vidyapeetham, India

Lakshmy K.V.
Amrita Vishwa Vidyapeetham, India

M. Sethumadhavan
Amrita Vishwa Vidyapeetham, India

ABSTRACT

Boolean functions are used in modern cryptosystems for providing confusion and diffusion. To achieve required security by resistance to various attacks such as algebraic attacks, correlation attacks, linear, differential attacks, several criteria for Boolean functions have been established over years by cryptographic community. These criteria include nonlinearity, avalanche criterion and correlation immunity and the like. The chapter is an attempt to present state of the art on properties of such Boolean functions and to suggest several directions for further research.

1. INTRODUCTION

In stream cipher cryptography a pseudorandom sequence of bits of length equal to the message length is generated. This sequence is then bitwise XORed (addition modulo 2) with the message sequence and the resulting sequence is transmitted. At the receiving end, deciphering is done by generating the same pseudorandom sequence and bitwise XORing the cipher bits with the random

bits. The seed of the pseudorandom bit generator is obtained from the secret key. For some recent proposals of stream ciphers refer the eSTREAM Project (The ECRYPT Stream Cipher Project). Linear (non-linear) Feedback Shift Registers (LFSRs) and Boolean functions are important building blocks for stream cipher systems. A standard model of stream cipher by Siegenthaler (1984, 1985) combines the outputs of several independent LFSR sequences using a nonlinear Boolean function to produce the keystream. Design and analysis of stream ciphers was kept

DOI: 10.4018/978-1-60960-123-2.ch015

confidential for a long time and was made public in the 1970's, when several research papers on the design of LFSR-based stream ciphers occurred. Cryptanalysis techniques discovered during the NESSIE and eSTREAM projects (Bernstein (Report 2008/010), The ECRYPT Stream Cipher Project) have made it possible to strengthen cipher designs to a large extent, and attacking new algorithms has become more difficult. Till the end of 1990's there are no standards for stream ciphers and the advent of these projects standardized the design of stream ciphers (Chris & Alexander 2004, The ECRYPT Stream Cipher Project). An LFSR is essentially an elementary algorithm for generating a keystream, which has the following desirable properties:

- Easy to implement in hardware.
- Produce sequences of long and deterministic period.
- Produce sequences with good statistical properties.
- Can be readily analyzed using algebraic techniques.

In this chapter section 2 gives an insight into Boolean functions and its different forms of representations, section 3 gives details of different complexity measures that a Boolean functions has to satisfy, section 4

2. BOOLEAN FUNCTIONS

Boolean functions play a central role in preserving the security of stream ciphers and block ciphers. Let n be any positive integer. We denote by B_n the set of all n-variable Boolean functions from the vector space F_2^n of binary vectors of length n to F_2. We denote $\oplus$ by the additions in F_2. The representation of Boolean functions which is mostly used in cryptography is the algebraic normal form (ANF) as given in Equation (2.1) and the truth table representation (TT):

$$f(x_1, x_2, ..., x_n) = \bigoplus_{u \in F_2^n} a_u x^u, \ a_u \in F_2, x, u \in F_2^n$$

(2.1)

The unique degree of ANF for a Boolean function is called the algebraic degree of the function. The Boolean functions whose algebraic degrees do not exceed 1 are called the affine functions. The TT of an n variable Boolean function is the 2^n length bit binary sequence obtained from the output of a Boolean function. There are also algorithms for getting one form of representation of Boolean functions from its other form of representation. The Trace representation of a Boolean function also plays a vital role in studying and defining these functions. The trace function $tr: F_2^n \to F_2$ is defined as $tr(x) = x + x^2 + x^{2^2} + ... + x^{2^{n-1}}$. Every Boolean function f can be written in the form $f(x) = tr(F(x))$ where F is a mapping from F_2^n into F_2^n. The numerical normal form (NNF) representation of Boolean functions is not discussed in this chapter. The sign function of a Boolean function f is defined as $(-1)^f$.

The Walsh Transform of a function f on F_2^n is the map $W_f: F_2^n \to$ R (set of real numbers), defined by:

$$W_f(a) = \sum_{x \in B_n} (-1)^f (-1)^{a.x},$$

(2.2)

where $a. x = a_1 x_1 \oplus a_2 x_2 \oplus ... \oplus a_n x_n$. The nonlinearity of f is:

$$NL(f) = 2^{n-1} - \frac{1}{2} \max_{a \in F_2^n} \left| W_f(a) \right|$$

(2.3)

Parseval's equation:

$$\sum_{a \in F_2^n} (W_f(a))^2 = 2^{2n}$$

(2.4)

The derivative of a Boolean function f with respect to a vector $a \in F_2^n$ is the Boolean function $D_f(a) = f(x) + f(x + a)$. The periodic autocorrelation function of f is a real-valued function defined on all $a \in F_2^n$

$$\Delta_f(a) = \sum_{a \in F_2^n} (-1)^{f(x) \oplus f(x \oplus a)} \qquad (2.5)$$

3. COMPLEXITY CRITERION FOR BOOLEAN FUNCTIONS

3.1 Nonlinearity

The main criteria for evaluating the cryptographic complexity of Boolean functions on F_2^n is the nonlinearity. Nonlinearity is closely related to the principle of confusion introduced by Claude Elwood Shannon (1949). Since then nonlinearity is used as a measure of complexity of Boolean functions and for measuring linear attacks involved in stream ciphers and block ciphers. The Hamming weight of a Boolean function f is the size of its support $\{ x \in F_2^n : f(x) = 1 \}$ and the Hamming distance between two functions f and g is the Hamming weight of the Boolean function $f \oplus g$. The nonlinearity $NL(f)$ of a Boolean function f is its minimum Hamming distance to affine functions. The Hamming distance is a natural measure to evaluate the difference between complex and simplest (i.e. affine) Boolean functions. This notion given by Rothaus (1976) has been considered as the main criterion for quantifying the resistance of ciphers using those functions to several kinds of attacks like linear and correlation attacks.

Covering radius bound (universal bound):

$$NL(f) \leq 2^{n-1} - 2^{\frac{n}{2}-1} \qquad (3.1)$$

Bent Functions

The equality in (3.1) holds only for even n and the functions which achieve this are called Bent functions. Bent functions were introduced by Rothaus (1976). Its distance to affine functions equals $2^{n-1} \pm 2^{n/2-1}$. Bent functions can be characterized in terms of their autocorrelation function, which means that a Boolean function f is Bent if and only if all of its derivatives $f(x) \oplus f(x \oplus a)$, $a \in F_2^n$ are balanced which implies $\Delta_f(a) = 0$ for all nonzero $a \in F_2^n$. Bent functions with high degrees are preferred from cryptographic viewpoint and for $n \geq 4$, the inequality given by Rothaus (1976) states that any bent function has algebraic degree at most $n/2$. Bent functions have a lot of useful applications in different fields, but in cryptography they have the drawback of being unbalanced. But these bent functions can be used to construct balanced Boolean functions with high nonlinearity (Dobbertin, 1995). Some of the constructions of bent functions are due to Adams & Tavares (1990), Carlet (1994, 1996), Dobbertin (1995), Dillon (1974) and Maiorana (1970). Monomial bent functions are Boolean functions of the form:

$$f : F_2^n \rightarrow F_2$$

defined as $f(x) = tr(\alpha x^d)$.

If there exits an α such that the $tr(\alpha x^d)$ is bent, then the exponent d is called a bent exponent. Most of the known cases of constructions of bent functions can be discovered from monomial functions. The nonlinearity being an affine invariant, so is the notion of bent function. Also if f is bent and l is affine, then $f \oplus l$ is bent. A class of bent functions is called a complete class of functions if it is globally invariant under the action of the general affine group and the addition of affine functions

Higher Order Nonlinearity

Let $NL_r(f)$ denote the distance between f and the set of all functions of degrees at most r (the so-called Reed-Muller code), we call $NL_r(f)$ the r-th order nonlinearity of f. For $r > 1$, it must be large and the maximum possible value of $NL_r(f)$ is unknown for $r > 1$ and $n \geq 8$ and also for $r = 1$ and $n \geq 9$ odd. The best known asymptotic upper bound has been given by Carlet and Mesnager (2006) as:

$\text{Max } NL_r(f)$

$$\leq 2^{n-1} - \frac{\sqrt{15}}{2} \cdot \left(1 + \sqrt{2}\right)^{r-2} \cdot 2^{\frac{n}{2}} + O(n^{r-2})$$

$$(3.2)$$

The upper bound for higher order nonlinearity of a balanced function f is given in [7]

$$NL_r(f) \leq 2^{n-1} - 2^{n-r} \qquad (3.3)$$

Linear Structures

Differential cryptanalysis is the process to discover statistical patterns in the output distribution by having x and $x + a$ as an input pair and trying to analyse the difference in their output $f(x) + f(x + a)$. A Boolean function f has resistance to differential cryptanalysis if for most nonzero a, $|\Delta_f(a)|$ is either zero or very close to zero, which implies the Boolean function $f(x) + f(x + a)$ will be balanced or close to be balanced. If the Boolean function $D_f(a) = f(x) + f(x + a)$ is a constant function, then the vector a is called a linear structure of f. In other words, $a \in F_2^n$ is a linear structure of f if $|\Delta_f(a)| = 2^n$. It is trivial to say that an all zero vector is a linear structure. The set of all linear structures of a function f form a linear subspace of F_2^n, the dimension of which is called the linearity of f. A nonzero linear structure is cryptographically undesirable. Also the existence/non-existence of nonzero linear structures is clearly affine invariant.

Affine Invariance

Two functions f and g on F_2^n are called affinely equivalent if there exists a linear isomorphism L from F_2^n to F_2^n and a vector a such that $f(x) = g(L(x)+a)$ for every input $x \in F_2^n$. The algebraic degree and the number of monomials in ANF of a Boolean function are some other complexity criteria which requires a study. High algebraic degree provides high linear complexity. Therefore high algebraic degree is desirable in stream ciphers. The general complexity criteria which are mostly interesting in cryptographic framework are affine invariant, because the attacks on cryptosystems using Boolean functions often work with the same complexity when the functions are replaced by affinely equivalent ones. Nonlinearity and algebraic degree are affine invariant. The notion of bent function is invariant under affine equivalence. But the number of monomials in the ANF is not affine invariant, so the number of monomials in the ANF of the function is not a proper criterion. So it is desirable that a complexity criterion to remain invariant under a large group of transformations.

Non-Normality

Dobbertin (1995) introduced the concept of normal Boolean functions in relation to the construction of bent functions. A Boolean function f on F_2^n is called k-normal (resp. weakly k-normal) if there exists a k-dimensional flat on which f is constant (affine). Here k-normality implies weak-k-normality and weak-k-normality implies $(k-1)$ normality. Non-normality is a natural complexity criterion to consider in cryptography. Moreover, there is a relation between non-normality and nonlinearity which shows that for a function to have high nonlinearity, it must be non-(weakly) normal at a reasonable level. Given a flat U of dimension k in F_2^n, $n = 2k$, there are exactly

$b_k = 2^{2^{2k}-2^k+1}$ Boolean functions that are constant on U. Let f be a weakly k-normal Boolean function on F_2^n (Carlet, 2006a). Then

$$NL(f) \leq 2^{n-1} - 2^{k-1} \qquad (3.4)$$

Nonnormal Boolean functions exist on F_2^n, $n = 2k$. An upper bound for the number of normal Boolean functions exists and Canteaut, Daum, Dobbertin, & Leander (2006) proved the existence of nonnormal bent functions for $n \geq 10$ and weakly nonnormal for $n \geq 14$ on F_2^n. Consequences of normality on bent functions is that if a bent function $f \in F_2^n$ is constant on an $\frac{n}{2}$ - dimensional affine subspace, then f is balanced on each proper coset of the subspace. Also most of the known constructions of bent functions lead to normal bent functions (Canteaut, Daum, Dobbertin, & Leander, 2003).

3.2 Correlation Immunity

The concept of correlation immune functions was introduced by Siegenthaler (1984). A Boolean function f is called k^{th} order correlation immune iff $W_f(a) = 0$ for all vector $a \in F_2^n$ with hamming weight less than or equal to k. Correlation immune functions are used in the design of pseudorandom number generators in stream ciphers to resist a correlation attack (Siegenthaler, 1985). A balanced m^{th} order correlation immune Boolean function f is called m-resilient. The bound given by Siegenthaler (1984) states that an n variable, m^{th} order correlation immune Boolean function f has degree at most $n - m$. Moreover, if f is balanced and $m < n - 1$, then the degree d of f satisfies

$$d \leq n - m - 1 \qquad (3.5)$$

According to Siegenthaler (1984), the functions achieving the equality in (3.5) are called optimized functions and Sarkar and Maitra (2000) constructed optimized functions.

3.3 Avalanche Criterion

A Boolean function f satisfies the avalanche criterion with respect to a if $f(x) \oplus f(x \oplus a)$ is a balanced function for all vectors a in F_2^n. Furthermore, f is said to satisfy the avalanche criterion of order l or propagation criterion of order l (Preneel, Leekwijck, Linden, Govaerts, Vandewalle, 1991) if it satisfies the avalanche criterion with respect to every nonzero vector whose Hamming weight is not larger than l. It is to be noted that the strict avalanche criterion (SAC) given by Maiorana (1970) is the same as the avalanche criterion of order one. In other words a small change in the input to the function leads to a large change in the output and so the word avalanche effect and a large change of uniform kind in the output corresponding to small changes in the input implies SAC. The SAC was first defined by Webster and Tavares (1986). The Avalanche Criterion and its generalizations are based on the properties of the derivatives of Boolean functions. They are related to the property of diffusion, which a cryptosystem must satisfy.

Global Avalanche Charecteristics (GAC)

A Boolean function satisfying avalanche criterion of order k does not have linear structures with Hamming weight less than or equal to k and which does not prevent the possibility of having linear structures with Hamming weight greater than k. This suggests that avalanche of order k for a Boolean function is not a sufficient indicator to identify the possibility of differential cryptanalysis. This encouraged Zang and Zeng to propose GAC indicator. GAC indicators consists of a *sum of squares indicators* and *absolute indicators* defined respectively as

$$\sigma_f = \sum_{a \in F_2^n} (\Delta_f(a))^2$$

$$\Delta_{\max} = \max_{a \in F_2^n, a \neq 0} \left| \Delta_f(a) \right|$$

The smaller σ_f and Δ_f the better f will be resisting differential cryptanalysis, that is in order to achieve good diffusion, cryptographic functions should have low sum-of-squares indicators and absolute indicators. Since Boolean functions does not guarantees satisfying the avalanche criterion and so the avalanche property for functions can be reflected by these two GAC indicators σ_f and Δ_f. Both the indicators are affine invariant.

3.4 Algebraic Immunity

Let f be any n-variable Boolean function. Its algebraic immunity $AI(f)$ equals the minimum algebraic degree of all the nonzero annihilators of f and of all the nonzero annihilators of $f \oplus 1$. Since f is an annihilator of $f \oplus 1$ and $f \oplus 1$ is an annihilator of f, the algebraic immunity is upper bounded by the algebraic degree of f. But we have got a tight bound on algebraic immunity (Curtois & Meier, 2003) given as

$$AI(f) \leq \left\lceil \frac{n}{2} \right\rceil \tag{3.6}$$

And for all $a < 1$, the lower bound for $AI(f)$ refered from Didier (2006) is as

$$\frac{n}{2} - \sqrt{\frac{n}{2} \log_e \left(\frac{n}{a \log_e 2} \right)} \tag{3.7}$$

Let A be the set containing all annihilators with degree atmost k of a Boolean function f. For a Boolean function f of degree r, the dimension of A is atmost

$$\sum_{i=0}^{k} \binom{n}{i} - \sum_{i=0}^{k} \binom{n-r}{i} \tag{3.8}$$

Algebraic immunity of a Boolean function is affine invariant.

4. BOUNDS AND RELATIONS ON VARIOUS COMPLEXITY MEASURES: BOUNDS ON NONLINEARITY

The universal bound (or covering radius) for Boolean functions over F_2^n is given by:

$$N_f \leq 2^{n-1} - 2^{\frac{n}{2}-1}$$

The equality holds if and only if f is a bent function. This bound is not tight for Boolean functions with n being odd. For odd n, one can find Boolean functions with nonlinearity satisfying

$$2^{n-1} - 2^{\frac{n-1}{2}} \leq N_f \leq 2^{n-1} - 2^{\frac{n}{2}-1} \tag{3.9}$$

The nonlinearity value $2^{n-1} - 2^{\frac{n-1}{2}}$ is achieved by quadratic functions (Carlet, 2006) and so this value is called quadratic bound. This value is also achieved by any n variable Boolean function resulting from the concatenation of two $n-1$ variable Boolean function. For n odd, the Boolean functions with nonlinearity $\geq$ the *quadratic bound* has been described in papers by Carlet (1999), Patterson and Wiedemann (1983) and Kavut, Maitra, Yucel (2007)

Nonlinearity of Balanced Boolean Functions

Balanced functions with high nonlinearity is of interest in cryptography. But balanced functions never achieves the universal bound of nonlinearity given in (3.1). The upper bound for balanced functions given by Seberry, Zhang and Zheng (1994) is as follows:

$$N_f \leq \begin{cases} 2^{n-1} - 2^{\frac{n}{2}-1} - 2, & \text{if } n \text{ is even} \\ \left\lfloor\!\left\lfloor 2^{n-1} - 2^{\frac{n}{2}-1} \right\rfloor\!\right\rfloor, & \text{if } n \text{ is odd} \end{cases} \quad (3.10)$$

where $\lfloor\lfloor x \rfloor\rfloor$ denotes the largest even integer less than or equal to x.

The maximum nonlinearities achieved by balanced Boolean functions for $n\leq 6$ equals the quadratic bound given above. But for balanced Boolean functions over F_2^n with $n = 7$ and $n = 8$, the maximum nonlinearity achieved is 56 and 116 respectively instead of 58 and 118 which are the upper bounds (quadratic bound). So finding balanced Boolean functions with maximum nonlinearity (ie. achieving the upper bound given above) using some deterministic process for $n\geq 8$ still remains an open problem

4.1 Nonlinearity vs. Algebraic Immunity

Relationship between the rth order nonlinearity and a recent cryptographic criterion called the algebraic immunity strengthens the reasons why the algebraic immunity can be considered as a further cryptographic complexity criterion.

In the paper of Dalai, Gupta and Maitra (2004) a lower bound on the (first order) nonlinearity of Boolean functions with its algebraic immunity $AI(f)$ is given as

$$NL(f) \geq \sum_{i=0}^{AI(f)-2} \binom{n}{i} \quad (4.1)$$

we have

$$\sum_{i=0}^{AI(f)-1} \binom{n}{i} \leq wt(f) \leq \sum_{i=0}^{n-AI(f)} \binom{n}{i} \quad (4.2)$$

Improved lower bound (Lobanov, 2005)

$$NL(f) \geq 2 \sum_{i=0}^{AI(f)-2} \binom{n-1}{i} \quad (4.3)$$

Let f be a Boolean function in n variables and let r be a positive integer. The nonlinearity of order r of f satisfies:

$$NL_r(f) \geq 2 \sum_{i=0}^{AI(f)-r-1} \binom{n-r}{i} \quad (4.4)$$

4.2 Nonlinearity vs. Avalanche

A function f on F_2^n is bent iff f satisfies the avalanche criterion of order n.

For an f satisfying avalanche criterion of order k, the nonlinearity N_f of f satisfies

$$N_f \leq 2^{n-1} - 2^{n-1-\frac{k}{2}} \quad (4.5)$$

- The equality in (4.5) holds if f is a bent function for $n = k$ even
- Let $g_1(x)$ be a bent function on F_2^{n-1} and $g_2(x)$ be any affine function on F_2^n. Then for $k = n-1$ with n odd, $f(x) = g_1(x) \oplus g_2(x)$, defined by

$$f(x) = g_1 (x_1 \oplus x_n,\ldots, x_{n-1} \oplus x_n) \oplus g_2 (x_2, x_2,\ldots, x_n) \quad (4.6)$$

satisfies the equality in (4.5). Here f is a nonbent function which satisfies avalanche criterion of order $n-1$. To get a nonbent and balanced function f which satisfies avalanche criterion of order $n-1$, choose the affine function $g_2(x)$ with coefficients in F_2 xored to 1.

General bounds for the sum of squares indicator and absolute indicator of a Boolean function f is given repectively as follow

$$2^{2n} \leq \sigma_f \leq 2^{3n}$$

$$0 \leq \Delta_{max} \leq 2^n$$

Based on the autocorrelation of a function, the two upper bounds on the nonlinearity of a Boolean function f:

$$N_f \leq 2^{n-1} - \frac{1}{2}\sqrt[4]{\sigma_f}$$

$$N_f \leq 2^{n-1} - \frac{1}{2}\sqrt{2^n + \Delta_{max}}$$

The two lower bounds on the nonlinearity of a Boolean function f:

$$N_f \geq 2^{n-1} - \frac{1}{4}\Delta_{min},$$

where

$$\Delta_{min} = \min\left\{ \left|\Delta_f(a)\right|, \alpha \in F_2^n, \alpha \neq 0 \right\} \quad (4.7)$$

If a Boolean function f satisfies avalanche criterion with respect to all vectors except for a subset $\Re$ of vectors in F_2^n, then:

$$N_f \geq 2^{n-1} - 2^{\frac{n}{2}-1}\sqrt{|\Re|} \quad (4.8)$$

A shortcoming of the above equation is that $|\Re|$ is large and this problem is addressed through the following bound given by Seberry, Zhang and Zheng (1994):

$$N_f \geq 2^{n-1} - 2^{n-\frac{1}{2}\rho-1}$$

where ρ is the dimension of the maximal linear subspace of the space $E = \{0\} \cup \Re^c$, where $\Re^c$ is the complement of $\Re$ in F_2^n.

A more improved lower bound on nonlinearity given by Zhang & Zheng (1996) is as follows:

$$N_f \geq 2^{n-1} - 2^{\frac{1}{2}(n-r)-1}\sqrt{2^n + (|\Re \cap W| - 1)\Delta_{max}}$$
$$(4.9)$$

where W is any r-dimensional linear subspace of F_2^n, $r = 0, 1, \ldots, n$ and $\Re$ is as in Equation (4.8).

4.3 Nonlinearity vs. Correlation Immunity

Let f be an n variable m^{th} order correlation immune function. Sarkar and Maitra (2000) gave the following upper bounds on nonlinearity:

$$N_f(m,c) \leq \begin{cases} 2^{n-1} - 2^m, \text{ if } m > \frac{n}{2} - 1 \\ 2^{n-1} - 2^{\frac{n}{2}-1} - 2^m, \text{ if } m \leq \frac{n}{2} - 1 \end{cases} \quad \text{for } n \text{ even}$$

$$N_f(n,m,c) \leq \begin{cases} 2^{n-1} - 2^m, \text{ if } N_f > 2^{n-1} - 2^m \\ \max_{h \geq 0}\{h2^m\} \leq N_f, \text{ if } N_f \leq 2^{n-1} - 2^m \end{cases} \quad \text{for } n \text{ odd}$$

where $N_f(n, m, c)$ denotes the nonlinearity of an n variable m^{th} order correlation immune function f.

The following upper bounds were given by Sarkar and Maitra (2000) for an n variable m-resilient function f:

$$N_f(n,m,r) \leq \begin{cases} 2^{n-1} - 2^{m+1}, \text{ if } m+1 > \frac{n}{2} - 1 \\ 2^{n-1} - 2^{\frac{n}{2}-1} - 2^{m+1}, \text{ if } m+1 \leq \frac{n}{2} - 1 \end{cases} \quad \text{for } n \text{ even}$$

$$N_f(n,m,r) \leq \begin{cases} 2^{n-1} - 2^{m+1}, \text{ if } N_f > 2^{n-1} - 2^{m+1} \\ \max_{h \geq 0}\{h2^{m+1}\} \leq N_f, \text{ if } N_f \leq 2^{n-1} - 2^{m+1} \end{cases} \quad \text{for } n \text{ odd}$$

where $N_f(n, m, r)$ denotes nonlinearity of n variable m-resilient function.

Seberry, Zhang and Zheng (1994) were the first to do research into relationships between nonlinearity and correlation immunity. The bound given in Equation (3.5) suggests that there is a trade-off between the algebraic degree and correlation immunity stating that a cryptosystem with high algebraic degree shows resistance to linear complexity attack but having low correlation immunity and hence weak against correlation attacks.

Let f be an mth order correlation immune function on F_2^n. If m and n satisfy the condition of (Zheng & Zhang, 2001b):

$$0.6n - 0.4 \le m \le n - 2, \text{ then } N_f \le 2^{n-1} - 2^{m+1}$$

(4.10)

Zheng and Zhang (2001b) proved that nonlinearity of f, $N_f = 2^{n-1} - 2^{m+1}$ if and only if the mth order correlation immune functions on F_2^n are plateaued functions (Zhang & Zheng, 2001a). Boolean functions whose Walsh spectrum takes only three values $\{0, \pm 2^i\}$, $0 \le i \le n$, are plateaued functions.

Claude (2006b) suggested a bound on $N_f(n, m, c)$ and $N_f(n, m, r)$ respectively as follows:

$$N_f(n, m, c) \le 2^{n-1} - 2^m \left\lceil \frac{2^{n-m-1}}{\sqrt{2^n - \sum_{i=1}^m \binom{n}{i}}} \right\rceil$$

$$N_f(n, m, r) \le 2^{n-1} - 2^{m+1} \left\lceil \frac{2^{n-m-2}}{\sqrt{2^n - \sum_{i=0}^m \binom{n}{i}}} \right\rceil$$

Carlet (1999) also suggested an upper bound for m-resilient Boolean functions f with algebraic degree d as follows:

$$N_f(n, m, r) \le 2^{n-1} - 2^{m+1+\left\lfloor \frac{n-m-2}{d} \right\rfloor},$$

for $n < 2(m + 2 + \left\lfloor \frac{n-m-2}{d} \right\rfloor)$

If $n \ge 2(m + 2 + \left\lfloor \frac{n-m-2}{d} \right\rfloor)$ then:

$N_f(n, m, r)$

$$\le \begin{cases} 2^{n-1} - 2^{\frac{n}{2}-1} - 2^{m+1+\left\lfloor \frac{n-m-2}{d} \right\rfloor} & \text{if } n \text{ is even} \\ 2^{n-1} - 2^{m+1+\left\lfloor \frac{n-m-2}{d} \right\rfloor} \left\lfloor 2^{\frac{n}{2}-m-2-\left\lfloor \frac{n-m-2}{d} \right\rfloor} \right\rfloor & \text{if } n \text{ is odd} \end{cases}$$

Suppose m-resilient Boolean function f achieves the nonlinearity bound $N_f = 2^{n-1} - 2^{m+1}$ for $m > \frac{n}{2} - 2$, then the f also achieves the Siegenthaler's degree bound $d = n - m - 1$ (Fontaine, 1999).

4.4 Avalanche vs. Correlation Immunity

For a balanced k^{th} order correlation immune function f on F_2^n, satisfying the avalanche criterion of degree m, we have:

$$m + k \le n - 2, \text{ if } f \text{ is balanced and } k \ne 1 \quad (4.11)$$

$$m + k \le n, \text{ if } f \text{ is unbalanced} \quad (4.12)$$

Equality holds in Equation (4.11) for odd n, $m = n - 1$, $k = 1$ and for functions of the form given in (4.6) with affine functions $g_2(x)$, whose coefficients in F_2 are xored to zero.

CONCLUSION

Boolean functions are used in coding theory for designing optimal error correcting codes, in combinatorics, in telecommunications for generating sequences for CDMA and Cryptography for designing secure cryptosystems. In this chapter we have made a survey on the complexity measures of cryptographically secure Boolean functions and have shown the major tradeoffs between them, which may help the beginners to get an insight into complexity measures of Cryptographic Boolean functions.

REFERENCES

Adams, C. M., & Tavares, S. E. (1990). The structured design of cryptographically good S-boxes. *Journal of Cryptology, 3*(1), 27–41. doi:10.1007/BF00203967

Bernstein, D. J., (Report 2008/010). Which eSTREAM ciphers have been broken?. *eSTREAM, the ECRYPT Stream Cipher Project.*

Canteaut, A., Daum, H., Dobbertin, H., & Leander, G. (2006). Finding nonnormal Bent functions. *Discrete Applied Mathematics, 154,* 202–218. doi:10.1016/j.dam.2005.03.027

Canteaut, A., Daum, M., Dobbertin, H., & Leander, G. (2003). Normal and Non-Normal Bent Functions. *Proceedings of the Workshop on Coding and Cryptography (WCC),* Versailles, France, pp. 91-100.

Carlet, C. (1994). Two new classes of bent functions. In *Adv. In crypt.-Eurocrypt, 93, LNCS, 765* (pp. 77–101). Berlin: Springer.

Carlet, C. (1996). A construction of bent functions. *Finite Fields Appl, 233,* 47–58. doi:10.1017/CBO9780511525988.006

Carlet, C. (1999). On the coset weight divisibility and nonlinearity of resilient and correlation immune functions. *In Proceedings of the 2nd international conference (SETA'01), Discrete Mathematics and Theoretical Computer Science,* 131-144.

Carlet, C. (2006a). Boolean functions for cryptography and error correcting codes. In Crama, Y., & Hammer, P. (Eds.), *Chapter of the monography Boolean methods and models.* In Cambridge, UK: Cambridge University Press.

Carlet, C. (2006b). On Bent and highly nonlinear balanced / resilient functions and their algebraic immunities. *In Proceedings of AAECC 16,* LNCS 3857, 1-28.

Carlet, C., & Mesnager, S. (2006c). Improving the upper bounds on the covering radii of binary Reed-Muller codes. *IEEE Transactions on Information Theory, 53*(1), 162–173. doi:10.1109/TIT.2006.887494

Chris, J. Mitchell & Alexander W. Dent (2004). International standards for stream ciphers: A progress report. *In SASC - The State of the Art of Stream Ciphers,* pp. 14-15.

Courtois, & Meier, W. (2003). Algebraic attacks on stream ciphers with linear feedback. *In Advances in Cryptology - EUROCRYPT 2003,* LNCS, Springer-Verlag, *2656,* 345-359.

Dalai, D. K., Gupta, K. C., & Maitra, S. (2004). Results on Algebraic Immunity for Cryptographically Significant Boolean Functions. *Indocrypt International Conference,* LNCS, *3348,* pp.92-106. New York: Springer Verlag.

Didier, F. (2006). A new upper bound on the block error probability after decoding over the erasure channel. *IEEE Transactions on Information Theory.*

Dillon, J. F. (1974). Elementary Hadamard difference sets. *Ph. D thesis, University of Maryland.*

Dobbertin, H. (1995). Construction of bent functions and balanced Boolean functions with high non-linearity. In *Fast software encryption-Leuven 1994. LNCS, 1008* (pp. 61–74). Berlin: Springer.

eSTREAM – The ECRYPT Stream cipher project.(2008). Retrieved from http://www.encrypt.eu.org/stream.

Fontaine, C. (1999). On some cosets of the First-Order Reed-Muller code with high minimum weight. *IEEE Transactions on Information Theory, 45*(4), 1237–1243. doi:10.1109/18.761276

Kavut, S., Maitra, S., & Yucel, M. D. (2007). Search for Boolean functions with excellent profiles in the rotation symmetric class. *IEEE Transactions on Information Theory, 53*(5), 1743–1751. doi:10.1109/TIT.2007.894696

Lobanov, M. (n.d.). *Tight bound between nonlinearity and algebraic immunity.* Retrieved from http://eprint.iacr.org/2005/441.pdf

Maiorana, J. A. (1970). A class of bent functions. *R41 Technical paper.*

Patterson, N. J., & Wiedemann, D. H. (1983). The covering radius of the [215, 16] Reed-Muller code is at least 16276. *IEEE Transactions on Information Theory, IT-29,* 354–356. doi:10.1109/TIT.1983.1056679

Preneel, B., Leekwijck, W. V., Linden, L. V., Govaerts, R., & Vandewalle, J. (1991). Propagation characteristics of Boolean functions. In *Advances in Cryptology–EUROCRYPT'90, LNCS, 437* (pp. 155–165). New York: Springer.

Rothaus, O. S. (1976). On Bent Functions. *Journal of Combinatorial Theory, 20A,* 300–305.

Sarkar, P., & Maitra, S. (2000). Construction of Nonlinear Boolean Functions with Important Cryptographic Properties. *Advances in Cryptology - EUROCRYPT 2000.* Springer Berlin / Heidelberg, LNCS, *1807.*

Sarkar, P., & Maitra, S. (2003). Nonlinearity bounds and construction of resilient Boolean functions. *In Advances in Cryptology - Crypto 2000,* LNCS, Springer-Verlag, Berlin, *1880,* pp.515-532.

Seberry, J., Zhang, X. M., & Zheng, Y. (1994a). Nonlinearly balanced Boolean functions and their propagation characteristics. *In Advances in Cryptology - CRYPTO'93,* LNCS, Springer-Verlag, Berlin, *773,* pp.49-60

Seberry, J., Zhang, X. M., & Zheng, Y. (1994b). On constructions and nonlinearity of correlation immune functions. *In Advances in Cryptology-EUROCRYPT'93,* LNCS, Springer, Berlin, Heidelberg, New York, *765,* pp.181-199.

Shannon, C. E. (1949). Communication theory of secrecy systems. *The Bell System Technical Journal, 28,* 656–715.

Siegenthaler, T. (1984). Correlation-immunity of nonlinear combining functions for cryptographic applications. *IEEE Transactions on Information Theory, IT-30*(5), 776–780. doi:10.1109/TIT.1984.1056949

Siegenthaler, T. (1985). Decrypting a class of stream ciphers using ciphertext only. *IEEE Transactions on Computers, C-34*(1), 81–85. doi:10.1109/TC.1985.1676518

Webster, A. F., & Tavares, S. E. (1986). On the design of S-boxes. In *Adv. In crypt.-Crypto'85. LNCS, 218* (pp. 523–534). Berlin: Springer.

Zhang, X. M., & Zheng, Y. (1996). Autocorrelation and new bounds on the nonlinearity of cryptographic functions. *Advances in Cryptology, Eurocrypt 96. LNCS, Springer-Verlag, 1070,* 294–306.

Zhang, X. M., & Zheng, Y. (2001a). On plateaued functions. *IEEE Transactions on Information Theory, IT-47*(3), 1215–1223.

Zheng, Y., & Zhang, X. M. (2001b). Improved upper bound on the nonlinearity of high order correlation immune functions. *In Selected Areas in Cryptography, 7th Annual International Workshop, SA5000,* LNCS, Springer, Berlin, Heidelberg, *2012,*264-274.

Chapter 16
Einstein–Podolsky–Rosen Paradox and Certain Aspects of Quantum Cryptology with Some Applications

Narayanankutty Karuppath
Amrita Vishwa Vidyapeetham, India

P. Achuthan
Amrita Vishwa Vidyapeetham, India

ABSTRACT

The developments in quantum computing or any breakthrough in factorization algorithm would have far-reaching consequences in cryptology. For instance, Shor algorithm of factorizing in quantum computing might render the RSA type classical cryptography almost obsolete since it mainly depends on the computational complexity of factorization. Therefore, quantum cryptography is of immense importance and value in the modern context of recent scientific revolution. In this chapter, the authors discuss in brief certain fascinating aspects of Einstein-Podolsky-Rosen (EPR) paradox in the context of quantum cryptology. The EPR protocol and its connections to the famous Bell's inequality are also considered in here.

INTRODUCTION

The potential power of quantum approach to computing would render the classical cryptology almost superfluous in the not too far away future. The main problem of cryptography is that of key distribution (hereafter KD). KD can be broadly classified into public KD and private KD. In conventional classical cryptography it is the private KD of RSA type algorithms that assumes the computational complexity of factorization. Quantum computing and computational algorithms would make things possible compared to that which cannot be even imagined by conventional means. For instance, Shor quantum algorithm, defined in Shor (1997), would make an unparalleled and unheard of quantum leap as far as factoring is concerned. As an illustration, if one wants to factor a very large integer (say, having 250 digits) what the existing very fast super computers might take is a time of the order of the age of the Universe

DOI: 10.4018/978-1-60960-123-2.ch016

($\approx$ 13.6 billion years!). But it would only be the matter of a few seconds or at the maximum a few minutes for a quantum computer equipped with quantum polynomial algorithm for factoring like that of Shor, defined in Julian (2001). Similarly the Grover's new efficient quantum search algorithms also would speed up searching phenomenally, Grover (1996), Grover (1997). If N is number of the possible keys then Grover's quantum search algorithm can speed up the time from $O(N)$ to $O(N^{1/2})$ for a thorough exploration of the public keys. That is, searching could be speeded up millions fold for very large value of N. Modern conventional classic cryptography makes use of a trap door algorithm for its public key. The assumption is on the complexity of computation like that it is difficult to factor a very large integer. But any break-through in mathematics or leap in computation would invalidate such an assumption. Even private key or symmetric key distribution can be jeopardized by the eavesdropper. So, any cryptography scheme based on the assumption of complexity of algorithm has a very high chance of being letting down. Private key distribution runs the risk of being intercepted which cannot simply be wished away. More importantly, one is never sure if someone had eavesdropped or not, be it public or private KD scheme of the conventional classic cryptography. Additionally, as said above, quantum crypto analysis poses extremely high degree of potential threat to the present classical encryption systems. The extreme exigency of the matter becomes severely felt when one considers the possibility of quantum retro-crypto analysis (or retroactive decryption) that would spell havoc. The evil Eve might copy the existing public keys and information and create a bank of it, for potential quantum retro analysis of the future. Hence, even the present state-of-the-art cryptology methods are neither fool proof nor future proof. Ironically quantum cryptography provides a solution for the same. This fact has to be taken utmost seriously.

Modern fields like Quantum Cryptology, Quantum Teleportation, Quantum Computing, Quantum Dense Coding and the like exploit the quantum properties of individual systems rather than those of large ensembles. Historically this became possible as follows. The most celebrated Einstein-Bohr debate culminated in the ubiquitous paper by Einstein, Podolsky and Rosen which paved way to deeper understanding of the weird aspects of quantum phenomena, though the new perspectives that resulted from the testing of Bell's inequality were in a contrary manner to the expectations of EPR, Narayanankutty and Achuthan (2005), Achuthan and Narayanankutty (2009). The development of Bell's inequality was described as the most profound discovery of science (not of physics alone!) by Henry Stapp. The non-intuitive feature of quantum mechanics is being exploited in quantum cryptography just as quantum computing. A future resistant way of crypto-scheme is what is aimed at by Quantum cryptology.

The subject of Cryptology, both classical and non-classical (quantum) can be seen firmly founded on many very fundamental mathematical concepts and theories. The following brief listing gives an idea of the coverage of topics as per the latest well-known Mathematical subject classification scheme brought out under Zentralblatt (MATH) edited by European Mathematical Society and Heidelberger Academie der Wissenschaften with B. Wegener, Berlin, Germany, as editor-in-chief. We give here the relevant information:

A few features of relevance to the topic under discussion can be given.

a) Cryptography is the art and science of sending a message unintelligible and indecipherable to any unauthorized party. It is a subset of the wider field of cryptology which includes as well cryptoanalysis, the art of code breaking. In order to succeed in this, an algorithm (also called a cryptosystem or cipher) is utilized for scrambling a message with what is known as the "key". Thus a cryptogram is produced. Such a procedure

Table 1. Sections and topics from the Maths. Classification of Zentralblatt MATH, Berlin

Section Number	Page	Subject
11T71	7	Algebraic Coding Theory-Cryptography
14G50	10	Applications to Cryptography (of Diophantine geometry)
11 D	5	Diophantine Equation, Inequalities
11G	5	Arithmetic, Algebraic Geometry
94 A60	57	Cryptography
94 B27	57	Geometric methods (Application of algebraic geometry)
94 B40	54	Arithmetic codes
68 P25	47	Data encryption
81 P68	52	Quantum Cryptography (and quantum computation)
68 Q05	47	Models of Computation (Turing machine etc.)
14 H 52	11	Elliptic curves
11 G 05	5	Elliptic curves over global field
11 G 07	5	Elliptic curves over local fields

is known as encryption. For a cryptosystem to be secure, it should be impossible to unlock the cryptogram without the proper key. The whole idea is to safeguard the secrecy of the original information of the message from any intrusion called eavesdropping. Confidentiality is the traditional application aim of cryptogram. It has wider objectives now. Cryptography is also used in achieving broader objectives such as digital signatures, authentication, non-repudiation and so on.

b)   Number theory is one of the major pillars of mathematics David (1989), Everest and Ward (2007), Andreescu (2009). Fundamental theorems of Arithmetic, thanks to mathematicians down from Euclid, have helped to have Number theory as a coherent and interconnected theory. There are a number of different approaches to the field. Apart from several standard aspects of number theory there are its modern computational

features and applications to physics, elliptic curves, cryptography and so on.

c)   Information communication is closely related to cryptography Biggs (2008). Mathematics of optimal coding, that is, replacing information expressed in qubits, such as natural language or a sequence of bits, by another message using different qubits-is required for economy, reliability and security. Many further topics are important: data compression, public key cryptology encryption standards, authentication schemes, elliptic curve cryptography etc.

d)   Group theory-based Cryptology as given in Myasnikov (2008) is central to the study of relations between a few different areas of mathematics and theoretical computer science: combination of group theory, cryptography and complexity theory. How can non-commutation graph be used in public key cryptology with a feedback to combinational group theory? Complexity theory, notably generic-case complexity of algorithms, is employed for crypto analysis of various cryptographic protocols based on infinite groups. Ideas and machinery from the theory of generic-case complexity are used to study asymptotically dominant properties of some infinite groups that have been applied in public key cryptography so far.

e)   Mathematical Cryptography is a fast growing modern subject. There is good amount of mathematics behind the theory of public key cryptosystem Wegner (2000), Hoffstein (2008). Digital signature schemes-construction and security analysis of diverse cryptosystem attract much attention from active students and researchers. Knowledge of Linear algebra, number theory and probability is required to work in this area. Modern Cryptography uses such good mathematical- foundations as are at present possible.

f)   Study of Cryptology is not new. However, only in 1970's the research in Cryptology, Cryptanalysis and related areas has picked up visible momentum Shaska (2007). The coming into existence of the International Association for Cryptologic Research has considerably changed the situation. Modern information theoretic, complexity theoretic perspectives as well as implementation, application, standard issues, public keys convention of algorithms and their implementation, crypto-analytic attacks, pseudo-random sequences, computational number theory, cryptographic protocols, untrace-ability, privacy, key management etc form realistic subjects of deep interest Wiesner (1983), Chaum (1988), Nicolas (2009).

WHAT IS QUANTUM CRYPTOLOGY?

Quantum Cryptology is quite different from the classical one. It relies more on the features of quantum physics rather than on some kind of specific mathematics, as a key feature of its security models to develop an undefeatable cryptosystem, that is, a cryptosystem that is completely secure and safe against eavesdropping without the knowledge of the sender or receiver of the concerned messages. Further, quantum cryptography offers ideally secure encryption of data and transfer. Quantum Cryptology is based on intrinsic quantum properties of individual particle like photon to develop an unbreakable crypto system.

The following properties are basic and unique to quantum systems: a) Linearity, b) Superposition, c) Unitarity of evolution, d) No-cloning theorem. Whereas it is possible to distinguish between two orthogonal quantum states, any attempt to distinguish between two non-orthogonal states would irrevocably destroy the original state. This is called the irreversibility of measurement. This is because a state can be represented by a vector in a complex Hilbert space and measurement on

a quantum system is nothing but a projection operator operating on this vector in Hilbert space. The projected state loses track of its original state. Thus any information on the past of the system is lost for good - a property when properly manipulated, gives rise to the phenomenon of quantum erasing. If cloning of an unknown quantum state were possible, it would amount to faster than light transmission of information violating Einstein's strict causality principle, as required by special relativity theory Herbert (1982). The last property, namely the impossibility of cloning an unknown quantum state (no-cloning theorem) is mainly exploited in quantum cryptography which, in fact, is only a corollary of the other three conditions. An infringement on no-cloning theorem would be a breach of linearity, causality and unitarity all together. This property makes the passive listening by Eve impossible. In principle, any quantum particles can be used but photons are most suited as they are the reliable information carriers in the optical fibre cables. Optical fibre cables are the most promising medium for extremely high band width communications. The polarizations of a set of the photons sent from Alice (sender) to Bob (receiver) form the coded information of the key. The actual encrypted message is transmitted via a public classic channel. Any attempt to measure the states of the photons would invariably disturb the state and hence will be noticed by the parties concerned. The sender and the receiver would compare their measurements of the polarizations of the photons to check for any potential eavesdropping. Thus quantum key distribution cannot prevent eavesdropping but can surely be detected with 100 percent efficiency. The key can then be discarded.

Quantum Cryptology works according to specific models, a famous one being due to Bennett and Brassard as described in Ekert (1991), Bennett and Brassard (1992). Detection of intrusion by eavesdropper is vital to Quantum Cryptography. It is a way to combine the relative convenience and ease of key exchange in public key cryptography

(PKC) with the ultimate security of a one time pad. Heisenberg's Uncertainty Principle plays a dominant role in actual practice here. Historically Quantum Cryptology was first proposed by Stephen Wiesner in early 1970's introducing the concept of quantum conjugate coding. In 1990 Arthur Ekert as given in Ekert (1991), developed a different approach to Quantum Cryptology based on peculiar quantum correlation known as quantum entanglement. Prospects for use of Quantum Cryptology are bright. Quantum Cryptology has the ability to detect any interception of the key, whereas with classical ones the key security cannot be proved or faulted. Quantum Key Distribution (QKD) would mean secure communication though not guaranteed against jamming. It enables two parties to produce a shared random bit string known only to them, which can be used as a key to encrypt and decrypt messages. QKD systems are automatic with greater reliability factor.

THE EPR PARADOX

We would like to give here briefly the essentials of the original work of EPR. It is crucial to the understanding of quantum cryptography that uses what is known as EPR pair. The most illustrious debate between Einstein and Bohr culminated in the famous paper of EPR paradox in 1935 described in Einstein, Podolsky and Rosen (1935). Their attack on the orthodox interpretations of quantum mechanics by the Copenhagen school was to bring out what later became famous as the EPR paradox. These deliberations were followed by others and are still being pursued. Experimental verifications of the violations of Bell's theorem became central to the discussions on the bizarre nature of the quantum phenomena. The insight into these gave rise to the above mentioned modern applications that exploit properties of quantum entanglement. Fundamentally an EPR system consists of a pair of quantum particles that have interacted in the past and are being space-like

separated. This means that they do not interact nor do exert any causal influence on each other. Now, there are three significant fundamental features of such a system.

Having interacted in the past and undisturbed so far, the two particles of the EPR pair will have correlated physical attributes even if they are separated by space-like regions. This means that there is an apparent non-local correlation between these EPR pairs as explained below.

Another property even for a single quantum particle is that unlike classical one the exact value of a physical attribute is undefined before measurement and the act of measurement disturbs the state. Trying to discern non-orthogonal quantum systems always result in loss of information about the past. In an empirical sense it has no definite real value but a possible combination or a 'mixture' of different possible values are having different probabilities. This strange fact is well-brought out by the Schrödinger's cat paradox in a picturesque manner. This peculiar characteristic, when viewed from a classical perspective, is an absolute absurdity. It would mean that there is no absolute reality to a dynamic variable in a classical sense unless measured or observed. This very bizarre quantum feature is corroborated and sheltered by the celebrated uncertainty principle and relations of Werner Heisenberg.

The third feature is the consequence of combination of the above two. A measurement on any one of the pairs could though yield a random result would nevertheless be correlated with that of the other member of the pair in a peculiar way. But, what can be controlled is the experimental set up at both space-like separated ends. The experimental arrangement would seem to influence in some way the overall results though not conclusively since the outcome of individual measurement is always random. Thus there seems to be a non-local correlation (no influence on the individual result) between the results of measurements on the two individual particles of the EPR pair. The two particles are said to be entangled then. Consider an EPR pair consisting of particle 1 & 2. Mathematically the entangled state can be represented as follows:

$$\frac{1}{\sqrt{2}}[(\uparrow)_1(\downarrow)_2 + (\downarrow)_1 + (\uparrow)_2], \qquad (1)$$

where $(\uparrow)$ and $(\downarrow)$ stand for the amplitudes for spin up and spin down, respectively. Curiously the combined state is the sum of amplitudes for both. The system is now in a 'mixed state'. The measurement actualizes the spin values. Whether it is really so or not is being highly debated but it is immaterial to our present discussions. The state 'jumps' to a 'pure' state, either $(\uparrow)_1(\downarrow)_2$ or $(\downarrow)_1(\uparrow)_2$ upon measurement, but one cannot predict with certainty which one of the two. Yet the spins of both particles are in perfect correlation as can be seen from above. If the spin of one particle upon measurement is found to be 'UP' then definitely that of the other one must be 'DOWN' and vice versa. This correlation is perfect. For our purpose, it is not necessary to be spins of particles or polarizations of photons but can be any two-valued state for illustration; it can be the two quantum states of an ammonia molecule. The representation of an EPR pair in (1) can be modified by slightly different notation:

$$\frac{1}{\sqrt{2}}[(1)_1(0)_2 + (0)_1(1)_2]. \qquad (2)$$

Now, $(1)_1(0)_2$ or $(0)_1(1)_2$ represents the two possibilities after measurement. It is now straight forward to translate these states to qubits (quantum version of bit) of information. The above mentioned property of entanglement of an EPR pair is exploited in some of the later versions of quantum cryptography whereas the older version made use of single particle superposition. There are three-particle and higher number entangled states (like GHZ states) which may also be put to some application in future.

These peculiar characteristics of quantum systems were topics of continual debate, the surprise over which is not yet subsided. The argument of EPR was that any one or more of the obvious, accepted and commonsense principles like Reality, Locality or Causality has to be abandoned in order to explain the above paradox. Hence EPR concluded that quantum mechanics is incomplete. Einstein argued that quantum mechanics is only a statistical theory pertaining to ensembles rather than individual particles. It is just like thermodynamics that does not deal with individual particles but a collection of them.

Bell's theorem gives a new twist to the problem making it possible to experimentally distinguish between classical deterministic theories and quantum theory. Motivated by the EPR and von Neumann's work on QM Bell published his landmark paper in 1964 Bell (1964), Bell (1993) on his famous inequality. Bell found that the EPR pairs would have a different statistical correlation upon measurement, if quantum behavior were true and not the classical deterministic one. Hidden variable theory was proposed to bring in back the classical feature of absolute determinism. The gist of the Bell's theorem is that classical deterministic type hidden variable theory cannot mimic the quantum features completely in every situation and range of parameters. This theorem is a generalization of the fact that quantum systems, like entangled EPR pairs, unlike the classical ones, would violate Bell's inequality giving away its quantum nature.

The experimental confirmations of violations of Bell's inequality and others and several other experiments have since seemed to be underlining the special nature of individual quantum particles. It is generally believed that these results vindicate Bohr's stance at least partially and demolished the EPR stance. Yet, there are a few twists to the problem to be really conclusive. Bohr's position was that quantum mechanics was the true description of nature, not just an approximate or incomplete one. (There are valid and sensible challenges to this stance that would be too much of a digression from the present topic.) The most important conclusive evidences of violations of Bell's inequality were experimental results of Aspect given in Clauser, Horne, Shimony and Holt, (1969), Freedmann and Clauser (1972), Clauser and Shimony (1978), Aspect, Dalibard and Roger (1982) and others. Later several other experiments using three-particle entangled systems (like GHZ states) repeatedly confirmed the quantum properties. There are several other phenomena experimentally verified to prove the quantum behavior like Bohm-Aharonov described in David and Aharonov (1957), George and Arthur (2006), Newton (2008) effect and so on. The above mentioned distinguishing traits are the basis of all the modern applications of quantum including in the quantum cryptology.

APPLICATIONS OF QC

Here we point out rather briefly the immense scope for applications of this important topic. In 1984, Bennett and Brassard proposed a scheme for quantum key distribution known as BB84 scheme as shown in Bennett, Brassard and Ekert (1992). It is a procedure using a set of individual photons. BB84 solves Quantum Key distribution problem but storage of the key was still a problem. Therefore Ekert proposed EPR-based protocol for key distribution as in Ekert (1991). The photons of EPR pair have undefined polarizations. Yet the polarizations of both are in orthogonal directions. These two properties together are mysterious and is the basis of many modern quantum applications not involving an ensemble.

Cryptography is the science and study of protecting data and secret messages in computer and communication systems from unauthorized disclosure, intrusion, modification and the rest. Developments in public key cryptography (PKC) have been taking place from about 1978. Commu-

nication between parties through insecure channels is the central problem. Data security issues have considerably increased the importance of the subject of late. There are several applications of cryptography in the present information-driven society. In addition to application to authentication, digital signature, user identification, protection of privacy, mail protection, zero-knowledge proof etc. there are further areas also to be investigated where Quantum Cryptology/cryptography is finding itself very useful.

CONCLUDING REMARKS

Quantum Cryptology is of really great merits and possesses much practical advantage. However, there are also some factors preventing wider adoption of Quantum Cryptology outside high security areas. They include equipment costs, lack of demonstrated threat to existing key exchange protocols etc. Nevertheless we must feel satisfied that with fiber optic networks presently already prevalent in many countries the required infrastructure is in good place for more and efficient usage of Quantum Cryptology. Very much like in the case of quantum computation and related matters the rich field of quantum safety related researches are all along bound to further flourish in the days to come. Even sky is not the limit for progress as anyone can forecast at the present juncture. In any case since quantum mechanics has proved itself to be so far a grand success in ever so many practical situations in science and technology, though it may not be complete, we can envisage its further utility in increasing measure in the future also.

Quantum cryptology is one of the useful modern applications of EPR and Bell states which do assume greater significance in several other technological contexts as well. What started as a pure philosophical debate between the two giants, Albert Einstein and Niels Bohr several decades ago gave technological spin-offs in modern times.

Several noted physicists considered the interpretational aspect of QM only of academic interest with very little experimental content in those days. Bell's theorem changed the whole situation quite considerably. The bottom line is not to neglect the 'understanding' aspect of science. It will definitely pay off well, even as technological spin offs, if not immediately, at least in future, quantum cryptology being clearly a glaring example. Quantum Teleportation, Quantum Computing, Quantum Dense Coding, Quantum Currency and the like are related potential fields. The quantum aspect has got a lot more potential to be exploited for technological gains. Though the single particle application is demonstrated in the laboratory over quite large distances, it is still riddled with technical problems to make it viable for practical applications. Commercial feasibility is to be thought of only after achieving that. Quantum Cryptology is a highly potential field capable of taking over the classical one also. This and quantum information theory together would surely bloom into highly useful and popular fields in the next decades, necessitated by the unprecedented growth of quantum computation and the related progress.

REFERENCES

Achuthan, P., & Narayanankutty, K. (2009). On Mathematical Modeling of Quantum Mechanical Systems. *Am. Inst. of Phys., Conf. Proc., 1146* (1),105-112

Andreescu. (2009). *Number Theory – Structures.* New York: Springer.

Aspect, A. (1804-1807). Dalibard, J. & Roger, G. (1982). Experimental Test of Bell's Inequalities Using Time-Varying Analyzers. *Physical Review Letters*, 49.

Bell, J. S. (1964). On the Einstein Podolsky Rosen Paradox. *Physics, 1*(3), 195–200.

Bell, J. S. (1993). *Quantum Mechanics: Speakable and Unspeakable in Quantum Mechanics.* Cambridge, UK: Cambridge Univ. Press.

Bennett, C. H. & Brassard, G. (1984). *Quantum Cryptography.* Conference Proc., Bangalore.

Bennett, C., & Brassard, H., G. & Ekert, A. K. (1992). Quantum Cryptography. *Scientific American*, 50–57. doi:10.1038/scientificamerican1092-50

Biggs. (2008). *An introduction to Information Communication and Cryptography.* New York: Springer.

Bohr, N. (1935). Can Quantum-Mechanical Description of Physical Reality be Considered Complete? *Physical Review, 48*, 696. doi:10.1103/PhysRev.48.696

Chaum, D, J. (1988*). Cryptography. 1(*1), 65 .

Clauser, J. F., Horne, M. A., Shimony, A., & Holt, R. A. (1969). Proposed experiment to test local hidden variable theories. *Physical Review Letters, 23*, 880–884. doi:10.1103/PhysRevLett.23.880

Clauser, J. F., & Shimony, A. (1978). Bell's theorem: experimental tests and implications. *Reports on Progress in Physics, 41*, 1881–1927. doi:10.1088/0034-4885/41/12/002

David, B., & Aharonov, Y. (1957)... *Physical Review, 108*, 1070. doi:10.1103/PhysRev.108.1070

David, M. B. (1989). *Factorization and Primality Testing.* New York: Springer.

Einstein, A., Podolsky, B., & Rosen, N. (1935). Can Quantum-Mechanical Description of Physical Reality be Considered Complete? *Physical Review, 47*, 777. doi:10.1103/PhysRev.47.777

Ekert, A. K. (1991). Quantum Cryptography Based on Bell's Theorem. *Physical Review Letters, 67*, 666. doi:10.1103/PhysRevLett.67.661

Everest, G., & Ward, T. (2007). *An Introduction to Number Theory*. New York: Springer.

Freedmann, S. J., & Clauser, J. F. (1972). Experimental test of local hidden variable theories. *Physical Review Letters*, *28*, 938–941. doi:10.1103/PhysRevLett.28.938

George, G., & Arthur, G. Z. (2006). *The Quantum Challenge-Modern Research on the Foundations of Quantum Mechanics* (2nd ed.). New Delhi: Narosa Publ.

GroverL. K. (1996) quant-ph/9605043.

Grover, L. K. (1997)... *Physical Review Letters*, *79*, 325. doi:10.1103/PhysRevLett.79.325

Herbert, N. (1982)... *Foundations of Physics*, *12*, 1171. doi:10.1007/BF00729622

Hoffstein. (2008). *An introduction to Mathematical Cryptography*. New York: Springer.

Julian, B. (2001). *The Quest for Quantum Computing*. New York: Simon and Shuster.

Myasnikov. (2008). *Group-Based Cryptography*. New York: Springer.

Narayanankutty, K., & Achuthan, P. (2005). *On Bell's theorem and inequality*. Abst. of the Natl. Symp. Mathematical Methods and Applications, (NSMMA-2005), IIT Madras.

Newton, R. G. (2008). *The Truth of Science*. New Delhi, India: Viva Books.

Nicolas. G., et al. (2009). Quantum Cryptography. Rev. Mod. Phys., and 207 references cited therein.

Shaska, T. (2007). *Advances in Coding Theory and Cryptography*. Singapore: World Scientific.

Shor, P. W. (1997). Algorithms for Quantum Computation: Discrete Algorithms and Factoring. *SIAM Journal on Computing*, *26*, 1484–1509. doi:10.1137/S0097539795293172

Strocchi, T. (2005). *An Introduction to Mathematical Structure of Quantum Mechanics*. Singapore: World Scientific.

Wegner, B. (2000) (Ed.in-chief), *Zentralblatt MATH*, Berlin.

Wiesner, S. (1983). Conjugate Coding. *Sigact News*, *15*, 1. doi:10.1145/1008908.1008920

Chapter 17
Error Linear Complexity Measures of Binary Multisequences

Sindhu M.
Amrita Vishwa Vidyapeetham, India

Sajan Kumar S.
Amrita Vishwa Vidyapeetham, India

M. Sethumadhavan
Amrita Vishwa Vidyapeetham, India

ABSTRACT

The joint linear complexity and k - error joint linear complexity of an m - fold 2^n periodic multisequence can be efficiently computed using Modified Games Chan algorithm and Extended Stamp Martin Algorithm respectively. In this chapter the authors derive an algorithm which, given a constant c and an m – fold 2^n periodic binary multisequence S, computes the minimum number k of errors and the associated error multisequence needed over a period of S for bringing the joint linear complexity of S below c. They derived another algorithm for finding the joint linear complexity of 3. 2^v periodic binary multisequence.

INTRODUCTION

In complexity measures for sequences over finite fields, such as the linear complexity and the k – error linear complexity is of great relevance to cryptology, in particular, to the area of stream ciphers. There are basically two types of requirements for suitability of a keystream generated by a stream cipher. One of the requirements is the keystream sequence must pass various statistical tests for randomness. This is to make it difficult to capture any information about the plaintext by an attacker from any possible statistical deficiencies in the keystream. The second is that it should be very hard to predict the entire keystream from the knowledge of a part of it. For this purpose, one is interested to know how hard a sequence might be to predict. This requirement leads to the study of several complexity measures for sequences. The most significant complexity measure is the linear complexity: length of the shortest linear recurrence relation satisfied by the sequence and

DOI: 10.4018/978-1-60960-123-2.ch017

related concept of k-error linear complexity (see Kaida, T. (1999)).

The major problem in stream cipher cryptography is generating a pseudorandom sequence of elements from a short random key. We mainly use LFSRs for the construction of stream ciphers. On the other hand, LFSRs can also be used to mount attacks on stream cipher systems. This attack is based on the Berlekamp-Massey algorithm: given a sequence S with terms in a finite field F_q of length n, the Berlekamp-Massey algorithm computes the feedback polynomial of the shortest LFSR that can generate the sequence S in $O(n^2)$ time. In fact, if the shortest LFSR is of length ℓ, then the algorithm needs just 2ℓ consecutive terms of the output sequence to determine its feedback polynomial. So this algorithm forms a universal attack on keystream generators since it carries the potential of substituting any keystream generator by its shortest linear equivalent. This leads to the concept of linear complexity of sequences. For a stream cipher system to be secure against the Berlekamp-Massey attack, it must not be possible to approximate the keystream sequence closely with a sequence of significantly smaller linear complexity. This means that changing a few terms in the keystream sequence must not cause a significant decrease of the linear complexity. This requirement leads to the concept of k-error linear complexity.

To take advantage of the general purpose processing units employed in the present day computers over public/private networks, we need the keystream to be a sequence of a few bytes, instead of bits. Such keystream generators are better suited for software implementation, and provide high throughput. Such ciphers are called word based (or vectorized) ciphers since they produce more than one bit per clock cycle. The theory of such stream ciphers requires the study of the complexity measures for multisequences, i.e., for parallel streams of finitely many sequences. In this direction, the joint linear complexity and the joint linear complexity profile of multisequences

have been investigated. The theory of k-error joint linear complexity of multisequences has been investigated recently.

An m fold N periodic multisequence S can be interpreted as an $m \times N$ matrix over F_q. For defining the k-error joint linear complexity of multisequences, we need the following definitions of term distance and column distance.

1.1 Definition: Let $S=(S^{(1)}, S^{(2)},\ldots,S^{(m)})$ and $T=(T^{(1)}, T^{(2)},\ldots,T^{(m)})$ be two m fold N periodic multisequences over F_q. We define the term distance $\delta_T(S,T)$ between S and T as the number of entries in S that are different from the corresponding entries in T, and the column distance $\delta_C(S,T)$ as the number of columns in S that are different from the corresponding columns in T. We define the individual distance vector by $\delta_V(S, T) = (\delta 1, \delta_2, \ldots, \delta_m)$, where δ_j is the Hamming distance between the jth rows of S and T for $1 \leq j \leq m$.

1.2 Definition: Let $S=(S^{(1)}, S^{(2)},\ldots,S^{(m)})$ be an m fold N periodic multisequences over F_q. For an integer k with $0 \leq k \leq mN$, the k-error joint linear complexity $L_{N,k}(S)$ of S is the smallest possible joint linear complexity obtained by changing k or fewer terms of S in its first period of length N and then continuing the changes periodically with period N. In other words, $L_{N,k}(S) = \min_T L(T)$ where the minimum is taken over all m fold N periodic multisequence T over F_q with term distance $\delta_T(S, T) \leq k$.

1.3 Definition: Let S be an m fold N periodic multisequence over F_q. For an integer k with $0 \leq k \leq N$, the k-error F_q linear complexity $L^q_{N,K}(S)$ of S is the smallest possible joint linear complexity obtained by changing k or fewer columns of S in its first period of length N and then continuing the changes periodically with period N. In other words, $L^q_{N,K}(S) = \min_T L(T)$ where the minimum is taken over all m fold N periodic multisequences T over F_q with column distance $\delta_C(S,T) \leq k$. Alternatively, if S is the N periodic sequence with terms in F_{q^m} corresponding to the given multisequence S, then $L^q_{N,K}(S)$ is the k-error F_q linear complexity of S defined by $L^q_{N,K}(S) = \min_T L^q(T)$ where the minimum is taken over all N periodic sequences T over F_{q^m} with Hamming distance less than or equal to k between the first periods of S and T of length N.

1.4 Definition: Let $S=(S^{(1)}, S^{(2)},...,S^{(m)})$ be an m fold N periodic multisequences over F_q. For $K = (k_1, k_2,..., k_m)$ with $(k_1, k_2,...,k_m) \in Z^m$ with $0 \leq k_j \leq N$ for $0 \leq j \leq m$, the K error joint linear complexity $L_{N,K}(S)$ of S is the smallest possible joint linear complexity obtained by changing k_j or fewer terms of $S^{(j)}$ in its first period of length N and then continuing the changes periodically with period N for each $j = 1, 2, ..., m$. In other words $L_{N,K}(S) = \min_T L(T)$ where the minimum is taken over all m fold N periodic multisequences T over F_q with $\delta_V(S, T) \leq K$.

The k-error joint linear complexities of the following type of sequences were discussed by Ayineedi Venkateswarlu (2007). For multisequences over F_q with period p^v, char $(F_q)=p$ and for multisequences over F_q with Period p^n, q is a Primitive Root Modulo p^2, algorithms for computing the k-error joint linear complexity has been established by Ayineedi Venkateswarlu (2007). These are the currently known algorithms for finding the k-error joint linear complexity of multisequences. Here we are discussing an algorithm for computing an error multisequence of minimum cost such that the joint linear complexity $JLC(S+e) \leq c$. Also we are discussing an algorithm for computing the joint linear complexity of m - fold 3.2^v periodic multisequence in an efficient manner.

1. An Algorithm for Computing an Error Multisequence E of Minimum Cost Such That $JLC(S+e) \leq c$

Ana Salagean (2005), derived an algorithm for computing an error sequence e of minimum cost for a binary sequence of period 2^n such that

$LC(S+e) \leq c$. Here we derive an extension of above algorithm to the case of multisequences. Given an m − fold binary multisequence of period 2^n and a given constant c, this algorithm computes the minimum number k of errors needed so that the joint linear complexity of given multisequence is less than or equal to c and the corresponding error multisequence. For this purpose we suitably modified the Extended Stamp Martin algorithm derived by Sethumadhavan, M., Sindhu, M., Chungath Srinivasan, & Kavitha, C (2008). (See Algorithm 1.1)

We prove this algorithm using the principle of mathematical induction on n. We can easily see that the cost vector values $cost[i][j]$ is updated at any step so that this value reflects the cost of changes in the original multisequence S in order to change the current element $s[i][j]$ without disturbing the results of the previous steps.

We are going to show that the quantity k' computed by the above algorithm is minimal such that $LC_{k',2^n}(S, \cos t) \leq c$. When $n = 0$, the result is obvious. Now suppose that the result is true for $n − 1$. Consider the first execution of the main *for* loop, when $j = 0$. We denote by $S(0)$ and $cost(0)$ the values of S and $cost$ at the beginning of the first run of the *for* loop, and by $S(1)$ and $cost(1)$ their values at the end of the first run. The value T represents the minimal cost of making changes in the current sequence $S(0)$ such as to make its left half multisequence equal to the right half. The condition "if $T = 0$ or $c' + l \geq c$" will decide whether we make these changes or not. If $T = 0$, we obviously should make these changes, as they decrease the complexity of the multisequence at no cost. If $c' + l \geq c$ it means $S(0)$ has to be changed so that it has period 2^{n-1} or less. So we have to force the left half to be equal to the right half. Now we are left with the case when $T > 0$ but $2^{n-1} < c$. Not doing changes in this case will mean that we add 2^{n-1} to the current value c' of the complexity and then process the sequence $S(1)=b$, effectively computing the value k' as the minimal quantity such that

Algorithm 1.1.

Consider an m - fold $l=2^n$ periodic multisequence $S=(S^{(1)}, S^{(2)},...,S^{(m)})$ where
$S^{(h)}=\left(s_0^{(h)},s_1^{(h)},....,s_{l-1}^{(h)}\right)$, $h=1, 2,...,m$

Initialize $l=2^n$, $c'=0$, $k'=0$,

cost $[i][j]$ = 1 for i = 1 to m, j = 0 to $l - 1$
flag $[k][j]$ = 0 for k = 1 to m, j = 0 to $n - 1$
error$[k][j][i]$ = 0 for k = 1 to m, j = 0 to $n - 1$ and i=0 to $2^{n-j}-1$
  for j = 0 to $n - 1$, $l = l/2$
    for p = 0 to $l - 1$
      Compute $b = L(S) \oplus R(S) = (b^{(1)}, b^{(2)}, ..., b^{(m)})$ where
      $b^{(h)}=\left(b_0^{(h)},b_1^{(h)},...,b_{l-1}^{(h)}\right)$ and $b_p^{(h)}=s_p^{(h)} \oplus s_{p+l}^{(h)}$

$$T=\sum_{k=1}^{m}\sum_{p=0}^{l-1}b[k][p]\min\left(\cos t[k][p],\cos t[k][p+l]\right)$$

      If T = 0 or $c'+l \geq c$, then
      $k'=k'+T$
        flag $[k][j]$ = 1 for k = 1 to m
          for k = 1 to m
            for i = 0 to $l - 1$
              If $b[k][i]$ = 1, then
                If cost $[k][i] \leq$ cost$[k][i + l]$
                $s_i^{(k)}=s_{i+l}^{(k)}$, cost$[k][i]$ = cost$[k][i + l]$ - cost $[k][i]$
                  error $[k][j][i]$ = 1
                else
                  $s_i^{(k)}=s_i^{(k)}$, cost $[k][i]$ = cost $[k][i]$ - cost $[k][i+l]$
                  error $[k][j][i + l]$ = 1
        else
        $c'=c'+l$
          For k = 1 to m
           For i = 0 to $l - 1$
            $s_k^{(i)}=b_k^{(i)}$
             If cost $[k][i] \leq$ cost $[k][i + l]$, then error$[k][j][i]$ = 1
            else cost $[k][i]$ = cost $[k][i + l]$, error$[k][j][i + l]$ = 1
for i = 1 to m
  $e[i][0]$ = 0
for i = 1 to m
    If $s_0^{(i)}=1$ and $c'+1>c$
      $k'=k'+\cos t[i][0]$, $e[i][0]$ = 1

continued on the following page

Algorithm 1.1.

```
    else e[i][0]  = 0
for k = 0 to m - 1
  p = 1;
    for j = n - 1  to 0
      p = p * 2;
      for i = p/2  to p - 2
        e[k][i] = e[k][i-1];
      if flag[k][j] =1
        for i = 0 to p - 1
          e[k][i] = e[k][i] + error[k][j][i]
      else
        for i = 0 to p - 1
          e [k][i] = e [k][i]*error[k][j][i].
```

$LC_{k',2^{n-1}}(S(1),\cos t(1)) \le c - 2^{n-1}$. By the induction hypothesis, this algorithm computes k' correctly. Note that T is exactly the minimum cost of changing all entries of $s(1)=b$ to 0. Hence $k' \le T$. That is not doing changes at this step is guaranteed to lead to a final cost no greater than the cost of doing changes at this step, while still keeping the complexity below the target c. The correctness of the computation of the error multisequence follows directly from the correctness proof as in the single sequence case. This algorithm has the time complexity O(mN), where m is the number of sequence in the given multisequence and $N = 2^n$.

2. An Algorithm for Computing the Joint Linear Complexity of M - Fold 3.2^v Periodic Multisequence

Now we modify an algorithm due to Wilfried Meidl (2008) derived for single sequences of period 3.2^v to the case of m-fold multisequences of period 3.2^v. Here we establish that the joint linear complexity of m − fold 3.2^v periodic binary multisequences can easily be calculated from the joint linear complexities of m − fold 2^v periodic binary multisequences with the help of Modified Games Chan algorithm (See Algorithm 2.1).

It is possible to reduce the calculation of the joint linear complexity of un periodic sequence over a finite field F_{p^m} to the calculation of the joint linear complexities of u multisequences over F_{p^m} of period n under the condition that u divides p^m-1 and $gcd(n, p^m-1) = 1$. These conditions guarantee that there exist exactly u distinct u^{th} roots of unity $x_0 = 1, x_1,..., x_{u-1}$ in $S=(S^{(1)}, S^{(2)},...,S^{(m)})$ and we can find unique $b_i \in F_{p^m}$ such that $b_i^n = x_i, i = 0,1,..., u-1$. Following proposition is a generalization of a result in Wilfried Meidl (2008).

Proposition 2.1:

Suppose $p, m, u, n, x_0, ..., x_{u-1}, b_0, ..., b_{u-1}$ are given as above. Let $S=(S^{(1)}, S^{(2)},...,S^{(m)})$ be a multisequence over F_{p^m} where $S^{(h)} = \left(s_0^{(h)}, s_1^{(h)},...., s_{n-1}^{(h)}\right)$ $h = 1, 2, ..., m$. For $i = 0,1, ..., u-1$ and let $S_i^{[h,u]} = \left(s_0^{(h,i)}, s_1^{(h,i)},..., s_{n-1}^{(h,i)}\right)$ for $h = 1, 2, ..., m$ be

Algorithm 2.1.

> Consider an m-fold $N = 3.2^v$ periodic multisequence $S = (S^{(1)}, S^{(2)}, ..., S^{(m)})$ where
> $$S^{(h)} = \left(s_0^{(h)}, s_1^{(h)}, ..., s_{N-1}^{(h)}\right), \quad h = 1 \text{ to } m$$
>
> for $i = 0, 1, 2$
> $$S_i^{[h,3]} = \left(s_0^{(h,i)}, s_1^{(h,i)}, ..., s_{N-1}^{(h,i)}\right)$$
>
> where
> $$s_p^{(h,i)} = \begin{cases} s_p^{(h)} & \text{if } p \text{ is not congruent to } i \pmod 3 \\ 0 & \text{otherwise} \end{cases} \quad \text{for } h = \text{to } m, \; p = 0 \text{ to } N-1$$
>
> Build m fold 2^v periodic multisequences as follows.
> $$T^{(h)} = \left(t_0^{(h)}, t_1^{(h)}, ..., t_{2^v-1}^{(h)}\right), \quad \text{where } t_p^{(h)} = s_p^{(h)} + s_{p+2^v}^{(h)} + s_{p+2*2^v}^{(h)} \quad \text{for } h = 1 \text{ to } m \text{ and } p = 0 \text{ to } 2^v-1$$
>
> For $i = 0, 1, 2$ compute
> $$T_i^{[h,3]} = \left(t_0^{[h,i]}, t_1^{[h,i]}, ..., t_{2^v-1}^{[h,i]}\right) where$$
> $$t_p^{[h,i]} = s_p^{(h,i)} + s_{p+2^v}^{(h,i)} + s_{p+2*2^v}^{(h,i)},$$
> $$for \; h = 1 \; to \; m \; and \; p = 0 \; to \; 2^v - 1$$
> $$JLC(S) = JLC(T) + \max\left(JLC\left(T_1^{[h,3]}\right), JLC\left(T_0^{[h,3]}\right)\right)$$
> $$+ \max\left(JLC\left(T_2^{[h,3]}\right), JLC\left(T_0^{[h,3]}\right)\right)$$

the n periodic sequence with k^{th} term
$$s_k^{(h,i)} = s_k^{(h)} b_i^k + s_{n+k}^{(h)} b_i^{n+k} + ... + s_{(u-1)n+k}^{(h)} b_i^{(u-1)n+k}$$
for $0 \le k \le n-1$. The joint linear complexity of S is given by

$$JLC(S) = JLC(S_0^{[h,u]}) + JLC(S_1^{[h,u]})$$
$$+ ... + JLC(S_{u-1}^{[h,u]})$$

From this we can observe that this proposition can be utilized for finding the joint linear complexity of a *un* periodic multisequence over a finite field F_q if u does not divide $q - 1$. In practice we want to obtain all binary component multisequences directly from the 3.2^v periodic binary m fold multisequence. The smallest integer such that $3|2^m - 1$ is $m = 2$. We will get $b_0 = 1$,

$b_1 = \alpha$ and $b_2 = \alpha^2$. Since $b_0 = 1$ the multisequence is binary. Rest of the proof follows from that for the single sequence case as the results used there can be extended directly to the multisequence case. Time complexity of this algorithm is $O(mN)$ where m is the number of sequence in the given multisequence and $N = 2^v$.

CONCLUSION

In this Chapter we derived two algorithms for finding the joint linear complexity of 3.2^v periodic binary m-fold multisequences and for finding error multisequence needed over a period of S for bringing the joint linear complexity of S below c, which are extensions of algorithm for the case of single sequence to the multisequence.

REFERENCES

Games, R. A., & Chan, A. H. (1983). A fast algorithm for determining the linear complexity of a pseudorandom sequence with period 2^n. *IEEE Transactions on Information Theory, IT-29,* 144–146. doi:10.1109/TIT.1983.1056619

Kaida, T. (1999). *On Algorithms for the k-Error Linear Complexity of Sequences over GF (p^m) with Period p^n*. Ph. D. Thesis, Kyushu Institute of Tech.

Meidl, W. (2008). Reducing the calculation of the linear complexity of $u2^v$ - periodic binary sequences to Games Chan algorithm. *Designs, Codes and Cryptography, 46,* 57–65. doi:10.1007/s10623-007-9134-x

Meidl, W., & Niederreiter, H., & Ayineedi Venkateswarlu. (2007). Error linear complexity Measures for Multisequences. *Journal of Complexity, 23*(2), 169–192. doi:10.1016/j.jco.2006.10.005

Salagean, A. (2005). On the computation of the Linear Complexity and the *k*-Error Linear Complexity of Binary Sequences with Period a Power of Two. *IEEE Transactions on Information Theory, 51,* 1145–1150. doi:10.1109/TIT.2004.842769

Sethumadhavan, M., & Sindhu, M., Chungath Srinivasan, & Kavitha, C. (2008). An algorithm for *k*-error joint linear complexity of binary multisequences. *Journal of Discrete Mathematical Sciences & Cryptography, 11*(3), 297–304.

Venkateswarlu, A. (2007). *Studies on error linear complexity measures for multisequences.* Ph.D Thesis, National University of Singapore.

APPENDIX A

Computing a Sequence *e* of Minimum Cost Such That *LC*(*s* + *e*) ≤ *c*

Consider a $l = 2^n$ periodic sequence $S = \left(s_0, s_1, \ldots, s_{2^n-1}\right)$, initialize the cost vector *cost*[*i*] and the error vector *error* [*j*] as follows:

```
cost [i] = 1 for i = 0 to l - 1
flag [j] = 0 for j = 0 to n - 1
error[j][i] = 0 for j = 0 to n - 1 and i = 0 to 2^{n-1} -1
for j = 0 to n - 1, l = l/2
    Compute b = L ⊕ R = (b_1, b_2, ..., b_{l-1}),where L is the left half of the se-
quence
    S and R is the right half. Compute
```

$$T = \sum_{i=0}^{l-1} b_i \min(\cos t[i], \cos t[i+l])$$

```
    If T = 0 or c' + l ≥ c, then
```
$$k' = k' + T$$
```
      flag [j] = 1
      for i = 0 to l - 1
            If b[i] = 1, then
            If cost [i] ≤ cost [i + l]
                s_i = R_i, cost[i] = cost[i + l] - cost [i]
                              error [j][i] = 1
                    else
            s_i = L_i , cost [i] = cost [i] - cost [i+l]
                        error [j][i + l] = 1
                else
                  s_i = L_i , cost [i] = cost [i] + cost [i+l]
        else
```
$$c' = c' + l$$
```
      for i = 0 to l - 1
            s_i = b_i
            If cost [i] ≤ cost[i + l ] , then error[j][i] = 1
      else cost[i] = cost [i + l ], error[j][i + l] = 1
  e = 0
If s_0 = 1 and c' + 1 > c, then
```
$$k' = k' + \cos t[0], \quad e = 1$$
```
else e = 0
for j = n - 1 to 0
```

```
e ← duplicate (e)
if flag[j] =1 then  e = e XOR error[j]
else  e = e AND error [j].
```

APPENDIX B

Extended Stamp Martin Algorithm

An algorithm for finding the *k*-error joint linear complexity of *m* - fold $N = 2^n$ periodic multisequence

Algorithm:

1. Consider an *m* -fold *N* periodic multisequence $S = (S^{(1)}, S^{(2)}, ..., S^{(m)})$, where $S^{(h)} = \left(s_0^{(h)}, s_1^{(h)}, \cdots, s_{N-1}^{(h)} \right)$, $h = 1, 2, ..., m$.

2. Initialize D (i, j) = 1 for i = 1, 2,..., m and j = 0, 1, ..., N-1 and LC_k = 0

3. Do the following until N = 1

   (a). Compute b = L(S) ⊕ R(S) = $(b^{(1)}, b^{(2)}, ..., b^{(m)})$ where
   $b^{(h)} = (b_0^{(h)}, b_1^{(h)}, ..., b_{N/2-1}^{(h)})$ and $b_i^{(h)} = s_i^{(h)} \oplus s_{N/2+i}^{(h)}$

   Compute $TB = \sum_{i=1}^{m} \sum_{j=0}^{N/2-1} b_i \min(D(i.j), D(i, j + N/2))$

   (b). If TB ≤ k then k = k - TB, N= N/2

      (i). If $b_j^{(i)} = 1$ = 1 and D(i, j) ≤ D(i, j+N), then D(i, j) = D(i, j+N) - D(i, j)
         and $s_j^{(i)} = s_j^{(i)} + 1$

      (ii). If   = 1 and D(i, j) > D(i, j+N)
         then D(i, j) = D(i, j) - D(i, j+N)

      (iii). If $b_j^{(i)} = 0$ then D(i, j) = D(i, j) + D(i, j+N)
         and S = $(S^{(1)}, S^{(2)}, ..., S^{(m)})$

   (c)   If TB > k then N = N/2, LC = LC + N and
   D(i, j) = min (D(i, j), D(i, j+N))
   and $s_j^{(i)} = s_j^{(i)} + s_{j+N}^i$ i.e. (S = b).
      If N ≠ 1then goto (a).

4.   If S ≠ 0 and $\sum_{i=1}^{m} D(i,0) > k$ for N = 1, Then $LC_k = LC_k + 1$

This final Linear Complexity is the *k*- error Joint Linear Complexity of given *m*-fold 2^n periodic multisequence.

APPENDIX C

Algorithm for Computing the Linear Complexity of 3.2^v Periodic Sequence

Step 1.

Consider an $N = 3.2^v$ periodic sequence where $S = \left(s_0, s_1, \ldots, s_{2^n-1}\right)$ for $i = 0, 1, 2$ define

$$S_i^{[3]} = \left(s_0^i, s_1^i, \ldots, s_{N-1}^i\right)$$

where

$$s_n^i = \begin{cases} s_n \ if \ p \ is \ not \ congruent \ to \ i\left(\mathrm{mod} \ 3\right) \\ 0 \ \ otherwise \end{cases}$$

Step 2.

Build the 2^v periodic binary sequences $T = \left(t_0, t_1, \ldots, t_{2^v-1}\right)$ where $t_n = s_n + s_{n+2^v} + s_{n+2.2^v}$
For $i = 0, 1, 2$ compute the 2^v periodic binary sequence

$$T_i^{[3]} = \left(t_0^i, t_1^i, \ldots, t_{2^v-1}^i\right) \ \ where \ \ t_p^i = s_n^i + s_{n+2^v}^i + s_{n+2.2^v}^i, \ n = 0, 1, 2, \ldots.$$

Step 3.

With the algorithm by Games, R. A., & Chan, A. H., (1983) determine $L(T)$, $L(T_0^{[3]})$, $L(T_1^{[3]})$ and $L(T_2^{[3]})$. Then the linear complexity L(S) of S is given by

$$L(S) = L(T) + \max(L(T_1^{[3]}), L(T_0^{[3]})) + \max(L(T_2^{[3]}), L(T_0^{[3]})).$$

Chapter 18
A Survey on Digital Image Steganographic Methods

Amritha P. P.
Amrita Vishwa Vidyapeetham, India

Gireesh Kumar T.
Amrita Vishwa Vidyapeetham, India

ABSTRACT

Steganography is the art of hiding information in ways that prevent the detection of hidden message, where as cryptographic techniques try to conceal the contents of a message. In steganography, the object of communication is the hidden message while the cover data is only the means of sending it. The secret information as well as the cover data can be any medium like text, image, audio, video etc. The objective of this chapter is to report various steganographic embedding schemes that can provide provable security with high computing speed and embed secret messages into images without producing noticeable changes.

The embedding schemes utilizes the characteristic of the human vision's sensitivity to color value variations and resistant to all known steganalysis methods. The main requirement of steganography is undetectability, which loosely defines that no algorithm exists that can determine whether a work contains a hidden message.

1. GENERIC EMBEDDING AND EXTRACTING SCHEME

Many approaches and techniques are available in the literature for information hiding. Figure 1 shows a generic embedding and extracting scheme. The inputs to the embedding scheme are the hiding message, the cover data and an optional public or secret key K. The output is stego data, also called stego object. Inputs to the generic extracting scheme are the tested data, the secret or public key, and the original cover data besides information about steganographic scheme used. The output is the extracted message.

Steganographic techniques can be divided into various categories. The basic and most common

DOI: 10.4018/978-1-60960-123-2.ch018

Figure 1 Generic embedding and extracting scheme

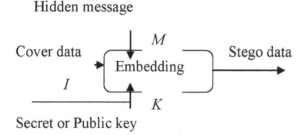

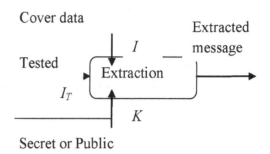

approach in partitioning of hiding techniques is in the spatial domain, frequency domain. Another way for categorization of steganographic methods is based on the condition whether or not they use the original data for extraction of hiding message from tested data. The third method is based on with or without encryption. Three types of steganography can be identified based on their difference in the nature and combination of inputs and outputs (Cox, Miller, Boom, & Fridrich, 2008)

- Pure Steganography

    We call a steganography system pure when it doesn't require prior exchange of some secret information before sending message. The pure steganography can be defined as the quadruple $(C, M, D,$ and $E)$ where:

    C: the set of possible covers.

    M: the set of secret massage with $|C| \geq |M|$.

    E: $C \times M \rightarrow C$ the embedding function.

    D: $C \rightarrow M$ of the extraction function with the property that

    $D(E(c, m)) = m$ for all $m \in M$ and $c \in C$

- Secret key steganography

    We call a steganographic system a shared-secret or shared-key or secret when it requires prior exchange of data like shared keys. Here the sender chooses a cover and embeds the secret message into the cover using a secret key. If

the secret key used in the embedding process is known to the receiver, he can reverse the process and extract the secret message. The secret key steganography can be defined as the quintuple (C, M, K, D_K, E_K) where:

C: the set of possible covers.

M: the set of secret message.

K: the set of secret keys.

E_K: $C \times M \times K \rightarrow C$ with the property that

$D_K(E_K(c, m, k), k) = m$ for all $m \in M$, $c \in C$ and $k \in K$

- Public key Steganography

    This kind of steganography does not rely on shared key exchange. Instead it is based on the public key cryptography principle in which there are two keys, one being the public key which can be usually obtained from a public database and the other a private key. Usually in this case the public key is used in the embedding process and the private key in the decoding process.

Steganography has to guarantee these requirements

- Undetectability: Embedded information is undetectable if the image with the embedded message is consistent with a model of the source from which images are drawn.

- Robustness: The embedded information is said to be robust if its presence can be reliably detected after the image has been modified but not destroyed beyond recognition.
- Perceptual transparency: It is based on the properties of the human visual system or the human audio system. The embedded information is imperceptible if an average human subject is unable to distinguish between carriers that do contain hidden information and those that do not.
- Security: The embedding algorithm is said to be secure if the embedded information cannot be removed beyond reliable detection by targeted attacks based on a full knowledge of the embedding algorithm and the detector, and the knowledge of at least one carrier with hidden message.

The above mentioned requirements are mutually competitive and cannot be clearly optimized at the same time. If we want to hide a large message inside an image, we cannot require at the same time absolute undetectability and large robustness. A reasonable compromise is always a necessity. On the other hand, if robustness to large distortion is an issue, the message that can be reliably hidden cannot be too long.

1.1. The Building Blocks

The main building blocks of any steganographic algorithm are:

1. The choice of the cover work

   A steganographic message says nothing about the cover work in which it is hidden. Consequently, the steganographer is free to choose a particular cover work from their source of covers. The main restriction is the source of cover works, which is determined by the resources available.

2. The embedding and extracting algorithms, which might include
   a. symbol assignment function.
   b. The embedding modification.
   c. The selection rule.

   The primary goal of steganography is to design embedding functions that are statistically undetectable and capable of communicating practical (i.e., large) payloads.

3. Stego key management.

   It is important to choose strong stego keys; otherwise it is easy to attack the steganographic scheme simply by trying to read messages from the stego work using all possible stego keys. Thus the scheme should adopt a more sophisticated key management and periodically change the key according to some pre agreed protocol. For example, the message may be communicated using a session key that is different for each cover and communicated in the cover itself.

2. SPATIAL DOMAIN EMBEDDING TECHNIQUES

The most common method in spatial domain is least significant bits (LSB) embedding (Walton, 1995) which utilizes some least bits of pixels in the cover image to embed secret data. This technique could not resist visual and histogram attack. A generic algorithm for optimal LSB substitution is obtained (Wang, Lin, C. F., & Lin, J .C., 2001) by hiding important data in the rightmost k LSBs of the host image, to improve the stego image quality of the simple LSB method. The method of randomized process and the optimal LSB substitution was introduced in this method. This method increases the system performance and prevents illicit access of data. Even though this method prevents visual attack, it could not completely prevent histogram steganalysis. In addition, (Chang, C. C., Hsiao, & Chan, C. S., 2003) presented a fast and efficient optimal LSB method based on the dynamic programming strategy that improves the computation time of Wang et al.'s (2001) scheme. Further, giving importance to embedding the variable sizes of the LSB's (Lee, & Chen, 2000) proposed a method based on variable size LSB insertion, to maximize the embedding capacity while maintaining image fidelity. Even though this method minimizes the embedding error, it could eliminate the false contours and made the steganalysis difficult, but could not resist RS steganalysis (Fridrich, & Goljan, 2002). Fu, and Au (2002). proposed a data hiding method for halftone images that not only can embed a large amount of secret data but also maintain good visual image quality. For embedding data into image by increasing the payload capacity, and to ensure more security, better quality of stego-image was obtained using the steganographic technique presented in (Tseng, Chen, & Pan, 2002). This scheme is capable of hiding a large amount of data by changing a small number of bits in the original binary image. Specifically, given an $m \times n$ image block, this scheme can conceal as many as $\lfloor \log_2(mn+1) \rfloor$ bits of data in the block by changing, at most, two bits in the block. This approach is much more efficient than available schemes, which can hide, at most, one bit in each block by changing, at most, one bit in the block.

Wu, & Tsai (2003) propose an efficient steganographic method to hide data into gray level images by multi pixel differencing. It is based on the concepts of human visual system, which points out that changing in smooth area is more sensitive than changing in edge area. It processes a block with four neighboring pixels at a time. This approach provides a large embedding capacity and remains acceptable image quality. Each block form three two pixel groups and the difference between two pixels within a group is used to embed data.

Wu et al.'s (2003) scheme possesses both high capacity of secret data and high quality of the stego image. It can embed much greater amounts of

secret data, if the high quality of the stego image is disregarded. For this reason, another method (Suk-Ling, Leung, Cheng, & Chan, 2006), was proposed that can hide double the capacity of the secret data in Wu and Tsai's (2003) scheme with an acceptable quality of the stego image. In this method, pixel value differencing (PVD) algorithm is used to discriminate between edged areas and smooth areas. The capacity of hidden data in edged areas is higher than that of smooth areas. However, to take into account of the capacity of hidden data in the smooth areas, a fixed size least significant bits method was proposed, but this method also could not resist RS steganalysis. To resist RS steganalysis, another steganographic approach using tri-way pixel value differencing (TPVD) was proposed by Chang, K. C., Chang, C. P., Huang, and Tu (2008). In this scheme to increase the hiding capacity of original PVD method, referring to only one direction, three different directional edges are considered and effectively adopted to design the tri-way differencing scheme. Also, to reduce the quality distortion of the stego image due to larger embedding capacity, an optimal approach of selecting the reference point and adaptive rules were presented. This can maintain the stego image at an acceptable and satisfied quality and this method survives RS steganalysis attack. Chao, Wu, Lee, and Chu (2009) proposed a scheme for gray scale images with diamond encoding which is an efficient steganographic technique in spatial domain and could resist all known steganalysis attacks. The diamond encoding method produces a diamond characteristic value (DCV) of the pixel pair block, and the DCV is revised as the embedded secret digit after data embedding procedure. For each block, the diamond encoding technique addresses the minimal changes of two pixel values under the embedding parameter k. In other words, the difference between the cover block and the stego block is never more than k, and the embedding capacity of a block equals $\log_2(2k^2+2k+1)$. The diamond encoding technique minimizes the distortion after the DCV alteration to perform better visual quality.

Zhang, X., Wang, and Zhang, W. (2009) developed a steganography scheme, combining data decomposition mechanism and stego coding method. In this scheme, a secret message is represented as a sequence of digits in a notational system with a prime base. Each digit block is decomposed into a number of shares. By using stego coding technique, these shares are then embedded in different cover images respectively. In each cover, a share is carried by a group of cover pixels and, at most, only one pixel in the group is increased or decreased by a small magnitude. That implies a high embedding efficiency, and therefore distortion introduced to the covers is low, leading to enhanced imperceptibility of the secret message. A further advantage of the scheme is that, even a part of stego images are lost during transmission, the receiver can still extract embedded messages from the surviving covers.

Another steganographic embedding by Exploiting Modification Direction was proposed by Zhang, and Wang (2006). The main idea of this method is that each secret digit in a $(2n + 1)$-ary notational system is carried by n cover pixels, where n is a system parameter and at most one pixel is increased or decreased by 1. For each group of n pixels, there are $2n$ possible ways of modification. The $2n$ different ways of alteration plus the case in which no pixel is changed to form $(2n+1)$ different values of a secret digit. Before data embedding, a data-hider can conveniently convert a secret message into a sequence of digits in the notational system with an odd base $(2n + 1)$. If the secret message is a binary stream, it can be segmented into many pieces with L bits, and the decimal value of each secret piece is represented by k digits in a $(2n + 1)$-ary notational system. This method provides more selectable cases so that the secret message can be conveniently hidden irrespective of the ratio between the payload and the size of cover signal.

Wet Paper Codes with improved embedding efficiency was proposed by Fridrich (2006). In this scheme, a coding method that empowers the steganographer with the ability to use arbitrary selection channels while substantially decreasing the number of embedding changes, assuming the embedded message length is shorter than 70% of maximal embedding capacity was proposed. This method can be flexibly incorporated as a module into majority of existing steganographic methods.

Image steganographic scheme using Tri-way Pixel-Value Differencing and adaptive rules was proposed by Chang, K. C., Huang, Tu, and Chang, C. P. (2007). This approach uses the tri-way differencing scheme with an optimal selection approach for the reference point and adaptive rules to reduce distortion from setting larger embedding capacity.

3. TRANSFORM DOMAIN EMBEDDING TECHNIQUES

Traditionally, JPEG steganography had focused on hiding data in the least significant bit of the quantized discrete cosine transform (DCT) coefficients. In order to avoid inducing significant perceptual distortion in the image, many available methods avoid hiding in DCT coefficients whose value is zero. While detecting the presence of data embedded in this manner, steganalysis algorithms exploit the fact that the DCT coefficient histogram gets modified, when hiding random information bits. Hence all steganographic approaches attempt to match, as closely as possible, the original DCT histogram or its model. In F5 algorithm proposed by Westfield (2001), the coefficient value increases, decreases, or keeps unchanged, based on the data bit to be hidden, so as to better match the host statistics. *OutGuess* (Provos, 2001) was the first attempt at explicitly matching the DCT histogram. Sallee (2003) proposed a model based approach in which the DCT coefficients were modified to hide data such that they follow an underlying model. *Steghide* (Westfeld, 2001) is another method that is able to hide data in various kinds of image and audio files. Perturbed quantization method introduced by Fridrich, Goljan, Lisonek, and Soukal (2004).attempts to select for embedding those DCT coefficients whose unquantized values lie "close to the middle" of quantization intervals. Intuitively, perturbing the rounding process at such coefficients will be harder to detect than modifying the coefficients that experienced a small rounding error during quantization.

Statistical restoration method proposed by Solanki, Sullivan, Madhow, Manjunath, and Chandrasekaran (2005, 2006) focused on Quantization Index Modulation (QIM) based data hiding. QIM allows the embedding of large volumes of data in a manner that is resistant to a variety of attacks. To ensure that the restoration does not interfere with decoding, a fixed percentage of host symbols are set aside for restoration, while the rest are used for embedding. A secret key, shared between the encoder and the decoder, determines the embedding and compensation locations.

High performance JPEG steganography using quantization index modulation in DCT domain was proposed by Hideki, Niimi & Kawaguchi (2005). This presents two steganographic methods using QIM in the DCT domain. In both methods, embedding is carried out just during quantization of DCT coefficients (not after quantization step). The first one is a histogram preserving method using two quantizers, where the representatives of each quantizer are given in advance and the intervals for each representative are set so as to preserve the histogram of cover image. The second one is a histogram quasi-preserving method which uses QIM in a straightforward way with a device not to change the after-embedding histogram excessively.

Cheng, Chung and Wang (2006) developed high capacity steganographic approach for 3D polygonal meshes. This approach combines both the spatial domain and the representation domain for embedding. In the spatial domain, this scheme uses a Modified Multi Level Embed Procedure (MMLEP) that can embed at least three bits per vertex with little visual distortion. In the representation domain, the representation order of vertices and polygons and even the topology information of polygons can be represented with an average of six bits per vertex using the Representation Rearrangement Procedure (RRP). This is the first 3D polygon model steganographic approach that can use the representation information to embed messages. This procedure efficiently increases the capacity from three fixed bits to around nine bits per vertex depending on the number of vertices and polygons of a model; this increases capacity about 200%. This scheme can achieve high capacity with little or no visual distortion. In addition, a secret key is used on the embedding sequence lists for more security.

Yet Another Steganographic scheme (YASS) (Solanki, Sarkar, & Manjunath, 2007) is a method for secure steganography that can successfully resist the blind steganalysis schemes. This technique is based on a simple idea of embedding data in random locations within an image, which makes it difficult for the steganalyst to get a good estimate of the cover image features via the self calibration process. Although data is hidden in randomly chosen blocks in the image, the image must be advertised in JPEG format. This leads to errors in the recovered data bits, which are dealt with by using erasure and error correcting codes. YASS is completely undetectable for most of the embedding configurations, while the competing algorithms, OutGuess and StegHide, are detectable at the same hiding rates. Almohammad, Robert, Hierons and Ghinea (2008) proposed a high capacity steganographic approach based on DCT and JPEG compression. This method divides the cover image into non overlapping blocks of 16×16 pixels. For each quantized DCT block, the least two significant bits of each middle frequency coefficient are modified to embed two secret bits. This approach can provide higher information hiding capacity and the produced stego images are almost identical to the original cover images.

There are a number of recent information theoretic results demonstrating (under certain conditions) a sub linear relationship between the number of cover objects and their total steganographic capacity. In the paper by Andrew, Pevny, Jan, Kodovsky and Fridrich (2008). explores the sub linear relationship. The main result of this paper states that the steganographic capacity of imperfect stegosystems with Markov covers and mutually independent embedding operation only grows with the square root of the number of cover elements. Probably the most remarkable one is that steganographic capacity exhibits quite different properties when compared with capacity of noisy channels or lossless compression. Hence they concluded that the sub linear relationship may be adapted to the steganographic capacity of a single cover object, which under the right conditions should be proportional to the square root of the cover size.

Multiple Messages Embedding (MME) using DCT based Mod4 Steganographic Method was proposed by Wong, Tanaka, and Xiaojun, Qi. (2006). This method is an extension of DCT based Mod4 steganographic method to realize MME. This method is an implement MME, utilize the structural feature of Mod4 that uses VGQC (valid group of 2×2 adjacent quantized DCT coefficients) as message carrier. VGQC's can be partitioned into several disjoint sets by differentiating the parameters where each set could serve as an individual secret communication channel. In this method, it is possible to embed a maximum number of 14 independent messages into a cover image without interfering one message and another.

4. CONCLUSION

This chapter provides a state of the art review of the different existing embedding methods of steganography drawn from the literature. We have seen from the survey that steganography methods usually struggle with achieving a high embedding rate and good imperceptibility. The challenge however, is to be able to embed into a group of images which are highly intercorrelated.

REFERENCE

Almohammad, A., & Robert, M. Hierons & Ghinea, G. (2008). High capacity steganographic method based upon JPEG. *The Third International Conference on Availability, Reliability and Security*, 544-549.

Andrew, D. Ker., Pevny, T., Jan, Kodovsky, & Fridrich, J. (2008). The square root law of steganographic capacity. *MM&Sec '08,* 22–23.

Chang, C. C., Hsiao, J. Y., & Chan, C. S. (2003). Finding optimal least significant bit substitution in image hiding by dynamic programming strategy. *Pattern Recognition, 36*(7), 1583–1595. doi:10.1016/S0031-3203(02)00289-3

Chang, K. C., Chang, C. P., Huang, P. S., & Tu, T. M. (2008). *A novel image steganographic method using Tri-Way Pixel-Value Differencing. National Science Council, R.O.* C, Academy Publisher.

Chang, K. C., Huang, P. S., Tu, T. M., & Chang, C. P. (2007). Image Steganographic Scheme Using Tri-way Pixel-Value Differencing and Adaptive rules. In Proc. of the Third International Conference on International Information Hiding and Multimedia Signal Processing, 2.

Chao, R. M., Wu, H. C., Lee, C. C., & Chu. Y. P. (2009). A novel image data hiding scheme with diamond encoding. *EURASIP Journal on Information Security, 9* .

Cheng, Y. M., Chung., & Wang, C.M. (2006). A high-capacity steganographic approach for 3D polygonal meshes. *The Visual Computer, 22,* 845–855. doi:10.1007/s00371-006-0069-4

Cox, I. J., Miller, M. L., Boom, J. A., & Fridrich, J. (2008). *Digital watermarking and steganography.* Reading, MA: Morgan Kaufmann publishers.

Fridrich, J. (2006). Wet paper codes with improved embedding efficiency. *IEEE Transactions on Information Forensics and Security, 1*(1), 102–110. doi:10.1109/TIFS.2005.863487

Fridrich, J., & Goljan, M. (2002). Practical steganalysis of digital images – state of the art. *Proceedings of the Society for Photo-Instrumentation Engineers, 4675*, 1–13.

Fridrich, J., & Goljan, M. Lisonek. P., & Soukal, D. (2004). Writing on wet paper. *In ACM Workshop on Multimedia and security.*

Fu, M. S., & Au, O. C. (2002). Data hiding watermarking for halftone images. *IEEE Transactions on Image Processing, 11*(4), 477–484. doi:10.1109/TIP.2002.999680

Hideki, N., Niimi, M., & Kawaguchi, E. (2005). *High performance JPEG steganography using quantization index modulation in DCT domain.* Amsterdam: Elsevier Science.

Lee, Y. K., & Chen, L. H. (2000). High capacity steganographic model. *IEEE Proc. Visual Image Signal Process, 147*(3), 288–294. doi:10.1049/ip-vis:20000341

Pevny, T., & Fridrich, J. (2006). *Multi-class blind steganalysis for JPEG images.* In Proc. of SPIE.

Pevny, T., & Fridrich, J. (2007). *Merging markov and DCT features for multi-class JPEG steganalysis.* In Proc. of SPIE.

Provos, N. (2001). Defending against statistical steganalysis. *In Proc. USENIX Security Symposium.*

Sallee, P. (2003). Model-based steganography. *In IWDW. LNCS, 2939*, 154–167.

Solanki, K., Sullivan, K., Madhow, U., Manjunath, B.S., & Chandrasekaran. (2006). Probably secure steganography: Achieving zero K-L divergence using statistical restoration. *In Proc. ICIP*, 125–128.

Solanki, K., Sarkar, A., & Manjunath, B. S. (2007). *YASS: Yet another steganographic scheme that resists blind steganalysis. Lecture Notes in Computer Science.* New York: Springer.

Solanki, K., Sullivan, K., Madhow, U., Manjunath, B.S., & Chandrasekaran.(2005). Statistical restoration for robust and secure steganography. *In Proc. ICIP*, 1118–21.

Suk-Ling. Li., Leung, K. C., Cheng, L. M., & Chan, C. K. (2006). Data hiding in Images by Adaptive LSB substitution based on the Pixel-Value Differencing. *International Conference on Innovative Computing, Information and Control, 3*, 58-61.

Tseng, Y. C., Chen, Y. Y., & Pan, H. K. (2002). A secure data hiding scheme for binary image. *IEEE Transactions on Communications, 50*, 1227–1231. doi:10.1109/TCOMM.2002.801488

Tseng, Y. C., & Pan, H. K. (2002). Data hiding in 2-color images. *IEEE Transactions on Computers, 51*(7), 873–878. doi:10.1109/TC.2002.1017706

Walton, S. (1995). Image authentication for a slippery new age. *Dr. Dobb's J, 20*(4), 18–26.

Wang, R. Z., Lin, C. F., & Lin, J. C. (2001). Image hiding by optimal LSB substitution and genetic algorithm. *Pattern Recognition, 34*(3), 671–683. doi:10.1016/S0031-3203(00)00015-7

Westfeld, A. (2001). High capacity despite better steganalysis (F5- a steganographic algorithm). In Lecture notes in computer science: 4th International Workshop on Information *Hiding, 2137*, 289–302.

Wong, K. S., Tanaka, K., & Xiaojun, Qi. (2006). Multiple messages embedding using DCT Based Mod4 steganographic method. *International Workshop on Multimedia Content Representation, Classification, and Security, LNCS, 4105*, 57-65.

Wu, D. C., & Tsai, W. H. (2003). A steganographic method for images by pixel-value differencing. *Pattern Recognition, 24*(9-10), 1613–1626. doi:10.1016/S0167-8655(02)00402-6

Zhang, X., & Wang, S. (2006). Efficient steganographic embedding by exploiting modification direction. *IEEE Communications Letters, 10*(11), 781. doi:10.1109/LCOMM.2006.060863

Zhang, X., Wang, S., & Zhang, W. (2009). Combining data decomposition mechanism and stego-coding method. *Informatica, 33*, 41–48.

Compilation of References

A. Perrig, B. Przydatek, D. Song,(2003). *SIA: Secure Information Aggregation in Sensor Networks.*ACM SenSys 2003.

Aad, I., Hubaux, J.-P., & Knightly, E. W. (2004). *Denial of service resilience in ad hoc networks*. Proc. Of ACM MobiCom '04, 202- 215.

Aadel, L. (2007). *Are National and Local Information and Communication Technology Policies Based on Adequate Assessment of Real Situation?*Tallinn University of Technology.

Absinthe. (2007). Retrieved from http://www.security-database.com/toolswatch/Absinthe-1-4-1-available.html.

Achuthan, P., & Narayanankutty, K. (2009). On Mathematical Modeling of Quantum Mechanical Systems. *Am. Inst. of Phys., Conf. Proc., 1146* (1),105-112

Acquisti, A., & Gross, R. (2009). Predicting Social Security numbers from public data. *Proceedings of the National Academy of Sciences of the United States of America, 106*(27), 10975. doi:10.1073/pnas.0904891106

Adam Dunkels & Thiemo Voigt. "Distributed TCP Caching for wireless sensor networks", Third Annual Mediterranean Ad Hoc Networking Workshop (MedHocNet 2004), June 2004.

Adams, C. M., & Tavares, S. E. (1990). The structured design of cryptographically good S-boxes. *Journal of Cryptology, 3*(1), 27–41. doi:10.1007/BF00203967

Adleman, L. M. (1988). An abstract theory of computer viruses.*Crypto '88, Advances in Cryptography*, Lecture Notes. In *Computer Science*. New York: Springer.

Adrian Perrig, Ran Canetti, J. D. Tygar, Dawn Song,(2002). *The TESLA Broadcast Authentication Protocol.* RSA Cryptobytes, Summer 2002.

Agrawal, P., & Ghosh, R. K. (2008). *Cooperative black and gray hole attacks in mobile ad hoc networks.* Proceedings of the 2nd International Conference on Ubiquitous Information Management and Communication, 310–314.

Ahluwalia, K. S. (2007). *Scalability Design Patterns.* In Proceedings of 14th Pattern Languages of Programs (PLoP 2007)

Ahuja, V. K. (2006). Importation of Pirated Copyright Articles into India: Powers of Customs Authorities to Confiscate. *E.I.P.R. 2006, 28*(8), 429-432

Alan, G., & Konheim (2007). *Computer Security and Cryptography*. New York: John Wiley and Sons.

AL-Shurman, M., Yoo, S. M., & Park, S. (2004). *Black hole attack in mobile ad hoc networks.*ACMSE'04, 96 - 97.

Anderson, R., Chan, H., & Perrig, A. (n.d.). *Key Infection: Smart Trust for Smart Dust.* 12th IEEE International Conference on Network Protocols (ICNP'04), pp. 206-215.

Andreescu. (2009). *Number Theory – Structures*. New York: Springer.

Anonymous,. (2008). *Why did NSG take 10 hours to arrive?*Mumbai, India: The Economic Times.

Anonymous,. (1999). *Wireless LAN medium access control and physical layer specifications. IEEE 802.11 Standards.* IEEE Computer Society LAN MAN Standards Committee.

Anonymous. (1999). Draft international standard ISO/IEC 8802-11 IEEE P802.11/D10. *LAN MAN Standards Committee of IEEE Computer Society.*

Arora, S. (2008). *Review and Analysis of Current and Future European e-ID Card Schemes.* London: University of London. Belgium. (2010). Taalkeuze eid.belgium.be.

Aspect, A. (1804-1807). Dalibard, J. & Roger, G. (1982). Experimental Test of Bell's Inequalities Using Time-Varying Analyzers. *Physical Review Letters*, 49.

Aurrecoechea, C., Campbell, A. T., & Hauw, L. (1998). A survey of QoS architectures. *Multimedia Systems*, 138–151. doi:10.1007/s005300050083

Austin, G. W. (2000). *Copyright Infringement in New Zealand's Private International Law*, 19 NZULR 1.

Awerbuch, B., Holmer, D., Nita-Rotaru, C., & Rubens, H. (2002). *An on-demand secure routing protocol resilient to byzantine failures.* ACM Workshop on Wireless Security (WiSe*)*, 21 - 30.

Axelrod, C. W. (2004). *Outsourcing Information Security.* Boston: Artech House.

Axelrod, C. W. (2009b). Investing in Software Resiliency. *CrossTalk Magazine*, *22*(6), 20–25.

Axelrod, C. W. (2009a). An Adaptive Threat-Vulnerability Model and the Economics of Protection. In Gupta, M., & Sharman, R. (Eds.), *Social and Human Elements of Information Security: Emerging Trends and Countermeasures.* Hershey, PA: IGI Global.

Axelrod, C. W. (2008). Security and Change (pt. 1): Blackouts. Retrieved from www.bloginfosec.com

Axelrod, C. W. (2008b). Security and Change (pt. 2): Black Swans. Retrieved from www.bloginfosec.com

Axelrod, C. W. (2008c). Security and Change (pt. 3): White Knights. Retrieved from www.bloginfosec.com

Axelrod, C. W. (2008d). Security in Times of Crisis. Retrieved from www.bloginfosec.com

Axelsson, S. (2000). Intrusion detection systems: A survey and taxonomy. *Technical Report 99-15*, Department of Computer Engineering, Chalmers University, March 2000.

Aycock, J. (2006). *Computer viruses and malware.* New York: Springer Science.

Azer, M. A., El-Kassas, S. M., Hassan, A. W. F., Magdy S., & El-Soudani. (2008). *Intrusion detection for wormhole attacks in ad hoc networks: A survey and a proposed decentralized scheme.* The Third International Conference on Availability, Reliability and Security, 636-641.

B. Krishnamachari, D. Estrin & S. Wicker,(2002). *Modelling Data-Centric Routing in Wireless Sensor Networks.* IEEE INFOCOM 2002.

Baker, B. S. (1995). *On finding duplication and near-duplication in large software systems.* In WCRE '95: Proceedings of the Second Working Conference on Reverse Engineering, page 86. Washington, DC, USA, Washington, DC: IEEE Computer Society.

Banerjee, S. (2008). *Detection/removal of cooperative black and gray hole attack in mobile ad-hoc networks.* Proceedings of the World Congress on Engineering and Computer Science, 337-342.

Baxter, I. D., Yahin, A., Moura, L., Sant'Anna, M., & Bier, L. (1998) *Clone detection using abstract syntax trees.* In Software Maintenance, 1998. Proceedings. International Conference on, pp. 368–377.

Bayuk, J. (2009). Vendor Due Diligence. *ISACA Journal, 3*, 34-38. Available at www.isaca.org (membership required).

Behera, L. (2009). Force equipped. *Kerala Calling*, 28-29.

Belgium eID card Website. (2010). Retrieved from http://eid.belgium.be/

Bell, J. S. (1964). On the Einstein Podolsky Rosen Paradox. *Physics, 1*(3), 195–200.

Bell, J. S. (1993). *Quantum Mechanics: Speakable and Unspeakable in Quantum Mechanics.* Cambridge, UK: Cambridge Univ. Press.

Bellardo, J., & Savage, S. (2003). *802.11 Denial-of-service attacks: Real vulnerabilities and practical solutions.* Proceedings of The 12th Conference on USENIX Security Symposium, 15 – 28.

Belzley, S. R. (2005).*Grokster and Efficiency in Music,* 10 Va. J.L. & Tech. 10.

Bennett, C., & Brassard, H., G. & Ekert, A. K. (1992). Quantum Cryptography. *Scientific American,* 50–57. doi:10.1038/scientificamerican1092-50

Bennett, C. H. & Brassard, G. (1984). *Quantum Cryptography.* Conference Proc., Bangalore.

Bergeron, J., Debbabi, M., Erhioui, M. M., & Ktari, B. (1999). *Static analysis of binary code to isolate malicious behaviors* (pp. 184–189). DC, USA: IEEE Computer Society Washington.

Berinato, S. (August, 2001). Security Outsourcing: Exposed! *CIO Magazine.* Available at www.cio.com.

Berkeley, U. C. The EECS department.(n.d.). *Cotsbots: The mobile mote-based robots.* Retrieved from http://www-bsac.eecs.berkeley.edu/projects/cotsbots/

Bernstein, D. J., (Report 2008/010). Which eSTREAM ciphers have been broken?. *eSTREAM, the ECRYPT Stream Cipher Project.*

Beynon-Davies, P. (2006). Personal identity management in the information polity: The case of the UK national identity card. *Information polity, 11*(1), 3-19.

Bialkowski., et al. (2004). *Application Vulnerability Description Language v1.0, OASIS Standard.* Reference from http://www.oasis-open.org

Biggs. (2008).*An introduction to Information Communication and Cryptography.* New York: Springer.

Bigley, G. A., & Roberts, K. H. (2001). The Incident Command System: High Reliability Organizing for Complex and volatile task environments. *Academy of Management Journal, 44*(6), 1281–1299. doi:10.2307/3069401

Biometric Identification and Personal Detection Ethics (HIDE) project. (2010) Retrieved from http://www.hideproject.org/

Biometric Identification Technology Ethics (BITE) project. (2010). Retrieved from http://www.biteproject.org

Birch, D. (2007). *Digital Identity Management: technological, Business, and Social Implications.* Aldershot, UK: Gower Publishing.

Bohr, N. (1935). Can Quantum-Mechanical Description of Physical Reality be Considered Complete? *Physical Review, 48,* 696. doi:10.1103/PhysRev.48.696

Bonfante, G., Kaczmarek, M., & Marion, J. Y. (2008). *Morphological detection of malware* (pp. 1–8). DC, USA: IEEE Computer Society Washington.

Bonfante, G., Kaczmarek, M., Marion, J.Y.,(2007). *Control flow graphs as malware signatures.*

Braginsky, D., & Estrin, D. (2002). Rumor Routing Algorithm for Sensor Networks.In the Proceedings of the First Workshop on Sensor Networks and Applications (WSNA), Atlanta, GA, October 2002.

Brank, J., Grobelnik, M., & Mladenic, D. (2005). A survey of ontology evaluation techniques. In *Proceedings of the Conference on Data Mining and Data Warehouses* (SiKDD05), Ljubljana, Slovenia, 2005.

Browning, D., & Mundy, J. (2001). *Data Warehouse Design Considerations.* Microsoft Corporation MSDN Library.

Bruschi, D., Martignoni, L., & Monga, M. (2007). Code normalization for self-mutating malware. *IEEE Security and Privacy, 5*(2), 46–54. doi:10.1109/MSP.2007.31

BSQL Hacker. (n.d.). Reference from http://labs.portcullis.co.uk/application/bsql-hacker/.

Bu, T., Norden, S., & Woo, T. M. (n.d.). *Detection of power-drain denial-of-service attacks in wireless networks.* European Patent: EP1708538.

Buchegger, S., & Le Boudec, J. (2002). *Performance analysis of the CONFIDANT protocol: Cooperation of nodes - Fairness in dynamic ad-hoc networks*. Proceedings of the 3rd ACM International Symposium on Mobile Ad hoc Networking and Computing (MobiHoc,) 226-236.

Budha Deb, Sudeept Bhatnagar, & Badri Nath,(2003). *REinform: reliable information forwarding using multiple paths in sensor networks*LCN 2003.

Campbell, G. K., & Lefler, R. A. (2009). Security Alert: When the economy's down – and budgets are stressed – the threat level rises. *Harvard Business Review,* ▪▪▪, 104–105.

Canteaut, A., Daum, H., Dobbertin, H., & Leander, G. (2006). Finding nonnormal Bent functions. *Discrete Applied Mathematics, 154*, 202–218. doi:10.1016/j.dam.2005.03.027

Canteaut, A., Daum, M., Dobbertin, H., & Leander, G. (2003). Normal and Non-Normal Bent Functions. *Proceedings of the Workshop on Coding and Cryptography (WCC)*, Versailles, France, pp. 91-100.

Carlet, C. (1994). Two new classes of bent functions. In *Adv. In crypt.-Eurocrypt, 93, LNCS, 765* (pp. 77–101). Berlin: Springer.

Carlet, C. (1996). A construction of bent functions. *Finite Fields Appl, 233*, 47–58. doi:10.1017/CBO9780511525988.006

Carlet, C., & Mesnager, S. (2006c). Improving the upper bounds on the covering radii of binary Reed-Muller codes. *IEEE Transactions on Information Theory, 53*(1), 162–173. doi:10.1109/TIT.2006.887494

Carlet, C. (2006a). Boolean functions for cryptography and error correcting codes. In Crama, Y., & Hammer, P. (Eds.), *Chapter of the monography Boolean methods and models.* In Cambridge, UK: Cambridge University Press.

Carlet, C. (1999). On the coset weight divisibility and nonlinearity of resilient and correlation immune functions. *In Proceedings of the 2nd international conference (SETA'01), Discrete Mathematics and Theoretical Computer Science*, 131-144.

Carlet, C. (2006b). On Bent and highly nonlinear balanced / resilient functions and their algebraic immunities. *In Proceedings of AAECC 16*, LNCS 3857, 1-28.

Carter, S., & Yasinsac, A. (2002). *Secure position aided ad hoc routing*. Proceedings of the IASTED International Conference on Communications and Computer Networks.

Chan, H., Perrig, A., & Song, D. (2003). *Random Key Predistribution Schemes for Sensor Networks*. IEEE Symposium on Security and Privacy 2003.

Chang, W. Y., Wu, T.-K., Cheng, R. H., & Chang, S. C. (2007). *A distributed and cooperative black hole node detection and elimination mechanism for ad hoc network. Emerging Technologies in Knowledge Discovery and Data Mining* (pp. 538–549). New York: Springer-Verlag.

Chaum, D, J. (1988*). Cryptography. 1(*1), 65.

Checkstyle.(2001-2010) Reference from http://checkstyle.sourceforge.net/.

Chen, R., Sharman, R., & Chakravarti, N., R. H. R. & S. Upadhyaya. (2008). Emergency Response Information System Interoperability: Development of Chemical Incident Response Data Model. *Journal of the Association for Information Systems*, 9.

Chen, R., Coles, J., Lee, J., & Rao, H. R. (2009). *Emergency Communication and System Design: The Case of Indian Ocean Tsunami.* ICTD Conference. Doha, Qatar.

Chieh-Yih Wan. Andrew T. Campbell, Lakshman Krishnamurthy. (2002). *PSFQ: A Reliable Transport Protocol for Wireless Sensor Networks.* WSNA 2002, Atlanta, GA.

Choi, Y. S., Kim, I. K., Oh, J. T., & Ryou, J. C. (2008). PE File Header analysis-based packed PE file detection technique (PHAD). *International Symposium on Computer Science and its Applications*.

Chouchane, M. R. Lakhotia, A.(2006). *Using engine signature to detect metamorphic.*

Chris, J. Mitchell & Alexander W. Dent (2004). International standards for stream ciphers: A progress report. *In SASC - The State of the Art of Stream Ciphers*, pp. 14-15.

Christodorescu, M., Jha, S., & Kruegel, C. (2007). *Mining specifications of malicious behavior*. In ESEC-FSE '07: Proceedings of the the 6thjoint meeting of the European software engineering conference and the ACM SIGSOFT symposium on The foundations of software engineering, pp. 5–14, New York:ACM.

Christodorescu, M., Kinder, J., Jha, S., Katzenbeisser, S., Veith, H.,(2005). Malware

Citizen's service number. (2009). *Gemeente Amstelveen*, from http://www.amstelveen.nl/web/show?id=174916&langid=43&dbid=850&typeofpage=44744

Clauser, J. F., Horne, M. A., Shimony, A., & Holt, R. A. (1969). Proposed experiment to test local hidden variable theories. *Physical Review Letters*, *23*, 880–884. doi:10.1103/PhysRevLett.23.880

Clauser, J. F., & Shimony, A. (1978). Bell's theorem: experimental tests and implications. *Reports on Progress in Physics*, *41*, 1881–1927. doi:10.1088/0034-4885/41/12/002

Cloud Security Alliance. (2009). *Security Guidance for Critical Areas of Focus in Cloud Computing v2.1.* Reference from http://www.cloudsecurityalliance.org/csaguide.pdf.

Collberg, C., & Thomborson, C. (1999). *Software watermarking: models and dynamic embeddings.* In POPL '99: Proceedings of the 26th ACM SIGPLAN-SIGACT symposium on Principles of programming languages, pp. 311–324, New York:ACM.

Collberg, C., Carter, E., Debray, S., Huntwork, A., Kececioglu, J., Linn, C., & Stepp, M. (2004). *Dynamic path-based software watermarking*. In PLDI '04: Proceedings of the ACM SIGPLAN 2004 conference on Programming language design and implementation, PP. 107–118, New York:ACM.

Collberg, C., Thomborson, C., & Low, D. (1997). *A taxonomy of obfuscating transformations*. Technical Report 148, Department of Computer Science, University of Auckland.http://www.cs.auckland.ac.nz/ ~collberg/Research/ Publications/ Collberg ThomborsonLow 97a/index.html.

CoMo. (n.d.). *Design the fundamental building block of a network monitoring infrastructure*. Retrieved from http://como.sourceforge.net.

Computer Economics. *(2010).2007 Malware report: The economic impact of viruses, spyware, adware, botnets, and other malicious code.* Retrieved from http://www. computer economics.com/ page.cfm?name =Malware%20Report

Cooke, E., Myrick, A., Rusek, D., & Jahanian, F. (2006). Resource-aware multi-format network security data storage. *In Proceedings of the 2006 SIGCOMM workshop on Large -scale attack defense - LSAD '06*, 177-184.

Corman, T. H., Leiserson, C. E., Rivest, R. L., & Stein, C. (1990). *Introduction to algorithms*. Cambridge, MA: MITPress.

Courtois, & Meier, W. (2003). Algebraic attacks on stream ciphers with linear feedback. *In Advances in Cryptology - EUROCRYPT 2003*, LNCS, Springer-Verlag, *2656*, 345-359.

Cppcheck. (2010). *A tool for static C/C++ code analysis*. Reference from http://cppcheck.wiki.sourceforge.net/.

Crocker, S. (1969). Request for Comments: 1, Host Software, Reference from http://www.faqs.org/rfcs/rfc1.html

CROSSBOWTECHNOLOGY INC. (n.d.). *Wireless sensor networks*. Retrieved from http://www.xbow.com/Products/Wireless Sensor Networks.htm.

Crowley, P. (2005). *Phishing Attacks on OpenID*. Available at http://lists.danga.com/pipemail/yadis/2005-June/000470.html

Curtmola, R., & Nita-Rotaru, C. (2007). *BSMR: Byzantine-Resilient Secure Multicast Routing in Multi-hop Wireless Networks*.IEEE SECON 2007, June 2007, San Diego, CA.

Dalai, D. K., Gupta, K. C., & Maitra, S. (2004). Results on Algebraic Immunity for Cryptographically Significant Boolean Functions. *Indocrypt International Conference*, LNCS, *3348*, pp.92-106. New York: Springer Verlag.

David, B., & Aharonov, Y. (1957)... *Physical Review*, *108*, 1070. doi:10.1103/PhysRev.108.1070

David, M. B. (1989). *Factorization and Primality Testing.* New York: Springer.

Dean, M., & Schreiber, G. (2004). OWL Web Ontology Language Reference. *World Wide Web Consortium, Recommendation REC-owl-ref-20040210*, February 2004.

Deb, B. (2003). Information assurance in sensor networks. In *WSNA 2003.* San Diego, CA: Sudeept Bhatnagar & Badri Nath. doi:10.1145/941350.941373

Deb, M. (2008). *A cooperative blackhole node detection mechanism for ad hoc networks.* Proceedings of the World Congress on Engineering and Computer Science, (pp. 343 – 347).

Deering., et al. (1998). *Internet Protocol, Version 6 (IPv6) Specification, RFC2460.* Reference from http://www.faqs.org/rfcs/rfc2460.html

Deng, H., Li, W., & Agrawal, D. P. (2002). Routing security in wireless ad-hoc network. *IEEE Communications Magazine, 40*, 70–75. doi:10.1109/MCOM.2002.1039859

Denning, D. E. (1987). An Intrusion-Detection Model. *IEEE Transactions on Software Engineering, SE-13*(2), 222–232. doi:10.1109/TSE.1987.232894

Department of Homeland Security (2003). *National Response Plan.*

Deri, L., & Netikos, S. P. A. (2003). Passively Monitoring Networks at Gigabit Speeds Using Commodity Hardware and Open Source Software. *In Passive and Active Measurement Workshop.*

Designing and Building Parallel Programs v1.3, An Online Publishing Project of Addison-Wesley Inc., Argonne National Laboratory, and the NSF Center for Research on Parallel Computation.

Desilva, S., & Boppana, R. V. (2005). Mitigating malicious control packet floods in ad hoc networks. *Proceedings of IEEE WCNC, 05*, 2112–2117.

Desilva, S., & Boppana, R. (2004). On the impact of noise sensitivity on performance in 802.11based ad hoc networks. *Proceeding of International Conference on Communications 7*, 4372- 4376.

Diallo at al. (2006). A Comparative Evaluation of Three Approaches to Specifying Security Requirements, presented at 12th Working Conference on Requirements Engineering: Foundation for Software Quality, Luxembourg.

Didier, F. (2006). A new upper bound on the block error probability after decoding over the erasure channel. *IEEE Transactions on Information Theory.*

Dierks., et al. (1999). *Request for Comments 2246, The TLS Protocol Version 1.0.* Reference from http://www.faqs.org/rfcs/rfc2246.html

Dillon, J. F. (1974). Elementary Hadamard difference sets. *Ph. D thesis, University of Maryland.*

Disclaimer. *Expat Guide Holland*(n.d.). Retrieved from http://www.expatguideholland.com/disclaimer/?region=tilburg

Dobbertin, H. (1995). Construction of bent functions and balanced Boolean functions with high non-linearity. In *Fast software encryption-Leuven 1994. LNCS, 1008* (pp. 61–74). Berlin: Springer.

Donner, M. (2003). Towards a Security Ontology. *IEEE Security and Privacy, 1*(3), 6–7.

Dreger, H., Feldmann, A., Paxson, V., & Sommer, R. (2004). Operational experiences with high-volume network intrusion detection. *In Proceedings of the 11th ACM conference on Computer and communications security - CCS '04, 2.* Kornexl, S. (2005). *High-Performance Packet Recording for Network Intrusion Detection.* Master Thesis.

Dutta, S. (2006). Estonia: A Sustainable Success in Networked Readiness? *The global information technology report, 2007*, 81-90.

Earl, M. J. (1996). The risks of outsourcing IT. *Sloan Management Review, 47*(3), 57–74.

Edwards, L., & Waelde, C. (2009). *Law and the Internet* (2nd ed.). Houston, TX: Hart Publications.

eID - Easier Access to Public Services Across the EU. (2010). European Commission – Information Society and Media.

Einstein, A., Podolsky, B., & Rosen, N. (1935). Can Quantum-Mechanical Description of Physical Reality be Considered Complete? *Physical Review*, *47*, 777. doi:10.1103/PhysRev.47.777

Ekert, A. K. (1991). Quantum Cryptography Based on Bell's Theorem. *Physical Review Letters*, *67*, 666. doi:10.1103/PhysRevLett.67.661

Endace, D. A. G. API (libtrace).(n.d.). Retrieved from http://researchwand.net.nz/software/libtrace.php

Endace, D. A. G. Card.(n.d.). Retrieved from http://www.endace.com/endace-dag-high-speed-packet-capture-cards.html

Engestrom, Y., Miettinen, R., & Punamaki-Gitai, R.-L. (1999). *Perspectives on activity theory*. Cambridge, UK: Cambridge University Press.

Engestrom, Y. (1999). *Outline of three generations of activity theory*. Retrieved 05/04/2010, from http://www.bath.ac.uk/research/liw/resources/Models%20and%20principles%20of%20Activity%20Theory.pdf.

Enhanced Social Security Number. (n.d.). *National Committee on Vital and Health Statistics*, from http://www.ncvhs.hhs.gov/app7-1.htm

Ergun, F., Kannan, S., Kumar, S. R., Rubinfeld, R., & Viswanathan, M. (1998). *Spot-checkers*. JCSS, 60:717-751. Preliminary version in Proc. STOC'98.

Ergun, F., Kumar, R., & Rubinfeld, R. (1999). *Fast approximate PCPs*. In Proc. 31st STOC, pp. 41-50.

Essam, Al.D., Ahid, Al.S., Adaan, M.A.(2009). Detecting metamophic viruses by using arbitrary length of control flow graphs and nodes alignment. *Ubiquitous Computing and Communication Journal*, *4*(3),628-633.

eSTREAM – The ECRYPT Stream cipher project.(2008). Retrieved from http://www.encrypt.eu.org/stream.

Everest, G., & Ward, T. (2007). *An Introduction to Number Theory*. New York: Springer.

Farrow, R. (2009). musings, LOGIN: VOL. 33, NO. 5, 2. Reference from http://www.usenix.org/publications/login/2009-10/openpdfs/musings0910.pdf.

FBI. (2009). *Next Generation Identification*. Retrieved from http://www.fbi.gov/hq/cjisd/ngi.htm

FG- Injector Framework. (2010). Reference from http://sourceforge.net/projects/injection-fwk/.

Filiol, E.(2007). Concepts and future trends in computer virology. *20th CISE Plenary Talk*.

Flawfinder.(n.d.). Reference from http://www.dwheeler.com/flawfinder/.

Fontaine, C. (1999). On some cosets of the First-Order Reed-Muller code with high minimum weight. *IEEE Transactions on Information Theory*, *45*(4), 1237–1243. doi:10.1109/18.761276

Ford, R., Howard, M.(2007). Revealing packed malware. *Proceedings of Security & Privacy*. IEEE Computer Society.

Fredrik, M. (2000). *Security Analysis of an Information System using an Attack tree-based Methodology*. Master's Thesis.Goteborg, Sweden: Chalmers University of Technology.

Freedmann, S. J., & Clauser, J. F. (1972). Experimental test of local hidden variable theories. *Physical Review Letters*, *28*, 938–941. doi:10.1103/PhysRevLett.28.938

Frohlick, A. B. (2009). *Copyright Infringement In The Internet Age--Primetime For Harmonized Conflict-Of-Laws Rules?*, 24 Berkeley Tech. L.J. 851.

Games, R. A., & Chan, A. H. (1983). A fast algorithm for determining the linear complexity of a pseudorandom sequence with period 2^n. *IEEE Transactions on Information Theory*, *IT-29*, 144–146. doi:10.1109/TIT.1983.1056619

Ganesan, D., Govindan, R., Shenker, S., & Estrin, D. (2002). Highly-Resilient, Energy-Efficient Multipath Routing in Wireless Sensor Networks. *Mobile Computing and Communications Review*, *1*(2), 2002.

Gao, L. (2006). *Intellectual Property Rights In The Internet Era: The New Frontier*, 5 J. *Marshall Rev. Intell. Prop.*, L, 589.

Garfinkel, T., Pfaff, B., Chow, J., Rosenblum, M., & Boneh, D. Terra (2003). *A virtual machine-based platform for trusted computing*. In SOSP '03: Proceedings of the nineteenth ACM symposium on Operating systems principles, pp. 193–206, New York:ACM.

Garhwal, T. (2009). Logical building blocks in n-tier application architecture. *Tejpal Garhwal*.fRetrieved from http://tgarhwal.wordpress.com/

Gaurav. (2009). *Shiv Sena's Orkut Campaign: The Limits to Freedom of Expression in an Intolerant India*. Retrieved February 20, 2010, from http://www.gauravonomics.com/blog/shiv-senas-orkut-campaign-the-limits-to-freedom-of-expression-in-an-intolerant-india/.

Gemalto. (2009). *Belgium – the national eID Card: A true e-Government building block*. Retrieved from http://www.gemalto.com/brochures/download/belgium.pdf

George, G., & Arthur, G. Z. (2006). *The Quantum Challenge-Modern Research on the Foundations of Quantum Mechanics* (2nd ed.). New Delhi: Narosa Publ.

GII. (1998). *Global Information Infrastructure principles and framework architecture*.ITU-T Recommendation Y.110.

Gonzalez, J. M., Paxson, V., & Weaver, N. (2008). *Shunting: A Hardware / Software Architecture for Flexible, High-Performance Network Intrusion Prevention*. In Proceedings of 14th Annual ACM Computer and Communication Security Conference, 139-149

Goodman, M. D., & Brenner, S. W. (2002). The Emerging Consensus on Criminal Conduct in Cyberspace. *UCLA Journal of Law and Technology*, 6(1), 153.

Groot, P., Bruijsten, F., Oostdijk, M., Dastani, M., & Jong, E. (2007, November 5-6). *Patient Data Confidentiality Issues of the Dutch Electronic Health Care Record*. Paper presented at the Proceedings of the 19th Belgium-Netherlands Artificial Intelligence Conference, Utrecht, The Netherlands.

GroverL. K. (1996) quant-ph/9605043.

Grover, L. K. (1997)... *Physical Review Letters*, *79*, 325. doi:10.1103/PhysRevLett.79.325

Gruber, T. R. (1993). Toward principles for the design of ontologies used for knowledge sharing. In Guarino, N., & Poli, R. (Eds.), *Formal Ontology in Conceptual Analysis and Knowledge Representation*. Amsterdam: Kluwer Academic Publishers.

Gu, Q., Liu, P., Zhu, S., & Chu, C. H. (2005). Defending against packet injection in unreliable ad hoc networks. *Proc. of IEEE GLOBECOM '05, 3*, 1837 - 1841.

Guarino, N. (1998). Formal Ontology and Information Systems. In N. Guarino (Ed.), *Proceedings of Formal Ontology and Information Systems* (pp. 3–15), 1998, Trento, Italy. Amsterdam: IOS Press, Amsterdam

Gummadi, R., Wetherall, D., Greenstein, B., & Seshan, S. (2007). *Understanding and mitigating the impact of RF interference on 802.11 networks.* Proceedings of the ACM SIGCOMM, 385–396.

Gupta, V., Krishnamurthy, S., & Faloutsous, M. (2002). *Denial of service attacks at the MAC layer in wireless ad hoc networks.* Proceedings of MILCOM. http://www.ietf.org/html.charters/manet-charter.html

H. Chan, A. Perrig, (2005). *PIKE: Peer Intermediaries for Key Establishment in Sensor Networks*. Infocom 2005.

Halderman, J.A., & Felten, E. W. (2006). *Lessons from the Sony CD DRM episode*. In USENIX-SS'06: Proceedings of the 15th conference on USENIX Security Symposium, Berkeley, CA:USENIX Association.

Han, S. Jang.K., Moon.S. & Park,K. (2010). Packet Shader: A GPU-Accelerated Software Router, *In Proceedings of 10th ACM SIGCOMM Conference.*

Hari Rangarajan, J. J. Garcia-Luna-Aceves,(2004). *Reliable Data Delivery in Event-Driven Wireless Sensor Networks*. The Ninth IEEE Symposium on Computers and Communications (ISCC2004).

Heavens, V. X. http://vx. netlux. org/lib.

Heinzelman, W. (2000).*Application-specific protocol architectures for wireless networks*. PhD Thesis, Massachusetts Institute of Technology.

Herbert, N. (1982)... *Foundations of Physics, 12*, 1171. doi:10.1007/BF00729622

Hernan, S., et al. (2006). *Uncover Security Design Flaws using The STRIDE Approach*. Reference from http://msdn. microsoft.com/en-us/magazine/cc163519.aspx.

Hill, J., Szewczyk, R., Woo, A., Hollar, S., Culler, D., & Pister, K. (2000). *System Architecture Directions for Networked sensors*. ASPLOS IX.

Hill, M. D., & Marty, M. R. (2007). *Amdahl's Law in the Multicore Era*. Reference from http://www.cs.wisc.edu/ multifacet/papers/tr1593_amdahl_multicore.pdf

Hindu. (2009). Businesses will gain from Unique ID project. *The Hindu*.

Hoffstein. (2008). *An introduction to Mathematical Cryptography*. New York: Springer.

Horrigan, J. B. (2008). *Use of Cloud Computing Applications and Services, Data Memo*. The Pew Internet & American Life Project. September 2008, Reference from http://www.pewinternet.org/Reports/2008/Use-of-Cloud-Computing-Applications-and-Services.aspx.

Horrocks, I., Patel-Schneider, P. F., Boley, H., Tabet, S., Grosof, B., & Dean, M. (2004). *SWRL: A semantic web rule language combining OWL and RuleML*. Retrieved on May 10, 2010 from http://www.w3.org/Submission/ SWRL/

HTTPattack. (2009). *An Open source web stress tool*. Reference from http://isea.nitk.ac.in/HTTPattack/.

Hu, Y. C., Perrig, A., & Johnson, D. B. (2003). Packet leashes: A defense against wormhole attacks in wireless networks. *Proc. of IEEE INFOCOM '03, 3*, 1976 - 1986.

Hu, Y. C., Perrig, A., & Johnson, D. B. (2003). Rushing attacks and defense in wireless ad hoc network routing protocols. *Proc. of ACM WiSe*, 30 - 40.

Hu, Y., Perrig, A., & Johnson, D.B. (2005). Ariadne: A secure on-demand routing protocol for ad hoc networks. *Wireless Networks, 11(1 – 2)*, 21 – 38.

Huang, Q., Avramopoulos, I. C., Kobayashi, H., & Liu, B. (2005). Secure data forwarding in wireless ad hoc networks. *IEEE International Conference on Communications, ICC 2005, 5*, 3525-3531.

IC3 Report. (2007). Retrieved January 18, 2010, 2010, from http://www.ic3.gov/media/annualreport/2007_ IC3Report.pdf.

ICT for Government and Public Services. (2010). European Commission Information Society.

ID-ticket. (2007). *Sertifitseerimiskeskus*

IEEE. 802. (2003). Retrieved from http://www.ieee802. org/15/pub/TG4.html

Information Security Research Labs. (2009).*Suraksha: A Security Aware Application Developers' Workbench*. Reference from http://isea.nitk.ac.in/suraksha/.

Internet History. (2010). *Computer History Museum*. Reference from http://www.computerhistory.org/internet_history/internet_history_80s.html

Internet2.(2010). Reference from http://www.internet2. edu/

Isaza, G., Castillo, A., & Duque, N. D. (2009). An Intrusion Detection and Prevention Model Based on Intelligent Multi-Agent Systems, Signatures and Reaction Rules Ontologies. In *Advances in Intelligence and Soft Computing - 7th International Conference on Practical Applications of Agents and Multi-Agent Systems (PAAMS 2009)* (pp. 237-245). New York: Springer.

ISO-7498 (1998) - Information processing systems -- Open Systems Interconnection -- Basic Reference Model

Jain, A., Flynn, P., & Ross, A. (2008). *Handbook of biometrics*. New York: Springer. doi:10.1007/978-0-387-71041-9

Jain, R. (2009). *Internet 3.0: The Next Generation Internet*. Reference from http://www.cse.wustl.edu/~jain/ talks/in3_bng.htm

Jeong, K., & Lee, H. (2008). Code graph for malware detection. *International conference on Information Networking, ICOIN*, 1–5.

Jiang, X., Wang, X., & Xu, D. (2007). Stealthy malware detection through VMM-based "Out-of-the-box" semantic view reconstruction.*Proceedings of the 14th ACM conference on Computer and communications security*, pp.128–138, New York.

Jin, R., Wei, Q., Yang, P., & Wang, Q. (2007). Normalization towards instruction substitution metamorphism based on standard instruction set. *IEEE, International Conference on Computer Intelligence and Security (CIS) Workshop*.

Johnson, D. B., Maltz, D. A., & Hu, Y. (2007). The dynamic source routing protocol for mobile ad hoc networks. *IETF RFC 4728*.

Jonathan, M. (2005). *McCune, Elaine Shi Adrian, Perrig Michael K.* Reiter.

Jordan, M. (1998, 1998, April 24). Especially in India/ Fair Color as a Cultural Virtue: Creams for a Lighter Skin Capture the Asian Market. *The New York Times*. Retrieved from http://www.nytimes.com/1998/04/24/news/24iht-light.t.html

Joseph, A. E. (2006). *Cybercrime definition*. June 28, 2006. Retrieved January 28, 2010, from http://www.crime-research.org/articles/joseph06/.

Julian, B. (2001). *The Quest for Quantum Computing*. New York: Simon and Shuster.

Just, M., Kranakis, E., & Wan, T. (2003). *Resisting malicious packet dropping in wireless ad hoc networks*. Ad – Hoc, Mobile, and Wireless Networks, 2865. Berlin: Springer Berlin/Heidelberg, 151-163.

Kaida, T. (1999). *On Algorithms for the k-Error Linear Complexity of Sequences over GF (p^m) with Period p^n*. Ph. D. Thesis, Kyushu Institute of Tech.

Kamiya, T., Kusumoto, S., & Inoue, K. (2002). Ccfinder: a multilinguistic token-based code clone detection system for large scale source code. *Software Engineering. IEEE Transactions on, 28*(7), 654–670.

Karlof, C., & Wagner, D. (2003). *Secure Routing in Wireless Sensor Networks: Attacks and Countermeasures. Ad Hoc Networks, 1, (2—3) (Special Issue on Sensor Network Applications and Protocols)* (pp. 293–315). Amsterdam: Elsevier.

Karnik, A., Goswami, S., & Guha, R. (2007). Detecting obfuscated viruses using cosine similarity analysis. *IEEE AMS '07: Proceedings of the First Asia International Conference on Modelling & Simulation*, pp.165–170, Washington, DC, USA.

Kavut, S., Maitra, S., & Yucel, M. D. (2007). Search for Boolean functions with excellent profiles in the rotation symmetric class. *IEEE Transactions on Information Theory, 53*(5), 1743–1751. doi:10.1109/TIT.2007.894696

Kennell, R., & Jamieson, L. H. (2003). *Establishing the genuinity of remote computer systems*. In SSYM'03: Proceedings of the 12th conference on USENIX Security Symposium, pp. 21–21, Berkeley:USENIX Association.

Kent., et al. (2005). *Security Architecture for the Internet Protocol*. Reference from http://www.faqs.org/rfcs/rfc4301.html

Khalil, I., Bagchi, S., & Nina-Rotaru, C. (2005). *DICAS: Detection, Diagnosis and Isolation of Control Attacks in Sensor Networks*. In the IEEE Conference on Security and Privacy for Emerging Areas in Communication Networks (SecureComm). Athens, Greece from 5 - 9 September, 2005.

Kinder, J., Katzenbeisser, S., Schallhart, C., & Veith, H. (2005). Detecting malicious code by model checking. In Klaus Julisch & Christopher Krügel (eds).*DIMVA*, (Vol. 3548 LNCS,pp.174–187). New York: Springer.

Kirda, E., Kruegel, C., Banks, G., Vigna, G., & Kemmerer, R. A. (2006). *Behavior-based spyware detection*. In USENIXSS'06: Proceedings of the 15th conference on USENIX Security Symposium. Berkeley, CA:USENIX Association.

Koninkrijksrelaties, M. v. B. Z. e. Frequently Asked Questions. *Burgerservicenummer*

Kontogiannis, K., Galler, M., & DeMori, R. (1995). *Detecting code similarity using patterns.* In Working Notes of the Third Workshop on AI and Software Engineering: Breaking the Toy Mold (AISE),pp. 68–73.

Kornexl, S., Paxson, V., Dreger, H., Feldmann, A., & Sommer, R. (2005). *Building a time machine for efficient recording and retrieval of high-volume network traffic.* In Proceedings of the 5th ACM SIGCOMM conference on Internet measurement - IMC '05.

Kosar, T., Christodorescu, M., & Iverson, R. (2003). *Opening pandora's box: Using binary code rewrite to bypass license checks.* Technical Report 1479, University of Wisconsin, Madison.

Kostyu, J.L. (1999). *Copyright Infringement on the Internet: Determining the liability of Internet Service Provider*, 48 Cath. U. L. Rev. 1237.

Krinke, J. (2001). *Identifying similar code with program dependence graphs.* In WCRE '01: Proceedings of the Eighth Working Conference on Reverse Engineering (WCRE'01), page 301, Washington, DC:IEEE Computer Society.

Kruegel, C., Kirda, E., Mutz, D., Robertson, W., & Vigna, G. (2005). Polymorphic worm detection using structural information of executables. *RAID*, 207–226, New York: Springer-Verlag.

Kruegel, C., Kirda, E., Mutz, D., Robertson, W., & Vigna, G. (2007). Metaaware: Identifying metamorphic malware. *Twenty-Third Annual IEEE Conference Proceeding on Computer Security Applications Conference, ACSAC.*

Kulik, J., Rabiner, W., & Balakrishnan, H. (1999).Adaptive Protocols for Information Dissemination in Wireless Sensor Networks. 5th ACM/IEEE Mobicom Conference, Seattle, WA, August 1999.

Kurosawa, S., Nakayama, H., Kato, N., Jamalipour, A., & Nemoto, Y. (2007). Detecting blackhole attack on AODV-based mobile ad hoc networks by dynamic learning method. *International Journal of Network Security*, 5(3), 338–346.

Kuutti, K. (1995). Activity Theory as a potential framework for human computer interaction research. In Nardi, B. A. (Ed.), *Context and consciousness: activity theory and human-computer interaction* (pp. 17–44). Cambridge, MA: Massachussetts Institute of Technology.

Lakhotia, A., Kapoor, A. Uday Kumar,E. (2004). *Are metamorphic computer viruses really invisible?* Part 1.

Liberty Alliance. (n.d.). Reference from http://www. projectliberty.org

Libpcap, a system-independent interface for user-level packet capture. Retrieved from www.tcpdump.org/

Lie, D., Thekkath, C., Mitchell, M., Lincoln, P., Boneh, D., Mitchell, J., & Horowitz, M. (2000). Architectural support for copy and tamper resistant software. *SIGPLAN Not.*, 35(11), 168–177. doi:10.1145/356989.357005

Lie, D., Thekkath, C., & Horowitz, M. (2003). *Implementing an untrusted operating system on trusted hardware.* In SOSP '03: Proceedings of the nineteenth ACM symposium on Operating systems principles, pp.178–192. New York: ACM.

Lindsey, S., & Raghavendra, C. S. (2002). *PEGASIS: Power Efficient GAthering in Sensor Information Systems.* 2002 IEEE Aerospace Conference, March 2002, pp. 1-6.

Liu, C., Chen, C., Han, J., & Yu, P. S. Gplag (2006). *Detection of software plagiarism by program dependence graph analysis.* In KDD '06: Proceedings of the 12th ACM SIGKDD international conference on Knowledge discovery and data mining, pp.872–881, New York:ACM.

Liu, D., & Ning, P. (2003). *Establishing pairwise keys in distributed sensor networks.*ACM Conference on Computer and Communications Security 2003, pp. 52-61.

Liu, D., Ning, P., & Sun, K. (2003). *Efficient self-healing group key distribution with revocation capability.* ACM Conference on Computer and Communications Security 2003, pp. 231-240.

Lobanov, M. (n.d.). *Tight bound between nonlinearity and algebraic immunity.* Retrieved from http://eprint. iacr.org/2005/441.pdf

LSE. (2005). *The LSE Identity Project Report*. LSE Information Systems and Innovation Group.

Lucchi, N. (2006). *Digital Media & Intellectual Property*. New York: Springer.

Maier, G., Sommer, R., Dreger, H., Paxson, V., Berkeley, I. U., & Schneider, F. (2005). Enriching Network Security Analysis with Time Travel. *ACM SIGCOMM Computer Communication Review*, *38*(4), 183–194. doi:10.1145/1402946.1402980

Maiorana, J. A. (1970). A class of bent functions. *R41 Technical paper*.

Malomsoky.S., Molnar.S., Veeres.A. & Szabo G (2010). Traffic Classification over Gbit Speed with Commodity Hardware. *Journal of Communications Software and Systems*.

Manders-Huits, N., & van den Hoven, J. (2008). Moral identification in Identity Management Systems. *The Future of Identity in the Information Society*, 77-91.

Marhusin, M. F., Larkin, H., Lokan, C., Cornforth, D. (2008). An evaluation of API calls hooking performance. *CIS '08: Proceedings of the 2008 International Conference on Computational Intelligence and Security*, pp. 315–319. Washington, DC: IEEE Computer Society. Metamorphism in practice or How I made Metaphor and What I've Learnt. http://vx. netlux. org/lib, February 2002.

Marti, S., Giuli, T. J., Lai, K., & Baker, M. (2000). *Mitigating routing misbehavior in mobile ad hoc networks*. Proceedings of the Sixth Annual ACM/IEEE International Conference on Mobile Computing and Networking (MOBICOM 2000), 255 - 265.

Martimiano, A. F. M., & Moreira, E. S. (2005). An owl-based security incident ontology. In *Proceedings of the Eighth International Protégé Conference* (pp. 43–44) Poster.

Martin, T. S. (n.d.). *Vicarious and Contributory Liability for Internet Host Providers: Combating Copyright Infringement In The United States, Russia, And China*, 27 Wis. Int'l L.J. 363

Martin, T., Hsiao, M., Ha, D., & Krishnaswami, J. (2004). *Denial-of-service attacks on battery-powered mobile computers*. Proceedings of the Second IEEE Annual Conference on Pervasive Computing and Communications, 309.

Math, P. http://planetmath.org/encyclopedia/ChebyshevsInequality.html

McElroy, D. (2008). *Mumbai attacks: foreign governments criticize India's response*. The Telegraph.

Meidl, W. (2008). Reducing the calculation of the linear complexity of $u2^v$ - periodic binary sequences to Games Chan algorithm. *Designs, Codes and Cryptography*, *46*, 57–65. doi:10.1007/s10623-007-9134-x

Meidl, W., & Niederreiter, H., & Ayineedi Venkateswarlu. (2007). Error linear complexity Measures for Multi-sequences. *Journal of Complexity*, *23*(2), 169–192. doi:10.1016/j.jco.2006.10.005

Meier., et al. (2003). *Improving Web Application Security: Threats and Countermeasures*. reference from http://www.msdn.microsoft.com/en-us/library/aa302419.aspx.

Michiardi, P., & Molva, R. (2002). CORE: A collaborative reputation mechanism to enforce node cooperation in mobile ad hoc networks. *IFIP-Communication and Multimedia Security Conference*, 107 – 121.

Moberg, F. (2000). *Security Analysis of an Information System using an Attack tree-based Methodology*.Master's Thesis. Goteborg, Sweden: Chalmers University of Technology.

Moreau, R., & Mazumdar, S. (2008). The Pakistan Connection. *Newsweek*.

Moser, A., Kruegel, C., & Kirda, E. (2007). Exploring multiple execution paths for malware analysis. *Security and Privacy, SP '07. IEEE Symposium on*, 231–245. MSDN library. http://msdn. microsoft. com/en-us/library. normalization. Technische Universitt Mnchen.

Multiple (2008). Important developments in the Mumbai terror attack. *The Hindu*. Chennai, India.

Multiple (2009). Mumbai Terror attacks - Dossier of evidence. *The Hindu*. Chennai, India.

Myasnikov. (2008). *Group-Based Cryptography*. New York: Springer.

Myers, M., Ankney, R., Malpani, A., Galperin, S., & Adams, C. RFC 2560: X. 509 Internet Public Key Infrastructure Online Certificate Status ProtocolñOCSP, 1999. *Found at*http://www. faqs. org/rfcs/rfc2560. html.

Myles, G., & Collberg, C. S. (2005). K-gram based software birthmarks. In Haddad, H., Liebrock, L. M., Omicini, A., & Wainwright, R. L. (Eds.), *SAC* (pp. 314–318). New York: ACM.

Myles, G., & Collberg, C. S. (2004). *Detecting software theft via whole program path birthmarks.* In Kan Zhang and Yuliang Zheng, editors, ISC, volume 3225 of Lecture Notes in Computer Science, pp. 404–415. New York: Springer.

Nandan, K. (2007). *Law Relating to Computers Internet & E-Commerce* (3rd ed.). New Delhi, India: Universal Law Publishing Co.

Narayanankutty, K., & Achuthan, P. (2005). *On Bell's theorem and inequality*. Abst. of the Natl. Symp. Mathematical Methods and Applications, (NSMMA-2005), IIT Madras.

Nardi, D., & Brachman, R. J. (2002). An introduction to description logics. In Baader, F., Calvanese, D., McGuinness, D. L., Nardi, D., & Patel-Schneider, P. F. (Eds.), *The Description Logic Handbook: Theory, Implementation and Applications* (pp. 1–40). Cambrdige, UK: Cambridge University Press.

Nardi, B. A. (1995). Activity Theory and Human-Computer Interaction. In Nardi, B. A. (Ed.), *Context and consciousness: activity theory and human-computer interaction.*Cambridge, MA: Massachussetts Institute of Technology.

Nardi, B. A. (1995). A Comparison of Activity Theory, Situated Action Models, and Distributed Cognition. In Nardi, B. A. (Ed.), *Context and consciousness: activity theory and human-computer interaction* (pp. 69–102). Cambridge, MA: Massachussetts Institute of Technology.

Nessus. Network Vulnerability Scanner.(2010) Reference from http://www.nessus.org/nessus/.

NetFPGA(n.d.). *A line-rate, flexible, and open platform for research.* Retrieved from http://netfpga.org/

Network Instruments. (2007), Network Security Forensics, *white paper.*

NetworkStumbler. (n.d.). Reference from http://www. netstumbler.com/.

Newsome, J., Shi, E., Song, D., & Perrig, A. (2004). *The Sybil Attack in Sensor Networks: Analysis and Defenses.* Third International Symposium on Information Processing in Sensor Networks (IPSN 2004).

Newton, R. G. (2008). *The Truth of Science*. New Delhi, India: Viva Books.

Nicolas. G., et al. (2009). Quantum Cryptography. Rev. Mod. Phys., and 207 references cited therein.

Noda, N., & Kishi, T. (2001). *Implementing Design Patterns Using Advanced Separation of Concerns.* Object-Oriented programming, Systems, Languages, and Applications (OOPSLA 2001).

Noordergraaf, A. (2000). *Enterprise Engineering Sun-blueprints™Online.* Retrieved from http://www.sun,com/blueprint

Noy, N., & McGuiness, D. (2001). Ontology Development 101: A Guide to Creating Your First Ontology. *Stanford Knowledge Systems Laboratory Technical Report KSL-01-05.* Retrieved on May 10, 2010 from http://protege.stanford.edu/publications/ontology_development/ontology101-noy-mcguinness.html.

O'Carroll, P. (2004). *Testimony Before the Subcommittee on Social Security of the House.* Committee on Ways and Means. Social Security Administration.

Oasis. (2007). Retrieved from http://docs.oasis-open.org/ws-sx/ws-trust/v1.3/ws-trust.html

Oh, O., Agrawal, M., & Rao, H. R. (in press). Information Control and Terrorism: Tracking the Mumbai Terrorist Attack through Twitter. *Information Systems Frontiers.*

Oh, J., Kim, B., Yoon, S., & Jang, J. (2008). A Novel Architecture and Mechanism for High Performance Real-Time Intrusion Detection and Response System. *Journal of Computer Science*, 8, 155–162.

Open, I. D. (n.d.). Retrieved from http://www.openid.org.

OWASP JBroFuzz. (n.d.). Reference from http://www.owasp.org/index.php/Category:OWASP_JBroFuzz.

Owen, C. A. (2007). Analysing the activity of work in emergency incident management. *Activités (Vitry-sur-Seine)*, 4(1), 217–225.

Park, D. (1981). *Concurrency and automata on infinite sequences*. In Proceedings of the 5th GI-Conference on Theoretical Computer Science, pp. 167–183, London: Springer-Verlag.

Parno, B., Perrig, A., & Gligor, V. (2005). *Distributed Detection of Node Replication Attacks in Sensor Networks*. IEEE Symposium on Security and Privacy 2005.

Patterson, N. J., & Wiedemann, D. H. (1983). The covering radius of the [215, 16] Reed-Muller code is at least 16276. *IEEE Transactions on Information Theory*, IT-29, 354–356. doi:10.1109/TIT.1983.1056679

Perdisci, R., Lanzi, A., & Lee, W. (2008). McBoost: Boosting scalability in malware collection and analysis using statistical classification of executables.*Annual Computer Security* Applications Conference, ACSAC.

Perkins, C., Belding-Royer, E., & Das, S. (2003). Ad hoc on-demand distance vector routing. *IETF RFC 3561*.

Perrig, A., Szewczyk, R., Wen, V., Culler, D., & Tygar, J. (2001). *SPINS: Security Protocols for Sensor Networks*Seventh Annual ACM International Conference on Mobile Computing and Networks (Mobicom 2001), Rome Italy.

Phil Williams, C. C. C. (n.d.). *Organized Crime and Cyber-Crime: Implications for Business*. Retrieved February 21, 2010, 2010, from www.cert.org/archive/pdf/cybercrime-business.pdf.

Ping Identity. (2007). *Internet-Scale Identity Systems: An Overview and Comparison*. White paper, Available at http://www.pingidentity.com/information-library/resourcedetails.cfm?customel_data pageid_1296=1738.

Prabhakar, S., Pankanti, S., & Jain, A. (2003). Biometric recognition: Security and privacy concerns. *IEEE Security & Privacy*, 1(2), 33–42. doi:10.1109/MSECP.2003.1193209

Prechelt, L., Malpohl, G., & Philippsen, M. (2002). Finding plagiarisms among a set of programs with jplag. *J. UCS*, 8(11), 1016.

Preneel, B., Leekwijck, W. V., Linden, L. V., Govaerts, R., & Vandewalle, J. (1991). Propagation characteristics of Boolean functions. In *Advances in Cryptology–EUROCRYPT'90, LNCS, 437* (pp. 155–165). New York: Springer.

Press Information Bureau. (2008). *Home Minister announces measures to enhance security*. New Delhi, India.

Project Liberty. (n.d.). Retrieved from http://www.projectliberty.org.

ProxyStrike. (2008). Reference from http://www.edge-security.com/proxystrike.php.

Puckett, C. (2009). Story of the Social Security Number, The. *Social Security Bulletin*, 69, 35.

R. Gandhi, S. Khuller, A. Srinivasan, (n.d.). *Approximation Algorithms for Partial Covering Problems*. Lecture Notes in Computer Science, Springer-Verlag GmbH, (Vol. 2076, pp. 225-236).

Rabasa, A., Blackwill, R. D., Chalk, P., Cragin, K., Fair, C. C., & Jackson, B. A. (2008). *The lessons of Mumbai*. RAND.

Rai, A. (2009). Here to make a difference, not to give Infy contracts: Nilekani. *The Times of India*.

Raj, P. N., & Swadas, P. B. (2009). DPRAODV: A dynamic learning system against blackhole attack in AODV based manet. *IJCSI International Journal of Computer Science Issues*, 2, 54–59.

Ralph, C. (1989). A certified digital signature. In *Proc. Crypto '89* (pp. 218–238). Merkle.

Ralph, C. Merkle.(1980). *Protocols for public key cryptosystems*. In Proceedings of the IEEE Symposium on Research in Security and Privacy, pages 122-134.

Ramaswamy, S., Fu, H., Sreekantaradhya, M., Dixon, J., & Nygard, K. (2003). *Prevention of cooperative black hole attack in wireless ad hoc networks*. Proceedings of International Conference on Wireless Network.

Raskin, V., Hempelmann, C. F., Triezenberg, K. E., & Nirenburg, S. (2001). Ontology in information security: A useful theoretical foundation and methodological tool. In [New York: ACM.]. *Proceedings of, NSPW-2001*, 53–59.

Reddy, D. K. S., & Pujari, A. K. (2006). *N-gram analysis for computer virus detection* (pp. 231–239).

Reed, C. (2004). *Internet Law: Text and Materials 96* (2nd ed.). New Delhi, India: Universal Law Publishing Co.

Rengamani, H., Kumaraguru, P., Chakraborty, R., & Rao, H. (2010). The Unique Identification Number Project: Challenges and Recommendations. *Ethics and Policy of Biometrics*, 146-153.

RHIOs. (2006). Using the SSN as a Patient Identifier. *Journal of AHIMA, 77*(3), 56A-D.

Rhodes, K. (2003). *Information Security: Challenges in Using Biometrics*. United States General Accounting Office.

Rost, J. (2005). *The Insider's Guide to Outsourcing Risks and Rewards*. Boca Raton, FL: Auerbach Publications.

Rothaus, O. S. (1976). On Bent Functions. *Journal of Combinatorial Theory, 20A*, 300–305.

Rowland, D., & Macdonald, E. (2005). *Information Technology Law*. Singapore: Cavendish Publishing Limited.

Ryder, R. D. (2002). *Intellectual Property and the Internet*. New York: Lexis Nexis Butterworths.

Sailer, R., Zhang, X., Jaeger, T., & van Doorn, L. (2004). *Design and implementation of a tcg-based integrity measurement architecture*. In USENIX Security Symposium, pp. 223–238. USENIX.

Salagean, A. (2005). On the computation of the Linear Complexity and the *k*-Error Linear Complexity of Binary Sequences with Period a Power of Two. *IEEE Transactions on Information Theory, 51*, 1145–1150. doi:10.1109/TIT.2004.842769

Salow, H.P. (2001). *Liability Immunity for Internet Service Providers--How is it working?,* 6 J. Tech. L. & Pol'y 0.

Sankarasubramaniam, Y., Akan, O. B., & Akyildiz, I. F. (2003). *ESRT: Event-to-Sink Reliable Transport in Wireless Sensor Networks*.Proc. of the ACM MobiHoc Conference, Annapolis, Maryland, June 2003.

Sanzgiri, K., Levine, N., Shields, C., Dahill, B., & Belding-Royer, E. M. (2002). *A secure routing protocol for ad hoc networks*. ICNP, Proceedings of the 10th IEEE International Conference on Network Protocols, 78 – 89.

Sarkar, P., & Maitra, S. (2000). Construction of Nonlinear Boolean Functions with Important Cryptographic Properties. *Advances in Cryptology - EUROCRYPT 2000*. Springer Berlin / Heidelberg, LNCS, *1807*.

Sarkar, P., & Maitra, S. (2003). Nonlinearity bounds and construction of resilient Boolean functions. *In Advances in Cryptology - Crypto 2000*, LNCS, Springer-Verlag, Berlin, *1880*, pp.515-532.

Sathyanarayan, V. S., Kohli, P., & Bruhadeshwar, B. (2008) Signature generation and detection of malware families. *ACISP '08: Proceedings of the 13th Australasian conference on Information Security and Privacy*, 336–349, Berlin: Springer-Verlag.

Savage, M. (Ed.). (2009). Security challenges with cloud computing services. *Information Security magazine*.

Schleimer, J. D. (2008). *Protecting Copyrights at The "Backbone" Level of the Internet*, 15 UCLA Ent. L. Rev. 139.

Schleimer, S., Wilkerson, D. S., & Aiken, A. (2003). *Winnowing: local algorithms for document fingerprinting.* In SIGMOD '03: Proceedings of the 2003 ACM SIGMOD international conference on Management of data, pp. 76–85. New York: ACM.

Schneir, B. (1999) *Modeling Security Threats.* December 1999. Reference from http://www.schneier.com/paper-attacktrees-ddj-ft.html

Schuler, D., Dallmeier, V., & Lindig, C. (2007). *A dynamic birthmark for Java.* In ASE '07: Proceedings of the twenty-second IEEE/ACM international conference on Automated software engineering, pp. 274–283. New York: ACM.

Schurgers, C., & Srivastava, M. B. (2001) Energy efficient routing in wireless sensor networks. In the MILCOM Proceedings on Communications for Network-Centric Operations: Creating the Information Force, McLean, VA.

Seberry, J., Zhang, X. M., & Zheng, Y. (1994a). Nonlinearly balanced Boolean functions and their propagation characteristics. *In Advances in Cryptology - CRYPTO '93,* LNCS, Springer-Verlag, Berlin, *773,* pp.49-60

Seberry, J., Zhang, X. M., & Zheng, Y. (1994b). On constructions and nonlinearity of correlation immune functions. *In Advances in Cryptology-EUROCRYPT '93,* LNCS, Springer, Berlin, Heidelberg, New York, *765,* pp.181-199.

Security and Privacy Challenges in the Unique Identification Number Project,. (2010). Data Security Council of India.

Sekar, R., Gupta, A., Frullo, J., Shanbhag, T., Tiwari, A., Yang, H., & Zhou, S. (2002). Specification Based Anomaly Detection: a New Approach for Detecting Network Intrusions. In *Proceedings of the 9th ACM conference on Computer and communications security* (pp. 265-274). New York: ACM.

Seshadri, A., Luk, M., Perrig, A., van Doorn, L., & Khosla, P. (2006). Externally verifiable code execution. *CACM, 49*(9), 45–49.

Seshadri, A., Luk, M., Shi, E., Perrig, A., van Doorn, L., & Khosla, P. (2005). Pioneer: verifying code integrity and enforcing untampered code execution on legacy systems. In Herbert, A., & Birman, K. P. (Eds.), *SOSP* (pp. 1–16). New York: ACM.

Seshadri, A., Perrig, A., van Doorn, L., & Khosla, P. (2004). *Swatt: Software-based attestation for embedded devices.* In IEEE Symposium on Security and Privacy, p. 272. Washington, DC: IEEE Computer Society.

Sethumadhavan, M., & Sindhu, M., Chungath Srinivasan, & Kavitha, C. (2008). An algorithm for *k*-error joint linear complexity of binary multisequences. *Journal of Discrete Mathematical Sciences & Cryptography, 11*(3), 297–304.

Severino, H. Gana, J.(n.d.). *Prosecution Of Cyber Crimes Through Appropriate Cyber Legislation In The Republic Of The Philippines.* Retrieved February 20, 2010, 2010, from http://www.acpf.org/WC8th/AgendaItem2/I2%20 Pp%20Gana,Phillipine.html

Shannon, C. E. (1949). Communication theory of secrecy systems. *The Bell System Technical Journal, 28,* 656–715.

Shaska, T. (2007). *Advances in Coding Theory and Cryptography.* Singapore: World Scientific.

Shawn., et al. (2006). *Uncover Security Design Flaws using The STRIDE Approach.* Retrieved from http://msdn.microsoft.com/en-us/magazine/cc163519.aspx.

Shieh, A., & Williams, D. GünSirer, E., & Schneider, F. B.(2005). *Nexus: a new operating system for trustworthy computing.* In SOSP '05: Proceedings of the twentieth ACM symposium on Operating systems principles, pp. 1–9, New York: ACM.

Shila, D. M., & Anjali, T. (2008). Game theoretic approach to gray hole attacks in wireless mesh networks. *IEEE Military Communications Conference,* 1 – 7.

Shor, P. W. (1997). Algorithms for Quantum Computation: Discrete Algorithms and Factoring. *SIAM Journal on Computing, 26,* 1484–1509. doi:10.1137/S0097539795293172

Shyamasundar, R. K., Shah, H., & Narendra Kumar, N. V. (2010) *Malware: From modelling to practical detection.* In Proc: International Conference on Distributed Computing and Internet Technology, to appear, Lecture Notes in Computer Science. New York: Springer.

Siegenthaler, T. (1984). Correlation-immunity of nonlinear combining functions for cryptographic applications. *IEEE Transactions on Information Theory, IT-30*(5), 776–780. doi:10.1109/TIT.1984.1056949

Siegenthaler, T. (1985). Decrypting a class of stream ciphers using ciphertext only. *IEEE Transactions on Computers, C-34*(1), 81–85. doi:10.1109/TC.1985.1676518

Sindre, G., & Opdahl, A. L. (2005). Eliciting security requirements with misuse cases. *Requirements Engineering, 10*(1), 34–44. doi:10.1007/s00766-004-0194-4

Sindre, G., & Opdahl, A. L. (2001a). *Capturing Security Requirements by Misuse Cases.* In Proceedings of 14th Norwegian Informatics Conference (NIK'2001), Troms, Norway.

Sindre, G., & Opdahl, A. L. (2001b). *Templates for Misuse Case Description.* Proceedings of the 7th International Workshop on Requirements Engineering, Foundation for Software Quality (REFSQ'2001), Interlaken, Switzerland.

Skoudis, E., & Zeltser, L. (2003). *Malware: Fighting malicious code.* Upper Saddle River, NJ: Prentice Hall.

Sniffer, S. D. K. (n.d.). *Packet Sniffer SDK.* Retrieved from http://www.microolap.com/products/network/pssdk/

Solley, T. (2008). *The Problem and the Solution: Using the Internet to Resolve Internet Copyright Disputes,* 24 Ga. St. U. L. Rev. 815.

Song, N., Qian, L., & Li, X. (2005). *Wormhole attacks detection in wireless ad hoc networks: A statistical analysis approach.* 19th IEEE International Parallel and Distributed Processing Symposium (IPDPS'05) Workshop. 289a.

Spike Proxy. (2004). Reference from http://www.immunitysec.com/resources-freesoftware.shtml.

Splint - Secure Programming Lint. (n.d.). Reference from http://www.splint.org/.

Sqlmap - A SQL Injection Tool. (2010). Reference from http://sqlmap.sourceforge.net/.

Stann, F., & Heidemann, J. (2003). *RMST: Reliable Data Transport in Sensor Networks.* 1st IEEE International Workshop on Sensor Net Protocols and Applications (SNPA). Anchorage, AK, May 2003.

Stann, F., & Heidemann, J. (2005). *BARD: Bayesian-Assisted Resource Discovery In Sensor Networks.* IEEE Infocom, Miami, FL, March 2005.

Starre, L. (2006). *The electronic government and its client systems.* University of Groningen.

Steinberg S. G., Bellheads vs. Netheads (2006), Wired, Issue 4.10, Oct 1996.

Strocchi, T. (2005). *An Introduction to Mathematical Structure of Quantum Mechanics.* Singapore: World Scientific.

Sun, B., Guan, Y., Chen, J., & Pooch, U. W. (2003). Detecting black-hole attack in mobile ad hoc network. *5th European Personal Mobile Communications Conference,* 490 - 495.

Sung, A. H., & Xu, J. Chavez, P., Mukkamala, S.(2004). Static analyzer of vicious executables (SAVE). *20th Annual Computer Security Applications Conference ACSAC'04,* 2004.

Swami, P. (2009). *Mumbai investigators found key clues in cyberspace.* Chennai, India: The Hindu.

Swiderski, F., & Snyder, W. (2004). *Threat Modeling.* Washington: Microsoft Press.

Switching, Circuit switching vs. Packet switching. (n.d.). Retrieved from http://voip.about.com/od/voipbasics/a/switchingtypes.htm

Sz"or, P. (1997). *Virus Analysis 3.* Oxford, UK: Virus Bulletin.

Sz"or, P. (2000). *The new 32-bit Medusa.* Oxford, UK: Virus Bulletin.

Sz"or, P., & Ferrie, P. (2001). *Hunting for metamorphic* (pp. 123–144). Oxford, UK: Virus Bulletin.

Tabatabai, F. (2005). *A Tale of two countries: Canada's Response to the Peer-To-Peer Crisis and What it Means for The United States,* 73 Fordham L. Rev. 2321.

Talukder, (2010a). *Mobile Computing – Technology, Application, and Service Creation* (2nd ed.). New York: McGraw-Hill.

Talukder, (2010b in press). *Cloud Economics: Principles, Costs and Benifits, Cloud Computing: Principles, Systems and Applications.* New York: Springer.

Talukder, A. K., & Chaitanya, M. (2008). *Architecting Secure Software Systems.* Amsterdam: Auerbach Publications. doi:10.1201/9781420087857

Talukder, A. K. (2009a). *Tutorial on Next Generation Internet through Next Generation Networks.* WOCN2009, Cairo, 28th April, Reference from http://www.geschickten.com/NGI-through-NGN.pdf

Talukder, A. K., & Prahalad, H. A. (2009c). *Security & Scalability Architecture for Next Generation Internet Services.* IEEE International Workshop on Emerging Internet Applications (WEIA2009), 9th December 2009, Bangalore, India

Talukder., et al. (2009b). *Security-aware Software Development Life Cycle (SaSDLC) - Processes and tools.* Proceedings of IEEE Conference on Wireless and Optical Communications Networks, 28-30.

Tamada, H., Nakamura, M., & Monden, A. (2004). *Design and evaluation of birthmarks for detecting theft of java programs.* In M. H. Hamza, (ed). IASTED Conf. on Software Engineering, pp.569–574. IASTED/ACTA Press.

Tamada, H., Okamoto, K., Nakamura, M., Monden, A., & Matsumoto, K. (2004). *Dynamic software birthmarks to detect the theft of windows applications.* In Proc: International Symposium on Future Software Technology.

Tamilselvan, L., & Sankaranarayanan, V. (2008). Prevention of co-operative black hole attack in MANET. *Journal of Networks, 3*(5), 13–20. doi:10.4304/jnw.3.5.13-20

Thapar, K. (2009). *Unique ID will enable more effective public delivery.* The Hindu.

Tho, I. (2005). *Managing the Risks of Outsourcing.* Burlington, MA: Elsevier.

Thomas, B. (2004). *Fact Sheet: Social Security Identity Theft.* Committee on Ways and Means.

Todorova, A. (2009, July 24). Is Hiding Your Social Security Number Worth It? *The Wall Street Journal.*

Toledo, A. L., & Wang, X. (2008). Robust detection of MAC layer denial-of-service attacks in CSMA/CA wireless networks. *IEEE Transactions on Information Forensics and Security, 3*(3), 347–358. doi:10.1109/TIFS.2008.926098

Treadwell, S., & Zhou, M. (2009). *A Heuristic approach for detection of obfuscated malware.* IEEE Xplore.

Tsoumas, B., & Gritzalis, D. (2006). Towards an Ontology-based Security Management. In *Proceedings of the 20th International Conference on Advanced Information Networking and Applications (AINA'06)* (Vol. 1, pp. 985-992). Washington, DC: IEEE Computer Society.

UK 'national identity register' is a national database of fingerprints. (2005). Privacy International.

Undercoffer, J., Joshi, A., & Pinkston, J. (2003). Modeling computer attacks: An ontology for intrusion detection. In *Proceedings of the 6th International Symposium on Recent Advances in Intrusion Detection (RAID'03),* Pittsburgh, PA (LNCS 2820, pp. 113-135).

United States Department of Justice. Computer Crime & Intellectual Property Section. (n.d.). Retrieved from http://www.justice.gov/criminal/cybercrime/ccips.html

Unni, V.K. (2001). *Internet Service Provider's Liability for Copyright Infringement- How to Clear The Misty Indian Perspective,* 8 Rich. J.L. & Tech. 13.

van der Ploeg, I. (2007). Genetics, biometrics and the informatization of the body. *ANN IST SUPER SANIT, 43*(1), 44–50.

Vasiliadis, G., Antonatos, S., & Polychronakis, M. (2008) Gnort: High Performance Network Intrusion Detection Using Graphics Processors. *In Proceedings of the 11th international symposium on Recent Advances in Intrusion Detection,* 116-134.

Venkateswarlu, A. (2007). *Studies on error linear complexity measures for multisequences.* Ph.D Thesis, National University of Singapore.

Venkatraman, J., et al. (2004). *Trust and Security Realization for Mobile Users in GSM Cellular Networks.* AACC Conference, Kathmandu October 29-31, LNCS 3285 pp-302-309.

Verma, S. K., & Mittal, R. (2004). *Legal Dimensions of Cyberspace 147.* New Delhi, India: Indian Law Institute.

Vinod Shukla and Daji Qiao Distinguishing Data Transience from False Injection in Sensor Networks. In *Proc. IEEE SECON'2007*, San Diego, CA, June 18~21, 2007

Vinod, P., Laxmi, V., & Gaur, M. S. Phani Kumar, GVSS., Chundawat, Y.S.(2009). Metamorphic virus detections through static code analysis. *Indo-US Workshop and Conference on Cyber Security, Cyber Crime and Cyber Forensics.*

Virendra, M., & Upadhyaya, S. (2004). SWAN: A secure wireless LAN architecture. *Proceedings of the 29th Annual IEEE International Conference on Local Computer Networks*, 216 – 223.

Virendra, M., Upadhyaya, S., Kumar, V., & Anand, V. (2005). SAWAN: A survivable architecture for wireless LANs. *Proceedings of the Third IEEE International Workshop on Information Assurance*, 71 – 82.

W. Zhang, H. Song, S. Zhu, G. Cao,(2005). Least Privilege and Privilege Deprivation: Towards Tolerating Mobile Sink Compromises in Wireless Sensor Networks ACM Mobihoc'05, UIUC, May 2005.

Walenstein, A., Chouchane, M.R., Lakhotia, A.(2007). Statistical signature for fast filtering of instruction-substituting metamorphic malware. *Proceedings of Worm'07.*

Walenstein, A., Mathur, R., Chouchane, M. R., & Lakhotia, A. (2007). The Design space of metamorphic malware. *2nd International Conference on Information Warfare.*

Wang, X., & Wong, J. (2007). An end-to-end detection of wormhole attack in wireless ad-hoc networks. *31st Annual International Computer Software and Applications Conference, 1,* 39-48.

Wang, X., Jhi, Y., Zhu, S., & Liu, P. (2009*). Behavior based software theft detection.* In CCS '09: Proceedings of the 16th ACM conference on Computer and communications security,pp. 280–290. New York: ACM.

Web 3.0.(n.d.). Reference from http://en.wikipedia.org/wiki/Semantic_Web

Webster, M., & Malcolm, G. (2006). Detection of metamorphic computer viruses using algebraic specification. *Journal in Computer Virology, 2*(3), 149–161. doi:10.1007/s11416-006-0023-z

Webster, A. F., & Tavares, S. E. (1986). On the design of S-boxes. In *Adv. In crypt.-Crypto '85. LNCS, 218* (pp. 523–534). Berlin: Springer.

Wegner, B. (2000) (Ed.in-chief), *Zentralblatt MATH,* Berlin.

Wei, W. (2006). The Liability of Internet Service Providers for Copyright Infringement and Defamation Actions in The United Kingdom and China: A Comparative Study. *E.I.P.R. 2006, 28*(10), 528-534.

Wenbo, M. (2003). *Modern Cryptography theory and Practice.* Upper Saddle River, NJ: Prentice Hall PTR.

White paper (2001, December). Impact of Electronic Signatures on Security Practices for Electronic Documents. *A National Electronic Commerce Coordinating Council White Paper.*

White Paper. (2009, August) *Cloud Computing Security.* A Trend Micro White Paper.

White Paper. (2009, June). *Introduction to Cloud Computing architecture. 1st Edition.*

Wiesner, S. (1983). Conjugate Coding. *Sigact News, 15,* 1. doi:10.1145/1008908.1008920

WiFiHopper. (2006). Reference from http://wifihopper.com/.

Wikipedia, The Free Encyclopedia.(n.d.). reference from http://en.wikipedia.org/.

Williams, C., Holz, T., & Freiling, F. (2007). Toward automated dynamic malware analysis using CWSandbox. *Security & Privacy, IEEE, 5*(2), 32–39. doi:10.1109/MSP.2007.45

Williams, B., & Camp, T. (2002). Comparison of broadcasting techniques for mobile ad hoc networks. *Proceedings of the 3rd ACM International Symposium on Mobile Ad hoc Networking and Computing*, pp. 194-205. New York: ACM Press.

Wong, W., & Stamp, M. (2006). Hunting for metamorphic engines. *Journal in Computer Virology, 2*(3), 211–229. doi:10.1007/s11416-006-0028-7

Woo., et al. (1994). *SNP: An interface for secure network programming.* Proceedings of the USENIX Summer 1994 Technical Conference, Boston, Massachusetts, USA

Wu, K., Dreef, D., Sun, B., & Xiao, Y. "Secure data aggregation without persistent cryptographic operations in wireless sensor networks", 25th IEEE International Performance, Computing, and Communications Conference, (IPCCC) 2006 Phoenix, AZ

Wybo, J. L., & Kowalski, K. M. (1998). Command centers and emergency management support. *Safety Science, 30*(1-2), 131–138. doi:10.1016/S0925-7535(98)00041-1

Xiaolong, L., & Zeng, Q. (2006). Capture effect in the IEEE 802.11 WLANs with rayleigh fading, shadowing, and path loss. *IEEE International Conference on Wireless and Mobile Computing, Networking and Communications*, 110-115.

Xiaopeng, G., & Wei, C. (2007). A novel gray hole detection scheme for mobile ad hoc networks. *IFIP international Conference on Network and Parallel Computing*, 209 - 214.

Xu, W., Ma, K., Trappe, W., & Zhang, Y. (2006). Jamming in sensor networks: attack and defense strategies. *IEEE Network, 20*(3), 41–47. doi:10.1109/MNET.2006.1637931

Xu, W., Trappe, W., Zhang, Y., & Wood, T. (2005). The feasibility of launching and detecting jamming attacks in wireless networks. *MobiHoc, 05*, 46–57.

Xu, J.-Y., Sung, A. H., Chavez, P., & Mukkamala, S. (2004). Polymorphic malicious executable scanner by API sequence analysis. *The Fourth International Conference on*

Xu, Y., Heidemann, J., & Estrin, D. (2001). *Geography-informed Energy Conservation for Ad-hoc Routing*. In Proceedings of the Seventh Annual ACM/IEEE International Conference on Mobile Computing and Networking 2001, pp. 70-84.

Yang, D. W. & Hoffstadt, B. M. (2006). *Countering The Cyber-Crime Threat, 43 Am. Crim. L. Rev. 201.*

Yen, A. C. (2000). *Internet Service Provider Liability for Subscriber Copyright Infringement, Enterprise Liability, And The First Amendment*, 88. *Geological Journal, 1833*, 1836.

Yi, P., Dai, Z., Zhong, Y., & Zhang, S. (2005). Resisting flooding attacks in ad hoc networks. *Proceedings of the International Conference on Information Technology: Coding and Computing, II*, 657–662.

Yi, S. Naldurg, & P. Kravets, R. (2001). Security aware routing protocol for wireless ad hoc networks. *Proceedings of ACM International Symposium on Mobile Ad Hoc Networking and Computing*.

Yoder, J. W. Barcalow J (1997). *Architectural Patterns for Enabling Application Security*. Proceeding of 4th Conference on Patterns Languages of Programs (PLoP '97) Monticello, Illinois.

Zapata, M. G., & Asokan, N. (2002). Securing ad hoc routing protocols. *Proc. ACM Workshop on Wireless Security* (WiSe), 1 – 10.

Zarrella, E. (2009). Managing IT Governance Through Market Turbulence. *ISACA Journal, 4*. Available at www.isaca.org (membership required).

Zhang, X. M., & Zheng, Y. (1996). Autocorrelation and new bounds on the nonlinearity of cryptographic functions. *Advances in Cryptology, Eurocrypt 96. LNCS, Springer-Verlag, 1070*, 294–306.

Zhang, X. M., & Zheng, Y. (2001a). On plateaued functions. *IEEE Transactions on Information Theory, IT-47*(3), 1215–1223.

Zhang, X., Tallam, S., & Gupta, R. (2006). *Dynamic slicing long running programs through execution fast forwarding.* In SIGSOFT '06/FSE-14: Proceedings of the 14th ACM SIGSOFT international symposium on Foundations of software engineering, pp. 81–91. New York: ACM.

Zheng, Y., & Zhang, X. M. (2001b). Improved upper bound on the nonlinearity of high order correlation immune functions. *In Selected Areas in Cryptography, 7th Annual International Workshop, SA5000,* LNCS, Springer, Berlin, Heidelberg, *2012,* 264-274.

Zhou, Y., Wu, D., & Nettles, S. (2004). Analyzing and preventing MAC-layer denial of service attacks for stock 802.11 systems. *Workshop on BWSA, BROADNETS.*

Zhu, S., Setia, S., & Jajodia, S. (2003). *LEAP: efficient security mechanisms for large-scale distributed sensor networks* (pp. 62–72). Washington, DC: ACM CCS.

Zhu, S., Setia, S., Jajodia, S., & Ning, P. (2004). *An Interleaved Hop-by-Hop Authentication Scheme for Filtering of Injected False Data in Sensor Networks.* IEEE Symposium on Security and Privacy 2004, pp. 259-271.

About the Contributors

Raghu Santanam is an Associate Professor of Information Systems and Director of the MSIM Program in the W. P. Carey School of Business at Arizona State University. His current research focuses on consumer related issues in pricing of digital products, Health Information Technology, Business Process Change, and Cloud Computing. Dr. Santanam has helped a number of organizations on Information Systems and Business Process related changes. He serves as an Associate Editor for Information Systems Research, Decision Support Systems, Journal of the Association for Information Systems and Journal of Electronic Commerce Research. He is an advisory editor of the Elsevier series on "Handbooks in Information Systems." He recently served as the Program Co-Chair for Workshop on E-Business, 2009. He facilitated the solutions and implementation work group proceedings in Arizona as part of the National Health Information Security and Privacy Collaboration project. Most recently, Dr. Santanam served as a co-PI on a research study entitled "Electronic Medical Records and Nurse Staffing: Best Practices and Performance Impacts." This study examined the impact of EMR systems on hospital performance in California State.

M. Sethumadhavan received his PhD (Number Theory) from Calicut Regional Engineering College (presently a National Institute of Technology). He is a Professor of Mathematics and Computer Science in Amrita Vishwa Vidyapeetham University, Coimbatore and is currently the Head, TIFAC CORE in Cyber Security. His area of interest is cryptography

Mohit Virendra received his Ph.D. in Computer Science and Engineering from the State University of New York at Buffalo in 2008. He currently works in the Software Design and Development team at Brocade Communications Systems in San Jose, CA. His research interests are Computer and Network Security, Wireless Networking and Storage Networks.

* * *

Manish Agrawal is an Associate Professor in the department of Information Systems and Decision Sciences of the College of Business Administration at the University of South Florida. His current research interests include Information security, Software quality and the development of application-specific Agent-based systems. He completed his Ph.D. at SUNY Buffalo and is a member of AIS and INFORMS.

P. Achuthan is Distinguished Professor in the Department of Amrita Vishwavidyapeetham. He is Professor Emeritus, IIT Madras, Chennai working there for 3 decades. He has taught at various levels, guided researchers towards PhD, published profusely, research papers, various articles, translation of W.Pauli's Quantum Mechanics from German, written books, edited proceedings of international conferences,… He has traveled widely visiting several academic institutions. While his mind is in Mathematics his heart is in physics. He is actively engaged in particles and their fundamental interactions. His interests extend to and cover social, cultural and spiritual matters as well.

C. Warren Axelrod, Ph.D., is a senior consultant with Delta Risk, a consultancy specializing in cyber defense, resiliency and risk management. Previously, he was the chief privacy officer and business information security officer for US Trust, the private wealth management division of Bank of America. He was a co-founder of the Financial Services Information Sharing and Analysis Center. Dr. Axelrod won the 2009 Michael Cangemi Best Book/Best Article Award for his article "Accounting for Value and Uncertainty in Security Metrics," published in the ISACA Journal, Volume 6, 2008. He was honored with the prestigious Information Security Executive (ISE) Luminary Leadership Award in 2007. He received a Computerworld Premier 100 IT Leaders Award in 2003.Dr. Axelrod has written three books, two on computer management, and numerous articles on information technology and information security topics. His third book is Outsourcing Information Security, published in 2004 by Artech House. His article "Investing in Software Resiliency" appeared in the September/October 2009 issue of CrossTalk magazine.He holds a Ph.D. in managerial economics from Cornell University, as well as an honors M.A. in economics and statistics and a first-class honors B.Sc. in electrical engineering, both from the University of Glasgow. He is certified as a Certified Information Systems Security Professional and Certified Information Security Manager.

Anup Kumar Bhattacharjee is a scientist in Bhabha Atomic Research Centre. He obtained his Ph.D in Computer Science from BITS (TIFR). His main interests are in Application of Formal Methods in the Design of Safety-Critical Systems.

Rajarshi Chakraborty is a third-year doctoral student of management science and systems in the School of Management at the University at Buffalo. His research interests include Internet privacy, cloud computing, digital forensics, intellectual property rights, and emergency response management. Rajarshi received his MS in computer science and engineering from the University at Buffalo. He can be reached at rc53@buffalo.edu.

Charulata Chaudhary is currently a Fourth Year Law student, BA LLB. (Five Year Integrated Course) at Rajiv Gandhi National Law University, Patiala, Punjab. Her research interests are in Criminal Law, Cyber Crimes and Constitutional Law. She has attended and presented articles and research papers at various national and international conferences and seminars. She can be contacted at charu.244@gmail.com.

Qi Duan got his Ph.D. degree in Computer Science from University at Buffalo in September 2008. Currently he is a postdoctoral research associate in Department of Software Information Systems, University of North Carolina Charlotte. His research interest is network security.

M.S.Gaur is a Professor in the Department of Computer Engineering at Malaviya National Institute of Technology Jaipur. he received his PhD from School of Electronics and Computer Science, University of Southampton UK in 2004. His research interests are in Information Security, Network Attacks Simulation and Countermeasures, Network on Chip Modeling and Simulation. He has published widely in refereed conferences, journals, and edited volumes. he has given a number of invited talks in his areas of interest. He is Program Chair for RASDAT workshop which is conducted in conjunction with VLSI Design Conference in India. He is reviewer and TPC member of a number of conferences.

Kenneth Giuliani received his Ph.D. in cryptography at the University of Waterloo and has worked as a postdoctoral fellow at the University of Toronto. He has worked in industry for IBM, Motorola, Ministry of National Defence (Canada), Certicom, and Prata Technologies.

Sukumar Haldar is currently serving as a Senior Program Manager with One Call Medical Inc. He received his Masters degree in Science from Kumaoun University in India and a DBMS from Harvard University. He has also provided consultancy services in the area of Enterprise & Credit risk management to the leading financial firms in US, Far East, Europe and South-Asian markets. He is an active member of GARP, ISACA and served as an Honorary Chairman of the Business Advisory Council for National Congressional Committee.

Harvey S. Hyman received his law degree from University of Miami in 1993. He is admitted to practice law in the State of Florida, United States Appeals Court in Atlanta Georgia, and The United States Supreme Court. He is currently a PhD student at University of South Florida, College of Business, and Director of Software Development at a small research firm in Tampa, Florida.

Lakshmy K. V. is a Junior Research Fellow at TIFAC CORE in Cyber Security, Amrita Vishwa Vidyapeetham University, Coimbatore. She received M Sc degree in Mathematics from Govt. Victoria College in 2007. She is pursuing PhD in Cryptography.

Ishupal S. Kang is an undergraduate law student studying in fourth year of BA LLB (Hons.) course at Rajiv Gandhi National University of Law. His primary research interests are in International Economic Law with focus on developing nations' concerns in the multilateral trading regime, Intellectual Property Laws, especially Copyright and Trademark Laws and Cyberspace laws. He has won several prizes in various competitions like National Level Moot Courts, International Essay Competitions etc. He has attended and presented papers at national and international conferences and also has international publications to his credit.

Narayanankutty Karuppath is a faculty at the Amrita Vishwa Vidyapeetham University where he is at present teaching Modern Physics and Astrophysics. He took his M.Sc in physics from Sardar Patel University and PhD from Amrita University. His research interests include quantum phenomena, its applications (including quantum cryptography and computation) and implications, the enigma of time in physics, Cosmology and scientific philosophy. He has published several papers in his area of interest. He has more than 3 decades of research, teaching and industrial experience.

Rajbir Kaur is PhD Scholar in the Department of Computer Engineering, Malaviya National Institute of Technology Jaipur (Rajasthan), India. Her research interests are in Information Security and Simulation Mobile Ad Hoc Networks.

Ponnurangam Kumaraguru ("PK"), is an Assistant Professor at Indraprastha Institute of Information Technology (IIIT), Delhi. PK received his Ph.D. from the School of Computer Science at Carnegie Mellon University (CMU). PK's research interests include developing technological and multi-disciplinary solutions to reduce computer crime, information security, cyber crime, trust, and human computer interaction. Of late, he has been working on Open Source Intelligence and analyzing online user-generated content to detect cyber crime. PK recently served as a Program Co-Chair for international conference on Collaboration, Electronic messaging, Anti-Abuse and Spam (CEAS) and was on the Program Committee of Symposium on Usable Privacy and Security (SOUPS). PK is also serving as a reviewer for International Journal of Information Security and ACM's Transactions on Internet Technology (TOIT). For more information, visit http://www.iiitd.edu.in/~pk and PK can be reached at pk@iiitd.ac.in.

N.V. Narendra Kumar is a Research Scholar at STCS, TIFR. His research interests are in Information/Network/Computer Security, with special focus on Analysis of Cryptographic Protocols; Access Control: Policies, Models and Mechanisms; Malware Detection and Protection; Operating System Protection; and Virtualization.

Vijay Laxmi is an Associate Professor in the Department of Computer Engineering at Malaviya National Institute of Technology Jaipur. She received her PhD from School of Electronics and Computer Science, University of Southampton UK in 2003. Her research interests are in Information Security, DRM Issues and Water Marking, Network on Chip Modeling and Simulation, and Algorithms. She has published widely in refereed conferences, journals, and edited volumes. She has given a number of invited talks in her areas of interest. She is reviewer and TPC member of a number of conferences.

Sindhu. M is a lecturer at TIFAC CORE in Cyber Security, Amrita Vishwa Vidyapeetham University, Coimbatore. She received M Sc degree in Mathematics from Govt. Victoria College in 2005 and MPhil Degree from Madurai Kamaraj University in 2008. She is pursuing PhD in Cryptography. Her research interests are Stream Ciphers, Block Ciphers and Linear Complexity

Himanshu Maheshwari has an MBA degree in Finance and MIS from the University of South Florida. He worked for JP Morgan Chase in India on various Operations, IT & Finance projects. Among these projects, he helped in the migration of processes to locations such as Mumbai and Manila. Currently, he is a financial Consultant for JP Morgan Chase working with HNI clients on money saving operations.

R.S. Mundada is leading Supercomputing and Information Security group at Bhabha Atomic Research Centre, Mumbai, India. He received his Bachelor of Engineering degree in Electronics and Communication discipline from Nagpur University, Nagpur, India in 1979. He has expertise in designing secure networks and building large HPC clusters. He has number of publications to his credit in areas of High Performance Computing and Information Security. His current research interests are High performance Computing, Grid Computing and Information security.

C.S.R.C. Murthy is senior scientific officer in Bhabha Atomic Research Centre. He is currently engaged in information security systems research and development. He received Bachelor of Technology degree in Electronics & Communication systems from Jawaharlal Nehru Technological University, Hyderabad, India in 1995. His research areas include cryptanalysis, intrusion detection systems, data leak prevention and web applications security. He has developed a number of software systems for information security enforcement and has served various committees on security audit. His current research works are on the study and improvements of TMTO cryptanalysis and development of faster cryptanalysis systems using High performance Computing.

V. Kumar Murty is Professor and Head of the Department of Mathematics at the University of Toronto. He is also the Director of the GANITA Lab. He received his Ph.D. from Harvard University. He is a Fellow of the Royal Society of Canada and a Fellow of the Fields Institute. He is the author of more than 80 papers and two books. His research interests are in number theory, algebraic geometry and their applications to information technology.

Sajan Kumar S is a Research Associate at TIFAC CORE in Cyber Security, Amrita Vishwa Vidyapeetham University, Coimbatore. He received M Sc degree in Computer Science from Amrita Vishwa Vidyapeetham, Amritapuri Campus in 2006. His research interests are Cloud Computing Security, Intrusion Detection Systems and Application Level Security.

Vinod P. is Research Scholar in Department of Computer Engineering, Malaviya National Institute of Technology, Jaipur (Raj.), India. His research interests are in Information Security, Metamorphic Malware Analysis and Detection methods.

Amritha P.P. is an Assistant Professor at TIFAC CORE in Cyber Security, Amrita Vishwa Vidyapeetham University, Coimbatore. She received her M Tech (Cyber Security) from Amrita Vishwa Vidyapeetham in 2009. She is pursuing PhD in Multimedia Security.

H. Raghav Rao is SUNY Distinguished Service Professor in the department of MSS, School of Management, SUNY Buffalo. His current research interests include Information Assurance, Security and Privacy Services and Emergency Response Systems. He completed his PhD at Purdue University.

Suja Ramachandran is working as Scientific Officer in Indira Gandhi Centre for Atomic Research, India. She received Bachelor of Technology degree in Computer Science & Engineering from Calicut University in 2006 and Master of Technology degree in Computer Science & Engineering from Homi Bhabha National Institute in 2009. Her areas of interest include information security systems, high performance computing systems, database systems and web applications.

Haricharan Rengamani has done his Masters in Management Information Systems from University at Buffalo. His adademic accomplishments and contribution to many projects nominated him for the coveted BETA 'Best Student Award' among all the WNY universities.Earlier he had completed his B.Tech in Information Technology from Vellore Institute of Technology,India.Before pursing his M.S, he was working as a Solution Definition Analyst earlier in a reputed IT firm and a certified Microsoft Technology Specialist,Microsoft Application Developer and ITIL V3.0. Currently he is working as a Lead Business Analyst for an IT firm. He writes many technical articles and participates activly in technical forums (MSDN,Code Project, DotnetGuru etc.,).

Harshit Shah is a PhD candidate at Amrita School of Engineering, Amrita Vishwa Vidyapeetham. He is jointly advised by Prof. R. K. Shyamasundar (TIFR, Mumbai) and Prof. M. Sethumadhavan (Amrita School of Engineering). His research interests include static and dynamic techniques for program analysis.

Divya Shankar completed her Masters in Information Systems from State University of New York at Buffalo in 2009. Her research interests are in the areas of emergency response management systems, decision support systems and information assurance. She is currently working as a Business data analyst in a leading financial organization.

Rohitashva Sharma is working as Senior Scientific Officer in Supercomputing and Information Security Group at Bhabha Atomic Research Centre, Mumbai. He received his Bachelor of Engineering degree in Electronics and Communication discipline from Rajasthan University, Jaipur, India in 1996. His research areas include web application security, secure information systems and data leak prevention. He has developed a number of software systems for monitoring and enforcement of information security policy in the organization. His current research interests are in the field of secure data storage to stop unauthorized access to information.

R.K. Shyamasundar a Ph.D.(Computer Science and Automation), from Indian Institute of Science, Bangalore is a Senior Professor and JC Bose National Fellow at the Tata Institute of Fundamental Research and was the Founder Dean of the School of Technology and Computer Science. His principle areas of research are: Specification, Design and Verification of reactive and real-time systems, Programming Languages, Logics of programs, Formal methods, Computer and Network & Information Security. He is a Fellow IEEE , Fellow ACM and serves on IEEE Esterel Standards Committee. He is a Fellow of the Indian Academy of Sciences, Fellow of the Indian National Science Academy, Fellow of the National Academy of Sciences, India, Fellow of the Indian National Academy of Engineering and Fellow of TWAS (Academy of Sciences for the Developing World, Trieste.)

Chungath Srinivasan is a lecturer at TIFAC CORE in Cyber Security, Amrita Vishwa Vidyapeetham University, Coimbatore. He received M Sc degree in Mathematics from Govt. Victoria College in 2005. He is pursuing PhD in Cryptography

Lalith Suresh P. is a Post Graduate at Portugal. He completed his B.Tech in Computer Engineering from Malaviya National Institute of Technology Jaipur in 2010. His research interests are in the area of Network Simulation and Computer Networking.

Gireesh Kumar T. received his M Tech (Computer and Information Science) from Cochin University of Science and Technology, Cochin, Kerala, in 2002. He is currently pursuing PhD (Artificial Intelligence) Anna University, Chennai. He is now an Assistant Professor (Sr. Grade) with TIFAC CORE in Cyber Security at Amrita Vishwa Vidyapeetham University, Coimbatore. His research interests are artificial intelligence, machine learning and algorithms.

Asoke K Talukder is the Chief Scientific Officer at Geschickten Solutions, Bangalore and Adjunct Faculty at ABV Indian Institute of Information Technology and Management, Gwalior, India. He received

M.Sc in Biophysics and Ph.D. in Computer Engineering from Calcutta University and IIIT Bangalore in 1976 and 2008 respectively. His research interests are in Cloud Computing, Security & Scalability, and Computational Quantitative Biology. He is associated with both in Education and Industry.

Shambhu Upadhyaya received his Ph.D. in Electrical and Computer Engineering from the University of Newcastle, Australia in 1987. He is currently a professor of computer science and engineering at the State University of New York at Buffalo. His research interests are computer security, information assurance, fault-tolerant computing, distributed systems and reliability. His research has been funded by National Science Foundation, U.S. Air Force Research Laboratory, DARPA and National Security Agency.

Index